THE COMPLETE GUIDE TO OFFSHORE MONEY HAVENS

How to Make Millions, Protect Your Privacy, and Legally Avoid Taxes

REVISED AND UPDATED 4TH EDITION

JEROME SCHNEIDER

PRIMA VENTURE
An Imprint of Prima Publishing

This book is about the profit, privacy, tax, and asset protection benefits available through offshore money havens. To get started, the author offers financial advice through seminar/workshops and one-on-one private consultation. For more information, Mr. Schneider invites you to contact him through his office in Vancouver, BC, Canada at (604) 682-4000 or fax (604) 682-7700.

Published by Prima Publishing, Roseville, California. Member of the Crown Publishing Group, a division of Random House, Inc.

PRIMA PUBLISHING, VENTURE, and colophons are trademarks of Random House, Inc., registered with the United States Patent and Trademark Office.

The names of the individuals referred to in this book have been changed in order to preserve their privacy.

Disclaimer

Investment decisions have certain inherent risks. Any investment a reader may make based on the information in this book must be at the reader's sole risk. You should carefully research or consult a qualified financial adviser before making any particular investment.

Furthermore, while efforts have been made to make this book complete and accurate as of the date of publication, in a time of rapid change, it is difficult to ensure that all information is entirely accurate, complete, or up-to-date. Although the publisher and the author cannot be liable for any inaccuracies or omissions in this book, they are always grateful for suggestions for improvement.

Library of Congress Cataloging-in-Publication Data

Schneider, Jerome.
    The complete guide to offshore money havens : how to make millions, protect your privacy, and legally avoid taxes / Jerome Schneider.—Rev. and updated 4th ed.
        p. cm.
Includes index.
ISBN 0-7615-3548-9
1. Banks and banking, International. 2. Tax havens. 3. Investments, American. I. Title.
    HG3881.S3714 2001
    332.1'5—dc21   2001036931

02 03 04 HH 10 9 8 7 6 5 4 3 2

Printed in the United States of America

Fourth Edition

Visit us online at www.primapublishing.com

CONTENTS

ACKNOWLEDGMENTS

The *Complete Guide to Offshore Money Havens* has become, in a way, part of my life. It has been a scrapbook for my experiences, observations, and exchanges with my clients. It has also been a lesson book on how to do business with offshore havens.

I give credit to my readers. It has been their enthusiasm that has motivated me to continue writing new editions. Credit goes to Jaqui Hofman, for keeping me organized. Thanks also to Linda Perigo for her expert guidance in editorial matters. And finally, to my agent, Al Zuckerman. His enthusiasm and optimism continue to enable me to write new material.

INTRODUCTION

As you begin reading this book, let your imagination run wild. Consider *The Complete Guide to Offshore Money Havens* as an opportunity to explore, expand, and bring about positive change to your life. Perhaps you're experiencing the much discussed midlife crisis—looking for a way to move out of a frustrating job and rejuvenate your energies. Maybe you're at another kind of crossroads—a marriage has ended and you're looking for a total life change that can bring you adventure and travel to exotic places. Or maybe all is great in your life, but each new professional challenge is beginning to seem like just more of the same—been there, done that. Whatever your present state of mind, picking up this book could be one of the best things you've done lately. I'm going to take you to exciting worlds just beyond the borders of the United States. Places where I, and thousands of my clients, have traveled, enjoyed incredible new adventures, and prospered. Whether lush and tropical, like Aruba, or stately European, like Liechtenstein, these are locales where you can not only vacation, but reap cultural, personal, and financial benefits as well.

All you need to know before deciding to turn the next page is that this adventure I'm offering is most certainly *not* restricted to just the super rich. You don't have to be a multimillionaire to take this journey. All you need is to determine that you are looking for one or more of what I call the "four Ps": profit, privacy, protection, and pleasure. For more than 27 years, I've been showing people where and how to invest and prosper in some of the most exciting, romantic, and relaxing pleasure spots on the globe. Sit back and enjoy the ride. You're bound to learn about some place you've been dying to visit.

For most of us, the words "offshore haven" bring to mind the Cayman Islands. Even though the vast majority of the business done in the Caymans is completely legitimate, the Islands have had difficulty shaking a reputation as being a haven for crooks. Some of this comes from the use of the locale as an exotic setting for fictional works. For example, you may remember the Caymans as the setting for John Grisham's bestselling novel *The Firm,* and for the subsequent movie starring Tom Cruise and Gene Hackman. In fact, the movie was actually filmed at the Hyatt Hotel in the Caymans, a beautiful spot I recommend to all of my clients who visit there. But even though the Caymans might be well known to you, it probably is *not* the best choice for an offshore involvement because of concerns that the U.S. government has penetrated the Islands with a mutual legal assistance treaty covering tax matters. Specifically, the government there now fully cooperates with the IRS when it comes to providing information about American account holders and money that is earned there. For more details of my analysis of the Cayman Islands, I invite you to read chapter 10, "Where to Go, Where Not to Go."

Next on my list of important offshore money havens of intrigue would have to be Switzerland. Certainly, this country is historically synonymous with banking and secrecy. But despite what you may have heard about Switzerland, it too is not my top choice, because it has become too over-regulated and too expensive to serve

U.S. investors in any meaningful way. Interest rates are low and service charges are high. Not many of my clients are able to make money there. And besides all of that, the wall of secrecy has eroded in Switzerland ever since the country entered into a number of information sharing and cooperation agreements with the U.S. government. Again, for more information, refer to page 275 of chapter 10.

So if neither the Cayman Islands nor Switzerland lives up to its reputation or fits your needs based upon what you will discover in my guide, then you may want to consider learning more about the "three Ns"—my favorite havens—Nevis, Nauru, and the Netherlands Antilles. Nevis represents the best of the Caribbean because of the simplicity the country offers for the creation of a company, the ease with which you can do business, and its ironclad secrecy. Nauru represents a premier offshore banking center where you can easily establish your own private, international bank. And finally, the Netherlands Antilles represents the best of Dutch culture and financial skill, while providing complete stability, privacy, and ease of incorporation. For more detailed information about my recommendations of the three Ns and almost 40 others, consult chapter 10 and chapter 5, "In Pursuit of True Financial Privacy." Looking at the complete picture, I think you'll find that you can easily obtain the four Ps in the three Ns.

■ ■ ■

One of the reasons I love my job as a financial adviser is that no two clients are alike. And when we meet for the first time, they often open up to tell me their life stories. They tell me where they've been, the problems they need solved, and where they want to go. I'm often amazed at the hard work and ingenuity they've shown in pursuing their dreams and achieving their successes. The qualities of creativity and tenacity these people possess are the things that have made the United States the success story it is today. Let me tell you about a few of them.

I first met Larry Lattimer in 1995 at a charity function I was chairing in San Francisco. He was a successful but stressed-out 37-year-old marketing executive for a computer software company. He had that "all-work-and-no-play" attitude that was quite typical for people from San Francisco's Montgomery Street business district. He told me his employer was going to give him a six-figure bonus, and he was struggling with the enjoyable problem of trying to figure out what to do with that sizable, lump-sum payment. He'd bought and read a copy of the first edition of *The Complete Guide to Offshore Money Havens*. Then he'd tracked me down to talk things over because he still wasn't sure offshore investing was right for him.

In a series of meetings, I uncovered Larry's concerns, gradually drawing him out, like a doctor coaxing a reluctant patient to reveal where it hurts. Eventually, both Larry and I came to agree that he fit the profile of the offshore investor: He was an experimenter, tax minimizer, privacy seeker, entrepreneur, and wealth maximizer.

Larry is an experimenter because he had bought my book. Experimenters try different things in order to be able to gain a specific outcome. For example, they will try investing in the stock market. If that doesn't work, they'll move on to real estate. They're always willing to open their minds to new perspectives and new ideas.

I believe that is why *you're* reading this book. As Larry was when he came to me, you're hoping to gain new perspectives and knowledge about the offshore process. That makes you an experimenter, too. You're willing to consider adopting a new value system. You believe in keeping an open mind. And you're prepared to entertain new strategies to become wealthier and better protected financially than you are right now.

By the way, *I'm* an experimenter as well. I'll try anything legal to achieve a goal for my clients or myself. I think all great inventors are experimenters. Take Thomas Edison. His method was to keep trying as many different filaments, or wires, as he could until he found the one that burned long enough to serve in the light bulb. He performed 1,200 experiments on 6,000 different types of material over two years before he finally came across carbonized cotton sewing thread in 1879.

Larry is also a tax minimizer, someone who seeks the friendliest and kindest way to structure his business dealings so as to ensure they don't result in excess taxes. Tax minimizers are people who always strive to reduce tax—as long as they can stay out of legal trouble while doing so. If you already have an IRA or any retirement plan that's tax-free, or you are already thinking about the principles of offshore, you, too, are a tax minimizer.

Finally, Larry is a privacy seeker. He was going through a messy time with a woman from whom he had been estranged for many years. Their marriage broke up long before he had made his fortune, and he had tried often to finalize the divorce, but she always stalled. Now that he had become successful, he feared she would try to clean him out financially. That certainly had been her threat.

So, given all of these factors, he decided to invest most of his money in the Cayman Islands, where he now has peace of mind that it's safe. Because his money is offshore, he has no reason to fear it would be seized if he were the victim of a lawsuit—something any of us with assets has to worry about in our litigious society. Moving his investments outside America—beyond the

> **Moving his investments outside America—beyond the reach of the U.S. legal system—gave Larry an advantage that most Americans don't have.**

reach of the U.S. legal system—gave Larry an advantage that most Americans don't have. That's why one of my first rules to offshore investing is to do your planning from outside the United States. When you personally experience the offshore advantage, and see for yourself how civilized and sane the world is beyond the U.S. borders, you'll feel calm and reassured that your money will be safe.

Edith Metcalfe had a strong feeling that her financial affairs and personal information were nobody else's business. In other words, she also was a privacy seeker. In my experience, privacy seekers are individuals who seek to maintain the lowest possible profile while going about their affairs. That includes accumulating their wealth without attracting notice or envy. A solid and soft-spoken Midwesterner, Edith found herself divorced in 1992 with no financial security and two small sons to raise alone. But she was smart and determined to create a new future for her family, and soon she established a small mail-order distribution company outside her home in Indianapolis. After years of dedication and scraping by, the business was beginning to pay off. Still, she knew it wasn't going to be enough. She needed to make some real money, and despite her creativity and tenacity, she knew this was unlikely to happen in the highly competitive U.S. marketplace. She decided to attend one of my seminars on offshore money havens. She waited until all the other participants had left before approaching me. It wasn't easy for her to share the details of her personal dilemma, but she had decided to come seeking advice. She was a struggling small business owner. How, she asked me, could *she* turn her then-small savings into real profit? And how could she keep these activities private from her large, wealthy competitors?

Once she had deposited a relatively small amount in the Freedom Bank of the British Virgin Islands, she asked the institution to act as financial intermediary as she approached two well-established mail-order publishers in Europe. Her plan was simple. She would help them create a catalog for distribution throughout the former Eastern bloc. The BVI bank even loaned her part of the costs of a glossy premier issue. In six months she was earning a profit in the low six figures. And her competitors never knew who was behind this bold maneuver.

Unfortunately, the United States makes privacy almost impossible. The federal government alone maintains about 50 separate files on you. Some levels of government are even starting to keep records of DNA. Soon, if not right now, the government will be able to pinpoint your life expectancy and your risk for developing diseases. This could happen without you knowing it.

Your state government, meanwhile, probably has another dozen or so files on you. Then think of the private agencies, such as credit rating firms, that are in the business of buying and selling your privacy. Taken together, these computer database records are an information trove for anyone wishing to snoop into your private affairs.

Edith wanted to set up a system that would let her make personal decisions that would not be mirrored by assorted databases. If you, too, desire privacy and protection, moving money offshore is a good way to accomplish the goal of secrecy.

But to Edith, perhaps the greatest offshore advantage may have been the time she and her sons spent in their beautiful island paradise. A collection of 36 islands in the Caribbean, BVI is inhabited by generous, well-educated people where the official language is English, and the official currency is the U.S. dollar. Most important, BVI is a perfect vacation spot for growing boys from Indianapolis. There they enjoyed swimming, boating, diving, fishing, and relaxing in the tropical sunshine. Edith could sit on the beach reading or wriggling her toes in the sand while the boys explored spectacular beaches or took diving tours of colorful coral formations of exotic undersea plant and animal life. She told me that during the harsh, gray Indiana winters, she would count the days until the next school vacation when she and the boys would slip away to what she called the "sapphire seas" so Mom could "do some banking."

When I first met Clayton Louis Young, I immediately spotted him as an entrepreneur—someone driven by a vision to achieve things on his own. Entrepreneurs think constantly about their businesses. They don't just work 9 to 5. Instead, they keep their senses alive to any new business opportunities. That's precisely the mindset you need to benefit from the opportunities available offshore.

Clayton was a young African-American inventor whose small electronics company was in seemingly perpetual litigation. If the larger companies weren't trying to harass him out of business with product duplication suits, he had to sue them for infringing upon his latest inventions. And they had the money to block him at every turn.

In Clayton's case, the offshore connection showed him opportunities beyond his borders. It gave him resources that weren't available from his conventional broker or banker. Like an artist who suddenly discovers hues beyond the primary spectrum, Clayton now had a full palette of colors to paint with. Foreign mutual funds, foreign real estate markets, currency exchange, and arbitrage were just some of the new investment tools now at his disposal—all of them, of course, tax-free and totally private.

Clayton was able to quickly adapt his thinking to include these new opportunities to get rich because he is also what I call a wealth maximizer. These are people who are absolutely focused on growing their wealth. In fact, pondering ways to increase their net worth becomes as natural a part of their day as brushing their teeth or eating.

The offshore process is the right course for the wealth maximizer. It presents opportunities that make it possible to grow your wealth and gain returns that far

Foreign mutual funds, foreign real estate markets, currency exchange, and arbitrage were just some of the new investment tools now at his disposal—all of them, of course, tax-free and totally private.

exceed those available within the United States. For example, offshore mutual funds, which are not encumbered by U.S. regulations or taxes, have continuously outperformed domestic mutual funds. In just the British Virgin Islands alone, there are more than 1,600 registered mutual funds with assets in excess of $60 billion. Funds there are exempt from all forms of BVI taxation, and the license fees are fixed and nominal. And in a 1998 report, non–U.S. equity mutual funds had a median expense ratio (what investors pay for operating expenses and management fees) of 1.78 percent. Offshore investing is all about moving your money out of the United States and into one of the several tax havens around the world. In Clayton's case, I helped him set up an offshore company in the Mariana Islands soon after we first met. The Marianas are an archipelago of 14 islands located in the western Pacific that was created 42 million years ago when volcanoes erupted up and out of the sea. Most islands have pristine beaches, mountains, waterfalls, rain forests, and a serene, welcoming population. Except for a short rainy season, the sun shines every day and the northeast trade winds always bring cool breezes. And after a short three-and-a-half-hour plane ride, Clayton and his wife are in the middle of Tokyo where they love to explore, dine on exquisite fare (both are epicureans), shop, and, of course, check out the latest Japanese electronics. Or as Clayton told me the last time he called, "A week unwinding in a tropical paradise, and then we recharge in one of the planet's most exciting cities. After that—I am juiced and ready to get back into my lab." Thinking about Clayton's success formula makes me smile. I love helping entrepreneurs and wealth maximizers to see the light.

Clayton Louis Young represents one of my most successful clients, and he created this success in the Mariana Islands. However, I must caution that this was some time ago—and at this time, the Marianas are no longer recommended. If Clayton were to come to me today for his first consultation, I would suggest he put his banking venture in Nauru. He still would be enjoying an exotic island paradise, and he would be able to fly easily to the cosmopolitan cities of Asia.

■ ■ ■

Now that we've put some of my clients under the microscope to understand what makes them tick, it's hopefully easier for us to understand what makes *us* tick. The offshore process is a new way of living by which my clients receive many desirable benefits. Not only are they able to protect their assets and solve tax problems, they are also able to lower their stress threshold. It's all part of the offshore connection.

When Larry Lattimer travels to the Cayman Islands, it isn't just a business trip, it's also a holiday. In the Caymans, Larry unwinds, making his investment decisions in a relaxed and contemplative atmosphere as he enjoys the beaches and the boats. To top it all off, Larry even enjoys a *tax deduction* for his travels. How's *that* for a cherry on top of the sundae that offshore investing can be!

During our meeting, Larry told me that offshore investing had changed his life. Now he feels a sense of empowerment, where before he felt victimized. Now he's able to use the money he's saved to generate more wealth, where before that money would have gone to fund wasteful federal programs. Now he enjoys the privacy that is his right as an American. Perhaps most important, now his wealth helps fuel the international economy. Larry has the satisfaction of knowing he is making a contribution to the world.

■ ■ ■

Now might be a good time to relate my own experiences and explain how I've come to develop my expertise in offshore investing. My career more or less began in 1974. I was in my early 20s, a stockbroker working in New York for a major Wall Street firm. I had a hunch that then-president Richard Nixon would be forced to resign because of the Watergate scandal. I reasoned that the resignation of a Republican president would play havoc with the stock market. I shared my hunch with a client, and suggested he should "short" some stocks—in other words, gamble that the stocks would drop in price if the president did actually resign. The client played my hunch—and made a whopping $10 million profit.

Pleased though he was with his profit, my client was then presented with a whole new problem: how to avoid paying the $6 million in taxes his accountant said he owed on his capital gains. He had read a magazine article about tax havens in the Cayman Islands. He decided to send me down there on a holiday, in part to thank me for my idea that had made him the money, and in part to have me look into a way to solve his tax problem.

> **I had a hunch that then-president Richard Nixon would be forced to resign because of the Watergate scandal. I reasoned that the resignation of a Republican president would play havoc with the stock market.**

When I got to the Caymans, I didn't have a clue where to look or whom to contact. But I was determined to solve my client's problem. A couple of days later I saw a huge black limousine drive past my hotel. In the little while I had been on the island, I hadn't seen too many limousines. Something told me the answer to my client's problem was somehow in that long, sleek black car. I quickly hailed a taxi and, just like in the movies, shouted, "Follow that car!" to the driver.

The limousine came to a halt near a Lear jet at the airport. I ran to the man in the three-piece suit getting out of the limo and breathlessly asked for his help. The man gave me the name of a trust company and a lawyer. I met with both that day. The trust company and the lawyer had the answers I needed, and so I was able to return to New York and tell my client how he could avoid his tax.

Are you ready for my story's fairy tale twist of good fortune? That client took it upon himself to pay me $100,000 for my advice! Being 22 at the time, I did the best thing I could think of with my newfound fortune. I took a leave of absence from my job and traveled the world, visiting all sorts of tax havens: the Caymans, the Bahamas, Hong Kong, and more. In every exotic and far-flung destination I visited, I took copious notes on laws and regulations. When I finally returned to New York and my old job, I was financially broke, but wealthy with priceless knowledge. In fact, I soon found everyone in the office wanted to pick my brain and copy my notes. Ultimately, I wrote my first book, *How to Profit and Avoid Taxes,* and moved back to my hometown, Los Angeles, where I opened a consulting business specializing in tax havens.

■ ■ ■

In *The Complete Guide to Offshore Money Havens, Revised and Updated 4th Edition,* I will show you the practical details of opening foreign accounts, how to best utilize the special services of these financial centers, and how to maximize your profits while keeping within the letter of U.S. tax laws. I will also discuss the latest developments to thwart money havens, for looming in the background is the specter of a global assault on offshore financial centers. These efforts are lead by the Paris-based Organisation for Economic Co-operation and Development (OECD), a group of almost 30 of the world's biggest and richest nations, jealous of the fact that certain smaller countries have carved out this financial niche. Because they have the flexibility to lower their tax rates to zero, the money haven countries are offering incredible advantages to the people of the world—and still raising the economic levels of their own people far above the subsistence levels they endured previously. The big countries, of course, don't have such a luxury because they must subsidize themselves through government revenues. In other words, the money haven countries are nibbling away at the world's profits—and the big guys are losing money. For the past two years, the OECD has been pushing hard for what it calls "tax harmony"—unanimity among all nations. Fortunately for all of us, it appears that money havens have escaped these OECD efforts. The OECD has lost.

This was primarily brought about because of a recent shift in U.S. policy as administered by George W. Bush. In a May 2001 statement, Treasury Secretary Paul H. O'Neill remarked, "The United States does not support efforts to dictate to any country what its own tax rates or tax system should be, and will not participate in any initiative to harmonize world tax systems."

Now that the coast is clear, this will—without question—generate the rise of even more money havens, as more and more smaller nations seek means of creating their own revenues. One good example is Fiji, which I predict will blossom within a few years to a major offshore financial center.

Do you fear the invasion of your privacy? Do you believe your wealth is growing? Are you satisfied with your lifestyle?

Today as I think back on my many years in this business and the thousands of clients I've helped, my message is very clear. I not only advocate offshore investing for you, I do it for myself, every day. After all, how could I expect you to trust me if I didn't "walk the walk" as well as "talk the talk."

Now it's time for you to evaluate your own personal situation. Do you share my concern about high taxes? Do you fear the invasion of your privacy? Do you believe your wealth is growing? Are you satisfied with your lifestyle?

If the answers to these questions tell you that it could be time for a change, then I believe the offshore lifestyle is something you should consider.

After all, the fact that you're reading this book already tells me you're an experimenter. Now it's time to read on.

CHAPTER 1

THE BRUISING OF AMERICA

The Red, White, and Blue is being beaten black and blue. All around us are signs of the nation's decay. The economy might look like it's booming, but in reality our standard of living is dropping. The proportion of two-parent families in which only one parent works outside the home is dwindling. The amount of leisure time available to the average American worker is shrinking. The percentage of citizens who can afford to own a home is dropping, and those who do buy are waiting longer to take the plunge. The lifestyle my parents might have been able to afford on $100,000 per year would now require an annual income of $700,000.

Baby boomers have led the United States through the largest productive cycle the nation has ever known. As they retire, the working energy of the country will have to come from their children. The trouble is that many of the baby boomers' children, or what sociologists call the "baby boom echoers," or the BBEs, don't want to

1

work. With the exception of that small group of kids who are pioneering Silicon Valley and the Internet, most of the BBEs seem to want to sit back and enjoy the wealth they'll inherit from their parents. The creative spark of the nation is fizzling out. We're entering an age where America is losing its productivity.

ROADBLOCKS

Consistent with that thought, I see eight reoccurring themes that spell disaster for America. Most people are unwilling to talk about what's going on. But I think we should put the spotlight on these problems so we can all see where the nation is heading. The eight problems we face are:

1. Invasion of Property

Our government and its army of bureaucrats have a frightening arsenal of powers aimed squarely at your property. For example, laws such as the Internal Revenue Code give the federal government a sweeping power to seize your property without due process. In law, this is called "asset forfeiture." I just call it outrageous.

I'll discuss asset forfeiture in detail in chapter 8, but let's look briefly now at how the process works. Forfeiture legislation often begins by invoking the magic Latin words "in rem." This creates a legal fiction whereby government is assumed to take action only against the property, and not against you. In order words, if the government wants to take your property, it need not charge you or anyone else with a crime because the "guilty" party is the property. Because the law targets the property and not the person, the government can act "ex

Our government and its army of bureaucrats have a frightening arsenal of powers aimed squarely at your property.

parte," which means it doesn't have to give you any notice or give you any chance to challenge the seizure in court before the government knocks on your door to cart your property away. The legal deck is stacked against you.

Sure, the government has to get a judge's permission before it takes your property. But the government can rely on pretty flimsy evidence, such as rumor, innuendo, hearsay, or hunches. If you want your property back, the burden falls on you to prove your innocence after the fact. Is your blood boiling yet? It will after you read on.

Seizures of private property by the U.S. Department of Justice grew 1,500 percent between 1985 and 1993, for a total of nearly $4 billion. More than $500 million was seized in 1993 alone. That same year, the United States held an inventory of almost $2 billion in real estate, cars, businesses, and other forms of property stolen from its owners. This doesn't even include the property seized by state and local governments.

Quite simply, forfeiture laws are a 500-horsepower engine where a 50-horsepower engine could do the job. It's true that there are some people, such as convicted drug dealers, who well deserve to have their ill-gotten gains seized by the government. But that should happen after a fair legal process. The harm and hassle caused by the present forfeiture laws far exceed the public good. Forfeiture laws give governments far too much power and are greatly abused. According to a 1991 story in the *Pittsburgh-Post Gazette,* in more than 80 percent of cases, the property owner is not even charged with a crime, even though government officials can and usually do keep the seized property. And if that doesn't leave you outraged, here are some examples of government abuse:

Murder by Forfeiture   Donald Scott and his wife woke up to the horrible reality of the government's forfeiture power at about 8:30 A.M. on October 2, 1998. A small army of local, state, and federal agents burst into the couple's home to seize their 200-acre Malibu ranch and search the property for drugs. Then things went even more terribly wrong. Scott, who seems to have mistaken the agents for illegal intruders, confronted them with a handgun. He was also likely confused, since he had just had eye surgery and couldn't see all that well. He was shot dead.

The events leading up to Scott's tragic death are a chilling testament to the abuse of government power. Most frightening of all is that it later came to light that police weren't really looking to bust Scott for growing pot on his property. The real prize was his $5 million ranch, which was located right beside the Santa Monica Mountains National Recreation Area. The U.S. National Park Service had identified the property as a welcome addition to the park. Ventura County District Attorney Michael Bradbury, who spent five months investigating the doomed raid, reached a conclusion that gives me shivers every time I read his report. "It is the District Attorney's opinion that the Los Angeles County Sheriff's Department was motivated, at least in part, by a desire to seize and forfeit the ranch for the government," he wrote.

The plans to turn Scott's ranch into federal parkland wouldn't seem so outrageous if police had credible evidence to suspect he really was some sort of marijuana kingpin. But District Attorney Bradbury later concluded that the evidence the police had presented to a judge in order to get the search warrant was highly suspect. In fact, D.A. Bradbury found that if police didn't intentionally lie to the judge, they were at least very misleading.

The warrant was riddled with errors. It wouldn't have stood up in court if Scott had been given a chance to challenge it. "This search warrant became Donald Scott's death warrant," D.A. Bradbury said.

Of course, the government doesn't want you to have the chance to fight these warrants in court before it bangs on your door. This is especially true in situations like Scott's, where the government was more interested in stealing his ranch than finding marijuana plants.

Grounded by Government The government's abuse of forfeiture laws cost Billy Munnerlyn his livelihood, his marriage, and his prized $500,000 airplane. Billy, a hardworking man from Las Vegas who had built a successful air charter business, saw his high-flying world come crashing down in 1989 after a ridiculous use of the federal government's forfeiture laws.

In 1989 a customer hired him to fly from Arkansas to California. At first it looked like Billy had scored a good fare. The customer, who Billy understood to be a legitimate businessman, paid $8,500 for the flight. But the trip had a sad ending. The Drug Enforcement Agency (DEA) stormed the plane after Billy landed in California. As it turned out, the passenger was a convicted cocaine dealer traveling with $2.7 million in cash. DEA agents seized Billy's plane and took the $8,500 he had been paid for the trip. Billy and his passenger were arrested.

Prosecutors soon realized Billy had no idea what his passenger was up to. Charges were dropped for lack of evidence. But did this mean the government was ready to return Billy's plane? No. Remember what I explained earlier. The way forfeiture laws work, Billy still had to go to court in order to fight to get his plane back. The complexity of fighting the government for the return of your own property is mind boggling. Billy's situation is a case in point. He ultimately spent $85,000 in legal fees fighting for the return of his plane.

The process was absolute hell. Even though prosecutors had admitted they had no case against him, the government fought Billy every step of the way. After a first trial, Billy thought he won when a jury decided he should get his plane back. But then a federal judge overturned the jury verdict. The battle over the plane continued. Finally, the government agreed to give his plane back, but only after he paid a $7,000 fine. This, even though he was supposed to have been declared innocent.

You'd think Billy's case would end with the return of his plane. Wrong. When Billy finally got his plane back, he realized DEA agents had trashed it to the tune of $100,000. But could he send the government a bill for the damage? No way. As if the painful $85,000 in legal fees and the ridiculous $7,000 fine weren't insulting enough, Billy found himself slapped with yet another abuse of government power. Under federal law, the DEA can't be held responsible for the damage it did to his airplane.

It was all just too much of a financial burden for Billy Munnerlyn. He was forced to file for personal bankruptcy and saw his government-instigated money troubles rip apart his marriage. Now he drives a truck instead of piloting his plane. Let's just hope the government doesn't decide to take that from him, too. While the government might justify its use of the forfeiture power as a way to fight the war on drugs, Billy's case shows how the use of forfeiture is really a war on working people and an invasion of your property.

Sunk by Forfeiture   In 1989 Craig Klein, a university professor from Jacksonville, Florida, had his new $24,000 boat raided by U.S. Customs Service agents looking for drugs. The search lasted seven hours. The boat was reduced to scrap after agents ripped it apart using axes, power drills, and crowbars. Agents punctured the boat with 30 holes, half of them below the waterline. Even though agents never found any drugs, Customs refused

Billy's case shows how the use of forfeiture is
really a war on working people and an
invasion of your property.

to reimburse Professor Klein. After years of debate and
pleading to Congress for reparations, Professor Klein was
finally paid $8,900.

Forfeiture Gets Fishy Another notorious case shows
how forfeiture laws ruined the life of an Ohio man simply
because he caught three fish illegally. State wildlife
agents seized the man's $6,000 boat after charging him
with illegal fishing. Like Professor Klein, he was practi-
cally sunk by the legal bills he booked fighting in court
for the return of his boat. In fact, he was forced to sell his
bait shop, hatchery business, and home in order to pay
the legal costs. Maybe the state thinks clamping down on
this man was necessary to protect other innocent fish.
Once again we have another example of the government's
forfeiture power throwing a man out of business simply
because he caught three illegal fish. And that stinks, like
. . . well, *you* know what.

When the Government Gets Its Beak Out of Joint
Sometimes the use of forfeiture power is more ridiculous
than tragic. Take the case of Judy Enright. She's an artist
from Brighton, Michigan, who thought she could liven up
one of her paintings with some feathers she found in her
backyard and a nearby forest. Unfortunately for her, the
U.S. Fish and Wildlife Service thought otherwise when
they saw her painting. They seized it because the feathers came from migratory birds.
     Judy's case is a strong example of how crazy the gov-
ernment's forfeiture power can be. She's made collecting

feathers her hobby. She finds hundreds of them in her backyard and a nearby forest. She's not really a bird-watcher. She just likes collecting feathers. You'd think that's no big deal. Yet it turns out that it's against the law to possess the feathers of migratory birds.

Judy had created a painting she titled *Rise of the Phoenix*. It didn't look right at first. Then she decided to stick some feathers from her collection on the painting. That did the trick, she thought. When the painting was done, she put it on display at a local art show. The painting caught the attention of officers from the U.S. Fish and Wildlife Service. Didn't she know the feathers in the painting came from migratory birds? And didn't she know that possession of the feathers violated the 1918 Migratory Bird Treaty? "I told them that I don't know one bird from another. I'm not a bird-watcher," Judy remembered.

There's no point arguing with a bureaucrat exercising the government's forfeiture powers. You are powerless to stop them. It doesn't matter how ridiculous your case is. It doesn't matter how innocent you are. The government's power to take your property is absolute, and there's nothing you can do about it.

As outrageous as the abuse of the forfeiture power gets, governments show no sign of backing away from it. In fact, governments are trying to beef up their powers. Right now New York City is experimenting with a new law that will allow police to seize the vehicles of sus-pected drunk drivers. This shows just how nefarious the forfeiture power gets. Everyone agrees police should have the right to clamp down on drunk driving. But to seize

---

There's no point arguing with a bureaucrat exercising the government's forfeiture powers. You are powerless to stop them.

property before people are convicted is simply going too far. The New York City law, just like every other example of forfeiture in the United States, will result in abuse and absolute invasions of property. Forfeiture laws are not fair. They punish the innocent. They give governments the right to steal your property, and there's nothing you can do about it. Forfeiture laws are an attack on hardworking people whose only crime is to own property envied by governments. More abuses are inevitable. Right now, boats are being confiscated for catching illegal fish. How long will it be before homes will be seized because they have illegal wiring? Cars impounded for having burned-out tail lights? Or your wardrobe seized because you are wearing the wrong color on St. Patrick's Day?

Does that sound ridiculous? Well, don't laugh too soon. Because the joke's on all of us as these outrageous forfeiture laws create a roadblock to the future growth and prosperity of America.

2. Invasion of Privacy

The government loves to snoop. Just think of the sheer number of databases and public records the government has compiled about you. The list is mind numbing: driver's license, professional licenses, business registrations, social security records, welfare payment records, tax returns, medical histories, school records, birth, marriage, and death certificates, military records, veterans benefits files, police records, court records . . . the list goes on and on. All of these records are computerized and easily searchable by government agencies. What's more, our governments are very creative at dreaming up new ways to snoop on us.

Right now, the federal government is considering legislation called the "know your customer" rule that would require banks to monitor their customers' transactions and financial dealings in order to report suspicious behavior. The government says it will use this information to track down smugglers, money launderers, and drug dealers. I bet! This is just another information grab on the part of the federal government. If governments abuse the forfeiture laws, governments will also abuse the information laws. A government that believes it has the right to confiscate your personal property via asset forfeiture isn't going to think twice before it trashes your personal privacy.

And privacy is more than just a fundamental part of your personal freedom. The loss of your privacy is a roadblock to economic growth, because it limits the control you have over your professional life. This is because your choices are restricted when your freedom is limited. Think about applying for a job. Your prospective employer will probably do some sort of background check. If you've kept your affairs private, you'll have more control over the hiring process because there's less chance your employer will have located some unflattering information that works against you.

Governments are robbing you of that control, by giving over your private life not only to faceless bureaucrats but also to companies that are out to make a quick buck by trading on your privacy. Driving records provide a hideous example of this. In March 1999, a New Hampshire company called Image Data said it wanted to buy four million driver's license photos compiled by the state of Tennessee. Image Data wants to put the photos in a database so it can sell the information to businesses that do credit card and check verifications.

Image Data has already bought 3.9 million driver's license photos from the South Carolina state government for $5,000. The company is now operating a trial program with 10 businesses across South Carolina, though the state is now suing the company to get out of the contract. A Florida judge barred a deal for that state to sell its driver's license photos, and the governor of Colorado is trying to block a similar deal in his own state. I don't know which is sadder: the absolute disregard these governments showed for our privacy for the sake of a few bucks, or the cold feet these states later developed when faced with the public outcry over their callous behavior. Incidentally, you might be interested to note that the U.S. Secret Service has provided technical assistance and $1.45 million in funding to Image Data. You can only guess what that's all about.

Computer databases make it easy for governments to compile files and sell them to interested buyers. They also make it easy for the government to develop an inability to forget. If you ever get into the slightest bit of trouble, governments will compile a file on you and store it in a database. There it will remain, no matter how hard you try to stay out of trouble. (More detail follows in chapter 5.)

And if the government has the information, it will use it. Just think what will happen if all governments start keeping track of DNA samples, something the state of Florida has begun doing with newborn infants. Florida says this information will be used to help track missing children. But just imagine what will happen when the government figures out how to use that data to determine when the newborn might die, to what diseases the baby would be susceptible, his future academic ability, and whether or not he would become manic-depressive. This was the horrific scenario depicted in the 1997 movie *Gattaca*. That was science fiction. What would happen if this scenario became science fact? Worse, just imagine how a government strapped for cash might be persuaded by insurance companies to sell such information.

If left unchecked, this invasion of our bodies will continue. In April of 2001, the Equal Employment Opportunity Commission (EEOC) sought a court order to stop Burlington Northern Railroad from using DNA testing on 40,000 employees to see which are genetically predisposed to carpal tunnel syndrome. As a result of the action, Union Pacific also stopped its own blood testing of employees; but officials deny that tests were ever intended for DNA screenings.

How can America grow when the most intimate details of our lives are becoming commodities ripe for government exploitation? We have to protect ourselves.

3. Assault on the Affluent

The United States punishes the affluent. The more successful you become, the higher your tax rate. This completely skews the political system in favor of the poor. It might not be a politically correct thing to say, but it's true.

Figures released by the Congressional Joint Committee on Taxation reveal that individuals making $200,000 or more in annual salary pay 42.7 percent of all taxes, while the so-called middle-income levels of $30,000 to $40,000 and $40,000 to $50,000 pay 4.4 percent and 3.4 percent, respectively. Those taxpayers in the highest 10 percent of all earners pay a whopping 66.4 percent of the nation's tax bill. As you see, there are basically two different types of people in the United States: those who produce more than they consume, and those who consume more than they produce. In other words, there are the people who make money, save it, and eventually become rich, and there are those who lose it, spend it, and stay poor. The progressive income tax system, by redistributing wealth, puts a heavier burden on the individuals who produce than it does on those who consume.

Now look at who has the voting power. It's not the wealthy people who produce more, but the masses of people who consume more. In the recent past that meant that the political power was in the hands of the takers, not the givers. At the time my book was first written, few

> The United States punishes the affluent. The more successful you become, the higher your tax rate. This completely skews the political system in favor of the poor. It might not be a politically correct thing to say, but it's true.

people in political power had the courage or the interest to stand up for the producers. Under President Clinton the government was largely unsuccessful at trying to cut the massive entitlement programs that stood to bankrupt the country. In 1998 social programs such as Medicare, Medicaid, and welfare accounted for 68 percent of the $1.7 trillion federal government budget. The government had not created those programs for the nation's wealth generators, but for the wealth consumers. However, now that we have elected George W. Bush, things are looking up. The landscape is changing and the numbers are sure to go down. After all, if no one in government looks out for your interests, you will be taxed without representation. Remember that our founding fathers established this nation in order to move away from such inequity.

What's worse from a national productivity perspective, the progressive income tax system is really an assault on affluence. The United States doesn't reward you for financial success. It punishes you by siphoning off a greater percentage of your income. To remain in the United States and succumb to this system is to enslave yourself. I don't think anyone should have to put up with slavery. Those individuals who are still in what I call "extreme discomfort" with the government should just leave. I, myself, experimented with changing my residence to Canada; however, I've come back to live in the States now because of the encouraging signs presently coming out of Washington.

There's another disturbing political force on its
way. The children of the baby boomer generation will
soon start to inherit their parents' wealth. The only reason they'll get that cash is because they were born at
the right time and into the right generation. With the
small exception of the technologically adept youngsters
I mentioned earlier, this generation of kids is growing
into a world where they are rewarded for doing nothing
except consume. They're not concerned with producing
wealth, just consuming it. This has perilous economic
ramifications. If our government is used to siphoning
off the wealth of producers, what's going to happen
when the producers disappear?

4. Government Waste

The U.S. government is addicted to spending and can no
more kick the habit than an alcoholic locked in a liquor
store. A nation with a government that wastes money like
ours is a nation whose future is bankruptcy. In fact, if the
U.S. government were a corporation, it would have gone
broke a long time ago due to financial mismanagement.

We've all heard about the "little" examples of government waste: hammers for $100 each, shower curtains for
$250 each, and $5,500 for a bronze fire hose cabinet. But
the real volume of government waste is staggering! For
example, there's a new federal courthouse in Boston that
is a monument to the U.S. government's ability to waste
money. This six-story office building cost $218 million. The
excesses started when the government paid $13 million to
have world-famous architect I. M. Pei design it. Then the
federal judges weren't shy when it came to requesting the
amenities: 63 private bathrooms, 37 libraries, and 33 private kitchens. The building also features $750,000 worth
of artwork and a $1.5 million boat dock. Not satisfied with

merely building the real thing, the government also commissioned a model of the new building. The model, which was made out of imported African wood, cost $80,000. At least we know where the new federal courthouse in Boston *is*. The government can't say the same thing about the billions of dollars in government property reported missing in a recent report from the General Accounting Office. Among the misplaced property is $636 million in military equipment, including a surface-to-air missile launcher worth $1 million, two harbor tugs worth $875,000 each, 15 jet engines (including two priced at $4 million), and a floating crane valued at $468,000.

Also revealed in a recent GAO report was that the Department of Housing and Urban Development is making $900 million a year in overpayments on rent subsidies and that the Health Care Financial Administration made more than $20 billion a year in Medicare overpayments.

Last year the United States Post Office lost $84 million on failed marketing campaigns to hawk not only stamps and envelopes but also T-shirts, mugs, baseball caps, and other various souvenirs. In Chicago postal officials paid $133 million for a building that had not been thoroughly inspected. The building was defective and later found to require an additional $23 million in repairs. In the waning months of the Clinton administration, the U.S. Navy paid a defense contractor a 280 percent markup for commercial parts and recorded 10 uninstalled aircraft engines (valued at $4 million each) as simply "missing." And in a 1999 report to Congress, the Department of Defense included an "unsupported adjustment" of $1.7 trillion. That's doublespeak for $1.7 trillion they can't account for!

How the heck can government stay in business when faced with such ridiculous waste? Simple. There's at least one thing the government can do with undeniable efficiency. It can keep tabs on us with a tremendously effective tax machine that makes government everyone's 50 percent business partner.

But change is in the air. As we go to press with this fourth edition, Congress has just passed a $1.35 trillion tax cut package to be phased in over the next 10 years. Although not quite as extensive as President Bush had requested, this tax relief will lower the top individual tax rate (paid by individuals with incomes over $300,000) from 39.6 percent to 35 percent by 2006. Other rates will also drop substantially. The old rate of 36 percent will drop to 33 percent, the 31 percent rate will drop to 28 percent, and the 28 percent rate will drop to 25 percent. The 15 percent rate remains unchanged, but the bill establishes a new 10 percent bracket on the first $6,000 of taxable income for singles and $12,000 for couples. Other provisions include the phasing out of the estate tax, increases to $5,000 per year in the amount that workers can contribute to an IRA, and a doubling of the $500-per-child tax credit to $1,000 for children under age 17.

5. America's Love Affair with Violence

If government is hooked on spending, our media is hopelessly addicted to violence. Just think about all the schoolyard shootings the United States has witnessed in the past couple of years. Each time a shooting takes place, we ask ourselves, "How could this happen? What drives our children to even think of such horrors?"

I think it comes back to a media obsessed with violence. Our children watch movies and television shows and listen to music glorifying death and mayhem.

And that's to say nothing of the *real* life pain, suffering, and horror our children watch on 24-hour news channels. The result is a numbing of our children's minds to the horror. The media tries to tell us that these incidents are isolated and abnormal. But there's so much of it. How many times must our children hear about these isolated situations before such things start to seem normal? Our teenage children, who are just starting to be capable of understanding how things work, will eventually become so desensitized to this onslaught of violence that it will seem normal to them.

Computer games are a horrible example of this. Ret. Lt. Col. David Grossman, a former psychology professor at West Point, is an expert in training soldiers on how to behave in combat situations and how to deal with death. The U.S. military trains soldiers with Doom, one of the most violent, and popular, computer games on the market. Lt. Col. Grossman is distressed at how popular these shoot-em-up "murder simulators" are with children. These games teach children to associate pleasure with death and human suffering. They also teach them the motor skills required for extremely accurate use of weapons. These games might be acceptable as tools for teaching soldiers how to kill as a conditioned response, according to Lt. Col. Grossman. However, they're horrible in the hands of children. "There are children in America who are spending countless hours and hours practicing and practicing on murder simulators," the lieutenant colonel warned. "When some go out and execute [what they've learned], we should not be surprised."

Lt. Col. Grossman served as an expert witness in a case in Paducah, Kentucky, where a teen went on a

Just think about all the schoolyard shootings the United States has witnessed in the past couple of years. Each time a shooting takes place, we ask ourselves, "How could this happen? What drives our children to even think of such horrors?"

shooting rampage, killing three and injuring five of his schoolmates. Grossman noted that the shooter used one bullet per victim; of eight shots fired, five struck victims in the head and three in the upper torso. Not even highly trained cops and soldiers shoot that well. This is the product of intensive computer game training, which rewards players extra points for head shots. The shooter, Michael Carneal (now 18), pleaded guilty and is serving a life sentence.

The American love affair with violence is becoming more passionate and will only get worse. This affair is grinding down the country by eroding our values. A prosperous nation needs to have children dreaming about a future in which they will become society's leaders—not dreaming about head shots for bonus points.

6. Increased Taxation

Historically, there's only one way for government to tackle its spending problem, and that's to tax more. Tax loopholes will be closed, new taxes will be created. People hoping to grow and prosper in America will bump into yet another roadblock. You can't invest in your nation's future when you don't have the money.

In 1960 middle-income Americans paid less than 30 percent of their earnings to local, state, and federal authorities. By 1992 that figure was up to 40 percent. In some states, such as New York and California, the tax burden is closer to 50 percent.

A recent study shows that the average American with a salary of $34,000 needs to earn about $17,000 to buy a $10,000 car. The extra $7,000 is needed for the sales, income, and payroll taxes on the earnings used to buy the car. This means it would take the average middle-income earner three and a half months to earn the money to buy the car.

As I mentioned earlier, entitlement programs such as Medicare, Medicaid, and welfare are responsible for sucking up more and more of the federal government's budget. If the current pace of growth in entitlement spending continues, federal entitlement programs will eat up all revenues by 2015. When we think how badly our governments mismanage themselves, we know this situation can only get worse. No government that pays $100 for a hammer or $250 for a shower curtain is going to be able to cut your taxes. Between 1988 and 1997, federal domestic spending shot from $622 billion to $1.1 trillion. The $7.6 trillion the federal government plans to spend between 1999 and 2002 is more than the U.S. government spent on everything between 1800 and 1970. Administration after administration promises tax cuts, but president after president actually raises them. They've got no choice.

The future prosperity and growth of the country will be stopped dead in its tracks by taxes that rob Americans of their desire to produce and contribute.

7. Red Tape

Increasing government spending also means bigger government. Unfortunately, the bureaucrats we *already have* don't want to work. One senator has repeatedly introduced bills calling on all federal government employees to remove computer games from their computers. "It is absolutely ludicrous that the taxpayers are paying people to play computer games," said Lauch Faircloth (R-NC). On the floor, the senator cited a study concluding that overall, U.S. workers spend an average of 5.1 hours per week playing games and performing other nonwork-related tasks on their computers. However, the *Washington Post* reported that the cost of removing these computer games from federal

One senator has repeatedly introduced bills
calling on all federal government employees to
remove computer games from their computers.
"It is absolutely ludicrous that the taxpayers
are paying people to play computer games,"
said Lauch Faircloth (R-NC).

government computers costs $200,000 a year. The news-
paper also interviewed two federal employees who
boasted that "cyberloafing" will continue no matter
what. Workers will simply download games off the Web
to replace any removed by managers.

Politician after politician promises to make government smaller and to get government off the backs of
working people. Indeed, President Clinton claims the federal government workforce is at its lowest level since the
days of the Kennedy administration. That sounds great.
Too bad it's not true. In November 1963 there were 2.3
million federal employees. At the end of 1999 there were
2.8 million. That doesn't sound smaller to me.

The federal government *has* been working to reduce
its payroll. But 90 percent of all recent federal job cuts
took place in a single agency, the Department of Defense.
That means that all the other federal departments are
doing nothing to reduce staff.

In fact, if you factor in state and local governments,
the total public workforce in this country grew by 700,000
during the term of Bill Clinton. Government jobs grew
more than employment in manufacturing, mining,
finance, insurance, and real estate combined.

Now ask yourself this: Is America getting the same
productivity from its government workers as it is from its
manufacturing, mining, finance, insurance, and real
estate workers? I don't think so. America's governments

are getting fat off the backs of hardworking wealth maximizers. What's more, the bigger governments get, the smaller the chances they can work as efficiently as private industry. The size of our government is grinding the nation's business to a halt. It's another roadblock on the way to prosperity.

8. Litigation

You are a target for a lawsuit. America has become one of the most litigious societies in the world. At least one lawsuit is filed every 30 seconds in this country. Your own chances of being sued within the next year are one in four. And if your net worth ranks within the top 20 to 30 percent of the country, you're even more at risk.

The worst thing you can do is think that it can't happen to you. Each day greedy plaintiffs and greedy lawyers are cooking up new reasons to sue innocent people. If you have any money at all, lawyers are looking for ways to take it away from you and give it to someone else—for a hefty commission, of course. Lawyers already know that if they sue you, you'll settle out of court, whether you're right or wrong, because it's too expensive to take the matter to trial. Lawyers are playing chicken with your wallet. How can America grow when lawsuits sap our vitality?

Maybe you think I'm exaggerating. But look at some of the ridiculous cases that have found their way before the courts. And here's another thing to stew over as you read on: Your tax dollars pay for the courthouses. So the problem isn't just that you're a target for one of these ridiculous suits. It's also that as a taxpayer, you're being duped into paying to fund this web of frivolous litigation.

A Real Beef?   I've got to hand it to the lawyers representing the California man who is suing Taco Bell. They've cooked up one of the most creative examples of

lawsuit abuse I've ever seen. The plaintiff is a Hindu. He
went to Taco Bell and ordered a bean burrito. Apparently
there was some sort of mix-up and the man, a vegetarian,
was served a beef burrito. The plaintiff took a bite and
was horrified to discover he had eaten some beef. "Eating
beef is like eating the flesh of my own mother," he said.

Chalk up a few points for hyperbole. But it goes farther. You might think the reasonable thing to do would be
to give the guy a free meal. Here's where his lawyers got
creative. They're asking Taco Bell to pay for a trip to
India. The plaintiff said he had to go there to purify himself for the sin of eating meat. His lawyers are milking
this situation like it's some sort of contest. Bite into the
wrong burrito, win a free trip to India. If this ridiculous
case ever goes to trial, remember that it will be the hardworking taxpayers of California that will have to pay for
this case.

Who's the Boss? A computer firm from Hopkins,
Minnesota, called Innovex Inc., gets a blue ribbon for its
recent settlement in a sex discrimination suit. The plaintiff wanted $10 million, but the company settled for
$750,000. Not bad. But read on and you'll see how wacky
this case gets.

The plaintiff was Mary Curtin, a former senior executive. She claimed the company made her life hell
because she was subject to sexist taunts at work. I think
we all agree that sexist behavior has no business in the
workplace. But this case takes a turn for the bizarre.
Curtin worked for her own husband, Innovex chairman
and CEO Thomas Haley. Why her own husband wasn't
able to step in and stop the alleged sexism at his own
company is anyone's guess. The result is another ridiculous example of lawsuits run amuck. One more point for
the record. Haley claims he won't personally benefit from
his wife's financial settlement with his own company.
Yeah, right.

Cover Your Ears   A music professor from Princeton University says the rock band Smashing Pumpkins trashed his hearing. Now he's taking on the band, concert promoters, and an earplug manufacturer and demanding they pony up.

Peter Jeffery, who teaches at Princeton but lives in Connecticut, decided to take his 12-year-old son to a 1997 rock concert in New Haven. He says the show was so loud he suffered permanent hearing loss. He says he now suffers from a persistent hissing sound in his ears and can't concentrate on his research.

By suing one of America's most successful rock bands, some concert promoters, and an earplug manufacturer, Professor Jeffery demonstrates the wisdom of shotgun lawsuit filing. It doesn't matter who really is at fault. It doesn't matter who will pay in the end. Professor Jeffery is trying at least three defendants. It would be fun to set up a pool to see who will settle first.

Milking It   Kerry Madden-Lunsford, a novelist, sued the second largest book retailer in the United States. You might think her case would have something to do with her work. If you do, you're wrong.

Madden-Lunsford was shopping at a Borders store in Glendale, California, when she decided it was time to breast-feed her baby. She claimed the store denied her permission to feed her baby in the store. So she took Borders to court, citing the loss of constitutional rights and saying that she suffered mental anguish and emotional

> **Professor Jeffery demonstrates the wisdom of shotgun lawsuit filing. It doesn't matter who really is at fault. It doesn't matter who will pay in the end.**

distress because she subsequently became wary of breast-feeding in public. She asked for unspecified damages plus a court order forcing Borders to allow breast-feeding in its stores. After three months of filing her lawsuit, Madden-Lunsford settled for an undisclosed amount of cold, hard cash.

Now which do you think is more important: collecting unspecified damages or breaking down the breast barrier at Borders?

Lonely Luis Makes New Friends   Thanks to the taxpayer-funded court and prison system, things are looking up for Luis Felipe. It seems good ol' Luis, leader of a violent drug gang called the Latin Kings, was feeling a little lonely at Supermax, the tough federal prison in Florence, Colorado. So Luis asked the court for some friends. In March 1999 he got his wish when a federal judge agreed to modify his exercise conditions. No more loneliness for Luis. The judge said it would be okay for Luis to spend his exercise breaks with Unabomber, Ted Kaczynski, and Oklahoma City bomber, Timothy McVeigh. The judge's ruling was far from perfect, though. Luis was barred from exercising with World Trade Center bomber Ramzi Yousef.

The judge decided it would be okay for Felipe to associate with Kaczynski and McVeigh, because both men kept to themselves and were considered less of a security risk than Yousef, who reportedly maintains contacts with international terrorist groups.

Maybe you're happy to know that the legal and prison system you work hard to pay for allows people like Luis to make new friends. Or maybe you're outraged to think that your tax dollars had to be wasted so that a gang leader can stretch his legs with two serial killers.

Crystal Ball   One of the most shocking things about frivolous litigation is that it isn't always the result of shady ambulance chasers. Judges get involved, too. Take the case of former California State Judge Bruce W. Dodds. He tried to sue the ABC television network, which is owned by Walt Disney Company. His suit went all the way to the U.S. Supreme Court, the highest court in the land, before the justices there finally threw out the case in January 1999.

Here are the ridiculous facts: The television show *PrimeTime Live* aired a segment in 1994 that suggested the judge was making rulings using a toy crystal ball. Indeed, the show featured an interview with a mother who had seen Judge Dodds and his crystal ball in action. In the mother's case, her child had been molested, and she'd sued the attacker. She said the case was settled only after Judge Dodds toyed with the crystal ball. She told the TV show she felt she had to accept the settlement after Judge Dodds pressed a button on the ball and said, "That's what you get."

Judge Dodds took ABC to court, arguing that he had the crystal ball "for levity only," not to decide legal issues. Don't ask me how Judge Dodds thought this poor woman's case was worthy of levity. And don't ask me how Judge Dodds thought he could somehow use this lawsuit to paper over his outrageous behavior. But what is clear is that he was suing defendants with very deep pockets. What does that tell you?

Judges in Action   Judge Dodds isn't the only example of disgraceful behavior from the bench. Take Judge John A. Clark. He "hired" a crew of probationers, used them to clean up his house for a summer party, then chalked up their labor to community service. Then there's Judge Bernard J. Avellino of the Pennsylvania Common Pleas Court. He resigned in 1998 after boycotting his own courtroom while still collecting his six-figure salary. It seems he had been assigned to cases he considered "demeaning." And Ralph T. Romano of West Haverstraw Village, New York, was removed from the bench in 1998 for offensive remarks he made from the bench. Facing a

> **Justice is no longer sought for its own sake, but for the sake of profit. And the greatest injustice of all is that America's prosperity is paying the penalty.**

defendant charged with beating his wife with a telephone, Judge Romano said, "What's wrong with that? You've got to keep them in line once in a while."

If only we could keep our legal system in line. Our notions of justice used to be the envy of the world. Now our nation is becoming a laughingstock. Every frivolous case that fills up the docket blocks a legitimate case from being heard. Justice is no longer sought for its own sake, but for the sake of profit. And the greatest injustice of all is that America's prosperity is paying the penalty.

CONCLUSION

The United States is a beautiful place to live, perhaps the most beautiful place on earth. But you have to look at what is going on in America. Currently we are at a crossroads. President Bush and his new budget bring hope, but government bureaucrats continue to dream up new ways to seize your property, to invade your privacy, and to waste your tax dollars. America's love affair with violence and abuses of the legal system continue unabated. In these ways, the growth of the United States still faces the roadblocks I've outlined in this chapter. For some, the only answer is to flee. However, you can still escape the brunt of these problems without becoming an expatriate. Don't give up hope, as there is a form of sanctuary offshore, and I'm about to show you how to find it.

Chapter 2

The Beacon Offshore

I'm often accused of using scare tactics to make my point. But no one could be more scared than I am, because I truly believe the United States is facing a pile of roadblocks that are making it impossible for the nation to grow. As I explained in the previous chapter, most of these roadblocks arise from the government's infiltration into every aspect of our daily lives. You can't even get a loan from a pawnbroker without filling in a form and leaving a thumbprint for the government!

Fortunately, I can show you how to lift the roadblocks to your personal growth. Just like a blinking lighthouse can guide a ship into the safety of an island harbor, I can show you how to physically and financially escape America's roadblocks by availing yourself of the sanctuary of the offshore world.

This world consists of a collection of exciting, profitable, and creative locations where you can earn a great deal of money in a short amount of time—all without excessive taxation, undue government interference, or fear for safety of your assets. The offshore world lets you make money anytime of the day or night. It lets you completely sidestep the suffocating red tape that has totally stifled the U.S. marketplace. It brings you into contact with businesspeople and investors from virtually every part of the world.

With all their boats, beaches, bars, and tropical settings, it's sometimes hard to believe these utopian outposts are for real! I can assure you they are. Foreign financial centers really do exist. What's more, many of them have been created expressly for people like you.

Beyond their physical reality, these offshore markets also exist as a state of mind. By that I mean that "offshore" is really a way of looking at the investment world. It's an all-encompassing financial perspective, liberated from territorial boundaries and legislative decrees. It transforms the globe into one enormous economic system made up of different but interdependent financial markets. In this world, your assets are entry tickets into one (or all) of these markets.

LOOK AT ALL THOSE WEALTHY PEOPLE OFFSHORE

It's a big mistake to think membership in the offshore club is restricted to the ultrarich jet set. Offshore havens are attracting more and more of what I call the "working affluent," possibly several million people in this country alone! The working affluent are wealth maximizers and tax minimizers, willing to experiment. I also call these men and women the "inventurers." Like trailblazing adventurers of the past, they are bold and self-confident. They prove you can try new things and come out ahead, time after time.

Even though I firmly believe the beacon of the off-shore world beckons you just as much as it does the super rich, I do want to tell you a little bit about how the extremely wealthy benefit from the offshore advantage. Actors like Sylvester Stallone have become tycoons by working for studios that finance films using offshore techniques. Billionaires like media mogul Rupert Murdoch save hundreds of millions of dollars each year by basing business deals in tax havens. Even counter-culture rock stars like the Rolling Stones have found they can get more satisfaction by moving their business dealings offshore. I think you'll see that the advantages these celebrities seek offshore differ little from your personal investment goals.

THE BIG BOYS TOOK THE FIRST DIP

First let's talk about the real pioneers of the offshore environment: the world's largest corporations. Virtually every Fortune 500 company today has tapped into the off-shore gold mine—McDonald's, Nike, Wal-Mart, DuPont, to name just a few. These companies were among the first to take the offshore plunge because they were big enough to risk a loss. If the offshore concept failed, they could lick their wounds and move on to experiment with other profit and tax protection methods.

But offshore didn't fail. In fact, it turned into a big hit. Companies soon realized that by operating from loca-tions such as the Cayman Islands or Bermuda they could better serve their customers and stockholders. Out went the onerous restrictions and red tape that slow down the release of new products. In came the tax advantages and the protection of assets and profits.

Take Jardine Matheson, for example. This huge multi-national conglomerate includes supermarkets, construction companies, financial services, hotels, and property investments, all primarily located in Asia. The company's official home base used to be Hong Kong, where it thrived under the low taxes and pro-business climate the former British colony made famous. But Jardine Matheson was worried its Hong Kong advantage would disappear after Communist China retook control of the colony on July 1, 1997. For Jardine Matheson, the answer was simply to move its official domicile from Hong Kong to Bermuda. That doesn't mean the company gave up its property in Hong Kong, where it still does piles of business. Changing domicile just means that the company decided to make Bermuda its official home. In fact, majority stockholders feel so strongly about the advantages of Bermuda that attempts by dissidents to scrap the company's cross-shareholding structure and move it back to the Hong Kong Stock Exchange have been defeated at the past two annual meetings.

Jardine Matheson isn't the only Hong Kong firm to have made the switch to Bermuda. More than 300 companies listed on the Hong Kong Stock Exchange now list Bermuda as their official domicile.

It's all a state of mind. Jardine Matheson was faced with repression from an authoritative and autocratic Beijing. It found sanctuary by following the beacon blinking across the world, to a freer and easier Bermuda.

RAMBO RAKES IT IN

Sylvester Stallone is one of Hollywood's highest-paid actors, often commanding tens of millions of dollars per movie. That kind of compensation, combined with today's expensive special effects budgets, requires a lot of creative financing in the movie business—something the offshore world has been quick to deliver.

More than 300 companies listed on the Hong
Kong Stock Exchange now list Bermuda as
their official domicile.

Carolco Pictures, which produced Stallone's highly
successful *Rambo* series of movies, financed the films
using a subsidiary set up in the Netherlands Antilles.
That's because the producers realized the films would
rake in piles of money outside the United States. Instead
of bringing that cash back to the United States where it
would be taxed, the offshore profits were parked in the
Netherlands Antilles company. As long as the money
stayed offshore, Uncle Sam couldn't touch it. The studio
then used the profits to make even more movies, including the Arnold Schwarzenegger hits *Total Recall* and
Terminator 2: Judgment Day.

By the way, the Netherlands Antilles is quite a hot
spot. Not only are private companies there producing some
of Hollywood's biggest films, Antilles-based companies own
one-third of all foreign-owned farmland in the United
States, and a good many of the office towers in Los Angeles.
That puts a whole new spin on the word "blockbuster"!

MEDIA MOGUL

Over the past four decades, Rupert Murdoch has transformed the two Australian newspapers he inherited into
a global multimedia empire. Chances are you read,
watch, or listen to one of Murdoch's business ventures
every day. He owns *TV Guide* magazine. He owns the
Fox television network and the Los Angeles Dodgers
baseball team.

Murdoch plays the offshore game like a pro. He pays almost no tax to Uncle Sam, even though he makes a good chunk of his change in the United States. Murdoch has set up a subsidiary in the Netherlands Antilles, a Caribbean tax haven with virtually no income tax. The offshore company is the legal owner of a stable of Murdoch's immensely successful and profitable magazines, among them *New York, Seventeen,* and *Soap Opera Digest.* When the magazines make a profit, the money is siphoned out of the United States and into the offshore holding company.

In 1989 Murdoch used this sweet system to avoid taxes on almost $100 million in publishing profit. And when Murdoch banked a profit of $325 million on the sale of a chain of travel magazines, he avoided most U.S. capital gains taxes by closing the deal offshore. "If you can move assets around like that, isn't that one of the advantages of being global," Murdoch said. Spoken like a pro.

ROLLING IN IT

A lot of my examples deal with successful Americans who've sought sanctuary offshore. But the crushing British tax system has resulted in the not-so-jolly exile of a host of the United Kingdom's wealthiest rock stars. Bill Wyman, who retired as the bass player for the Rolling Stones, said high taxes made it impossible for him to remain in England, when he fled to the south of France in 1971. Charlie Watts, drummer for the Rolling Stones, ditched England for Switzerland after his taxes had approached 100 percent! And Mick Jagger, leader of the band, quit living in England, though he decided he spent so much time on the road he declared that he doesn't live anywhere in particular.

You see, going global isn't reserved for people from a particular country. It's open to everyone because all sanctuary seekers are looking for the same goals. British rock stars, just like every other wealth creator, have their breaking points, too. "Why the hell should you put something out and come out of it with tuppence?" asked Robert Plant, the frustrated singer for 1970s supergroup Led Zeppelin.

RAMBO, RUPERT, THE ROLLING STONES . . . AND YOU

Now you're probably thinking that these examples don't apply to you. You're thinking that to build an offshore business program you have to be a superstar actor like Sylvester Stallone, a billionaire tycoon like Rupert Murdoch, or one of the Rolling Stones. Don't worry. If you think offshore is strictly for the super rich, I've got some good news for you.

In the offshore world, the same laws that apply to the big guys apply to the little guys. So if Rambo and Rupert can take advantage of the offshore world, you can, too. Indeed, I'm not writing this book for the multinational conglomerates who are already admitted users of offshore money havens. I'm writing this for you, the small business person with limited resources but an unbridled desire to grow.

OFFSHORE DEFINED

"Offshore" quite simply means banking, borrowing, and investing in countries with laws and regulations that are more favorable to you than the laws and regulations in the country where you currently operate.

A businessperson from Canada, for example, might decide to set up a manufacturing facility in the Caribbean because the labor laws there are a lot easier to comply with than at home. The added bonus is that he'd also get to benefit from the warmer weather!

But you don't actually have to move the physical *location* of your business offshore. You can do quite well simply by moving your business *deal* to a kinder and friendlier location. For example, when you borrow money from a bank, it doesn't matter where the transaction takes place. You can be in Alaska and your banker can be in Switzerland. The location the loan calls home can be wherever you and the bank decide to locate it in the lending contract.

This can afford you a considerable advantage. Take the issue of so-called safety in U.S. legislation. Safety might sound like a good objective, but what it really means is red tape and wasted time. When you're in the midst of a hot deal, the last thing you probably want is to have Uncle Sam poking his nose into things.

Let's say a lender agrees to loan someone $1 million. Then, for some reason, the lender decides to back out of the deal just before closing. In a country where securities laws are complex, such as the United States, it's not very hard for the lender's lawyers to bust the transaction using the numerous schemes and requirements packed into the Federal Securities Act. This doesn't happen in countries where the laws are less complex, such as the Cayman Islands. Accordingly, if you want to borrow

When you're in the midst of a hot deal, the last thing you probably want is to have Uncle Sam poking his nose into things.

money, why not do the deal in the Caymans, where the lender can't rely on red tape to back out of the deal?

As long as the local laws accommodate your needs, you can choose to base your business deal in any country you choose. I often use the example of the Caymans because they are not only a fun place to visit, but they have developed an excellent offshore infrastructure that, when used properly, can reduce taxes on an infinite number of transactions. These include selling products, selling your car, providing services, lending or borrowing money . . . you name it.

The offshore world is especially adept at banking. If you're talking about selling cars, you're talking about tangible products sold from specific locations. But banking is unique. The electronic network that makes up the world of international finance doesn't need a physical home base. So you can conduct banking free of physical constraints that pin you down in any one geographical location, and in that way get the deal done faster, with less hassle.

WHY HAVENS DO IT

Tax havens exist because serious investors and entrepreneurs need a kinder, gentler place to do their deals. They need sanctuaries where they can escape the taxes and excessive regulation that slow their growth in stodgier, more restrictive business centers like the United States. They also need places where they can enjoy privacy and the sense of well-being that comes from knowing their assets are protected.

Offshore tax havens are those countries that fulfill this need for privacy, asset protection, tax protection, and freedom from red tape. Tiny, resource-poor countries that once owed their livelihoods to banana trees and pineapple plants flexed the muscles of supply and demand by developing into thriving financial centers with wonderful futures. This explosion has been phenomenal, particularly throughout the Caribbean and the South Pacific. Only 15 years ago there were 450 offshore investments funds; today there are 6,000.

The real story goes back to the 1930s and the dark days of the Nazi terror in Europe. After Adolf Hitler became the dictator of Germany, he put in place a collection of laws that stripped the Jewish people of their rights. Hitler's goal wasn't just to extinguish the Jewish people as a race, but also to steal their property. The Nazi regime thought nothing of looting Jewish bank accounts and stealing Jewish businesses. Genealogy became a ticket to genocide. Heritage became a legal excuse for execution and expropriation.

Jews searched desperately for ways to protect the wealth they had built up over generations. The Jewish plight was noticed in Switzerland, a small country anxiously looking for ways to make money through products other than chocolate and cheese. So the Swiss government introduced the banking legislation that would change the tiny European country forever. Banks would be allowed to accept anonymous deposits. Under the new banking secrecy law, depositors would be assigned identification numbers. Under no circumstances would the Swiss government disclose the identity of the depositor. The assets on deposit would be safe until Hitler was gone and World War II was over.

We now know things didn't exactly work that way. A lot of Jewish depositors were murdered in the Holocaust, and the Swiss banks wound up stealing their assets. Only today some heirs are reclaiming those assets their ancestors deposited in secret. And we now know the secrecy laws didn't protect the identity of just Jewish depositors.

Nazi chieftains used Swiss banks as a dumping ground for the loot they stole from the Jews.

All of that said, the Swiss banking laws essentially did a good job when it came to providing depositors with true financial privacy and asset sanctuary. From the 1930s onward, Swiss banks became legendary for their love of secrecy. The system saved the financial skin of many individuals as the land of cuckoo clocks and wristwatches became a prime destination for the world's wealth.

New problems with the Swiss system popped up as time ticked on. By the mid-1970s, media reports linked Swiss banks to the piles of money Argentine dictator Juan Peron had looted from his country. It was the same thing in the 1980s, when word leaked out that Philippine despot Ferdinand Marcos had used Swiss banks to store wealth stolen from his impoverished nation. Switzerland started to feel pressure from the U.S. government to reveal the identities of some depositors. The veil of Swiss secrecy was lifted.

The privacy gap was soon filled by other small countries with no trade or aid on which to rely. Tiny islands without natural resources and tourism saw the opportunity: If the rich want privacy, why not give it to them? Soon tiny island nations became dynamic players in the world's financial scene. The Cayman Islands, for example, now boasts $800 billion on deposit and is the fifth-largest financial center in the world, providing global investors with ease of access, excellent professional services, and everything else one needs to get up and running. Not bad for a place where the chief economic resource used to be turtle farming!

Of course, technology has helped the offshore industry to flourish. When I started in this business, the Caymans and other Caribbean havens were without the speedy direct-dial telephone communications we take

> Typically, each haven—whether it's located in the Pacific, in the Caribbean, in the Mediterranean, or inland (such as Luxembourg)—specializes in a particular financial area and serves a specific market.

for granted today. Back in the 1970s, we relied on clunky old telex machines and "snail mail." Today we have fax machines and e-mail that can deliver information in the blink of an eye. Airline courier services can deliver documents overnight. With the world constantly getting smaller, little countries needed only the will and creative drive to elevate themselves to offshore money haven status.

Consider Malta, a country composed of three small islands just south of Sicily in the Mediterranean. Malta is just one of several new foreign financial centers that have transformed themselves from impoverished island states into thriving international business and vacation havens.

Like most other offshore centers, Malta is quite small (122 square miles). It has a modest population of a few hundred thousand residents. Among its citizens are many U.S. and European expatriates. That's because Malta has a generous tax system. Independent for more than 25 years, this former British colony also attracts a good number of tax exiles from the United Kingdom.

Malta's economy, like any other, requires capital. Following independence, its government needed to generate money in order to fund economic development. Unfortunately, the fledgling state went through a period of political upheaval during which its financial stability went from bad to worse. Malta learned its lesson, however. By the mid-1980s, it had established a sound government that sought to secure an influx of capital by offering an impressive tax break to individuals purchasing island property.

In the late 1980s, the Maltese government announced new regulations designed to compete with other money havens. The first of those regulations cut the jurisdictional income tax rate in half, from 30 to 15 percent for foreign investors residing on any of the three islands. Another of the regulations modified local inheritance tax rules to ensure that estate duty is payable on only a small percentage of a deceased resident's assets. (Again, the government's aim was obvious: to attract wealthy people from around the world who want to save taxes and leave the largest possible estate to their heirs.) Finally, financial services such as the cost of office rental and attorney's fees means that operating out of Malta is about half the price of mainland Europe. And if they're structured well, holding companies and international trading companies (ITCs) can have stockholders paying as little as 4.2 percent, explaining why there are presently more than 1,800 such companies registered in Malta.

Not every offshore haven contours its local laws and enforcement practices to this particular market. Still, such financial and legal accommodations are reflective of the economic benefits available through foreign financial centers. Typically, each haven—whether it's located in the Pacific, in the Caribbean, in the Mediterranean, or inland (such as Luxembourg)—specializes in a particular financial area and serves a specific market.

The bottom line is this: Offshore havens want the spending power that foreign investors and residents can bring. Without your wealth and the wealth of others like you, they would be forced to depend entirely on tourism for a capital base. And tourism could never begin to compare with the profits available through genuine foreign investment services. The result is that many places, Malta being just one example, deliberately and carefully develop into financial centers offering tax efficiency and state-of-the-art financial opportunity.

WHERE YOU FIT IN

It's funny how tiny nations with barely two coconuts to rub together can instantly reshape themselves into powerful offshore banking centers. Meanwhile, the United States, the most powerful nation on earth, seems stuck in a rut. In the blink of an eye, these miniature countries were able to adapt to the world demand for offshore havens. Meanwhile, the future growth and prosperity of America is blocked by a morass of bureaucratic red tape, violence, taxes, and government waste.

Oh well. We can't do much to solve America's problems. Fortunately, you can solve your own by seeking sanctuary offshore.

Don't get me wrong. I don't think all government is bad. For instance, I like the idea that I can get an ambulance to my house by dialing 911. I just don't want the government on my back, poking around in my private affairs, when it comes to my business.

An offshore business strategy gives you the power to choose how much government you want. It puts you in the driver's seat. And by choosing the location to base your business deal, you can choose the degree of regulation you wish to face, or the amount of tax you want to pay. It's all about choice.

The people who serve on a board of directors know they have a duty to shareholders. They have to find the cheapest way to do business so the company enjoys maximum profits. You owe yourself the same duty. You know that setting up an offshore business program will result in lower taxes, less regulation, greater privacy, and more asset protection. Don't you owe it to yourself to take true control of your life by moving offshore? The beacon is blinking. Look for it.

DON'T BE AFRAID

For many investors the biggest obstacle to venturing offshore is *fear.* A lot of them come to hear me speak. They read my books, as well as books on related topics. They talk with other independent financial consultants. They ponder the possibilities of involvement in an international market. But in the end, they weasel out of their own best plans because they're afraid.

"Who'll be out there with me?" one client asked not so long ago. "Sure, I want to make money, but I don't want to stalk the globe *alone* looking for the next big killing."

This fear comes from a lack of knowledge, and I understand it perfectly. When you grow up in the United States, you never truly realize there are other people and countries in the world. Your mind is closed to the global reality. My mind was opened when I was in my early 20s and had that great opportunity to travel the world, learning everything I could about tax havens. I lost my fear of the unknown and gained a sense of mission to share my knowledge with as many people as I can through my books.

I know you're worried that building up businesses in foreign countries means grappling with foreign languages and dealing with uncertainty. It's true you have to learn a new language when you create an offshore arrangement. But I'm not talking about French, Spanish, or

Chinese. I'm talking about the universal language of the offshore world. And as most of my clients found, it's easy! To master this new language, you have only to understand a few simple concepts. I call them the Five Easy Pieces. Master these Easy Pieces and ordering up business deals will be as simple as ordering a cup of coffee.

THE FIVE EASY PIECES: LOCKING UP

There's a reason I call these concepts the Easy Pieces: They're easy to remember. I meet a lot of complexity freaks in this business. These are people who take comfort in developing complicated solutions to simple problems. I take the opposite route. I want to solve problems as quickly and as simply as possible. That's why I've figured out that there are only five things you need to know to get yourself the key that can "lock up" your financial assets in the safety of an offshore money haven.

Location	First you decide which haven to use as your offshore venue.
Organization	Next you decide which legal structure to use. Should you park your assets in a trust, a bank account, or an offshore corporation?
Cost	An important question. If the annual maintenance costs of your arrangement far outweigh the benefits of the protection, why bother? Your goal is to save money, not spend it.

Kept At	Moving offshore doesn't necessarily mean physically moving your assets to the haven. You must decide where the assets will continue to reside.
Umbrella of Protection	The offshore umbrella of protection will keep you and your assets secure as long as you continue to make certain that your umbrella stays open. In other words, you must keep your organization in good working order and stay under the umbrella.

So all you have to do to develop a "Lock-Up" strategy is sit down and think about your needs. Remember Larry Lattimer, the executive we met in the introduction? His problem was what to do with the significant year-end bonus his company gave him. He was worried about taxes, wanted the government off his back, and wanted his assets protected. He resolved all these issues with an offshore program. He relied on me to explain how the system worked. Once I did, his fears went away, the mental cuffs came off, and Larry was ready to seek sanctuary.

Chances are, you are already well on your way to developing a strategy. Soon you will be wondering what you were ever afraid of in the first place!

BREAK DOWN THE BARRIERS

The very notion of tax havens and offshore investing raises some hackles. Some people turn negative right away. They think of media stories and reports that identify

anything offshore as being within the realm of drug dealers and money launderers. Nothing could be farther from
the truth. Remember that almost every Fortune 500 company reaps the benefits from their own offshore money
haven programs. Do you really think McDonald's or Wal-
Mart is involved in money laundering? There's no way
image-conscious corporations such as these would get
involved with anything so criminal.

You don't have to worry about being lonely, either.
In fact, the offshore community of successful foreign
investors and businesspeople gets bigger all the time. This
community includes people from all over, people starting
out with just a few thousand dollars, people with every
conceivable strike against them. What sets these people
apart is that when they see an opportunity, they seize the
initiative. Then, voilà: These rags-to-riches visionaries
find themselves on the leading edge of the world's profit-
making curve.

Face it. The possibilities within the United States for
truly profitable investing are dwindling. There just are
not that many Horatio Alger stories cropping up in this
country anymore.

On the other hand, wealth and security abound
offshore. There you can get extremely rich, in privacy,
and without unreasonable taxation.

YOUR ONE BEST OPTION

The beacon of the offshore world is sending you a light
beam. It's shining through the darkness to guide you to a
safe harbor. It's telling you that now is the time to put
your uncertainties aside and move out into the profitable
and less bureaucratic offshore world.

In order to be successful, you will need to combine
intelligence, instinct, and know-how. Intelligence is a

> **The sooner you get started, the faster your instinct for investments will develop.**

quality you're either born with or not. My sense is that if you've figured out that you need to read this book, you were born with it. Instinct exists in all of us. We just have to learn to trust it, and that comes with experience. The sooner you get started, the faster your instinct for investments will develop.

That leaves know-how. To acquire it in the offshore world, you have to be in the right place at the right time, talking with the right people. Helping you to acquire that kind of know-how is the purpose of this book. So let's keep going.

CHAPTER 3

BECOMING THE
INTERNATIONAL MAN

John Galt is the International Man. He is the mysterious entrepreneur that lurks largely unseen through Ayn Rand's influential novel *Atlas Shrugged*. John Galt thinks government should exist only to protect people and property. Yet he becomes convinced the U.S. government is destroying both him and his property through excessive taxation and regulation. Disgusted with the United States, he decides to go "on strike" by dropping out of sight. He lives in a world of total privacy—and total profit. He takes care of himself very well in the sanctuary he finds in the international world.

"Do not seek the favor of those who enslaved you," he says. "We are on strike against the creed of unearned rewards and unrewarded duties. We are on strike against the dogma that the pursuit of one's happiness is evil."

More and more, the United States we know is starting to resemble the country that earned the contempt of

John Galt. The reach of our government is growing. It's taxing us more. It's failing in its duty to protect us from violence. It's failing in its duty to protect our property—in fact, it's actually stealing our assets through forfeiture. While John Galt exists only on the page of a work of fiction, each day more and more real people decide to follow his example and make the exciting move into the international world.

And what makes the offshore world compelling? It certainly doesn't hurt that most of these havens are located on beautiful tropical islands! There's no question that it's more fun to do business while relaxing on the beach of some Caribbean paradise than while cooped up in your office back home.

But there's more to the offshore world than the sunny climate. There's freedom and privacy beyond your wildest imagination. Off come the shackles of government regulation and the handcuffs of excessive taxation. You become one of the new breed of entrepreneur, free to move through the world unburdened by the roadblocks that slowed personal growth at home. You become an International Man.

The International Man sees beyond borders. He believes that if government can't run its own affairs, it can't watch over his. He's fed up with producing wealth simply so it can be taken, with the notion that the harder he works, the more he's taxed. Like John Galt, he feels enslaved and seeks privacy, the unfettered pursuit of tax-free wealth and protection for his assets.

The International Man does business in the full confidence that his assets are completely impenetrable to attacks by asset forfeiture laws, lawsuits, and creditors.

Once he's broken free, the International Man quickly realizes that he and his assets are as liquid as mercury. He and his money can go anywhere. Even more important, the International Man knows *where* to go, which is wherever his money gets the kindest treatment. Once he's reached his destination, he knows how to keep a low profile. He's visible to his friends and invisible to his adversaries. He does business in the full confidence that his assets are completely impenetrable to attacks by asset forfeiture laws, lawsuits, and creditors. And he pays virtually no tax. Best of all, his stress evaporates as he begins to understand the truth behind the phrase "out of sight, out of mind."

MIGHT AS WELL GO FOR A SOLAS

Perhaps you think the world of the International Man is too good to be true. Maybe you think the International Man is, like John Galt, a fictional character who could only exist on the pages of a novel—or this book.

Not so at all. The International Man is very real. In fact, I've met him several times.

I'll never forget the first time I met Federico Solas. He walked into my office with tremendous resolve. Everything about him announced confidence. He dealt in certainties, not in the abstract. He knew how to reach you with a few well-directed words and a calm, determined matter. If you rank confidence on a scale of 1 to 10, with 10 being the highest, he was an 11.

Federico Solas lives in an Acapulco Spanish-style villa he designed himself. He wears custom-tailored suits and carries an elephant-hide briefcase. Behind his larger-than-life persona, Federico is a brilliant businessman. The son of a well-respected Mexican industrialist, he was already worth $30 million before we met.

I knew this man would be extremely successful in the offshore world from the first moment I saw him. And as things turned out after our consultation, Federico did make a $4.5 million profit in the first year of this offshore program.

Federico came to see me because he was interested in establishing an offshore bank that would serve as the intermediary for those whom he called "the big boys." He meant the largest American corporations and the biggest banks in Europe. His idea was completely original and opened my eyes to an entirely new way of using offshore banks. First, he would garner potential borrowers and then advise certain banks of their interest as a way of attracting sizable lenders. He reasoned that if an offshore facility was able to attract big-name borrowers—for instance, the Fortune 500 companies—it would automatically attract big-name lenders, such as Swiss Bank Corporation, Barclays, and Credit Lyonais. He was right, of course.

I found the idea as intriguing as I found Federico. He was so confident and clear on how his bank would work that before he came to see me he had printed up the letterhead of his bank's business stationery!

The first step in Federico's plan was to obtain financial mandates from several multinational corporations. With his Swiss-American Bank fully chartered and licensed to do business in Montserrat, he began work. Introducing himself as the Mexican representative for the Swiss-American Bank, he scheduled luncheon appointments with the treasurers of various Fortune 500 companies. After sundry business preliminaries, he would get to the real point: He could offer each treasurer lower borrowing rates than they were finding elsewhere. Needless to say, few said no.

Within 90 days, he had 10 letters in hand. Each was signed by the treasurer of a major corporation, and indicated that his or her organization was looking for funds at some specific interest rate. Federico then flew to

Europe and approached the leading banks on the Continent. He later told me that he made it a *rule* never to meet with anyone but an institution's top executive—or as he actually put it, he would only meet with the man who "cut the cheese." The results were impressive: Virtually every banker committed himself to extending loans—at the rates Federico had quoted to the Fortune 500 executives.

By using his offshore bank as a broker for the loans, Federico negotiated a small commission on each financial package. With every loan amounting to at least $15 million, his commissions were sizable. After just one year of such negotiations, his profits were almost $5 million.

I haven't talked to Federico in a while, but I do know he went on to bigger things. He ultimately sold his offshore bank and used the proceeds to buy one in the United States. He also went on to finance the construction of a $100 million office building in New York City. All of this grew out of his simple idea (putting lenders in touch with the right borrowers), which he merged with the basic principles of offshore banking, to generate profits beyond the wildest dreams of most investors.

Federico Solas is indeed an International Man. He makes quick decisions with enormous confidence. He doesn't let national borders stand in the way of his business plans. And he pursued those plans with a single-minded focus that is nothing short of inspiring.

We can all learn something from Federico. Think about his focus, his drive, his confidence, and his desire. Federico pursued his business with a sense of purpose. He operated from a mission statement, a set of rules and principles that guided his every step.

Federico Solas's Mission Statement

1. Always use my offshore accounts to receive and pay funds.

2. Always check every detail with my attorney.
3. Spend an extra day in Tahiti.
4. Loose lips sink ships.
5. Only deal with the top people.

Let's look at why Federico's mission statement was his road map to success. For each point in the mission statement, you should ask three questions: *Why is this statement important? How has the rule made Federico's life more beneficial or safer? What does this mean to me?*

1. Always use my offshore accounts to receive and pay funds. Why is this important? Federico came from an environment where every cent he made was accounted for. Before he became an entrepreneur, he worked as a salaried employee. He was used to having his expenses deducted from his paycheck. But once he made the move offshore, he didn't want to leave the same paper trail of accountability. He thought such a trail would be like a ball and chain. He wanted to make his life private.

How did this rule help? Federico had a great idea but he didn't have a lot of experience. Leaving behind a paper trail would generate a lot of evidence that would make it possible to verify his inexperience. (With digging, his prospective clients could easily figure out that he hadn't already done a number of deals with Fortune 500 companies.) Eliminating the paper trail and keeping his life private made it possible for him to fudge his lack of experience. It's not that he wanted to lie or con anyone. He knew he would eventually make the deals. He just needed privacy to give him a head start.

What does this mean to you? You could benefit from this rule for the same reason. Perhaps you have a great business idea that will get shot down if people realize your lack of experience. Perhaps you have other reasons to eliminate a paper trail. No matter what, you will find that enhancing your privacy will help you get on with business.

2. Always check every detail with my attorney. Why is this important? Because Federico realized *it's better to call a lawyer before something goes wrong than after!* Federico was not a legal expert. He figured the few dollars he'd have to spend to consult with a lawyer would be money well spent. His attorney translated the language of the offshore world into Federico's business language. He also confirmed that none of his deals or ideas would break the law. This further enhanced Federico's confidence.

Moving offshore was all about expanding Federico's freedom. The last thing he wanted to do was risk that freedom by getting into legal trouble. Federico was a good businessman and a brilliant entrepreneur. But good entrepreneurs usually make bad lawyers. Federico wanted to concentrate on his vision, and the best way to do that was to make sure a specialist was baby-sitting the pesky legal details of that big picture.

What does this mean to you? As the saying goes, keep the tigers in their cages. Let the lawyers prowl around their cage, while you prowl around yours. Work with a lawyer you can trust to keep you out of trouble, while you keep your eye on the ball.

3. Spend an extra day in Tahiti. Federico decided that if he was often in the South Pacific tending to his affairs, he might as well enjoy the beauty of it all. What's the point of visiting an island retreat if you don't take some time out to enjoy it?

> **No matter what, you will find that enhancing your privacy will help you get on with business.**

Federico knew he worked better and faster when he was relaxed and stress free. Learn from his experience. Going offshore is supposed to make your life better and reduce your stress. This is an offshore benefit just like privacy and tax relief, so don't shortchange yourself. Make sure you take advantage of your time spent offshore.

4. Loose lips sink ships. It turns out Federico had tried to arrange his bank loans before he came to see me. He had met with a big company in New York and secured a letter asking for credit. So far so good. Off he flew to Paris to meet some bankers. Following his "top people–only rule," he secured a meeting with the president of the Bank Nationale de Paris. Federico was closing in on his first deal! But here's where things ran amok. Federico had brought his wife with him to Paris. While Federico was in the bank president's office, his wife waited outside and struck up a friendly chat with the receptionist. The topic of conversation became Federico's inexperience in banking. After Federico and his wife left the bank, the receptionist dutifully repeated the conversation to the bank president. Not surprisingly, the bank turned Federico down.

Federico realized he'd never get anywhere unless people thought he was a seasoned financial pro. To project that image, he had to control the flow of information about himself. By strengthening his privacy, he got control of the image he wanted to convey.

Why is this important to you? Perhaps you lay out your business plan to a friend in a bar. Maybe you joke about your plans with your wife. Whenever you do something like this, you lose control over who people perceive you to be. You've got to stay in the driver's seat. Keeping things to yourself is the best way to do this.

5. Only deal with the top people. In the early stages of his plan, Federico found himself shuffled from one junior-level office manager to another. It was impossible to get things done. He was dealing with people who did not have the power to grant him what he sought.

Federico soon learned that he needed to deal with the decision makers in every organization. Doing so simplified Federico's life and saved him valuable time by eliminating his need to kibbitz with endless levels of impotent middlemen. Federico saved his energy for those who "cut the cheese."

Why is this important to you? Since decisions tend to be made only at the top, the simplest thing to do is to go directly there. That's how Federico got things done.

You probably think mission statements are insincere exercises in public relations. Often they are, but in Federico's case his mission statement was a serious tool. It's also what set him apart from the run-of-the-mill businessman.

Perhaps you're asking yourself whether a mission statement is for you. Before you answer, think how much good it did Federico.

MISSION POSSIBLE

Federico's experience shows that moving offshore isn't just a business deal, it's a mission. It's about learning how to think in a new way. It takes tremendous discipline and organization. But then, all important projects require a plan. Moving offshore is no different.

In the Ayn Rand novel, John Galt lived his life according to three guiding principles: reason, purpose, and self-esteem. When government interfered with the pursuit of his ideals, he abandoned government. His personal mission statement of reason, purpose, and self-esteem was so clear and concise that he had no trouble overcoming the roadblocks government placed in his way.

John Galt's guiding principles came to forge his character and personality.

Federico is another example of principles that define character and personality. His mission statement governed his whole outlook on life. They reflected his personal values and the goals he sought via his offshore strategy.

Perhaps you still have your doubts. Perhaps to you a "mission statement" is still merely a handful of insincere words that no one reads, hanging on an office wall. I understand. I know where you're coming from. You're a producer, a wealth maximizer. You believe in action, not words. So do I. But whenever I think the phrase "mission statement" is hokey, I'm reminded of my good friend Donald MacPherson from Phoenix.

Mac served with the U.S. Army Airborne Rangers in Vietnam. Now he's an attorney who defends clients from what he calls a new enemy, the IRS. His military training and experience have taught him the value of mission statements. When he was in the Army, he had to follow orders all the time. Those orders were mission statements. Focusing on his orders and doing whatever it took to reach that goal wasn't just the way to win the battle, it was also the way to stay alive. It's the same thing now that he's practicing law. When he maps out a strategy to defend a client, he develops a mission statement that simplifies his courtroom tactics. He says a good mission statement works like a road map. "It tells me where I want to be. I think about it and I never get stuck."

Mac's military approach is very useful, especially when it comes to the offshore world. He sees a parallel between offshore money havens and military fortresses. Which fortress should his military unit use to fight the enemy? That depends on things like intelligence reports, terrain, and enemy firepower. Which tax haven should his tax client use to fight the new enemy, the IRS? That depends on the information available from the haven, the

> **Developing your own personal mission statement simplifies your strategy and clarifies your vision. It gives you the map that shows you the easiest route offshore.**

degree of protection offered by the haven's laws, and whether the IRS has any weapons to penetrate the secrecy offered there. The answers to these questions find their way into Mac's mission statement. "It's the Bible."

Mac's experience shows us the real value in the mission statement. Moving offshore is a lot of fun, but it's also very serious business. Developing your own personal mission statement simplifies your strategy and clarifies your vision. It gives you the map that shows you the easiest route offshore.

Simplicity is very important here. One of the things I've noticed in my consulting business is the degree to which people love complexity. It's like a worn-out yet comfortable sweater: You get too attached to it to throw it out and buy a new one. People find the same comfort and security in complexity. They believe a complicated business arrangement will offer more choice, more flexibility. But this misses one of the beautiful reasons for moving into the offshore world. You don't need complexity because you don't have to deal with as much red tape. The international world offers enough choice as it is. So concentrate on the choices available in this world, and not on the minute details of complicated transactions.

In the offshore world, you need to take a focused and disciplined approach to your business. You can do that by boiling down your own rules and goals to your own personal, simple mission statement.

Then, with your mind focused on your goals, you can solve problems without worry. The answer you need will already be encoded into your business DNA. It's time to throw out that old sweater with the holes in the elbows and buy a new one.

ONE WORD: PLASTICS

Here's another example to illustrate what I'm talking about. Philip Evans Kamins walked into my office in 1979 with a copy of one of my books. He had a very clear mission. So clear, in fact, that he plopped the book open on my desk and pointed to a highlighted paragraph on page 65. "I want this," he said. "It will make my company $132,000 a day."

Kamins, who made his fortune in the plastics business, is a rags-to-riches success story. Since our meeting, he's moved onto the Forbes 400 list with a wealth of more than $500 million. Born in Chicago in the 1930s, Kamins's parents divorced when he was 12 and he had to go to work to help support the family. At 16 he got a job with a local plastics scrap dealer and, you might say, the rest is history.

Kamins is among this country's ultra-affluent, but he didn't do it through elite social connections or impressive academic credentials. In fact, he took night classes in finance at Northwestern, but never graduated. This is a guy who got rich by using his keen intuition for upcoming business trends. He got in on the ground floor of the plastics explosion, and he played all his cards right.

Kamins is an experimenter. He had come to see me to experiment with the idea of using a private international bank to pay domestic bills. The beauty of this is that checks written on foreign bank accounts take longer to clear. That means the money Kamins "paid" via check would sit in his bank account longer, earning Kamins extra interest.

Kamins was intensely focused on this idea. He knew exactly what he wanted to accomplish. He took me through a list of questions he had written out by hand. This was not a man who wasted time.

In the end, we decided to implement the plan. I recommended his company set up a private bank on the Caribbean island of St. Vincent. He took me to St. Vincent with him. He insisted on inspecting everything. It took only one day to complete the paperwork. Kamins then spent six days in St. Vincent enjoying the sun. Kamins has one specific interest that made offshore an outstanding option for him: He loves the beach.

Kamins doesn't have time to build personal relationships with even a fraction of his business contacts. Still, I do take a special interest in him and I've made it a point to keep track of his success. Has the bank worked? I am not in a position to say. However, I can say that someone like Kamins does not enter into this type of financial arrangement without it paying off for him in some tangible way. If nothing else, it allows him some measure of confidentiality in his bank-controlled business dealings.

Kamins had a very simple, two-step mission statement:

1. Generate more than $100,000 a day in interest income using the international bank.

2. Enjoy the sun and catch a game of tennis while down in St. Vincent. (He's a tennis buff.)

Now that's focus! Kamins planned it, then he did it. That kind of sense of mission is what it takes to crack the Forbes 400.

¿HABLA DINERO?

Another success story involves a man from Florida in his late 50s named Charles McKay. Based in south Dade

County, McKay has worked hard to be successful. He has almost three decades of experience with his offshore investment and business operation. When McKay talks about international moneymaking, a gleam comes to his eyes and his face beams. "There's nothing quite like it," he says proudly. For him, the initial allure was travel and big money. Always one who enjoyed foreign places, he was determined to find a way to make that enjoyment pay off.

Perhaps best described as an "international trader," McKay lives by a simple three-word mission statement: "Innovate or evaporate." By having a stake in the offshore market, he has managed to do much more than survive erratic shifts within the U.S. economy. He's capitalized on them. In effect, he is poised for future strategic investment, wherever it looks the brightest.

McKay started out back in 1963 with a small-sized company that manufactured building materials for Florida-based contractors. There was nothing particularly remarkable about the company, nor about McKay. But he had two things going for him: He spoke a little Spanish and he had a good idea. He wanted to take his product line and market it throughout Latin America. In the beginning, he hit the pavement himself—actually walking the streets of various South American nations, meeting potential clients and drumming up business.

His efforts succeeded. Today he trades commodities—everything from used factories and lumber to exquisite marble and frozen American orange juice. Like other global players, he doesn't need to speak Spanish anymore. And he doesn't have to leave the United States unless he wants to. Instead, he conducts business and monitors his

By having a stake in the offshore market, he has managed to do much more than survive erratic shifts within the U.S. economy.

offshore investments—which span the Western Hemisphere and the Middle East—from his home office via sophisticated communications technologies and various methods of instantaneous money transfer.

That's the simple yet elegant essence of the offshore option: being able to manage your business and personal affairs from the onshore location of your choice while continuing to enjoy the legal and tax benefits of offshore locales. McKay's current offshore operation is a company called International Equipment Services, which he describes as a "turnkey operation." It's a multifaceted venture based in Miami with activities that shift from country to country depending on need. For example, he might operate for a while in Ecuador, then move to Venezuela or Guatemala. He may make a deal to purchase a plant's industrial equipment in one country, dismantle the machinery and ship it to another for refurbishing, and then to somewhere else for reassembling.

Like many offshore strategists, McKay moves fast. Many find it difficult to keep pace with him. "He's a crazy man," one observer says. "He's running off in all directions at once and you think this guy is nuts, until you see him bringing home all the bacon."

The offshore option provides Charles McKay with the flexibility to adhere to that simple mission statement: Innovate or evaporate. This flexibility applies to all aspects of his business and personal financial affairs—including a safe harbor from taxes, and a relaxed legal environment where he can increase his profit margin tenfold.

MISSION STATEMENTS IN ACTION

You've seen how three individuals, Federico Solas, Philip Evans Kamins, and Charles McKay use mission statements to map their way to financial success. You've seen how the fictional character John Galt used his principles to decide to move offshore. And you've seen how Donald MacPherson uses mission statements to protect his tax clients from attacks by the IRS. So hopefully you're learning that mission statements are very practical business tools.

You can't argue with success. So here are more examples of successful organizations that have used mission statements to achieve their goals.

MISSION STATEMENTS ARE COOL

Childhood friends Ben Cohen and Jerry Greenfield started a small business together in 1978. They had only $12,000 to invest—and $4,000 of that was borrowed money. They used their little nest egg to renovate a gas station in Burlington, Vermont, and open a small ice-cream parlor.

More than 20 years after Ben Cohen and Jerry Greenfield opened their first shop, Ben & Jerry's scooped up $44 million in sales from a chain of ice-cream parlors that spanned all 50 states and had expanded into Canada, Israel, and Holland. And in April 2000 they sold the company to Unilever, the international conglomerate that also produces Breyers, Popsicle, and Klondike frozen desserts.

That's growth. From the first day of operation, Ben & Jerry's followed a clear mission statement. In fact, the company applied this mission statement to as many day-to-day business decisions as possible. For Ben & Jerry's, their mission statement is the foundation of their business. Here it is:

> Ben & Jerry's is dedicated to the creation and demonstration of a new corporate concept of

linked prosperity. Our mission consists of three interrelated parts:

Product—To make, distribute, and sell the finest quality all natural ice cream and related products in a wide variety of innovative flavors made from Vermont dairy products.

Economic—To operate the Company on a sound financial basis of profitable growth, increasing value for our shareholders, and creating career opportunities and financial rewards for our employees.

Social—To operate the Company in a way that actively recognizes the central role business plays in the structure of a society by initiating innovative ways to improve the quality of life of a broad community—local, national, and international.

Underlying the mission of Ben & Jerry's is the determination to seek new and creative ways of addressing all three parts, while holding a deep respect for individuals inside and outside the Company and for the communities of which they play a part.

There are concrete examples of how Ben & Jerry's turned its mission statement into action. The company gives away 7.5 percent of its pretax profit to projects that help children and families, disadvantaged groups, and the environment. It has established a charitable body called the Ben & Jerry Foundation, has set up "community action teams" throughout Vermont to help communities there, and even has a Director of Social Mission Development whose job it is to hand out grants. By putting their money where their mouths are, Ben Cohen and Jerry Greenfield prove that mission statements are a cool way to do business.

THE REAL THING

The world's most successful soft drink company says its mission is long-term growth for bottlers, shareholders, customers, and communities. Coca-Cola calls this mission statement Vision 2000. This statement clearly sets out how the company views itself in the business world:

> In creating value, we succeed or fail based on an ability to perform as worthy stewards of several key assets:
>
> 1. Coca-Cola, the world's most recognized trademark, and other highly valuable trademarks.
> 2. The world's most effective and pervasive distribution system.
> 3. Satisfied bottlers, who make a good profit selling our products.
> 4. Our people, who are ultimately responsible for building this enterprise.
> 5. Our abundant resources, which must be intelligently allocated.
> 6. Our strong global leadership in the beverage industry in particular and in the business world in general.

Sound insincere? Remember that Coca-Cola generates annual sales of more than $20 billion and is one of the most successful corporations in world history.

YOUR GOVERNMENT'S SECRET MISSIONS

The U.S. Marines are recognized as one of the world's most effective fighting forces. And because they're one of

> **There's absolutely nothing the U.S. government can do to stop you from joining the ranks of International Men.**

the best, they attract the best. This is similar to Federico's philosophy of only dealing with the top decision makers. Excellence breeds excellence. Federico only dealt with the best because he didn't have time to screw around. Marines pursue the best because they want to be in top form so they can handle any situation. They also learn to consider every possible option. To preclude one is ridiculous.

All of these principles can be summed up in the Marines' motto: *Semper Fidelis.* That's Latin for "Always Faithful." For Marines, the message is that they will always be true to their buddies in their unit, to their orders, and to their pledge to defend the United States. It means they will always be true to their mission.

I decided to include the Marines in this section not simply because of their motto. They provide us with a very interesting example of the way the offshore world works. I'm thinking specifically of retired Marine Lt. Col. Oliver North. Whether you like North's politics or not, his use of offshore bank accounts was meticulous, interesting, and exact. It also reveals a delicious irony: Several branches of the U.S. government, from the U.S. Army to the CIA, are active customers of offshore banks. Why? Because these institutions require secrecy. If the CIA wants to send socks to Iraqi Kurds rebelling against Saddam Hussein, they don't want nosy Congressmen or pesky investigative journalists to find out about it. The powers that be in the CIA and the Army use offshore banks because they're International Men.

But while the U.S. government relies on offshore banks to cover the tracks of its covert operations, it constantly works to erode this veil of secrecy for others. For example, the U.S. Justice Department decided to link businessman Albert Hakim to Oliver North's Iran-Contra dealings. The government lawyers had tried to get a court order forcing Hakim to turn over all records from his off-shore companies. But a judge tossed out the case. He said the U.S. government had absolutely no jurisdiction over anything outside the country. The U.S. government had absolutely no power to ask Hakim to turn over any off-shore business records. In fact, the court also noted that offshore banking records were so secret that the U.S. government hadn't even been able to prove Hakim had anything to do with any offshore companies!

Hakim walked free because he was an International Man. The U.S. government was unable to penetrate the veil of secrecy that protected Hakim's offshore dealings—assuming Hakim even had any offshore dealings. The beauty of the offshore world is that the same U.S. government that relies on this offshore world for its own covert dealings can't even prove the offshore world exists!

Your U.S. government would like you to think it can stop you from going offshore, but here's the truth: There's absolutely nothing the U.S. government can do to stop you from joining the ranks of International Men. In fact, we can start building your international personality right now. And we can start with nothing more complicated than a mission statement.

THE MISSION OF THE MISSION STATEMENT

For a company, a mission statement becomes its raison d'être, its collection of short- and long-term objectives. With the help of an effective mission statement, a company's employees, shareholders, and clientele know what the company's goals are and how it intends to teach those goals in the future.

Companies, after all, are diverse creatures. They are made up of people of various cultural, religious, and educational backgrounds, responsible for different tasks within the company and often working in different parts of the world. A mission statement plays an important role in uniting all this diversity under a common goal. It does not matter how diverse the staff is if everyone understands what the corporate team as a whole is trying to accomplish. Through a mission statement a company can achieve consistency, harmony, and better communication among its employees and its customers. The mission statement becomes the road map that will effectively lead the company to its goals.

By drawing up a mission statement for the International Man, we can develop a common set of standards, principles, and goals that will help anyone succeed offshore. We not only can identify what our International Man hopes to become, but will also set the standards by which he will do business.

One of the first things to think about is who the mission statement is written for. Companies write them not just for employees, but also for clients, shareholders, and the public at large. Take the Ben & Jerry's mission statement. A company that is committed to the community would want the neighborhood to know about it. To that end, Ben & Jerry's created a rather formal-sounding document.

But mission statements don't have to be formal. They can be as simple as a collection of phrases scribbled on a card in your wallet.

The length of mission statements can also vary greatly. Some are several pages long, others are only one page, while some condense their essence into one sentence. Remember the John Galt character. His mission statement consisted of a simple, three-word philosophy: reason, purpose, self-esteem.

The length of a mission statement is not important. What it says is. That, and the fact that it gets used. There's no sense in writing a mission statement that never gets read or implemented.

Let's look at how a mission statement can apply to someone who's moved offshore. You remember Larry Lattimer, the computer company executive mentioned in the Introduction. He came to me looking for advice on how to protect his assets from the U.S. legal system and how to reduce his tax burden on a six-figure bonus paid to him by his company.

Larry's mission statement boiled down to a set of five simple rules short enough to have been written on a scrap of paper and placed in his wallet. Nevertheless, these five rules defined Larry's actions.

Larry Lattimer's Mission Statement

1. Always deal face to face.
2. Only tell the government what it needs to know.
3. Don't panic.
4. Always keep the goal in mind.
5. Talk to Jerome first.

Let's look at Larry's rules in more detail:

1. Always deal face to face. Never deal by telephone. Only use the telephone to set appointments. Body language speaks volumes, and information can be lost when not speaking face to face.

2. Only tell the government what it needs to know. Don't volunteer information. The government doesn't give you brownie points for working hard, producing more, or revealing more information.

3. Don't panic. Ever. There's no need to worry once assets are offshore.

4. Always keep the goal in mind. Larry's ultimate goal was to start his own business. His mission was to build up capital to make the leap to self-employment.

5. Talk to Jerome first. Larry believes in advice. As an experimenter, Larry is eager to try new things. But before he makes a decision he consults with knowledgeable advisers to make sure he has the total picture.

Larry's mission statement rules gave him a framework in which to analyze and tackle every challenge. Using it, Larry knew what he wanted to do, and how to do it.

THE MISSION STATEMENT
OF THE INTERNATIONAL MAN

You have to adopt a focus similar to Larry's before moving offshore. You have to know what to do in any situation. For example, one of my rules is that I will never lie about my assets or my business dealings. That rule is ground into my psyche. It's a piece of my business DNA. Now, not lying doesn't necessarily mean I will fully answer every question I'm asked.

The International Man needs similar nuances to texture his sense of values. That's because the International Man must carry with him his own value system. This system is like a house that creates structure and order around your life. If you always put your socks in the same drawer, eventually you won't even have to think twice about where you store your socks. Your subconscious tells you where to find those socks. It becomes habit.

Through my experience, I've found that the following 10 rules define the essence of the International Man. This is his universal mission statement, if you will. It could apply to a Philip Evans Kamins working to save some money for his growing company. It could apply to a Federico Solas out to win business from "the big boys." It could apply to a John Galt who wants to lurk in the shadows of international commerce, unburdened by government taxes or regulation.

In fact, John Galt is precisely who I think of when I want to remember these 10 rules. The first letter of each rule spells out "John Galt, IM." The "IM" stands for International Man.

THE JOHN GALT INTERNATIONAL MAN RULES

1. Jail—never risk it.
2. Open your mouth to your advisers only.
3. Have control. Always.
4. Never lie.
5. Government is not for me!
6. Asset protection.
7. Legal—make sure it is.
8. Tax minimization or elimination.
9. Information on a need-to-know basis.
10. Make time for rest and relaxation.

Let's look at those in more detail:

1. Jail—never risk it. The whole point of moving offshore is to achieve freedom. The International Man never puts himself in a situation where his freedom could be compromised. That means never putting himself in a situation where his actions amount to a crime. If he does get in trouble, he negotiates a solution that keeps him out of jail. *The International Man understands that if he risks his freedom, he's already lost the game.*

2. Open your mouth to your advisers only. The International Man doesn't run around telling everyone what he's got. He realizes his property is no one else's business. *The International Man realizes that talking about his property provides others with information that could come back to haunt him.*

3. Have control. Always. The International Man always knows what's going on. He can delegate tasks to others, but he always retains control. In my experience, the clients I would describe as incompetent or unable to thrive in the offshore environment are those who weren't able to maintain control. They depended too much on others, forgetting that there's a fine line between soliciting advice and surrendering the authority to make decisions about one's own financial affairs. *The International Man craves independence and understands that like the captain of a ship or the captain of industry, the buck stops invariably with him.*

4. Never lie. One of your key values must be to always tell the truth. That doesn't mean you must volunteer information. You want to learn to create room for plausible denials. For example, what if someone asks you whether you've been sued, and the answer is you have been, but you don't want to admit previous legal troubles? You could answer this question in an ambiguous fashion. For example, you might respond, "It's true that I've made people upset . . ." and leave it at that. You've answered, but not directly enough to get you into trouble. *The International Man knows how to avoid falsehoods by answering questions so as to reveal the minimum amount of information.*

5. Government is not for me! When the International Man maps out his affairs, he selects the route that best avoids government. He views government as incompetent. Government bumbles, government loses, government hinders. The International Man knows he is better off on his own, relying on his own cunning, courage, and creativity, tempered by his own value system. *Wherever possible, the International Man avoids situations where his business plans require the approval or disapproval of government.*

6. Asset protection. The International Man wants to put his property beyond the reach of adversaries. He knows that leaving his assets in his home state could make him the target of frivolous lawsuits. If facing a possible legal claim in, say, California, he looks for any way he can move his assets either out of state or out of the country. Remember what I said about offshore havens being offshore fortresses? *The International Man makes sure his assets are behind the protective walls of his fortress, out of reach of his enemy, before he is attacked.*

7. Legal—make sure it is. This rule is an elaboration of Rule 1, because the concept is so important. There are absolutely no exceptions to it. Illegal activity means risking jail. The International Man never wants to take that chance. It's like L. Ron Hubbard, founder of the Church of Scientology, once said: "Subvert the legal system, but do it legally." *The International Man knows that any two-bit thief can break the law and make money, at least for a little while. The way to win is to bend the rules without breaking them.*

8. Tax minimization or elimination. The International Man is always looking for ways to cut taxes. He does not want to pay taxes in a system where the producers live at the mercy of the consumers. He'll contribute a little bit of his income to taxes, but the amount will be his decision, not the decision of some wasteful, greedy bureaucrat. *The International Man constantly organizes his affairs to pay minimum taxes.*

9. Information on a need-to-know basis. This is a rule I've adopted from the U.S. Army Rangers. Ask yourself whether anyone needs to know your dealings before you reveal information. Just think of the ridiculous things you're asked in surveys. (The warranty card that came with the vacuum cleaner I just bought asked me to fill in my income. Why the heck would the vacuum cleaner manufacturer need to know that?) You have to be very careful about telling anything to anyone. That said, remember Rule 2. You still need key advisers to consult with. Remember Captain Kirk from *Star Trek*? He never made any big decisions without consulting Mr. Spock and Dr. McCoy. You need to have your own Mr. Spock and Dr. McCoy. In my case, I trust my wife and my lawyer (who's also one of my closest friends) before I make any decision I think might amount to a material change in my life. *The International Man shares his confidences only with his inner circle of advisers.*

10. Make time for rest and relaxation. This might not sound like a very serious rule, but for me it's one of the most important. One of the key reasons to adopt an offshore program is to expand your horizons and travel a bit. If you travel to some tropical paradise for business and forget to take time out to enjoy the beaches and the boats, you've lost the game. Take Philip Evans Kamins, for example. Here's a very serious businessman who doesn't like wasting time. But he also understands the importance of taking time out. When we flew down to St.

Remember Captain Kirk from *Star Trek*? He never made any big decisions without consulting Mr. Spock and Dr. McCoy. You need to have your own Mr. Spock and Dr. McCoy.

Vincent, he made sure he spent time enjoying himself. Or consider Federico Solas, another hard-nosed business-man who didn't like to mess around. He, too, understands the value of rest and relaxation to keep himself operating at his peak. If the name of the game is achieving personal freedom, why not take time to enjoy it? If you don't have time for fun, what's the point? All work and no play does not result in personal growth. It results in stress, and stress breeds bad decision making. You don't prove anything by ignoring the opportunity for R&R that traveling offshore provides. *The International Man reserves at least 10 percent of his time to enjoy rest and relaxation because he understands the opportunity is part of his profit—and why would he leave part of his profit untapped?*

NOW IT'S UP TO YOU . . .

You want to do this. You need to do this. And you can do this.

It all starts with your personal mission statement. Individuals like Philip Evans Kamins, Federico Solas, and Charles McKay might seem exceptional. Institutions like Ben & Jerry's, Coca-Cola, and the U.S. Marine Corps might seem successful beyond the norm. But if you follow their examples, you can accomplish your own goals. You just have to focus your mind and your actions by drafting a simple mission statement of your own. This will help you find the inner strength, clear self-values, and self-image you need to become an International Man.

Ask yourself what you'd rather be: a sheep blindly following the flock, or a lone wolf prowling through the night. The choice is yours. The offshore world can be your dominion. You can be an International Man.

Chapter 4

Planning for Profit

In my quarter century of helping clients set up offshore programs, I'd have to say the most pervasive reason people make the move is the profit motive. That's not to say that privacy and asset protection aren't important to my clients. But the underlying incentive is the bottom line. People always want to use an offshore program to make a lot of money, and make it fast. While investors also find privacy and asset protection offshore, profit is definitely the silver lining.

Profit comes from an abundance of opportunity. The pioneers who settled the frontier challenged the notion that there was nothing west of Kansas City. By doing so, they found a new and exciting world bursting with opportunity and promise. To explore the offshore world you need to adopt the mindset of those western pioneers. Because this world is secretive and private, at first it might seem like there's nothing there. But once you break through that barrier of secrecy, you'll find yourself surrounded by new global opportunities offshore.

At the end of the process, you will find that you have become an International Man. You will have become an investor fully prepared to profit from any global business opportunity.

Start by following the advice of legendary investing guru Sir John Templeton. The founder of the Templeton Growth mutual fund empire, Sir John now races around the globe in his private jet, spreading a message that has for more than 40 years made him one of the world's hottest portfolio managers: *Treat the world as a single marketplace. Look for investment ideas everywhere and always be prepared to swoop down on any opportunity that creates the most bang for your buck.*

Sir John Templeton, you see, fits the definition of an International Man. He seeks to grow his fortune everywhere and all the time.

In my 27-year career I have also found that two categories of people respond to the beacon of profit that flashes offshore. I call one group the wealth maximizers and the other group the entrepreneurs. My most successful clients straddle both categories. But for starters, let's think of wealth maximizers and entrepreneurs as two distinct groups, and look at each in more detail.

WEALTH MAXIMIZING IS IN THE BONES

The International Man is a wealth maximizer. As I said in the introduction, wealth maximizers are people who are incredibly focused on growing their net worth. For wealth maximizers, thinking about ways to increase their fortunes is as much a part of their daily routine as brushing their teeth or taking their vitamins.

When I think of wealth maximizers, the first person who pops into my mind is a client of mine who contacted me after hearing me on the radio. By day, Dr. Steve Wilson is an orthopedic surgeon from the San Francisco area. After hours, Dr. Steve is one of the savviest investors I've ever come across. He is an investing genius whose batting average is 10 out of 10 when it comes to picking winners and making money. In just four years he ballooned $1 million into $18 million. I've often asked him why he doesn't give up his medical practice and devote all of his energy to managing his portfolio. I bet he could boost his holdings 1,000 times over if he worked on his portfolio full-time. He laughs at the suggestion. He says investing is just a small sideline. He enjoys orthopedic surgery more. I suppose I can understand. In both occupations he breaks bones!

I'm introducing you to Dr. Steve because he illustrates a point. Dr. Steve realizes he can't be a doctor and a full-time money manager at the same time. So he *delegates* and turns to professionals to give him advice and manage his fortune.

Dr. Steve understands this because of his own professional background. As an expert in orthopedic surgery, he realizes how counterproductive it is for his patients to tell him his business. His patients can tell him where it hurts, but they then must rely on his experience and expertise to advise them how to cure the problem. That doesn't mean patients lose control. They still have the ultimate say on whether Dr. Steve will perform the surgery. They can also set limits on what he should do. But it's up to Dr. Steve to apply his professional expertise to the problem and give patients his best advice.

When it comes to investing, Dr. Steve has learned to trust investment professionals the way his patients trust him. When I first met him, I was blown away by his degree of self-confidence, but I soon learned not to mistake that confidence for arrogance. Dr. Steve is willing to listen carefully to the suggestions and advice of his professional advisers.

In our first meeting, I couldn't resist the opportunity to get some free advice from Dr. Steve concerning my knee, which was hurting me after a long run that day. In about five minutes he told me how to get rid of the pain. Then he got right to the point and told me where *he* hurt: his tax bill. Like all wealth maximizers, Dr. Steve knew that if he could get rid of his tax burden, he would have more capital to work with. Access to more capital meant more opportunity to pursue profits. Eliminating taxes would give him the edge he needed to maximize his wealth.

My prescription, of course, was an offshore investing program that would keep Uncle Sam's greedy hands off his money. Once he told me he wanted to undergo the offshore treatment, we had to decide how Dr. Steve would go about managing his money. His directly overseeing his portfolio was not an option. Dr. Steve is far too busy with his medical practice to spend his days staring at computer screens or chasing down brokers on the telephone. So he decided to hire professional money managers to watch over his holdings.

That's not to suggest that Dr. Steve is meek and mild when it comes to investing. On the contrary, he issues very clear instructions to his investment professionals and monitors them regularly to ensure that his game plan is being followed. Just like that patient of his who has the final say before surgery, Dr. Steve makes sure he has the final say before his investment advisers operate on his accounts.

Dr. Steve does not consider himself an overly aggressive risk taker, but he is constantly on the alert for opportunities. That's why he was making money off Internet stocks long before most people had even heard of the World Wide Web. He is also an avid contrarian who believes the opposite of what he reads in the newspaper. If he hears that investors are flocking to buy stock in a particular company, he runs for the exit. If the word on the street is that a company is particularly undervalued and about to explode in value, he ignores the rumor and immediately sells the stock, locking in his profit. Likewise, Dr. Steve is quick to buy the stocks others disdain so he can build up his holdings at bargain prices, then sell once the price rebounds.

One thing Dr. Steve will never do is bet the house. He believes in diversification to reduce risk and protect himself. Dr. Steve has divided up his portfolio between stocks, bonds, and offshore investments. He reserves a good portion of his portfolio for relatively low-risk investments, such as bond mutual funds, which he knows will always be there. This gives him peace of mind. Dr. Steve knows that if even his most favorite stock plummets, he won't be wiped out.

"You have to be prepared for a stock to go to zero, otherwise it will drive you crazy," the good doctor explained to me. "You can't invest your grocery money, or your mortgage payment. It's got to be disposable income, otherwise you'll always be worried."

That's priceless advice from an orthopedic surgeon who's made an 1,800 percent return on his investments in four years.

ON THE ROAD TO PROFIT

Another client of mine, Bill Hollings, is a perfect example of the entrepreneurial spirit. Entrepreneurs are driven by a vision to achieve things on their own. They think constantly about their businesses 24 hours a day, 365 days a year. Their senses are razor sharp when it comes to the hunt for new business opportunities. They're great experimenters and tremendous free spirits who are willing to take great risks in the pursuit of wealth and reward.

I sensed these qualities in Bill when we first got together after a two-day seminar that I conducted in Dallas. In fact, he struck me as a classic American entrepreneur. Everything about him—his beige gabardine suit, his neat dark-brown mustache, his modest manner and cool Texas drawl—conveyed an image of honesty and exactness. He instantly came across as the kind of guy you'd trust with your money. I had a feeling even then that this relatively small businessman, who operated a limousine service in the Dallas–Fort Worth area, had the entrepreneurial drive to turn himself into an international financier.

Bill outlined a fairly simple international business plan at our first meeting. He intended to purchase an offshore bank and use it to increase his personal assets while he increased his company's visibility. At that time, remember, Bill was operating a limousine service. By establishing an offshore presence, he figured he could hobnob with the rich and famous and line up some clients looking for rides.

Within a few weeks Bill received the official license and charter for his bank in Vanuatu. Within months he had built it into a thriving, full-service financial center. He began by developing three zero-risk investment programs for people who wanted to benefit from an offshore involvement, but who were too cautious to purchase their own company or bank. These investment programs were

> **One thing Dr. Steve will never do is bet the house. He believes in diversification to reduce risk and protect himself.**

structured to let every client find his own level of comfortable risk.

Like most good businessmen, Bill had a sixth sense about promotion. It wasn't long before he had produced some really persuasive yet understated brochures and postcard mailings designed to add an extra level of professionalism and credibility to the well-conceived nature of his three offerings. For many investors, the promotional pieces were the initial contact with Bill's bank. What they saw through Bill's direct-mail efforts was a serious, sensible service institution that addressed their needs.

After only a year of successful operation, Bill decided to concentrate more of his energy on the offshore marketplace. It had already been very good to him, and he was now convinced that it could offer him much more than a means to promote his limousine service. He now believed his bank could be a phenomenally successful business in and of itself. He delegated a lot of his Texas limo operation to associates in order to free up his time for his offshore ventures.

He also began to get creative. His tendency to do things in the most traditional manner gave way to a more innovative business style. For instance, he started using his Vanuatu-based institution to structure and broker large transitional loans. It didn't take long before he was bringing together borrowers and lenders from all over the world in a wide array of interesting partnerships, mergers, acquisitions, and start-up ventures.

It was then that Bill grasped he had created an amazing financial instrument that could get him through any door. Soon after, Bill read in the Dallas newspapers that the famous Hunt family was running into some major financial problems and was facing bankruptcy. He instantly saw an opportunity. Never one to waste time, he picked up the phone and called them directly. Not only did he get through, but he designed a loan package that made the Hunts a bundle of money.

Three years after Bill's entry into the global arena, he called to tell me that since buying the bank he'd earned more than $25 million. Not bad for 36 months' work and an initial investment of $30,000. But what I like best about his story is the way it shows that offshore businesses can make millionaires out of fairly ordinary people. More important, it reveals the way that global moneymaking affects people. Bill did not enter the international marketplace as a dynamic man. He entered it as an intense, methodical entrepreneur who had very modest goals for an offshore banking business. Nevertheless, the power and vitality of the offshore environment itself had an effect on him. It freed him from the excessive restrictions that characterize business operations within the United States and gave him the tools to make more money than he had ever imagined.

These days, Bill is regularly invited to all the high-society balls in Dallas. He is no longer surprised but still elated to receive gold-engraved invitations to many of the premier events of the year. Of course, nowadays he isn't Bill the limo driver. He is William T. Hollings, a banker to be reckoned with and respected. Through the brilliant use of his offshore bank and his entrepreneurial drive, Bill has moved up into an entirely new social stratum, commanding a Texas-size dollop of influence and prestige.

BUILDING A STRATEGY

Wealth maximizers and entrepreneurs pursue profit in the offshore world in different ways. Dr. Steve Wilson, a classic wealth maximizer, was more passive in his investments. While he kept full control over his offshore portfolio, he was content to rely on professional advisers to manage the day-to-day operations of his equity, fixed income, and private investments. Bill Hollings, a classic entrepreneur, took a more hands-on approach. He didn't just make relatively liquid offshore investments, such as buying international mutual funds. He barged out into the banking world and created his own international business.

The wealth maximizer uses an offshore program as a platform to pursue profit in a relatively liquid investment portfolio. The entrepreneur uses an offshore program to create an international business. Of course, nothing stops the International Man from using the offshore world to pursue both objectives. In fact, the more the International Man establishes his offshore presence, the more intertwined his wealth maximizer and entrepreneur personalities become. For example, it would make perfect sense for a successful entrepreneur like Bill Hollings to safeguard a portion of his new personal wealth by investing it conservatively offshore. And it makes just as much sense for a successful wealth maximizer like Dr. Steve Wilson to set up his own offshore bank to pursue a more entrepreneurial line of investing.

It's all a question of strategy. And it's important for you to understand that all of my successful clients, be they wealth maximizers or entrepreneurs, have created strategies for themselves. A strategy is a way to organize your own resources to gain a specific outcome. My clients follow their strategies religiously, and they always achieve their goals.

Let's look at two sets of strategies the new offshore investor can employ in the pursuit of profit.

Let's look at two sets of strategies the new offshore investor can employ in the pursuit of profit. One strategy set is designed for the wealth maximizer, the other for the entrepreneur.

WEALTH MAXIMIZERS

Wealth maximizers usually work with three strategies. If you consider yourself a wealth maximizer, the first thing you should do is figure out how to set up your investment portfolio so you can make decisions and take action as quickly as possible. Specifically, I strongly urge you to learn how to use the Internet to research, buy, and sell securities. This is the future of investing. Secondly, you should line up professional money managers to give you good advice. This advice can be used to maximize wealth with the professional's account and on your own through the Internet. And thirdly, you should design your portfolio so that a significant portion of it remains liquid for immediate access. This liquid portion will be your offshore nest egg, safely tucked away offshore, yet readily accessible should you ever need cash quickly.

Conquer Your Computer

If you've put off buying that new computer or getting hooked up to the Internet, it's time to knuckle down and get online. For years I was a low-tech person, avoiding the Internet and computers at all cost. I thought there was no substitute for human-to-human contact. Then I found out that I could receive country and offshore banking information from great distance and without any costs on the Internet in a tenth of the time that I could using the phone and fax machine. So I became an instant believer.

If you followed the evolution of stock trading, you know that the Internet has revolutionized the brokerage industry. Trades and information are now just a few mouse clicks away. And when you couple the Internet with the offshore advantage, you've got an even more powerful tool. It allows you to take action on your investments quickly. It grants you instant access to research from an infinite number of sources, including news releases, analysts' reports, historical pricing data, and chat groups. Most important, it lets you monitor your account 24 hours a day without anyone trying to sell you anything.

Internet trading is a wonderful way to maximize wealth. Until recently, direct access to the stock market was limited to the exclusive club of the brokerage community. For wealth maximizers, this limited access meant delay. It meant nervously waiting for your stockbroker to return your telephone calls. Then it meant more delays as your broker sent your buy or sell order down to the order desk. And finally it meant paying your broker a hefty commission. The Internet changes all this. Now buying or selling stock is as easy and as instant as pointing and clicking on the computer screen.

This lightning-fast action is revolutionizing trading. It's now possible to buy a stock in the morning, then sell it for a profit later the same day. This process is called "day trading." You can't do it by trying to get through to a traditional stockbroker. By the time he returns your calls, the stock might have dropped again and wiped out your potential profit. Not so with the Internet. Your buy and sell orders are processed instantly. You have the speed you need to lock in those quick profits.

You can get even more out of Internet day trading by coupling it with the opportunities and advantages that lie waiting for you in an offshore program. By locating your

trading portfolio offshore, you can accumulate profit
without having to pay tax on your capital gains until
profit is removed from the account. Every penny you
make can go back into your portfolio to make even more
money for you. And remember that all of your trading
activity takes place under a veil of offshore protection. No
tax collector or nosy attorney is going to find a paper trail
leading to your offshore funds. You establish no accountability and have no responsibility to anyone but yourself.
You operate in perfect privacy. And profits are yours for
the taking. Taxes are paid when profits are spent. This
process is called "tax deferral."

Go with the Pros

Hiring a professional to manage your money offers you
peace of mind. If you're busy with another job, or if you're
busy enjoying a retirement, the last thing you want to do
is spend 24 hours a day worrying about your money.
That's the conclusion Dr. Steve Wilson came to. And quite
frankly, that's the conclusion any wealth maximizer
should come to. Don't be afraid to delegate responsibility,
and don't be afraid to receive expert advice. I know there's
a lot of things I'd rather do besides staring at a computer
terminal all hours of the day.

A lot of my clients are apprehensive about hiring professional money managers. They worry that this will
result in a loss of control—or even worse, account abuse,
such as churning. That's a point well taken, and you'll
remember from chapter 3 that I strongly advise you to
keep firm control over all your offshore activities. But hiring a professional adviser doesn't have to result in abuse
of your assets. Dr. Steve Wilson insists that his portfolio
manager report to him on a daily basis. He uses these
reports to ensure that his manager strictly adheres to the
diversification strategy he has in mind. Dr. Steve remains

in total control over his investments. He just delegates the nuts and bolts of the operation to professionals he can trust. The manager fears instant repercussions if he tries something funny.

By the way, I should mention that Dr. Steve has set up an Internet trading account and uses it regularly. In fact, that's how he reads the market reports he insists on inspecting each day. As soon as he told me about this, I contacted my personal money manager and asked to have the same feature set up for me. I think having instant access to performance reports is absolutely essential. Investing offshore means moving quickly to capitalize on quick information. Instant access to your account lets you know whether it's time to take the decisive action that will result in profit.

So for our wealth maximizer, hiring a professional should be a rule. And monitoring this account using the Internet on a daily basis is a great way to keep full control over the account your professionals manage on your behalf. If ever the reports reveal that your managers seem to have strayed from your diversification strategy, you can take care of the situation with a quick telephone call.

Your Offshore Nest Egg

The perfect privacy and the asset protection you enjoy in the offshore world create a wonderful opportunity for you to set up what I call an "offshore nest egg." Of course, by "nest egg" I'm talking about a pool of money that accumulates and grows for a rainy day. It's money that you don't intend to touch, at least not for a long time. You want it to grow at a conservative rate, say 10 percent a year. And while it should be separate from your more active investment account, your nest egg should also be highly liquid, in case you ever need to access it in a hurry.

Building up an offshore nest egg should be the crucial third leg to the strategy of the wealth maximizer.

Think of your nest egg as a security blanket. It enables you to go about your life knowing that no matter what happens to you financially, your monetary lifeline lies safely tucked away offshore.

Of course, by now you certainly understand that cash and investments kept in an offshore account remain absolutely private. Just imagine what would happen if you squirreled away your nest egg in a U.S. bank account! The government could steal it with its asset forfeiture power, or aggressive lawyers could grab it by hitting you with a civil lawsuit. A U.S. nest egg is as vulnerable as a real egg, and that's not much use to you if ever you should fall on hard times. Not so for the offshore nest egg. It remains safely and legally hidden from the prying eyes of the government, or anyone else that wants to get their hands on your capital.

This is why building up an offshore nest egg should be the crucial third leg to the strategy of the wealth maximizer. Someday it will serve you well as a source of funds for your retirement, in case of a serious accident, or should you want to go off and create a new life for yourself. That makes the litmus test of a good offshore nest egg—just how quickly you can tap into it in case of an emergency.

In my own case, I have two emergency tools in my wallet. One is a spare lightweight plastic key to my car. The other is a credit card that I've had set up so it's connected to my offshore nest egg. If ever I should find myself in need, I can use this card to quickly tap in to my emergency capital. I think of it as my "get out of trouble

free" card—just like in the board game Monopoly. I joke
with my wife about this. If she ever refuses to let me buy
something, I know I will still have access to the funds
from my personal nest egg via that card.

I recommend that you give yourself a 10 percent
rule. That is, take 10 percent of your annual earnings
and put it into your nest egg account. I can't emphasize
how important it is to invest these funds in a liquid
fashion. You can't struggle to get your money. If you do,
it's not much of a nest egg. One alternative would be to
place the money in an offshore bank account where it
can be accessed instantly. The downside to this is that
the interest this account would pay might be a little
less than you'd like to achieve for growth. So another
alternative is a leveraged bond fund or a money fund
that is quickly convertible to cash, but will also achieve
greater growth.

An offshore nest egg has tremendous psychological
power. Because it's safely protected offshore and because
it's always there in case you need it, you will find yourself
able to pursue your usual investing activities with
greater confidence and security.

STRATEGIES FOR THE ENTREPRENEUR

Now I'd like to tell you about three strategies that work
for entrepreneurs. These are people who want to use
the offshore process not just to maximize their wealth,
but also as their launching point into the international
business world.

The first thing the entrepreneur needs to do is to
develop an offshore idea. The second thing is to market
this idea as powerfully as possible. And the third is to use
his offshore accounts as a means to store and multiply the
profits acquired from that idea.

The Offshore Idea

Business ideas don't exactly fall out of trees, but entrepreneurs seem to find them everywhere they look. That's one of the things that separates entrepreneurs from other people. Maybe you've already got a business plan in mind and are simply looking for a way to turn your idea into action.

But if you're still looking for an idea, I suggest you learn as much about the offshore process as you can and set out to sell it to other people. If you think about the examples I've used in this book, you'll see how my entrepreneur clients have created their own offshore banks and used them to enter the world of international finance. There's nothing that's stopping you from becoming the next Bill Hollings or Federico Solas.

Suggesting that you pick up the offshore ball and run with it may sound reminiscent of a slick sales pitch. But as you'll remember from the introduction to this book, that is precisely what I did. It worked for me and my clients, and I encourage you to give it a try.

Whatever idea you come up with, don't forget how helpful the offshore process can be to getting your idea to market. There's always the obvious advantage that by operating from an offshore haven, you will benefit from lower or postponed taxes. This will free up capital. But don't forget that as an International Man you will additionally be freed from the government regulation that clogs our domestic markets.

For example, let's say you have an idea to set up a miracle drug clinic that will provide alternative medical treatments. Doing this in the United States would require you to satisfy a web of complex federal, state, and municipal regulations. Or maybe you'd like to set up your own offshore bank or mutual fund. Once again, you'd have to comply with an endless list of government regulations that will bring your wonderful new business plan to a

screeching halt. Your solution lies offshore, where regulations are less complex and more in tune with your desire
for quick action. You'll be up and running much sooner.

Perpetual Motion Marketing

Once you come up with your business idea, the next step
is to conquer the world with your new product. The way
to do that is to use your offshore program to market your
product as explosively and as extensively as possible.
Advertise in every media you can think of. Create a Web
page on the Internet. Buy classified ads in newspapers all
over the world. Set up a toll-free telephone number. Hold
seminars. Give speeches. Send press releases to every
publication and every television and radio station you can
find. Stop at nothing to get the message out.

The key element of this marketing strategy is
momentum. Every bit of publicity you get should be leveraged to breed even more publicity. After a while, this publicity becomes self-perpetuating. Your message takes on a
life of its own through inspiration or excitement. You
want those who learn about your ideas to feel inspired
enough to spread the word to their friends and colleagues,
creating an exciting story that becomes irresistible to
your target market.

The Wealth-Building Dividend

Once you begin to rake in the profits from your offshore
business idea, you'll need to do something with your
money. It would be a waste of a great business plan to
simply take your hard-earned cash and stuff it in a
domestic bank account. Doing so would leave your money
languishing at a low rate of interest. What's more, your
profits would be taxed at U.S. rates and would also be
liable for seizure by a government bent on exercising its

asset forfeiture power. And don't forget the lawyers who could greedily target you with frivolous lawsuits because of your deep pockets.

This is where offshore comes to the rescue. Remember, just as wealth maximizers should protect their savings from litigation or taxation in an offshore account, so too should entrepreneurs protect the profits of their business. Indeed, this third stage of managing your profits is to adopt the mindset—and protective strategies—of the wealth maximizer. Don't be afraid to fly, just make sure you've got a net to catch you should you fall— a net of protected profits.

So learn how to manage an investment portfolio using the computer, if you don't already have this skill. Learn to work with a professional money manager. And pause in your entrepreneurial endeavors long enough to build an offshore nest egg. If you don't practice wealth maximization, your hard-earned money garnered through your bright ideas isn't going to grow.

CONCLUSION

I've introduced you to two different types of offshore benefit seekers. Wealth maximizers use their offshore program as a means to manage their investment portfolios while reducing taxes. They also enjoy the benefits of financial privacy and protection from the seizure of their assets. Offshore entrepreneurs take things a step farther. They use the offshore process to bypass government regulation and take their money-making plan to market before using offshore resources to manage their profits and grow their wealth.

In short, I've shown you how the offshore concept is your gateway to profit. All you have to do is adopt a strategy that fits your needs. The money is out there. Now let's go get it.

CHAPTER 5

IN PURSUIT OF TRUE
FINANCIAL PRIVACY

After profit, the second major concern that brings prospective clients into my office is financial privacy. This doesn't surprise me. Over the years, I've heard a staggering number of horror stories from people whose lives have been indelibly marked by corporate and governmental intrusion. Based on what they've told me and on what I've read about U.S. law and economic policy, I am convinced that there is a complex, seemingly invisible information system in this country that has been set up to unearth, store, and disseminate even the most personal facts about your life. Hollywood seemed to have portrayed this in the 1998 movie *Enemy of the State*.

But this isn't Hollywood. I've seen the full power of this system unleashed on a good friend and client of mine. Tim Bradford is an animated, fun-loving man who runs a construction company near Los Angeles. I've always thought he looks like Flip Wilson. And he's as much fun. He enters the room with a confident gait and engages you in robust, enthusiastic conversation. A meeting with him isn't just a discussion, it's a concert.

Tim first came to see me about setting up an offshore bank. His reasons for doing so were purely economic. He thought the offshore bank would make it easier to deal with creditors. But precisely the day after we got the bank up and running, 30 federal agents and investigators from the IRS raided his offices, seized his business records, and chained his business shut. Needless to say, Tim was angry beyond words. Later that night he returned to his office and cut the chain off. That was a big mistake. Federal agents then broke into his home with a battering ram, arrested him, and carted him off to jail.

As things turned out, the IRS had been totally mistaken. The raid was the product of some sort of administrative mix-up. But because Tim had returned to his office and cut the chain, he was still prosecuted for tampering with seized property!

After this experience, Tim learned that the offshore bank wasn't just a handy way to deal with creditors, but a way to move his business affairs into a private realm where he could reduce his exposure to abuse by an incompetent government. Tim was emotionally devastated by his run-in with the IRS. He wanted nothing more to do with a government that had treated him like a convicted criminal.

Yet sometimes it seems the law isn't set up to protect people like Tim, but to persecute them. If you're like many Americans, you probably assume that the Constitution ensures your inalienable right to privacy. Unfortunately, you're wrong. The Fourth Amendment, most often cited as the national guarantee of confidentiality, specifies only that "the right of the people to be secure in their persons, houses, papers, and effects against unreasonable searches and seizures shall not be violated and no warrants shall issue, but upon probable cause."

The men of 1787 who drafted this legal tenet clearly meant to protect privacy as it pertained to property. They wanted an unquestioned right to ownership of land and personal possession. But as an article in *Time* magazine recently pointed out, our founding fathers lived in a world where people shared common norms of morality. They didn't need to sort through the questions that plague a global information service economy. They didn't need to worry about how one man might decide to use (or share) private financial information about another. They didn't foresee an era in which sophisticated communication systems could instantaneously interact—calling up, comparing, and exchanging information about you or me—within a matter of minutes.

In other words, they didn't foresee the new millennium. Today the greatest threat to your individual privacy may have nothing to do with property theft. It has to do with access to information about you and your activities. Where you live and work, the names of your children, your medical and psychiatric history, your arrest record, the phone numbers you dial, the amount of money you earn, the way you earn it, and how you report it to Uncle Sam after it's yours—these are the information tidbits that will undoubtedly remain stored in lots of different places as long as you keep your money within U.S. borders.

ESCAPE TO THE THREE NS

Much of the offshore world still offers you the one and only escape from this government-created conspiracy. Just as you can legitimately make more money overseas than you could ever hope to earn in this country, you can also look forward to enjoying your foreign profits in an atmosphere of confidentiality. In offshore money havens like Nauru, Nevis, or the Netherlands Antilles (what I call the "three Ns"), you can enjoy secrecy laws that strictly forbid any bureaucratic review of your personal financial records. That means you can legally guard your assets from the overzealous inspection that has become part and parcel of U.S. banking and investment portfolio management.

How Deep Can They Dig for Dirt?

It used to be that collecting information was a mysterious skill best left to private investigators. But these days anyone with about $100 and access to the Internet can unlock volumes of private information about people. Court records, now available online, are a window to some of your most intimate financial details. Civil lawsuit records make public scores of details you'd rather keep to yourself: income records, employment information, lists of assets and debts, and your Social Security information. Records in municipal databases can reveal both the value of your property and the amount you pay in property taxes.

If you're like most upper- and middle-income Americans, the federal government alone maintains nearly 50 separate files on you. According to one recent analysis, Uncle Sam currently has computer tabs on three billion files, a virtual treasure trove through which an army of eager bureaucrats can search and snoop. The state in which you reside probably holds another dozen or so active computer files on you. And the Census Bureau routinely updates its records. Any minute of any day, its computer system can spit out your basic data: sex, race, ethnic origin, marital status, employment situation, criminal records, and place in the household pecking order— and, coming soon, your DNA code. Most important, it can

> **According to one recent analysis, Uncle Sam currently has computer tabs on three billion files, a virtual treasure trove through which an army of eager bureaucrats can search and snoop.**

legally pass any or all of that information along to other interested branches of government.

For example, the Social Security Administration probably knows more than you do about your employment earnings history. If you served in the armed forces, you're permanently listed in the archives of the Veterans Administration as well as your service branch.

Then, of course, there's the IRS. It used to be that they only knew how much money you made, and where it came from. And yet, if you have ever borrowed money, an IRS agent can now—with a few computer keystrokes— neatly skirt the Privacy Act of 1974 and access a slew of information about your income, debts, employment history, marital status, tax liens, judgments, arrests, convictions, driving history, mailbox rentals, phone numbers, and other personal data. In 2000 the Justice Department spent $8 million purchasing such information from the publicly held data retrieval service ChoicePoint. Boasting a client list of 34 other federal agencies, including the FBI, ChoicePoint buys most of its information from the nation's three major credit bureaus: Equifax Credit Information (a division of ChoicePoint's former parent, Equifax Inc.), Experian Information Solutions Inc. (formerly TRW), and Trans Union LLC. The largest of these credit bureaus, Trans Union, maintains files on some 190 million Americans at any given time.

However, there is one small ray of hope. After a case brought by the Federal Trade Commission in March

2001, a federal appeals court in Washington, D.C., ruled that unless they have your written permission, Trans Union can no longer build and sell targeted marketing lists constructed from your credit report information. Predictably, Trans Union is mounting a vigorous court challenge. Stay tuned.

Still another category of consumer investigation companies collects information about the health habits and lifestyles of likely employment and insurance applicants. How do these agencies get their information? Mainly from the friends, neighbors, employers, landlords, and other casual professional associates of those they are investigating. The big daddy of this business is Equifax Incorporated based in Atlanta. Equifax sells reports to prospective employers and insurers on well over 20 million people each and every year.

This booming information industry has gone the way of all big business—toward specialization. For example, the Chicago-based Docket-Search Network sells a service called "Physician's Alert." It consists solely of information on patients who have filed civil suits. Its clients, naturally enough, tend to be doctors in high-risk specialties like obstetrics and orthopedics who are looking to refuse new patients with a history of suing for malpractice. Also in the arena of personal medical histories, the Department of Health and Human Services has just announced plans to spend $15 million over the next several years to create a new superdatabase that would integrate all patient-safety (that is, medical-error) data now being collected by four federal agencies. Plans call for possibly incorporating the data from state and private systems as well.

Then there's Moscom, the world's leading supplier of all accounting computer systems. Through Moscom's software system, employers can connect their workers' telephones to a personal computer system and track all on-the-job phone calls. The service gives executives a bird's-eye view of their company's telephone bill. But in the process they are spying on their employees' telephone practices. Is it such a stretch to envision a future in which employers eavesdrop on the actual conversations?

Sometimes the information that's conveyed through these personal records is painfully accurate. For example, I was once hired by a professional caterer named Suzie who had spent years living with the negative financial consequences of a past mistake. She was still fairly young when I first met her—maybe in her mid-30s. She came to see me because her five-year-old business, a good catering service hired primarily by the Los Angeles entertainment industry, had finally taken off and she was becoming quite successful. Along with her partner, she had nurtured a select clientele, and they were grossing about $1 million a year. They wanted to take a percentage of their profits and invest them offshore. Their goal was a healthy return with a fast turnaround.

During our second meeting Suzie happened to mention that she had actually started the business out of her small West Hollywood apartment. Now she leased a separate facility but still lived in the apartment. It seemed odd to me that someone making her kind of money—and obviously aware of strategic financial planning—wouldn't own a home. So I asked her about it. It turned out that while she was still in cooking school she had bought a brand-new Porsche sports car. "It was great while it lasted," she told me. "But on an assistant chef's salary, I couldn't keep up the payments for long." Before she could get out from under a mountain of unpaid bills, the car was repossessed.

In hindsight, of course, it's obvious that Suzie shouldn't have bought a car she couldn't afford. But by the same token, it doesn't seem fair that six and a half years later her credit rating was still suffering a deathblow from that earlier mistake. She had tried to buy a house, she told me, but the repossession of the Porsche was a red light to every potential lender. None of them was willing to take the risk.

I think it's even more shocking to learn about the victims of inaccurate information transfer. For example, one California woman was unable to buy health insurance because an emergency-room physician treating her after a diabetic attack wrongly diagnosed her as being an alcoholic. And not long ago, I read a story about a fellow in New York who had received a notice of his dishonorable discharge from the Army—a very odd occurrence since he'd never been in the service. Finally, he found the source of the problem: a former college roommate had been using his name. His ex-roommate had everything from bad credit to jail records, all under this unlucky guy's name. Unable to persuade credit agencies to change his records, he was forced to apply for a new Social Security number and driver's license. How's that for adding insult to injury?

TECHNOLOGY: BOON OR BANE?

The extent to which misinformation exists is, unfortunately, a matter of sheer speculation. According to some estimates, as much as 50 percent of all FBI records are inaccurate or incomplete. State criminal records are said to be anywhere between 12 and 49 percent accurate. And only 13 percent of all federal agencies bother to audit their own systems for accuracy.

That is particularly alarming when you stop to consider the following: It's Uncle Sam himself who weaves the most complex web of information on U.S. citizens. There are more than 85 federal databases on nearly 115 million people. And it's not just the volume of information that's frightening. Advances in computer technology are making it easy to do what was impossible just a decade ago: cross-match information at the touch of a keyboard.

A network of 18 federal regulatory and enforcement agencies routinely mixes and matches data—ostensibly

> **All this collecting, computerizing, searching, matching, merging, sifting, and reporting is meant to spot criminals, cut costs, and increase efficiency. Fine, but what about risk of error and intentional abuse?**

in an effort to detect fraud and waste in welfare and social service programs. Divorced fathers who fail to pay child support can be identified. The Department of Education can compare data that comes from various record systems to locate wage earners who have defaulted on their student loans. By comparing its lists with state driver's license records, the Selective Service can ferret out the names of young men who have failed to register for the draft. And the IRS can flag taxpayers who under-report by matching tax returns with information from employers, stockbrokers, mutual funds, and insurers of stocks and bonds.

In fact, the government's most aggressive investigating agency is the IRS. Its debtor master file, created in 1986, is routinely used to withhold tax refunds owed to borrowers who default on federal loans. So far it lists about 750,000 people who owe money to the Department of Education, the Department of Housing and Urban Development, the Veterans Administration, and the Small Business Administration.

Business Week reported that Uncle Sam even experimented briefly with buying lists from direct-mail companies, just to find out if the spending habits of targeted individuals were in sync with their reported income.

While that program was dropped almost immediately, the basic concept behind it—computer profiling—is now common practice within government. The idea is to spot combinations of data that characterize the types of individuals likely to engage in specific behaviors or activities. The Drug Enforcement Administration, for example, has worked up profiles of the types of people who are most apt to violate drug laws. The IRS knows the characteristics and behavior patterns of people most likely to underreport income. All this collecting, computerizing, searching, matching, merging, sifting, and reporting is meant to spot criminals, cut costs, and increase efficiency. Fine, but what about risk of error and intentional abuse?

And as our world catapults into the Internet Age, your privacy is likely to be compromised in yet another significant manner because of the apparent inability of our federal government to protect its own databases. In April 2001 Sallie McDonald, assistant commissioner of the Office of Information Assurance and Critical Infrastructure, told the House Energy and Commerce Committee's subcommittee on oversight and intrusions that during the previous year there had been 586 "incidents" affecting federal computer systems. Of these, 155 were defined as "root compromise" intrusions. Meaning that at least 155 computer hackers (and their buddy lists) also now have access to any information stored about you in any federal database.

THE LETTER OF THE LAW

What does the law have to say about this blatant invasion of privacy? What are your rights when it comes to keeping your financial life confidential?

The truth is, you don't have many. And the ones you do have are steadily eroding. The bottom line is that while the U.S. Supreme Court has recognized your constitutional right to privacy in some cases, it has repeatedly failed to extend that right to "informational privacy." In other words, you have very limited ability to curtail the collection, exchange, or use of information about you or your personal financial situation. There are, in fact, laws that authorize the *invasion* of your privacy. One of them is the Bank Secrecy Act of 1970 (Public Law 91-508). Its name is a deceptive misnomer because instead of protecting confidentiality, it gives our government outrageous authority to review and investigate personal and business bank accounts. The law requires all U.S. banks to maintain records of deposit slips and the front and back of all checks drawn over $100. Since it would cost so much to keep these records on hand, banks are allowed to routinely microfilm all your checks—regardless of value. So they do. All of them!

The law also demands that banks maintain records of any credit extension (other than a real estate mortgage) that exceeds $3,000. Banks must report all cash transactions, deposits, or withdrawals in excess of $3,000. They are required to ask you for your Social Security number or taxpayer identification number before any new checking or savings account can be opened. If you do not supply this number within 45 days of the request, your name, address, and account numbers are put on a list for inspection by the Treasury Department.

The law takes routine government inspection a few steps farther by requiring that you supply federal officials with your own share of sensitive information. For instance, you must report any transfer of cash or monetary instruments across U.S. borders if it exceeds $10,000. You must also acknowledge the existence of any foreign bank accounts valued over $10,000 when completing your 1040 tax return. And in fact, Americans voluntarily report an estimated $8 billion in offshore investments each year. A practice I hardly endorse.

Advocates of the Bank Secrecy Act like to say that it aims at fighting organized and white-collar crime. Maybe that's true, but I seriously question who suffers most from the letter of this law. Criminals and thugs, who are often masterminds at circumventing legal mandates, or innocent Americans who have never heard of the laws that conspire against their rights to privacy? I have to agree with the late Supreme Court Justice William O. Douglas who said, "I am not yet ready to agree that America is so possessed with evil that we must level all constitutional barriers to give our civil authorities the tools to catch criminals."

Several individuals and groups have challenged the constitutionality of the Bank Secrecy Act, but in each case the Supreme Court has ruled in favor of the federal government. In one of the most significant rulings, the highest court in this nation said categorically that we are not entitled to any "expectation of privacy" in bank accounts or records. Furthermore, one of the justices wrote that in each and every one of our banking transactions, we take the risk that the information will be conveyed by the banker to the government.

On the bright side, some action has been taken to reduce what privacy expert Mark Skousen calls the "wholesale government inspection of bank records." In his book *Mark Skousen's Complete Guide to Financial Privacy,* he reviews some of them. The most important of those he discusses, I think, is the Financial Privacy Act, passed by Congress in 1978. It requires that government investigators notify an individual and give him the opportunity to challenge the search of any bank, savings and loan association, or credit card record before that record is turned over to the government. If Uncle Sam wants to review records without notifying the customer, he must seek a court order barring the bank from notifying its customer of the investigation.

In actuality, a lengthy time delay is the only benefit of the law. Some of the people who have challenged the government's request to see bank records have waited up to nine months before their case was heard in court. And

once heard, virtually every judge has ruled in favor of
Uncle Sam.

You should also know about the Anti-Crime Act of
1986. In my view, it has given ominous new powers to
U.S. Customs, allowing agents the right to search
through baggage and mail without a warrant or permission. This new authority applies to departing as well as
returning travelers. So at their discretion, airport
Customs officials can now rummage through the things
you take out of this country as well as the things you
bring back into it.

The Money Laundering and Drug Control Act of 1986
is another frontal attack on personal privacy. This one
makes it illegal for bank employees, stockbrokers, real
estate agents, automobile dealers, jewelers, and other
businesses to accept deposits from anyone engaged in an
illegal business. Granted, it sounds fair so far. But the
law also states that deposits are outlawed even before
legal conviction. In effect, businesspeople and bankers
are being told to discriminate against anyone who
appears to be guilty! That seems diametrically opposed to
the principles upon which this nation was founded. Yet
it's now the law of the land, passed by Congress and
upheld by the courts.

The conspiracy continues. In August 1994, under
unrelenting pressure from the White House, Congress
passed another anticrime bill that contains provisions
that will further wipe away our precious constitutional
right of privacy. These new provisions will, in effect, take
us back to the worst consequences of the Bank Secrecy

**You deserve something better, and there are
plenty of foreign financial centers willing to
make you an offer that's hard to refuse.**

Act by allowing the Treasury Department and other federal agencies to forward to the Justice Department records of any "suspicious financial transactions" without notifying the bank customer.

Don't be mistaken about why all this concerns me. I don't condone illegality. I don't think people should evade the taxes they owe to this country; I certainly don't think that white-collar executives should be allowed to use public or private corporation funds to make outrageous and underhanded profits for themselves.

On the other hand, I wonder why our government has decided that the only way to identify bad guys is to snoop around freely through the personal business matters of law-abiding citizens.

Even more to the point, I wonder why any American with the economic option of moving offshore and into an atmosphere of utter financial privacy would choose to stick around and take the abuse. You deserve something better, and there are plenty of foreign financial centers willing to make you an offer that's hard to refuse.

An Ounce of Prevention

To ensure your own financial privacy, you must do two things. First, you must minimize the amount of information that gets created about you. Second, you need to verify and limit access to the information that already exists.

That may sound like elementary advice, but remember, the experts say that we ourselves provide government and private industry with most of the data they maintain on us. In fact, one study concludes that more than 72 percent of the time, investigators obtain their information from the very people they are monitoring.

Because you will probably want to keep some portion of your assets within the United States, I urge you to take a minute and consider ways that you can protect yourself from unnecessary invasion of privacy. Just to get you thinking along the right track, here are some practical suggestions.

First, be aware that not all domestic banks are alike. They all fall under U.S. banking regulations, but some are more privacy oriented than others. For example, a number of financial institutions have recently started photographing and fingerprinting customers before completing even the most routine transactions. I recommend avoiding that kind of a bank. Instead, look for a bank that's willing to ensure the highest possible level of financial confidentiality.

A good way to identify the right institution is to ask for a written contract that sets down the ground rules for your professional relationship. Make sure your contract includes at least these two provisions: (1) the bank must notify you whenever anyone asks to see your records; and (2) you reserve the right to periodically see and correct any records the bank may keep on you.

Secondly, when banking, try to keep a low profile. Think about it. By reviewing nothing more than your monthly checking account statement, an investigating agent could learn a lot about you—where you shop, the restaurants you frequent, the names of friends and relatives, your religious and political affiliations, even the private clubs at which you have a membership. On careful study, the account provides a panoramic view of your everyday lifestyle.

You should aim to reduce the clarity of that view. For instance, use your checking account for only ordinary, everyday expenses—mortgage or rent payments, utility bills, car loans. For more sensitive purchases, open and maintain a second account, preferably offshore. Better yet, handle these through a registered trade name. Simply set up a company and conduct your discreet transactions through its checking account. It's easy to implement this strategy. Your business must be registered, of course, either at the county or state level (or both). It's perfectly legal as long as you register it and use it without intent to defraud, and it will give you a flexible, low-key way to legitimately preserve your privacy.

To keep a low profile, you should probably avoid the wide array of privacy-insurance gimmicks that are around these days. Ultimately, things like invisible ink (meant to protect your checks from the bank's photocopy machine) and red checks (again, intended to limit reproduction) are only going to work against you because they bring attention to you and your account. That's not your goal. You want to preserve privacy, so you must try to blend in, become invisible within a system that constantly searches for the slightest deviation from routine procedure.

When it comes to investments, be forewarned that some—like interest on bank accounts and dividends from a brokerage account—are automatically reported to the government. Others are known only to brokers, bankers, and fund managers. Still others are not reported to anyone. Within this last (and most appealing) category, there are a number of subdivisions. For example, information about your commodity futures, options, and nondividend-paying stocks must be made available for disclosure, but only if someone asks for it. Data relevant to a foreign bank account is reportable to the government, but you are the one who reports it. And investments such as municipal bonds, gold and silver, foreign currency, diamonds, art, and other collectibles are not reportable to anyone, not necessarily known to anyone, and not available for disclosure until the investment is sold.

To maintain the privacy of your investments, consider the benefits of working through a fictitious business name or a corporation. Brokerage firms accept corporate accounts, and these accounts are used by individuals as well as by large corporations. A professional corporation can trade under its own name and, if titled properly, will ensure the anonymity of the real owner. You should know that your privacy is maintained only at the trading level. Outsiders can still gain access if the brokerage firm chooses to reveal the true owner.

To maintain financial and personal privacy in your correspondence, consider renting a post office box. This, together with a registered trade name, can do a lot to ensure at least a significant amount of confidentiality.

Finally, keep tabs on your credit records. There are about 2,000 separate credit bureaus in this country, and they all carry data that could potentially be used against you. Under the Fair Credit Reporting Act, you can demand to know what is in your file. If you disagree with any of the information you find in it, you can insist that another investigation be done. If that second go-around doesn't resolve the matter, you can enter your own statement of explanation as a permanent part of the credit file.

IN SEARCH OF THE REAL THING

To quote from Bill Petrocelli's excellent book *Low Profile,* "The greatest degree of privacy in this society is achieved by the very rich, the very poor, and the very crooked." His entire argument is wrapped up in that short excerpt.

Within the United States, it's possible to work diligently and ferociously to safeguard the limited privacy that our legal system still allows. Frankly, the incredibly rich don't need to bother. They're already protected by sophisticated investment plans—usually including off-shore involvements. The very poor don't make much effort either. They're too busy making ends meet, and Uncle Sam isn't vigorous in pursuit of information about them because they don't have enough money to make it worth his while. Finally, of course, there are the very crooked. They don't spend time protecting a legal right to privacy because illegal activity keeps them pretty well occupied and camouflaged.

That still leaves a lot of Americans who need to fight for privacy. This group includes people like you: upper-income professionals and businesspeople whose level of success makes them aware of how the government sys-tematically deprives them of personal financial privacy but who hesitate to take any drastic action.

It's for all those people that I've written this book. By moving a portion of your money offshore, you can give yourself an immediate escape route. You can stop chasing that elusive goal of onshore privacy and, in the process, you can walk away from the frustration and aggravation that are part of that quest. You can find out what life is like on the other side of excessive government regulation and bureaucratic red tape. You can, for the first time in your life, discover what true financial freedom feels like.

Again and again throughout this book I've said that if you want to design an international investment plan that's tailored to your specific needs, you must establish a one-on-one, professional relationship with an experienced offshore financial consultant. When it comes to structur-ing a foreign involvement that's sensitive to your genuine concerns about privacy, the same advice holds true.

A pro will help you implement and utilize the six basic privacy benefits that apply to almost every offshore

> **If you want to design an international investment plan that's tailored to your specific needs, you must establish a one-on-one, professional relationship with an experienced offshore financial consultant.**

venture and can be implemented in virtually any foreign financial center.

Privacy Benefit Number One: Reduce Your Internet Exposure

The Internet is a powerful research tool, especially when it comes to searching for new investment opportunities. Unfortunately, the tables can be easily turned and the Internet can be used to dig up information about *you.*

Everything you do on the Internet leaves an electronic footprint, and your electronic identity is a valuable piece of property to marketers and other individuals with an interest in snooping into your personal habits.

For example, if you send an e-mail, permanent copies of that message are left along the way. Your thoughts in chat groups and in bulletin boards can be recorded and stored indefinitely. Some Web sites innocently ask you to enter your e-mail address before letting you in. This creates another permanent record.

The most powerful aspect of this would be shopping. Let's say you buy your wife some lingerie over the Internet. A prospective employer might find this tidbit about your lifestyle rather interesting. Likewise, a prospective employer might like to study records of the movies you rent at the video store or the books you've bought from Web sites. And what if you buy groceries or food over the Internet? Insurance companies might be interested in this information to determine whether your eating habits suggest any health problems.

The moral of the story is don't underestimate the significance of the electronic footprints you leave behind when you surf the Web. Just think of all those junk e-mails you receive. The senders likely picked up your e-mail address from the electronic trail you leave on Web.

The future has set itself up for a more ominous Internet premise. The Personal Digital Shopping Assistant (PDSA) has just been released. This little gadget, about the size of a pocket calculator, will revolutionize the way you shop. You can carry it in your pocket and pull it out to scan the price codes of items at the store—just the same way the clerk does at the checkout of the grocery store. After you scan the price code, the PDSA displays what the product is, how much it costs, the date you might have last bought the same item, how much you last paid for it, and where you last bought it, and it questions whether you really need this product. It then—and this is the scary part—transmits this information to the Internet using the same technology you find in your cellular phone. The PDSA then surfs the Web to locate other stores that might be selling the same product for less money, then reports the results. All of this happens instantly, while you are in the aisle of the store.

That sounds remarkably convenient. But just think what would happen if this information got into the hands of an adversary! This information is extremely private. It reveals your personal shopping tastes and interests. All of this information is leaked out onto the Internet, where it can fall into the wrong hands. The future of personal shopping involves the sacrifice of your privacy. Do you really want to expose yourself to that world?

PRIVACY BENEFIT NUMBER TWO: PROTECTION OF YOUR BANK RECORDS

Government officials can gather the following information and material on you or just about anyone: checks (both front and back sides), bank statements, signature cards, loan applications, deposit and withdrawal slips, and all bank communications. Even more to the point, they can get it without their suspect ever knowing about the probe.

Domestic banks typically release records in the event of civil litigation, criminal proceedings, Securities and Exchange Commission investigations, and any IRS audit. A private foreign bank, on the other hand, can protect you from any such invasion. By owning your own offshore bank, for instance, you ensure that all your financial decisions (and the papers that authorize them) are beyond the reach of domestic rules and regulations. Provided your dealings are structured as bank transactions rather than as individual or corporate ones, Uncle Sam has virtually no authority over the size or frequency of your money maneuvers. You can also avoid reporting requirements by using offshore banks to transact your financial dealings in their name. Although the U.S. Treasury is informed of these dealings, it does not know the individuals involved—only the banks' names. The actual bank owners remain anonymous.

PRIVACY BENEFIT NUMBER THREE: LIMITS ON EXCESSIVE AND UNFAIR MARKETPLACE COMPETITION

One of the most important privacy benefits you get from an offshore involvement is protection against overly aggressive competitors. Countless fights have taken place in U.S. courtrooms, many of them involving large sums of money and vengeful antagonists. The inclination to sue at the least provocation is approaching an epidemic. And the likeliest targets are the people with the most money.

Let's say you become involved in a business situation that ultimately leads to a lawsuit. If you bank within the United States, a court may award your competitor legal access to any or all of your financial records. In the process, your privacy may be seriously jeopardized. If, however, your records are kept offshore, they are impervious to court orders.

PRIVACY BENEFIT NUMBER FOUR: SEPARATION OF YOUR PRESENT FROM YOUR PAST

Have you ever been the target of ugly gossip or intentional misinformation? It's sometimes based on nothing—just lies and innuendo. Other times, the story has a kernel (or more) of truth. And that's even more difficult to handle.

Most of us have a few skeletons in our closets. When it comes to financial privacy, however, those bones take on particularly ghoulish contours. Past mistakes—from a car repossession to a personal bankruptcy, draft evasion, or a minor criminal record—can haunt you for a very long time. Credit bureaus maintain all their information for at least seven years, often even longer.

If, for whatever reason, you are interested in separating your past from your present, financial privacy is a must. You will never have it within the domestic financial environment. Offshore centers, however, can guarantee your yesterdays will belong to you alone.

There is a more subtle concern that some people have about separating their personal identities. Even if they have no past mistake to hide, they want or need to make a clear distinction between various current financial involvements. For example, doctors have a very particular

> **Offshore centers, however, can guarantee your yesterdays will belong to you alone.**

professional image in this society. To protect their medical practice they must appear above and beyond many of the investment projects that the rest of us can implement.

What would you think of a doctor who decided to invest in a bar? Probably not much. Yet he has every right to experiment with such potentially profitable ventures. By handling his affairs offshore, he can keep a desirable distance between his Park Avenue medical practice and his South Beach bar and grill.

Privacy Benefit Number Five: Discrimination

History has also taught that discrimination can rise up and target even the powerful within a society. At various times, in various places, Jews, Blacks, Asians, Protestants, Catholics, and many other groups have been singled out for attack.

Unfortunately, governments are not immune to prejudice. Under federal authority, people around the world have had their property taken away. Sometimes they have also been imprisoned and even killed.

In times of trouble, governments tend to persecute the financially independent by means of price controls, rationing, foreign exchange controls, prohibition of foreign accounts, confiscation of property, and high taxes. War, and sometimes just the threat of war, can bring with it the sting of government restrictions.

That's why smart investors living in politically and socially explosive countries often keep the bulk of their money offshore. Overriding (and rational) fears of government expropriation push them into a no-choice position. As Americans, we can be far less fearful. Nevertheless, there is growing concern about creeping federal authority over individual economic liberty. As a result, quiet transfers of money and assets have become common.

If the essence of financial privacy means limiting the information that is available about you, then it seems wise to act before the fact. Don't wait until a period of unrest brings you and your assets under federal scrutiny. By then, it will be too late. You won't be able to protect what you've got because Uncle Sam will probably decide to "protect" it for you.

PRIVACY BENEFIT NUMBER SIX: LAYERING

An offshore program makes it easy to implement a powerful privacy strategy called "layering." This involves structuring property ownership to put as much distance as possible between you and the asset, without giving up any control over the property. The idea is to draw the scent of any search away from you by creating the illusion the property belongs to someone else. A simple strategy, referred to as a "Level One" layering, would be to list the ownership of an asset in the name of your spouse or a friend.

But if you don't want to involve those people, there are ways you can create even more distance from yourself. A "Level Two" strategy would list the property in the name of a corporation or business entity, then have an offshore mailing and legal address for the company. Moving to a "Level Three" strategy would involve registering the property in some offshore corporation, but then hiring employees or a management company to dress up the company and create the illusion that the corporation is much more than a shell.

CLEARING HIS NAME

At six-foot-five, Brian Donovan is a bear of a man who is honest to a fault. Back in the 1960s he was convicted of

> **The solution was to organize his life so he could keep his past his own business. I helped him set up an offshore bank. As an International Man, he was able to disconnect his identity from his finances.**

evading the draft, leaving him saddled with a criminal record. This was a travesty. He has deeply entrenched values and is incredibly committed to his family. Brian had evaded the draft due to his religious convictions. He decided it was more important to protect his family than his country. Whether or not you agree with Brian's decision, this deeply religious man was hardly a threat to society.

Back before President Reagan changed the law and granted clemency to all men convicted of draft evasion from the Vietnam War, Brian found himself unable to get a good job and get credit. His hands were tied by that felony conviction. Brian would try to be direct and tell people about the conviction up front in hopes they would understand. This is a fine example of why you should *never* volunteer information. Every time he would tell the truth of his past, he would be shown the door. No one would trust him because of his conviction. That meant he couldn't even get a loan or financing to launch his own business. He had enormous potential, but was going nowhere fast.

It took Brian a couple of hours to tell me his story. I found it exceptionally profound. I could tell that the black mark on his record did more than prevent him from getting credit or landing an important job. He bore this black mark like it was a scar. He couldn't forget it. It was always on his mind, wearing down his confidence and contributing to a mounting sense of defeat that was dragging him to the bottom. He poured his heart out to me, and I decided to return his openness by giving him 110 percent.

Despite his difficulties, Brian had achieved some success as a salesman. He was selling exotic cars, something for which he had a passion. He was clearly an able businessperson, a budding entrepreneur with the instincts and savvy that would have made him a fortune had he not been limited by his criminal record.

My job was to help him turn that around. The solution was to organize his life so he could keep his past his own business. I helped him set up an offshore bank. As an International Man, he was able to disconnect his identity from his finances. He was free and clear to make his mark in the world.

Brian was in a unique position. He came into contact with a lot of wealthy people by nature of his sales job. He saw an opportunity to invite his clients from the car dealership to invest in his bank. He used his private bank to provide more than just a release from his criminal identity as a draft evader. It also gave him an opportunity to step out in the world of international finance. He took his clients' money and invested it prudently. In this way he used his bank both to solve his identity problem and to provide an exciting service to others.

Soon after Brian's bank was up and running, President Reagan changed the law and expunged the criminal records of all convicted draft dodgers. This erased Brian's need for the bank, but he ran it for a while longer because it was making him so much money. Ultimately, he sold the bank for a substantial profit. The man, once shunned because of his criminal past, retired as a respected international banker. Now 62 years old, he spends a very comfortable retirement at the wheel of his sailboat. Free at last.

AS MUCH OR AS LITTLE AS YOU LIKE

Privacy is a relative concern. It can mean virtually nothing to one person while it means everything to the next. Only hermits know complete confidentiality, and they pay a high price for it. Most of us don't want privacy at such a terrible cost. At the same time, very few of us want to just hand over the details of our financial lives to the IRS and other federal officials. Instead, we want some middle ground, some halfway point between hypersensitive secrecy and flagrant economic exposure.

Offshore financial arrangements, which can be as simple as a checking account in some Caribbean tax haven or as complex as an international corporation, allow you to have as much privacy as you need. If you want to declare everything to Uncle Sam, you can do nothing. If, on the other hand, you want a strict guarantee of confidentiality in all your personal financial dealings, you can have it with a little effort.

By moving assets offshore, you can regain control of your privacy. Within the United States, you must play according to federal rules—rules that get a little less citizen-oriented every year. Offshore, there are entire jurisdictions organized to play by your rules. You design the game, and you get to be the winner.

CHAPTER 6

TRYING TO SAY GOODBYE TO THE IRS

Benjamin Franklin once said that there are only two absolutes in this world: death and taxes. That's certainly true in the United States, where concern over excessive taxation is the third major motivation for offshore banking. And so if you're reading this chapter, I will assume that you too are looking for ways to lower your taxes.

We have a new president and a new set of rules. What exactly does that mean? If you have had the perception that you can use offshore money havens in a way that would delay the payment of taxes, or even in ways that might provide privacy from the IRS—this perception must be scrupulously avoided now. I believe George W. Bush will keep his promises to bolster efforts to collect tax revenues. This means the IRS will receive increased staffing; we will see more audits; and prosecution of those convicted of tax evasion will be swift and sure. Most of my readers are aware that this has already begun. The IRS has embarked on a vigilant crackdown on all activities, both domestic and offshore, that permitted Americans to avoid paying taxes or hide income from the IRS. The approaches I recommended in the past have been, in my opinion, completely legal and aboveboard. However, the playing field has changed and it's time for a new game plan.

WHAT IS THIS NEW LANDSCAPE?

It's important to understand that none of the changes of the current administration prevent Americans from legally using offshore money havens. But the way in which they use them should be to shield their assets from creditors (but not from the IRS), to provide confidentiality from other businesses, and to take advantage of international global moneymaking opportunities. Thus you can still purchase offshore mutual funds and still earn greater interest and diversity for your assets when you invest in other countries. In fact, the legal opportunities for offshore investment are stronger now than ever before. The new landscape simply means that if you're an American and you want to stay at home, then you'd better be prepared to pay taxes on your offshore income. But what if you've had it with America? Then perhaps you should cash in your chips and repatriate.

BILL AND HILLARY SENT A LOT OF US PACKING

Even though I've moved my residence back to the United States, I still maintain an office in Canada; and this means I have dual citizenship. So I did acquire a valuable

But what if you've had it with America? Then perhaps you should cash in your chips and repatriate.

asset. Living abroad is a wonderful, enlightening experience that frequently helps to refocus your love and regard for your country of origin—your home. What have I personally gained from the experience? One fact is that I'm assured of medical attention for the rest of my life—because I'm a Canadian citizen. This is certainly one answer to Medicare. I may be in what some U.S. officials call "mediocre care," but it's still medical attention for anything that may arise for any catastrophic ailment—and at a lower cost. The systems to deliver health care eventually may change in America, but meanwhile, I'm covered.

Secondly, I gained enormous insight into what living in another country is like, and I think this is a benefit for anyone. I learned a new culture, how to meet challenges, my own strengths and weaknesses. I learned what it means to go into a supermarket and not find American brands like my favorite frosted flakes. I can recall how my wife and I used to go into the market and see all the boxes printed in French. Throughout the six and a half years we lived in Canada, we would still drive to the border towns of Washington to buy American products. I am an American, and a patriotic one—it was always difficult for me to completely make the transition.

Nevertheless, if the idea of giving up your U.S. citizenship and becoming a citizen of another country intrigues you (even for a short term), then you're not alone. There is an endless list of famous businesspeople who have given up their citizenship and moved offshore.

Kenneth Dart is a reclusive and privacy-loving tycoon who gave up his U.S. citizenship a few years ago to become a citizen of the tiny Central American country of Belize. Dart is the president of Dart Container, a company responsible for producing more than half of the 30 billion polystyrene cups sold each year in the United States. According to the Embassy of Belize in Washington, the tiny country taxes no income generated outside its borders. Dart has homes near Sarasota, Florida, and works out of the Cayman Islands. Dart's choice has saved him millions in taxes.

John "Ippy" Dorrance III, the billionaire heir to the Campbell Soup fortune, exercised his right to renounce U.S. citizenship to become a citizen of Ireland. He now divides his time between the Emerald Isle, the Bahamas, and Devil's Tower, Wyoming. Because Ireland levies an estate tax of only 2 percent, his heirs will escape the 55 percent tax bite Uncle Sam would have gouged from his fortune.

The list goes on. Ted Arison, founder of Carnival Cruise Lines, moved to Israel and became a citizen there. J. Mark Mobius, the famed money-market manager, was born a U.S. citizen but has now adopted the German citizenship of his ancestors. He lives in Hong Kong and Singapore. Sir John Templeton, whom we met in a previous chapter, gave up U.S. citizenship in 1962 and moved to Nassau. The move saved him $100 million in capital gains taxes when he sold his mutual fund management company in 1992.

So many important and immensely wealthy people have embraced this strategy that *Forbes* magazine published an article about it in 1994. This article attracted some very interested readers, not the least of which was a certain William Jefferson Clinton. After the president closed the magazine, he decided to take swift action to close what came to be known as the "expatriate's loophole."

CATCHING THE LAST BOAT

Floyd Sutcliff, a pistachio farmer originally from
California's agriculturally fertile Central Valley, literally
caught the last boat when he seized on the citizenship
abandonment strategy. I met Floyd in 1994 at one of my
seminars. He is a real old-fashioned American. In fact,
with his ambling walk and masculine presence, he
reminds me of John Wayne. One of the most interesting
things about Floyd is that up until the early 1990s, he
had an abiding faith in the U.S. economy. In fact, he was
almost religious in his passion for the American way of
life. Still, Floyd is nobody's fool, and at some point he
clearly saw the writing on the wall. Floyd's profits were
down. They'd been diminishing gradually over time, and
all projections indicated continued decline. Maybe that's
partly why he lost his faith in America. Floyd was convinced the federal government was incompetent; specifically, he was dismayed by the overall failure of
Washington to produce a balanced budget.

The country's continued fiscal irresponsibility had
thoroughly eroded the value of the dollar, and Floyd felt
bankruptcy snapping at his heels. "It's a damn shame," he
barked out at our initial meeting. "Hell, I used to be rich."

It didn't take much effort to convince Floyd that he
should diversify his assets and get a hefty chunk of them
offshore. Later, he decided to sell most of his family's
farming interests and he wanted to get the profits out of
the country tax-free. So I arranged for him to become a
citizen of St. Kitts. I completed the process on January
31, 1995, having no idea that for his February 6th budget
speech, President Clinton was planning to announce
actions leading to the Tax Compliance Law of 1995—a
law that would have prevented Floyd from proceeding.

The law was designed to make it more difficult to
give up U.S. citizenship without triggering some tax liabilities. Specifically, it provided that Americans giving up

citizenship must pay a 35 percent tax on appreciated assets at the time of relinquishment. The tax would apply only on gains greater than $600,000. The new law aimed at collecting $2.4 billion a year in new taxes over five years.

Floyd considers himself lucky to have made it under the deadline. This born and bred all-American took his money and his faith offshore where he thought both would be better appreciated and protected. "This isn't the America I used to know," Floyd once told me. So rather than wait for some fantasy turnaround by trickster politicians, he chose to become an International Man. That was seven years ago.

Today, from his Canadian home office, Floyd manages an offshore financial portfolio that includes partnerships with two Middle Eastern pistachio farmers, a small auto parts distributorship throughout Eastern Europe, and a chain of bed-and-breakfast hotels in British Columbia. Without outrageous taxation or government's economic bungling, he's making much more money than he ever could in the United States. And I would have to say, it is our country's loss.

More and more of my clients are anxious to make the move. They get their feet wet by first setting up an offshore arrangement to reduce taxes, and once they start to enjoy the benefits, they feel more comfortable about taking the plunge and moving offshore. This often leads to the third step—the high-board dive of renouncing their citizenship. And so, no book on the elimination of taxes

> **Specifically, [the Tax Compliance Law of 1995] provided that Americans giving up citizenship must pay a 35 percent tax on appreciated assets at the time of relinquishment.**

would be complete without exploring your right as a U.S. citizen to leave your country—and say goodbye to the IRS. The concept is simple. By exercising your choice to acquire citizenship in another country, registering your assets there, then proving that you have given up U.S. citizenship, you can relieve yourself of any obligation to pay Uncle Sam taxes.

EXPATRIATION—FOR SOME, IT'S THE ULTIMATE OFFSHORE OPTION

Let me begin by offering a definition:

Expatriation   To leave one's home country, and often renounce one's citizenship, to reside in another country

It sounds serious because it is serious. Expatriation is not for the fainthearted. Each year a few hundred Americans take this serious and ultimate step into the offshore world. These are Americans who have become tired of the taxes and economic mess here at home. They look around and realize that the Cold War is over. The Evil Empire has been defeated. Satellite communications means that they can be in touch with anyone, anywhere in the world, in an instant. And many offshore jurisdictions are quite comfortable and secure places to live.

Expatriation is the ultimate offshore option, and in many ways its time has come. Every year more and more Americans consider taking the plunge. It means renouncing your U.S. citizenship, taking up residence in another country, and obtaining a new citizenship. One tax planner calls it the "ultimate estate plan" because you can reduce your taxes considerably.

Expatriation is the ultimate offshore option, and in many ways its time has come.

Years ago, the actor William Holden made international headlines when he changed his legal residence or domicile from the United States to Kenya. Many wealthy Chinese Americans are making the switch back to Chinese citizenship for the simple reason that they can gain significant savings every year on income, gift, and estate taxes.

A recent expatriate is the billionaire Kenneth Dart. As mentioned earlier, he gave up his U.S. citizenship and became a citizen of the Central American country of Belize. He doesn't live there, though. He's domiciled in the Cayman Islands, a very comfortable island paradise. Other U.S. expatriates are headed to Ireland, Israel, Costa Rica, Canada, Portugal, Monaco, and any number of Caribbean money havens.

Expatriation is a complex process. I advise prudence and patience because a lot of careful legal and financial planning is involved if expatriation is really to work.

First of all, before you renounce your current citizenship, you should have already lined up a dependable citizenship with all appropriate documents in your new home country. Always remember that once you have renounced your citizenship, you immediately lose your passport. And renunciation involves signing an Oath of Renunciation with the U.S. State Department in a foreign country, not in the United States. In other words, renouncing your citizenship, obtaining your new citizenship, and setting up a legal residence in a new country must occur almost simultaneously.

Secondly, be sure that the benefits outweigh the disadvantages. Once you're no longer a citizen, you can stay in the United States for no more than 182 days per year. Any more than that and you will be considered a resident for tax purposes. On the plus side, once you've renounced your citizenship and set up a legal residence somewhere else, you will be seen as a nonresident alien and forced to pay estate taxes only on property actually located in the United States. And you can avoid further U.S. estate taxes by simply transferring all real U.S. property to a foreign corporation.

In terms of income tax, expatriation means that you will be taxed on U.S.-source income only—that is, income from assets geographically located in the United States. But it's important to know that there are special tax provisions intended to trap what the IRS calls "tax expatriates." Currently, if the IRS determines that your motive for leaving the country is to avoid tax, the Immigration and Naturalization Service can exile you from the country the same way it exiles convicted rapists and drug dealers. There are ways to avoid being banned, but they take careful planning. For example, if you pay less than $100,000 in taxes or move to a country with a higher tax rate, such as Canada, the IRS and the INS won't necessarily get together and assume that you've left the country to avoid taxes. This can be taken care of by receiving an advance ruling on your situation from the IRS before you leave.

Bottom line: Be very careful, and work with an experienced financial planner.

MORE ABOUT FOREIGN RESIDENCY

Americans also can take advantage of a tax benefit known as the "foreign-earned-income exclusion" covered under Section 911 of the Internal Revenue Code. This allows for U.S. citizens who live and work outside the country to exclude from gross income up to $80,000 of foreign-earned income. In addition, an employer-provided housing allowance can be excluded from income. There are other tax breaks available: Each member of a married couple working overseas, for example, can exclude annual salary of up to $80,000. That's a total of $160,000 plus housing allowances. It is important to note that this is not a deduction, credit, or deferral. It is an outright exclusion of the money from gross income.

Naturally, to get these benefits you have to meet certain requirements: You must establish a tax home in a foreign country; you must qualify for either the "foreign-residence test" or the "physical-presence test"; and you must have foreign-earned income. In the IRS view of the world, your tax home is the location of your regular or principal place of business. That is, the tax home is where you work, not where you live.

The definition goes farther for the foreign-earned-income exclusion. The problem is that many Americans think they are earning tax-free income. If you work overseas and maintain a principal place of residence in the United States, your tax home is not outside the United States. To qualify, you have to establish both your principal place of business and your residence outside the United States.

After establishing your tax home, you must pass one of two additional tests. The more straightforward of the two concerns your "physical presence." You must be outside of the United States for 330 days out of any 12 consecutive months. The days, of course, do not have to be consecutive. That sounds very simple, but there are a number of smaller rules that can complicate it. Few people begin their foreign assignments on January 1 and end them on December 31. For most people, therefore, the first and last 12 months of their overseas stay will occupy two tax years. This requires them to prorate their income and the $80,000 exclusion for those tax years.

THE BARRIERS AND THE EXEMPTIONS

There's an interesting history behind the tax advantages of offshore banking. Back in the late 1950s and early 1960s, federal officials became alarmed by the alluring tax benefits available to U.S. investors abroad. Their fear was simple enough: If too many investors moved assets offshore, the IRS could lose millions in annual revenue. So as a precautionary move, President Kennedy urged Congress in 1962 to prevent Americans from using tax havens. Within months, legislation was introduced that taxed every American citizen who owned a controlling interest in any foreign corporation.

It wasn't long before the U.S. banking industry got wind of the proposal and quickly moved to modify it. Virtually every major bank in this nation lobbied against the tax law. If their foreign subsidiaries were taxed at a shareholder level, they explained, then they would be unable to compete effectively against their foreign competitors.

Congress was convinced, and it basically built in a series of tax breaks for American-owned banks operating outside the United States. These special privileges continue to apply to any merchant bank that purchases and sells stocks as an underwriter; acts as an investment adviser, merger consultant, or business manager; or engages in a broad range of manufacturing and business activities outside U.S. borders.

Back in the late 1950s and early 1960s, federal officials became alarmed by the alluring tax benefits available to U.S. investors abroad. Their fear was simple enough: If too many investors moved assets offshore, the IRS could lose millions in annual revenue.

Let's take a look at some of the taxes you can effectively avoid by creating an offshore arrangement. I think the list is impressive:

- The Controlled Foreign Corporation (CFC) tax is a major barrier to tax avoidance. It applies to all foreign corporations closely held by either a U.S. corporation or individual. Normally, when no more than 10 U.S. citizens own such a foreign company, they are all subject to the current federal tax on their proportionate share of that company's worldwide interests, dividends, and royalties. In other words, the CFC tax allows Uncle Sam to take a hefty share of "passive income" from each of these shareholders—all of whom are treated as if the corporation (as a separate legal entity) did not exist. This barrier may be overcome by structuring ownership so that U.S. owners do not control the bank.

- The Foreign Personal Holding Company (FPHC) tax was adopted many years ago to attack incorporated pocketbooks that operate in tax havens and receive passive income. The tax is imposed only in the case of passive income generated by a foreign corporation that is owned by no more than five U.S. citizens. In such cases, each shareholder is taxed as if the corporation did not exist. Typically, this barrier to tax avoidance is insurmountable, but under its provisions foreign banks receive special exemption from the IRS if they can show that the bank was created for some express purpose other than pure tax avoidance.

- The Accumulated Earnings (AE) tax applies to both foreign- and U.S.-based corporations that are owned by U.S. citizens. Put simply, it taxes all accumulated earnings that are considered "unnecessary" for the business of the corporation. The AE tax burden can be as high as 38 percent on undistributed U.S.–source accumulated earnings in excess of $150,000 per year. It also imposes a penalty tax on those earnings that cannot be justifiably retained. An offshore bank can qualify for exemption from this tax because all banks—in the everyday course of business operation—accumulate earnings. That's the way they make the portfolio investments that keep them afloat.

- The Personal Holding Company (PHC) tax, imposed at the rate of 70 percent, applies to foreign- as well as U.S.–based corporations that are owned by fewer than 10 Americans. It is incurred directly by the company and not by its shareholders. In the case of a tax-haven corporation, it applies to closely held haven businesses and is imposed on all relevant U.S.–source passive income. Offshore banks may be able to avoid this tax if their income is not considered to be "passive."

- Foreign Investment Company (FIC) tax is imposed annually on U.S.–owned foreign corporations that exist primarily to invest in stocks or commodity futures. An offshore bank is exempt from this tax so long as it functions as more than an international brokerage house.

- Passive Foreign Investment Company (PFIC) tax was enacted in 1986 because Congress was concerned that some taxpayers were able to avoid many of the IRS traps by careful tax planning. The PFIC rules add a surtax on all distributions to U.S. shareholders from a foreign company unless the company is actively engaged in business and most of its assets are used in that business. A foreign bank registered in the United States can avoid the PFIC rule. Also, the PFIC rules can be avoided or their impact minimized through careful tax planning.

- Effectively-Connected-with-U.S. tax is a nebulous-sounding federal practice. It basically imposes a tax on the U.S.–source income of any foreign-based but U.S.–owned corporation if that income is "effectively connected with a U.S. business." An offshore bank is exempt from this tax because its activities, to a large extent, are treated as if they were conducted offshore through a resident agent.

JUST A WORD OF WARNING . . .

Remember that even within the international market, laws apply. A vast majority of the people I meet in my work see offshore banking and business as a legitimate escape from our overzealous U.S. tax system. Occasionally, however, I hear about someone who views it as something else: a way to conduct profitable but illicit business activity.

A story comes to mind about a famous offshore rogue. It shows how tempting it can be to break the law when you enter the foreign market. It's like being set free inside your favorite candy shop: With so much to choose from, it can be hard to watch your weight. I also like the story because it shows how offshore financial trouble can come from the least likely source. And, finally, the story shows how you can operate legitimately on all the major levels, but ultimately be destroyed by the small but illegal details.

Gucci is, for most discriminating shoppers, a familiar name. Luggage, briefcases, purses, and innumerable accessories—all of them expensive—are the products made by the firm. Most shoppers don't know, however, that the company's founder, Dr. Aldo Gucci, made part of his fortune with help from an illegal offshore scheme.

When Gucci entered the offshore market, he was a successful, middle-aged physician who wanted to use his hard-earned capital as a ticket into the lucrative world of foreign investment. So he hired a high-priced Manhattan tax attorney and told him to establish a company called

Gucci USA. It would design and market some of the most expensive leather accessories in the world, he said, and market them throughout the United States and the rest of the world.

Next, based on some very "creative" advice from his attorney, Dr. Gucci decided to establish a foreign-based subsidiary. The foreign company was to develop concepts for new products, research the marketability of those products, and attempt to sell the designs to interested manufacturers abroad. After considering the options, he selected Hong Kong as the offshore jurisdiction for the subsidiary because of its tax allure. Within a few months he had signed a licensing agreement with his own Hong Kong company, stipulating that it would receive 10 percent of Gucci USA's gross annual income to use as operational funds.

On one level, it was a brilliant scheme, but only on one level! Imagine being able to take 10 percent of an enormous gross annual income, move it out of this country without ever paying tax on it, use it to make millions offshore, and keep the money within a foreign financial center that imposes no tax on capital gains. It was illegal, of course, because the Gucci subsidiary never really functioned at all. It was a paper front that allowed Dr. Gucci to funnel unreported personal and corporate income into an offshore tax haven.

Nevertheless, the idea worked for 15 years.

And ultimately, when Dr. Gucci was caught, it had absolutely nothing to do with a thorough IRS investigation. He was caught because his own children turned him in. They felt that they were not getting their fair share of his burgeoning financial empire. So they decided to make money another way. They went to the IRS and gave them the name of their father's front company. They also provided the name of its bank, Chase Hong Kong, and its bank account number. In exchange, they asked to collect the reward that's typically given for such information: up

> **Imagine being able to take 10 percent of an enormous gross annual income, move it out of this country without ever paying tax on it, use it to make millions offshore, and keep the money within a foreign financial center that imposes no tax on capital gains.**

to 10 percent of the amount of unpaid tax due on accumulated profit.

As long as they were at it, the Gucci kids also decided to tell Uncle Sam who held the shares of the Hong Kong Company: two Panamanian-chartered companies. And if that wasn't good enough for the government, they even told officials where the actual shares were held.

Guess what the IRS did with all this information? Go directly after Dr. Gucci? No, because the government couldn't convince its star witnesses, Gucci's kids, to testify in open court. What's more, the IRS didn't have anything that could be used to indict Dr. Gucci. So Uncle Sam went after his bank. The IRS went to Chase Manhattan in New York, the parent bank company, and asked it to make Chase Hong Kong provide records on Dr. Gucci's transactions. When Chase New York refused to comply, the IRS decided to sue the bank.

Of course, the bank lost the case. So the bank took it all the way to the appellate court. And, again, it lost. In fact, I suspect that it knew all along that it would lose. But it also knew that if it rolled over too quickly on a big client like Gucci, its name would be mud with every major international investor.

To end the story, let me tell you how Dr. Gucci was ultimately nabbed. When all the dust settled, they got him on a technicality. He was shown to have had a "defective license agreement." In other words, they showed that there had not been enough activity within Gucci's Hong Kong subsidiary to prove it a legitimate business entity. In fact, during the 15 years that the agreement was in place, only three drawings or plans for new products had been produced by the firm. They had all been sent to the United States for approval, but none of the three ever resulted in an actual product. And the killer was that all three drawings had been prepared by an employee in New Jersey!

As soon as Chase New York turned over its records on Gucci USA, Dr. Gucci pleaded guilty and he wound up spending 18 months in a New York halfway house.

I've shared this story because it illustrates the fact that offshore crime really doesn't pay, at least not very often. And definitely not forever. Certainly there are international players who find illegitimate ways to make big money up front, but over the long haul, they pay a high price for the profit. They must constantly worry about exposure, and more often than not they end up paying Uncle Sam anyway—from a prison cell especially designed for white-collar crooks.

It's one thing to outsmart the IRS at its own game. It's another to break the law. How can you tell the difference? When you cannot comfortably trace your actions with clear explanations for why you did what you did, you've probably crossed the line from shrewd offshore venture strategy into criminal business operation. That's an extremely important distinction.

THE SPIRIT OF AMERICA

There are tens of thousands of people throughout this country who mind their own business, apply themselves, and make a real contribution to our economy. But with the passage of each new tax law, they must hold on tighter in the effort to keep an equitable fraction of the fruits of their labor.

Every year, the president, the Congress, and the Supreme Court give IRS officials more money, more laws, and more leeway to collect revenues from us all. They get better computers, more agents, and more auditors. It's a virtual army against each individual and each family.

Ironically, however, it's the very complexity of the U.S. tax system that offers wise Americans the one remaining way out from under excessive taxation. With the help of an experienced financial consultant, you can turn the ambiguities and inconsistencies of our tax code to your own advantage. You can break away from the uninformed majority and revolutionize your economic life. I believe that in making such a move, you reflect the finest spirit of this nation: individual ingenuity and the pursuit of personal betterment.

Right now, offshore banks and some foreign companies let you legally move assets outside the United States and benefit from this move. All you have to do is reap your profits and pay your taxes. There are still fortunes to be made abroad.

CHAPTER 7

PROTECTING YOUR ASSETS

Nuisance lawsuits are proliferating. Ridiculous and frivolous, they litter the courthouses of the nation. The odds you will be sued are about one in ten. Lawyers will target anyone with any money for any reason. A recent study suggests that one-fourth of all lawsuits filed in the United States are of the nuisance variety.

That statistic isn't hard to believe when you glance at some of the lawsuits filed during the past few years. A Florida man tried to sue a topless bar for $15,000. He claimed he got whiplash after being bonked on the head by a dancer's 66-HH bust. A man sued Anheuser-Busch for $10,000 for false advertising. He complained that drinking beer didn't improve his luck with women. An Ohio man wants $500,000 from the company that makes M&M candies and the Family Dollar Store because he found a plain M&M among his Peanut M&Ms.

That's not even the most nutty suit I could mention. What's less of a joke is the fact that you could be a target, and that one of these ridiculous suits can be a horrific drain on your wealth. Don't think a judge or a jury will simply laugh a nuisance suit out of court. Sometimes the plaintiffs win huge, lottery-size awards. And even if you prevail, your legal fees can be astounding.

For example, a West Virginia convenience store worker had to be tickled pink when she learned she won a whopping $2.7 million because she hurt her back opening a pickle jar. Fortunately, the West Virginia State Supreme Court decided to reduce this ridiculous sum. It cut the damages to a mere $2.2 million.

In another case, a 27-year-old Michigan man won a $200,000 jury award after he claimed a rear-end collision with a truck turned him into a homosexual. He sued the owners of the truck, claiming the accident caused him to lose interest in his wife. After the accident, he moved in with his parents, began frequenting gay bars, and reading gay literature. By the way, the jury also gave his wife $25,000 for the resulting loss of companionship.

Jury awards in hand, the lady from West Virginia and the man from Michigan have every right to force the unsuccessful defendants to pay up. And the legal ammunition they have available is extraordinary because they have the power of the state at their disposal. In the words of the law, the victorious plaintiffs become judgment creditors and the defeated defendants become judgment debtors. Judgment creditors can bleed judgment debtors dry until the full award is paid.

Judgment creditors can slap liens on defendants' real estate and personal business property. They can report the claim to a credit rating agency. They can haul the debtors back to court for a debtors' examination. This is where the creditors can ask the defendants about their finances under oath. The creditors can also obtain documents called "writs of execution" that allow them to seize the debtors' property. If a plaintiff's frivolous lawsuit isn't bothersome enough, a plaintiff with a judgment in hand

can make the rest of your life a living hell. Take O. J.
Simpson, for example, who will spend the rest of his life
appearing before Fred Goldman's lawyers and answering
questions about where he got the money to pay for his
last set of golf clubs.

This threatens the life you take for granted. Most
successful Americans want a very basic kind of financial
freedom. They want to be able to spend the largest possible percentage of the wealth they have accumulated in
whatever way they see fit, and they want to be able to
leave what remains upon their death to their heirs.

There's nothing terribly complex or bewildering
about such a liberty. In fact, it complements the economic ethics that built the United States of America: a
guarantee of free enterprise and the promise that every
generation might prosper beyond the previous, to ensure
a better life for those to come.

Unfortunately, it's only a small minority of affluent
Americans who ever manage to enjoy this kind of economic freedom. The reality for everyone else is far more
sobering and grim. Put simply, true asset protection does
not exist in this country, or anywhere in North America
for that matter.

We've already talked about taxes. After Uncle Sam
takes his share, you've probably lost more than one-third
of what you had to begin with. Then there's state tax to
pay, Social Security tax, gasoline tax, consumer tax, and,
of course, estate tax on anything you inherit. Figure in

Most successful Americans want to be able to
spend the largest possible percentage of the
wealth they have accumulated in whatever way
they see fit, and they want to be able to leave
what remains upon their death to their heirs.

the additional cost of liability insurance and loss—both
of which are everyday components of doing business for
a lot of wealthy and affluent Americans—and you begin
to see why even the most highly paid professionals don't
live as well as their parents did in the 1950s and 1960s.
In fact, they don't live as well as they themselves did in
the 1980s. Things just get worse and worse with no end
in sight.

All these irrefutable realities create the strongest
argument for developing an offshore financial strategy.
Outside the United States, beyond the reach of excessive U.S. government interference, there are little-
known ways to safeguard what you have and use it to
make more.

There are two kinds of people who need asset protection. I call them "principle seekers" and "insolvenites."
Let's look at each in turn.

PRINCIPLE SEEKERS: PROOF BEFORE ACTION

Principle seekers often have no trouble with money. They
work hard, save efficiently, and invest wisely. They guard
their fortunes very carefully. So if someone takes a stab at
their money, be it through a lawsuit or a bill for goods and
services rendered, they think carefully before paying. If
they owe the bill fair and square, they pay. But if for any
reason they believe the demand is unwarranted, unfair,
inaccurate, or outright frivolous, they don't roll over and
take it. They say, "Prove it."

This is especially the case when it comes to lawsuits.
Even if they agree they did something wrong, they still
insist the plaintiff take the case to court and go through
the motions of proving up the case. Divorces are a good
example. If the state divorce law contemplates splitting
the assets of the marriage into two pieces, the principle

seeker will insist his or her spouse prove the value of the assets in court before agreeing to any division of property. Business lawsuits are another good example. The principle seeker won't let his adversaries in business raid his finances without a fight. He won't settle any dispute until he's convinced his opponent has had to pay some money to take the case to court. For the principle seeker, offshore asset protection makes a lot of sense. It makes the creditor/attacker come in to a court, which is always friendlier to the accused.

INSOLVENITES: EXTRACTING BLOOD FROM A STONE

Insolvenites are people who are broke. They couldn't pay the claims leveled against them even if they wanted to. For example, an insolvenite might be facing a $1 million lawsuit even though his personal net worth is only $100,000.

The real problem insolvenites face is they can't afford to fight legal claims in court. Lawsuits cost thousands to defend, even frivolous ones. A writer was sued for $60 million after writing a book about a convicted serial killer. The death row inmate, convicted of 16 murders, claimed the book defamed his good name. The case was thrown out of court in 46 seconds, but months of trial preparation resulted in a $30,000 legal bill for the writer's publisher.

There is obviously a certain stigma that goes with being broke or being unable to pay all your bills. But there's no shame in fighting to get your life back in order. For example, the Chapter 11 bankruptcy system is designed to give insolvenites an option other than throwing in the towel by affording them a "time-out" to restructure their affairs and once again become productive members of society. It's okay to try to repair yourself. The problem is that it costs money. You don't want to put what little you have left at risk. You need your assets to fight for your survival.

THE SOLUTION LIES OFFSHORE

Whether you're a principle seeker or an insolvenite, placing your assets into the offshore world is a great way to protect yourself. For the principle seeker, it's a way of making it even more difficult for your adversaries to seize your cash. Locking up your money in an offshore bank gives you a contingency plan. If you stash your money in the Cayman Islands, for example, your adversaries will have to contend with tough banking secrecy laws. If your adversary tried to sue you in the Cayman Islands, he must first deposit with the court the full amount of your estimated legal costs. If your attacker loses his case, you get fully compensated from the court out of your adversary's pocket—for your inconvenience. If you're a principle seeker, this is a wonderful deterrent to ridiculous litigation. If you're an insolvenite, your adversaries will find it difficult, if not impossible, to seize whatever assets you've managed to stash in offshore money havens. You'll always have at least enough of a war chest to get you back on your feet.

WHEN IS SUCCESS A LIABILITY?

When I was a kid, my family lived next door to a man named Hal Leon. Mr. Leon was not a particularly exceptional guy, but he was one of the nicest people I've ever met. He seemed to love his family and like his neighbors. He was always the first to offer help when you needed it

> **If you're an insolvenite, your adversaries will find it difficult, if not impossible, to seize whatever assets you've managed to stash in offshore money havens.**

and the last to interfere otherwise. He was a lawyer, which in our neighborhood made him sort of a big shot, but he never held his credentials over anyone. As I recall, his only apparent source of pride was an enormous backyard garden that he tended himself.

I was in the fifth grade when I first overheard my parents talking about Mr. Leon's car accident. Later it came out that the incident had left a young girl blind in one eye. I remember that everyone talked about it a lot, but nobody ever seemed to approach him directly. So it was only through the neighborhood gossip that I learned, over the course of many months, that he was sued by the girl's parents, lost the case, and was hit with an overwhelming liability debt.

For a while, nothing seemed to change. But during my sixth-grade year, I remember that Mrs. Leon went to work—an odd development in our suburban area, where wives were inevitably full-time homemakers. Eventually, I heard that they had gone bankrupt. "Bankruptcy" was a word only uttered in hushed tones when I was a child, and at the time I wasn't really sure what it meant. I did know that it was the explanation for the Leons moving away and selling their big station wagon to someone else on the block.

When I was a child, lawsuits happened only to the very rich and the very delinquent. Millionaires were vulnerable because their pockets were so deep that they almost cried out to be pilfered. Ne'er-do-wells were vulnerable, too: drunks, quacks, and scam artists who either allowed bad habits to blur their better judgment or deliberately set out to deceive and steal. Today things are very different. Lawsuits affect just about everybody. Experts predict, in fact, that one out of every four adults in this country will be sued during the coming year alone. Some of those suits will be for wrongful damages, like the one against Mr. Leon, and like all spheres of economic activity, these lawsuits have "matured" over the past several years. For example, there will probably be 50,000 personal injury lawsuits involving damages of $1 million and more filed this year—twice as many as were filed even 15 years ago.

In 1990 the average general practice doctor (GP) spent between $10,000 and $15,000 a year on malpractice insurance to cover up to $1 million in award damages. Today that same doctor is paying at least $50,000 a year for coverage of up to $3 million! And that's just for GPs! Medical specialists such as heart surgeons and orthopedic surgeons pay far more.

Clearly, litigation is our newest craze, replacing baseball as America's favorite pastime. People sue their doctors, hospitals, general contractors, plumbers, electricians, gardeners, and television repairmen. They sue their landlords, and they sue their tenants. They sue their automobile dealers and their insurance companies. One group of failed investors recently sued their bank for lending them too much money—the cause, they argued, for their financial demise. One couple sued the Roman Catholic Church when their son committed suicide because, they maintained, he had received inadequate counseling from his local parish priest.

It's absurd, of course, but that doesn't make it funny. Lawsuits hang like a threatening storm cloud over most of us. It might not even be your own mistake that gets you in trouble. Negligence on the part of one of your employees—or even one of your customers—can do the job just as well.

Consider the following scenario: A midsize hardware store was sued for $1.4 million because a customer foolishly decided to test a power saw inside the crowded store. He hit another shopper—seriously cutting the other man's arms, leaving him unable to work for nearly two years and permanently disabled. The store owner, as it so happens, wasn't even in the store at the time of the tragic accident. But as the owner of the store, he was sued for negligence. Does it sound far-fetched? It shouldn't. Sad cases like this happen all the time, and they wipe out hard-earned fortunes in the instant it takes a judge or jury to rule in favor of the plaintiff.

By the way, lawsuits don't always result from a little guy suffering at the hands of a big guy. Sometimes, in fact, it's just the opposite. Strategic Lawsuits Against Public Participation (SLAPPs) are good examples of what I mean. Concerned citizens who campaign against local polluters or new developments are increasingly likely to be hit with one of these suits. They can be small, like the one filed against a West Virginia blueberry farmer. When he told local authorities that operators of a nearby coal mine had polluted a river and killed the fish in it, the mining company sued him for $200,000.

SLAPPs can also be quite big, like the one filed against the League of Women Voters in Beverly Hills. In a recent election, the league supported a ballot initiative to stop a fully planned condominium project. League officers also wrote two letters to a local newspaper criticizing the measure. The developers took decisive action: They sued the league for $63 million.

Perhaps the worst aspect of the lawsuit mania that plagues us is that it can be completely indiscriminate about whom it destroys. A woman named Violet Hanson once came to see me, desperately wanting to take advantage of her offshore options. In conversation it came out that her house and life savings were likely to be confiscated to pay off angry creditors. I should admit up front that I have a hard time accepting the legitimate right of a creditor to take such personal assets, regardless of the offense. But what was particularly frustrating about this case was the fact that Vi herself had not done anything wrong.

Years earlier, she had co-signed on a loan that her son-in-law took out to start his own graphic design and printing business. The company had been doing well, at least apparently, so Vi had forgotten about the loan. Well, in actuality, things were not going so well. The business failed, and along with her son-in-law's bankruptcy came her own. Vi's only crimes were a soft heart and poor judgment. But for those offenses, she paid through the teeth.

I remember how frantic and agitated she was. Her husband had worked his whole life to provide for their retirement. He had died just a few years before, and she was almost inconsolable at the thought of losing all he had left behind. Her idea was to quickly establish a legitimate offshore presence and then transfer nearly all her holdings into a welcoming foreign center.

The trouble was, her excellent idea had come too late. Offshore asset conservation can be legally offered only if there are no judgments or liabilities against your assets. Vi's assets were already under steady attack. Fortunately, with some careful planning, I was able to deal with her predicament, but she was definitely caught in a bad situation.

Perhaps one of the worst cases I've come across had to do with a client of mine named Oliver Webster. He had

Soon after he inherited the property, he was sued for $75 million by the local townspeople. The land had a gas storage tank buried on it.

inherited some virgin land in rural Tennessee from an uncle. Soon after he inherited the property, he was sued for $75 million by the local townspeople. The land had a gas storage tank buried on it. The tank was polluting the water for the whole area. The case went to court and Mr. Webster lost everything.

It is also possible to have all your assets frozen by police, not only for your own crimes but for other people's as well. By the stipulations of the Anti-Drug Act of 1988, authorities have the right to temporarily take or restrict your access to your own property (i.e., your house, your car, and all your bank accounts) if they think you received all or part of them from a relative or other associate who sold drugs. When will the assets be returned? When the suspect is found innocent or when you can prove that you had no reasonable way of knowing about the illegal activity and that the property was purchased with "clean" money. Even under the best of circumstances, that could take several months to prove. In the meantime, your financial ship is sunk.

BUMPS ARE BETTER

An offshore program gives you an effective strategy to chase away nuisance suits. Placing your assets offshore constructs a set of "speed bumps" that slow down your adversaries. The last thing creditors want is to run into obstacles that will cost them extra legal fees and delay, if not prevent their recovery claim. In addition, by using an offshore strategy, you can preserve more capital, which you can use to fight your adversaries harder. Fighting harder will slow your adversaries' momentum even more.

There's no end to the number of speed bumps you can create. Offshore banking laws might already provide enough secrecy to protect you. But within your offshore

> **Placing your assets offshore constructs a set of "speed bumps" that slow down your adversaries. The last thing creditors want is to run into obstacles that will cost them extra legal fees and delay, if not prevent their recovery claim.**

program, you can distance yourself from your business affairs using layers of trusts and blind corporations. There are many banks, management firms, and trust companies located in offshore money havens that specialize in helping you protect your assets. With their experienced assistance, you can develop a solid strategy that will force your opponents to conclude they can't afford to fight you.

A LITTLE PROTECTION IS BETTER THAN NONE

My advice is straightforward: Move as many of your assets offshore as you can. Why? Because the more you keep offshore, the better protected you are from attacks by nuisance lawsuits, the government, and the courts. Nevertheless, I realize that not everyone is initially willing to commit the bulk of their hard-earned assets to an offshore protection plan.

Frankly, I suspect that's only because they're new to the game. The more involved you become in foreign investment and business opportunities, the more confident you will become about seeing your money leave the veritable sieve that characterizes the domestic marketplace in North America. The conventional means of protection—for example, IRAs and savings accounts—no longer offer any real protection. In time, I predict that you will be reluctant to become involved in any domestic investing.

In the beginning, however, you will probably want to maintain a sizable onshore presence. So for those just starting the offshore adventure, I would like to offer some advice on how to best protect the assets you keep in the United States. My advice is limited because there are so few possibilities for genuine asset protection without extensive and creative planning. There are, however, four rules you should follow in all your onshore financial activities. If you adhere to them, your accumulated wealth will be as safe as it can possibly be within the United States.

RULE NUMBER ONE:
BEWARE OF JOINT RELATIONSHIPS

Marriage is a 50-50 proposition, right? And a 10 percent interest in a new venture means a 10 percent accountability for future losses and claims, right?

Wrong on both counts.

Most Americans suffer under the misconception that what is fair in one aspect of a relationship, whatever the nature of the association, is fair in all aspects of the relationship. Sadly, that doesn't hold true when it comes to the distribution of financial responsibility and accountability.

For example, a wife may have nothing at all to do with her husband's professional activities—in fact, they may be separated—but if his business gets into trouble, creditors will see her share of their jointly owned assets as fair game in their quest for recompense.

Likewise, if you are a 10 percent partner in a business venture that fails, you can be held 100 percent accountable for its losses. That means your home, IRA, stocks, bonds, savings accounts, and valuable investments are all up for grabs in the scramble to pay off bad debts.

So be cautious. "Joint tenancy," the fancy term for co-ownership, between spouses and relatives can sound great in the beginning, but it can turn very sour very fast. Prenuptial agreements, as unromantic as they are, can provide a good deal of asset protection down the line. Once dismissed in most court proceedings, many judges are now quite willing to review them and rule in accordance with the provisions they outline.

Be careful, too, about joint business ventures. Often they are held to be nothing more than simple general partnerships with open-ended liability for anyone involved. If that "anyone" is you, it could mean big losses down the line.

RULE NUMBER TWO: USE CORPORATIONS WISELY

One of the cornerstones to all asset protection is that you must separate yourself from your money in order to avoid paying it to people you don't like. By establishing a U.S.–based corporation through which you handle your business activities, you distance yourself somewhat from the liability that might result from those activities. There are other alternatives in Wyoming and Florida, where limited liability corporations and limited partnerships are available under special laws.

Years ago, when I first became involved in offshore financial consulting, I met a man at an international business seminar who kept telling me to incorporate. "Don't let the bastards get you," he said. "Make one mistake and you'll lose a little blood." Then he said something I'll never forget. "And they're all like sharks. They smell that little bit of blood and they go crazy."

He gave me good advice. I'm happy to report that I have not encountered trouble with my business associates. But that doesn't mean I couldn't. So for me, and for millions of other consultants and businesspeople, it's wise to operate through a corporation. If the time ever comes that a client or business associate does sue me, all my personal assets are independent of the business. Ultimately, they're still vulnerable by virtue of the fact that the same person owns them both. But they're not as immediately vulnerable.

By the way, it's possible to need more than one corporation. This would certainly be true if, let's say, your business has two facets, and one of them is far more likely to bring on lawsuits. For someone who operates an architectural firm and also runs a construction company, for example, two corporations would be in order—one for the relatively low-risk architectural venture and another for the high-risk construction business. With this arrangement, one business could remain, at least temporarily, unaffected while the other withstands the shock of a legal battle and possible liability.

RULE NUMBER THREE: SPREAD YOUR WEALTH

There's one surefire way to avoid paying costly tax and liability bills: Technically rid yourself of your most valuable assets. Give a lot of your money to your children, other relatives, or worthy social causes; put it in a trust; transfer it to a limited partnership of which you officially own just a small part. But get your name off it, somehow. In this way, if financial disaster hits, much of the wealth you have accumulated will be beyond the reach of your business or personal adversaries.

The problem with this arrangement is pretty obvious. How can you enjoy the pleasures of wealth you give away? Well, for starters, most people work hard—at least in part—because they want to pass along economic security to their kids, extended family, and important causes. In addition, it is quite possible that assets given to children (especially through an irrevocable trust) can be relied upon in times of future economic need.

For example, if you place 100 percent of your real estate assets in a trust for your kids, you could easily have more than a million dollars in equity stashed away for your heirs' financial future. If, however, you run into financial trouble yourself—even if you lose everything you own—the trust and all that's in it will belong legally and lawfully to your children. Creditors will have no claim to it.

Assuming you have a good relationship with the trust's beneficiaries, you can count on them to instruct their trustee to loan you some money to get you started again. If, on the other hand, you don't get along, you've got little recourse because nothing in the trust belongs to you. You have little or no control. As always, the key is planning.

RULE NUMBER FOUR:
INTELLIGENTLY DISTRIBUTE
ASSETS BETWEEN SPOUSES

Just as a couple can, to some extent, safeguard their assets by entrusting them to their heirs, they can also protect against potential loss by intelligently dividing

> Remember not to put 100 percent of your
> assets in just one spouse's name. A court of law
> would probably find that to be an attempt to
> defraud creditors.

their assets within the marriage. Let me use an example
to illustrate my point.

Lauren and Jake were in their early 40s when they
decided to initiate some careful estate planning. In talking with a number of consultants, they decided that Jake's
sports equipment rental business left him relatively open
to devastating lawsuits. So they strategically set up two
trusts. One was established in Lauren's name, and into it
they placed the bulk of their assets. The other was set up
in Jake's name, which held his office equipment and their
two cars.

It proved to be a brilliant move. Six years later,
Jake was sued for more than $4 million when two cus-
tomers had a fatal accident in a dune buggy he had
rented to them. Their widows won the case and had the
legal right to everything owned by the business and by
Jake. That meant the cars, of course. But virtually
everything else was held in trust under Lauren's name.
As a result, it was safe and provided a second economic
chance for the couple.

Thousands of married people lose everything each
year because of a lawsuit brought against just one spouse.
Don't let that happen to you. Plan wisely. And, while
we're on the topic, remember not to put 100 percent of
your assets in just one spouse's name. A court of law
would probably find that to be an attempt to defraud
creditors. If so, you could still lose everything.

THE OFFSHORE ADVANTAGE:
AN OFFSHORE ASSET PROTECTION TRUST

The idea of trust law comes from the time of the Crusades. Before the English knights left to fight in the Holy Land, they needed someone to look after their property while they were gone. So they often signed the title to their property over to their "trusted" friends. These trusted friends would then look after the knights' properties as if it was their own because, technically, it was.

After the knights came home from the wars, they returned to their estates and expected to have their trusted friends immediately hand back their properties. Trouble was, quite a few of these trusted friends turned out not to be so trustworthy. At first there wasn't much the knights could do about it. The law was straightforward: If the knights had transferred title, then the trusted friends were the legal owners of the property, period. But this didn't seem very just. Hadn't these good, brave, chivalrous knights gone off to fight for His Majesty? A priest eventually convinced the king that there had to be some new form of property ownership that would cure this injustice. The trust was born. Armed with this new law, a lot of angry knights were then able to go off and clobber those trusted friends who had tried to steal their property.

There are three parties to every trust. The "settlor" is the person, such as one of our brave knights, who has some property that he needs looked after. The "trustee" is the person who will be brought in to look after the property. And the "beneficiary" is the person who is supposed to enjoy the property. Sometimes the settlor and the beneficiary are the same person, as would be the case with one of our knights. Sometimes the beneficiary is a different person from the settlor, as often happens when a rich individual sets up a trust to care for his heirs. The key point is this: The trustee has an unflinching duty to protect that property for the sake of the beneficiary. If he should lose the property, the trustee becomes liable to compensate the beneficiary.

Let's look at a more practical example. If you want offshore protection using a trust, you want to create or "settle" a trust, so you are the settlor. You hire a trustee in the offshore money haven and sign over your property to that person "in trust." This gives the trustee the right to act on your behalf, though the trustee must also very closely follow your specific instructions, if any. If you name yourself as beneficiary, your trustee has an absolute obligation to protect your assets for your sake. This is an important thing to understand. The law protects beneficiaries. Trustees cannot be reckless with the property.

Now here's the practical point to all of this. By settling a trust, you can put the legal title to your property in the name of your trustee. And if you name yourself as your beneficiary, you can still retain possession of the property and enjoy it. In other words, you disown yourself from the asset, while at the same time still being able to control it.

You might settle a trust that names an offshore trustee owner of your car but names you as beneficiary, for example. That means you can drive your car and enjoy it to the fullest. Anyone who tries to trace the title will only be able to connect to the name of your trustee.

Don't confuse a trust with a bailment. That won't work for protection. An example of a bailment would be leaving your car with a valet parking service. The valet will take your keys and have full control over your car while you go off to the restaurant or the theater. While the parking service has your car, it will have certain legal responsibilities to care for it. But the parking lot will never have full, registered title to your car. So if an adversary had a judgment against you, and wanted to execute it by seizing your car while it was parked with the valet service, that adversary could legally take it. But if your car is registered with an offshore trustee, there's no way the car can be taken to satisfy the judgment. Therefore, in order to gain protection, title of ownership must be out of your name.

Admittedly, there are limitations to each of these domestic asset-protection plans. And in effect, all the limitations result from two mutually supportive conspiracies against American businesspeople and investors.

First, in any attempt to safeguard your money within the United States, you are up against the power of the federal government. Put simply, Uncle Sam doesn't want your assets to be protected because he wants the ability to get at them at any time.

Second, there is a relationship between U.S. banks and brokerage firms and the U.S. government that works against your efforts to keep assets free from excessive taxation and regulatory interference. At one time, American banks could operate independently of the federal bureaucracy. Today they cannot. The reporting requirements and legal restraints placed upon banks, brokerage firms, and thrift institutions make it truly impossible for you to have a private relationship with your financial institution. In fact, whether your onshore banker likes it or not, he is the greatest obstacle to your asset protection plan.

In the effort to circumvent these intricately inter-twined problems, many investors have relied on onshore trusts, into which they've placed the bulk of their assets. "Living trusts" are the newest rage, it seems. (These revocable trust agreements usually specify that all trust income be distributed to you, as the trust creator, during your lifetime. Then, upon your death, the trust's principal assets are left to your heirs.) I've personally seen a number of how-to paperbacks marketed specifically to affluent Americans who might want to investigate the trust as an appealing alternative to simple bank accounts and stock or real estate investment options.

Living trusts do offer one real benefit: They let your heirs avoid inconvenience, delay, and the cost of probate. (Many people are unaware that probate can be extremely expensive, up to 11 percent of the gross value of the estate in some parts of the country.) Nevertheless, if you are considering a living trust, my advice is to beware. For starters, revocable living trusts will not escape estate tax because by their very nature they let you keep control over the property—by being able to revoke or amend them and by retaining the power to withdraw any portion of the trust property at any time.

If that's not enough to dissuade you, there are other serious drawbacks to domestic trusts. For example, U.S. courts consider any trust that has been created by an individual for his own benefit—even if actual control of all assets has been surrendered—fair game in a creditor's quest for recompense. In other words, if you place your assets in trust but continue to benefit in any way from them, then someone who wins a legal judgment against you can go after those assets. And, in most cases, get them. Moreover, the U.S. courts have held that creditors can go after assets in a domestic trust if the trust creator retains any measure of control over them—even though he or she may not actually enjoy the benefits of the trust assets.

If your estate is worth $350,000 or more, I strongly suggest you consider one of the best asset protection strategies I know about: the asset protection trust. If properly executed and intelligently maintained, this single offshore venture can provide you with an unparalleled level of tax protection and financial invisibility. It may not protect you from becoming the target of a lawsuit or other claim. But it may place your assets substantially beyond the reach of any U.S. court, and severely limit anyone's ability to enforce a money judgment against you. In the process, it will also discourage potential creditors from making bogus claims, and save you the emotional and financial cost of addressing such claims.

As much as I like asset protection trusts, you should be very aware of their limitations. Make sure you discuss the trust with your American lawyer before you proceed, because the U.S. courts are starting to tear up flawed asset protection trusts—though I emphasize the word "flawed."

One of the keys to a successful foreign trust is the selection of a friendly host country. You should establish your trust within an offshore jurisdiction that, first and foremost, maintains stringent laws against enforcing foreign judgments. The whole notion of the trust is based on common law, which is applied in only some countries—those formerly or presently associated with Great Britain. Most other countries operate under a separate set of codes, and while they have arrangements similar to trusts, they have different names and varied structures.

For example, the British Virgin Islands (BVI) has a well-established body of trust laws that protect any BVI-based trust from the scrutiny of foreign courts and creditors. Presently, the BVI recognizes a properly structured trust as a separate legal entity—independent of its creators—and will not allow creditors of any of the parties to the trust to obtain the trust's assets. However, since 1998 the Organisation for Economic Co-operation and Development (OECD) has questioned such trust laws and threatened the BVI (and other countries) with economic sanctions unless they overhaul these practices. (Chapter 10 will address these developments more fully.)

One thing you must absolutely ensure is that the foreign site you choose has nothing equivalent to the U.S. laws on fraudulent conveyance. The Uniform Fraudulent Conveyances Act and the Uniform Fraudulent Transfers Act can void U.S. property transfers that are intentionally designed to hinder, delay, or defraud creditors. In other words, if you know you are being sued and suddenly transfer your assets into your spouse's name, U.S. law can be used to void that transfer. Your creditor can undo

the transfer and in that way seize your property. So you
want to be sure that you are transferring your assets into
a trust at an offshore center where the local laws do not
recognize the Uniform Fraudulent Conveyances Act and
the Uniform Fraudulent Transfers Act.

A basic foreign asset-protection trust can be set up
with anyone as the direct beneficiary (including you as
the creator of the trust). However, for maximum protection, it's better to choose someone else for that role.
(Otherwise you could be seen to have too much of a beneficial interest in the trust and its activities.) If, however,
you do decide to make yourself the beneficiary, be
absolutely sure that you are entitled only to the trust's
income and have no claim on its principal. That way, a
creditor can theoretically attack only your income stream
from the trust, not the actual assets.

Just like domestic trusts, all foreign asset-protection trusts have a trustee, someone to administer the
trust and hold its assets for the benefit of the beneficiaries. I have worked with clients who insist on being the
trustee to their own foreign trust, but in every one of
those cases I advised against it. Serving as your own
trustee can be extremely dangerous. A court is much
more inclined to invalidate a trust if its creator is also a
trustee or beneficiary.

So select an independent foreign trustee, either an
individual familiar with your personal life and business
needs or a financial institution with which you have an

In other words, if you know you are being
sued and suddenly transfer your assets into
your spouse's name, U.S. law can be used to
void that transfer. Your creditor can undo the
transfer and in that way seize your property.

ongoing relationship. If neither of those options seems appealing or appropriate, you can turn to one of many professional international management firms that specialize in the supervision of foreign trusts and other offshore entities. Management does not have to be in a remote island haven such as the BVI. It must just be out of the United States, like Canada. You may operate through a management firm in Vancouver or Toronto as an alternative.

When you initially establish the trust and name a foreign trustee, you should also name a committee of one or more "trust protectors" to serve as advisers to that trustee. And you should serve on that committee. Why? Because the protectors have the right to remove or replace the trustee, so, by remaining a part of the protector committee, you keep indirect but effective control over the trust's assets. And if a creditor should later decide to pursue you, you can simply resign as a protector, leaving the foreign trustee in sole control of the assets. (That way, there can be little merit in the argument that your resignation was somehow an impermissible transfer of assets after the creditor's claims were made.)

Establishing a foreign asset-protection trust is not a terribly complex or lengthy undertaking, but it does require expert legal advice from a trust attorney. There are a number of special features that should be included in the trust agreement: antiduress provisions and a spendthrift clause are just two examples. Don't risk making a mistake. Bring in a qualified specialist to work with you on the project. It will necessitate a financial outlay up front, but it's likely to save you untold headaches and expenses down the line.

Finally, the foreign asset-protection trust is usually best for holding liquid assets: cash, stocks, bonds, and certificates of deposit. In addition, assets transferred to a simple foreign asset-protection trust should generally be those not needed for your daily living or business needs.

In other words, they should be your "nest egg," which you have been setting aside for future security.

A WORD OF WARNING

I want to repeat a word of warning: Never set up an asset protection trust—nor any other form of offshore investment vehicle, for that matter—without first consulting your attorney. Recently, we've seen four important court decisions that challenge the validity of asset protection trusts. Some critics say these decisions prove that offshore trusts are not the watertight asset-protection vehicles we once thought. I disagree. These cases do show that offshore trusts can be ripped up by U.S. courts, but it appears to me that in each instance, the settlor's intentions were so flawed it should come as no surprise the courts were able to tear them down. These cases do not kill the offshore trust concept on the whole. They simply illustrate what can happen if the trust is created without proper planning.

Mary Reichers *v.* Dr. Roger Reichers, *New York State Supreme Court, July 1998*

This case involved a divorce action between Mary and Roger Reichers. Before the wife filed the divorce papers, Roger secretly moved $4 million into a Cook Islands trust. The trust did not name his wife as a beneficiary, but the court ruled that since the property moved into the trust included assets of the marriage, half the trust property belonged to Mary.

I'm not surprised by this outcome. No court was going to give the good doctor any preference or privilege he would not have been able to get under existing state law. If the trust was settled with property acquired during the marriage, that property belongs as much to her as it does to him. In this case, the good doctor didn't seek his wife's permission before he shipped the property offshore. Asset protection trusts are not vehicles by which you can legally steal or cheat other people out of their property. They are supposed to exist so you can protect that which you legally own and are entitled to.

The lesson to be learned from this case is that you need to be certain your actions are legally correct before you proceed. This is a classic example of why you should consult a lawyer first. Someone in Dr. Reichers's shoes should call his lawyer and explain why he wants to set up the trust. He should be frank with the attorney, explaining that the purpose of the trust is to avoid a situation where he has to pay his wife a large divorce settlement. There are ways, other than using an asset protection trust, in which he could have achieved his objective without getting himself in legal trouble. The court decision that went against him was simply the result of poor planning.

Dr. Reichers argued in court that he set up the trust in order to protect his family from malpractice suits. If this was the real purpose for the trust, all the more reason to have named his wife as a beneficiary—something the trust he settled didn't do. This is an omission that might have been caught with top-notch legal advice.

You need to consult a lawyer to verify whether the trust will withstand court scrutiny under domestic laws. This assessment must be a local one, because the lawyer consulted must have an intimate understanding of how local laws will treat your property.

Marina Papson *v.* Vazha Papson, *New York State Supreme Court, August 1998*

The facts here are almost identical to those in the Reichers case. The key difference here is that the husband secretly transferred $1.5 million in assets into a Cayman Islands trust *after* divorce proceedings were commenced.

The lack of wisdom exhibited by this move astounds me. As we've seen from the Reichers case, using a trust to sign away marital assets without your spouse's consent is fraud and will get you in trouble. That's like you "borrowing" $1 million from your business partners without bothering to let them know, then parking the money offshore.

The shocking thing here is that Vazha Papson went farther and moved the assets offshore after divorce proceedings had commenced and the property in question was clearly at dispute before the courts. The timing of Vazha's move made it so obvious he was out to deny his wife the property that the judge labeled his actions a clear violation of "public policy." The judge ordered the trust collapsed and the funds returned to New York.

So how might Vazha have legally moved these assets offshore? First, he could have consulted his wife before moving the property offshore. Since the point of his exercise was to keep some of these assets out of his wife's hands, the second thing he could have done was set aside some portion of the trust for her use. He still could have fought his wife in court over the division of the marital assets.

The lesson to be learned is that you should not get too greedy with your assets. If the purpose of your trust is to deal with marital property, make sure you leave at least something for your ex-spouse. Try to take it all, and you might wind up with nothing.

Stephan Jay Lawrence, U.S. Bankruptcy Court, Miami, September 1998

Stephan Jay Lawrence was an options trader who lost big-time in the 1987 stock market crash. Around 1991, just before an arbitrator ordered him to pay Bear Sterns and Co. just over $20 million, he moved the bulk of his $7 million estate into a trust in the Republic of Mauritius.

He filed for bankruptcy in 1997, arguing that he didn't have access to the money in the trust. The bankruptcy judge, Thomas S. Utschig, basically laughed in his face: "A bankruptcy discharge for a debtor who engages in this type of conduct should be as rare as the dodo bird that once graced the shores of Mauritius."

Lawrence's behavior was simply silly. It's like he thought he could make some vampire disappear by holding up a cross. If you think bankruptcy is a real threat to you, set up your trust *before* you find yourself in a position where your debts outweigh the value of your assets. Doing this after you've found yourself to be insolvent is ignorant.

Stephan Jay Lawrence didn't really need an offshore trust. What he really needed was a lesson in negotiation. Moving all of his property offshore was no way to deal with his situation. He should have offered at least part of his money to Bear Sterns as some sort of settlement. Moving the property offshore after he got into trouble only magnified Bear Sterns's desire to get at his money.

So remember this: Learn to negotiate. Settling cases is an option. It's better to reach a settlement that leaves something for yourself than to bet the house and walk away with nothing. And watch your timing. Don't make the move after you've found yourself in trouble.

Federal Trade Commission vs. Denyse and Michael Anderson, U.S. Ninth Circuit Court of Appeals, June 1999

This case is the most frightening example of what can go wrong when the purpose of your trust is illegal. Denyse and Michael Anderson sought investors in their 1997 scheme to sell water-filled dumbbells and something called "talking pet tags." The Federal Trade Commission argued that since the Andersons shipped $6 million in profits from the business to an offshore

> **If the purpose of your trust is to deal with marital property, make sure you leave at least something for your ex-spouse.**

trust they had set up, the operations was really a tele-marketing Ponzi scheme. Since the Andersons acted as the trust's protector, the Federal Trade Commission ordered them to repatriate the funds. The courts agreed, and a judge ordered the money returned to the United States. But the Andersons didn't comply with the ruling, arguing that it was impossible to comply with the court order because they could not access their property under the terms of the trust. A U.S. judge didn't buy that explanation. Because the Andersons didn't abide by the court order, he ruled them jailed for six months for contempt of court.

It's unfortunate for this case to be used as an example of how trusts fail. The problem here wasn't the trust. The problem was that the two people who settled the trust did so to protect their ill-gotten gains. The trust got the bad rap even though the Andersons did the wrong.

As you might well imagine, the point I want to leave with you is that you should consult a lawyer before settling your trust. A trust alone can't be used to magically convert illegal activities into legal ones.

ADDITIONAL LAYERS OF PROTECTION

A foreign asset-protection trust can be a vehicle for people seeking nothing more than the basic right to safeguard their money. As an irrevocable trust, it is an entirely independent entity, and recognized as such under the laws of all 50 states and the U.S. federal government. If you take care to distance yourself sufficiently from the trust—so that a court will not find that the arrangement is a sham for holding assets under your direct control—no judge or jury can legally give your creditors assets that you earlier contributed to the trust.

A number of recent court cases demonstrate exactly how the use of these irrevocable trusts can work. In one of those cases, a woman with two grown children established an irrevocable trust into which she transferred most of her assets. The trust provided for the distribution of the entire net income to the woman for life, with the remaining principal to go to her children upon her death. When the woman was later sued by a creditor, the court upheld the validity of the trust, saying, "A creditor has no more rights and can secure no greater benefit from a trust than the beneficiary of the trust can obtain for himself [or herself]." In other words, since the woman herself could not ignore the provisions of the trust or regain the principal for herself, then neither could her creditors have it set aside to obtain the assets it contained.

But for some people, an offshore trust alone does not offer enough asset control. Despite a trust's protective advantages, some people want (and need) more direct authority over how assets are maintained and profitably put to work. In particular, if you run your own business, have a professional corporation, or own real property within the United States, you will probably want to combine a foreign asset-protection trust with a domestic lim-

A foreign asset-protection trust can be a vehicle for people seeking nothing more than the basic right to safeguard their money.

ited partnership. Using both, you can ensure that your assets remain completely safe from creditors, and that you keep constant and total control over them.

Here's how it works. You establish an asset protection trust within a welcoming offshore jurisdiction, and you contribute virtually all of your property to that trust. Then, you set up a domestic limited partnership, personally taking just 1 percent interest in the partnership but designating yourself as general partner. The foreign trust takes 99 percent interest and pays for that interest by contributing to the partnership the following: your operating business, your family home, the title to your investment real estate, and any other nonliquid assets.

Once the trust and partnership are funded, your total assets will consist of just 1 percent interest in the limited partnership and the few personal belongings you have not contributed to the trust. As a result, very little of your total net worth is available to any potential creditor. Technically, 99 percent of that worth belongs to the foreign trust and has been contributed to the limited partnership.

So if a creditor were ever able to obtain a judgment against you, your only asset would be a small interest in the partnership.

Another big part of the system's appeal lies in the degree of control it gives you over assets that cannot be attached. Specifically, because of your role as a general partner, you will still be able to do with the trust's assets whatever you please as long as it's in the furtherance of the partnership's purpose. And as an additional perk, there is no authority that could allow a creditor to remove you as general partner of the partnership. So you would continue to control all of your assets all of the time.

You may even be able to get money out of the limited partnership held in your offshore trust if you have the ability, in arm's-length transactions, to draw funds from it as salary for services performed and as fringe benefits.

(If you go this route, however, be aware that these wages and benefits are vulnerable to creditors in any judgment against you.)

Even if there is a judgment against you, the most a creditor can obtain would be a so-called charging order against your partnership interest. True, the creditor could go after all the benefits that flow to you from the partnership, but because you own so small an interest, very little does flow to you. This charging order would also mandate that you treat the creditor only as an "assignee." That means he would have no vote in the management of the partnership and would not be able to force you to make distributions from the partnership.

This final provision allows you to create the "poison pill," something to discourage even the heartiest of creditors. You simply include a provision in the partnership agreement that allows the general partner to retain the earnings of the partnership and not make cash distributions. If a creditor gets a charging order against the partnership, you can stop making cash distributions. This move will no doubt irritate the creditor. But, frankly, that irritation pales in comparison to what next lies ahead for the creditor. Let me explain.

Under U.S. tax laws, a limited partnership is deemed to have distributed its income to the partners at the end of each fiscal year—even if no cash distributions were made. Thus the creditor is faced with the prospect of having to pay taxes on the income generated by his assigned share of the partnership's income despite the fact that he has not received any money at all! Faced with such a prospect, most creditors will not even bother to attack your interests in the foreign trust or the domestic limited partnership. Finally, because 99 percent of the partnership belongs to the foreign trust, the assets from the partnership all flow automatically offshore and back into a trust that is governed by extremely favorable foreign laws.

I should mention that there are even more elaborate offshore asset-protection plans. Of course, they involve more initial research and additional start-up revenue. Nevertheless, for investors with a lot of vulnerability and a high or professional profile, they can be very desirable. Unlike the foreign trust alone, a trust, partnership, and offshore bank can work hand in hand, forming a powerful triad. These complex protection strategies are not fixed plans. Instead, they constantly evolve and change to inhibit potential challenges of lawsuits directed against you. In essence, by keeping your money on the move, and circulating it through creative combinations of various off-shore financial ventures (e.g., trusts, consulting companies, holding companies, and banks), you can obliterate all traces of your financial activities.

For such total financial invisibility, you will have to relinquish virtually all personal affiliation with, and claim to, your assets. You can control them. In fact, you can make them grow beyond your wildest dreams. But you can't call them your own because they are all absorbed by the offshore plan, never to emerge for future creditors to see.

HAVE YOUR CAKE AND EAT IT TOO

There's a popular expression we've all heard at least once: Less is more. Well, when it comes to conservation and responsible ecology, this may be true. But when it comes to money—your money—only more is more.

So as you find yourself successfully accumulating more, don't forget that unless you do something to protect yourself, a hefty chunk of what you've worked to acquire will be sacrificed to the U.S. tax collector. And what's left could be lost overnight in an ugly, and perhaps even unfair, lawsuit.

But take heart. Asset protection is available. To a very limited extent it's even available onshore within the domestic marketplace. Unfortunately, however, as citizens of the world's great experiment in free enterprise, we Americans have to look offshore for the best, most effective safeguards.

That's the bad news.

The good news is that there really are places where you can protect your precious assets—and with some careful preplanning, you can gain all of the benefits of profit, privacy, asset protection, and tax protection. All you need is the commitment to give offshore money havens a try, and the willingness to work closely with a well-qualified professional consultant.

CHAPTER 8

PROTECTING YOURSELF FROM ASSET FORFEITURE

Despite the guarantees of due process contained in the U.S. Constitution, we are all subject to the government's sweeping power to take our property without due process of law. This concept is called "asset forfeiture." I introduced you to this assault on property rights earlier. It makes me angry because it is one of the most frightening and chilling abuses of government power. Asset forfeiture completely subverts the freedoms we are supposed to take for granted.

Asset forfeiture is a legal principle giving the government the right to seize property it believes is associated with crime. Beginning with the 1984 Comprehensive Crime Control Act, more than 200 federal laws now have provisions for the forfeiture of private property. Presently, the U.S. Marshals Service holds approximately $1 billion in such assets, and it has seized and sold more than $9 billion in property since the program began. The laws were designed to let authorities seize yachts and luxury cars belonging to drug dealers and other criminals. And at first blush, the principle seems like a good idea. Why not deny criminals the right to enjoy the fruits of their crimes? But there is one huge flaw: Forfeiture gives the government the right to seize your property without giving you so much as a single day in court. The litany of outrageous attacks on the innocent that have resulted from this misuse and abuse of this absolute power is a shame to the nation.

Remember Billy Munnerlyn from chapter 1? He was a pilot who lost his chartered airline business simply because one of his passengers turned out to be a drug dealer. Billy's business was destroyed through guilt by association. He had no reason to suspect the man he was flying from Arkansas to California was anything other than an ordinary businessman. But when the plane touched down, it was swarmed by federal authorities. They busted the drug dealer, and busted Billy simply because he was flying the plane. Even though Billy was later cleared by the courts, the costs of fighting to prove his innocence proved so great that he lost his business. Now he drives a truck.

Remember Judy Enright? She had her paintings seized because she had attached some feathers she had collected in her Michigan backyard. She collected a lot of them. She thought they looked pretty. When one of her paintings didn't look complete, she decided to attach some of the feathers from her collection. She thought they made for the perfect finishing touches. Trouble was, the feathers came from migratory birds that were protected by a federal law. Wildlife agents saw the painting at an art show and ordered it seized.

Remember Donald Scott? Government agents on false suspicions that he was growing marijuana murdered him. Police claimed they had flown over the property and seen pot growing on the ground. This was a ridiculous claim, since it would be next to impossible to detect tiny pot plants from the altitude they were flying at. But this ridiculous evidence was enough to get a warrant to raid the Scott home. His wife was first to hear the 30 armed agents burst in the door. At first she thought the police were burglars and screamed for Scott's help. He grabbed his gun to confront the intruders. Police shot Scott when they saw his weapon. A subsequent investigation revealed the federal government was interested in the Scott property because it would have made a wonderful addition to an adjacent federal park.

Forfeiture laws are the dark side of your government.

One of the most disturbing things about forfeiture is it gives government the legal right to presume *guilt*. In the cases I've just mentioned, innocent people were punished for charges that had not been proven in court. Essentially, asset forfeiture gives the government the power to punish without trial. That is a betrayal of the right we have to enjoy our property and live our lives without fear of the arbitrary exercise of government power. What's worse, it makes asset forfeiture a power that can't help but be abused.

And asset forfeiture is not just a power that belongs to the federal government. It's also available to municipal and state governments. Reporters from the *Kansas City Star* discovered that police in 24 states use the federal provisions to circumvent their own state laws regarding the unwarranted seizure of property. Driving the action is a practice called "handoffs," in which the feds allow local police to keep the majority of profits from such seizures. And if that doesn't turn your stomach, have a look at how the law enforcement community lobbies to ensure the legislature never turns off the asset forfeiture tap. The state legislature of Missouri tried to pass a law saying all proceeds from asset forfeitures would go to education. Believe it or not, law enforcement agencies were actually outraged! The police pay for a lot of their expenses through the sale of seized property. Police keep some of the property they seize, such as Mercedes and BMWs, which they actually drive in undercover and sting operations. The Missouri law would have thrown all this out the window.

So the law enforcement lobby went to work on the state legislature and got it to make a key amendment that opened the door for the federal government to come in and "adopt" the property seized by state police. This was a crafty move. The federal government funds state police. So under the adoption amendment, up to 80 percent of the property seized by Missouri and later adopted by the federal government came back to law enforcement officers in the state. This, of course, keeps the proceeds of this property away from the Missouri education system and illustrates some of the duplicity that underlies the forfeiture system. Police officers and other supporters of asset forfeiture might look like they are embracing a law-and-order agenda. Scratch the surface and you see a real agenda of budgeting battles, such as the one between Missouri police officers and Missouri educators. Now, two years later, state legislators have sent a bill to the governor that redesigns the law's language and once again sends the money from asset forfeiture back into the school districts.

In Detroit a man was convicted of engaging a prostitute in the front seat of his car. The car was seized as a "public nuisance" and sold at auction. But the man had a wife who was co-owner of the vehicle and who had actually purchased it with her baby-sitting fees. As a result of the seizure, she was no longer able to transport her five children to school. In a suit filed against local officials, she alleged that the action had violated both her property rights and her rights to due process. The Michigan Supreme Court ruled against her, and the United States Supreme Court upheld that decision.

In New Mexico, the Albuquerque City Council recently passed an ordinance empowering the police to confiscate any house in which they catch underage kids drinking beer. And one autumn day in 1999, a Minnesota man bought a shiny, new $40,000 2000 Ford Excursion. That night, he got drunk, climbed into the SUV, and cranked up its audio system with some Rolling Stones— all while simply sitting in his own driveway. A neighbor complained, after which the man was arrested and the vehicle was confiscated. The Minnesota Appeals Court has upheld the seizure.

New York City is the place where so many immigrants first glimpsed the Statue of Liberty and first set foot on the soil of the good, free United States of America. But the Big Apple is now experimenting with an example of asset forfeiture that is so atrocious it makes a mockery of everything the Statue of Liberty represents.

New York City has instituted a law that permits police to seize the vehicles of suspected drunk drivers. Note the key word here: *suspected.* It's hard to be opposed to any effort to get tough on drunk driving. We all know it's a serious problem. Drunk drivers deserve to be punished once they are convicted in a court of law. The problem with New York City's law is that it targets and punishes *suspects.* So much for the sacred belief that all are innocent until proven guilty.

The New York City law throws the presumption of innocence out the window. If the police have a good case, let them take the case to trial. Why should the suspect be punished before the police have been required to prove their case? There are legal defenses to charges of drunk

New York City has instituted a law that permits police to seize the vehicles of suspected drunk drivers. Note the key word here: *suspected.*

driving. Maybe the driver was unintentionally suffering the effects of prescribed medication. Maybe the police Breathalyzer was flawed. Maybe the police simply made a mistake. These things can and do happen. By allowing New York City to punish suspects prior to a trial, this law tramples the constitutional tradition that guarantees the presumption of innocence.

Just think of the lives that will be ruined by the inevitable abuse of these laws. There are people whose whole lives depend on their cars. They need them to take their kids to school. They need them to commute to work. For most Americans of average income, cars are, after their homes, one of the most valuable assets they own. This valuable, necessary asset can be seized by New York City police simply because they suspect the driver of a crime. And because the balance is tipped so far in the city's favor, there's little people can do about it.

"What we're talking about is draconian sanctions without due process of law," says Roger Pilon, a noted legal philosopher and constitutional scholar who has written about forfeiture laws. "This is the very thing we fought the Revolutionary War to prevent."

BLAME THE OX, NOT THE OWNER

It's difficult to believe that a country that is supposed to protect and nurture property rights would ever conjure up a law that puts our property at risk. Just where does this horrible law come from?

The historical roots of asset forfeiture lie, strangely enough, in the Old Testament. Exodus 21:28–29 says, "If an ox gore a man or a woman, that they die: then the ox shall be surely stoned, and his flesh shall not be eaten; but the owner of the ox shall be quit." In other words, the rule was that it was the property that should be punished, not the owner of the property. This biblical admonition found application in the Middle Ages. If ever an ox harmed someone, the ox was seized and sold. Some of the money it was worth would go to the church and some would go to the king. The legal principle was called "deodands," which means, "to give to God." The revenue potential of this biblical principle didn't go unnoticed by the king. A whole body of law developed in which the king could target guilty property "in rem" or "against the thing." The owner of the property didn't have to be punished, just the guilty property itself.

The forfeiture law practiced today in the United States is built on this same principle. U.S. Customs agents first used it. If a ship came into port and the skipper was unwilling or unable to pay customs duties, agents had no choice but to seize the ship in lieu of payment. It just wasn't practical to travel to the port of origin and demand the shipping company cough up the cash. That's still the case today.

During the prohibition of alcohol during the 1920s, federal agents used the forfeiture power in the battle against rumrunners. And the Drug Enforcement Agency (DEA) continues to apply the law today in the federal government's war on drugs. Indeed, the law has acquired a lot of strong supporters in Washington. A lot of politicians embrace the law as a chance to prove they support a strong law-and-order agenda. These politicians, of course, cling to the myth that the law is only unleashed on drug lords and money launderers. They conveniently forget about the countless innocent victims who find themselves preyed upon by government zealots and bureaucrats.

Here's a chilling passage that, I think, sums up the use of the law today. These are actual instructions Richard Thornburgh gave to his staff when he was attorney general. "We must significantly increase forfeiture production to reach our budget target," he said. "Failure to achieve the $470 million projection would expose the department's forfeiture program to criticism and undermine confidence in our budget predictions. Every effort must be made to increase forfeiture income in the three remaining months of fiscal year 1990." In effect, here's the nation's chief law enforcement officer telling his people to go out and steal from the rich in order to meet budget targets. This is the frightening reality of these arcane laws.

ENEMY OF THE STATE

Aside from this theme as a Hollywood movie illustrating abuse of government authority, it's awkward to look at government as your enemy. The U.S. Constitution is supposed to protect you from arbitrary and unjust abuses of government power. If you're a law-abiding, hard-working citizen, why should you have anything to fear? Because what happened to Billy Munnerlyn, Judy Enright, and Donald Scott can happen to you.

There's another reason. The American legal system is adversarial. If you ever get sued, it's the plaintiff *versus* you. If the police charge you with a crime, it's the state *versus* you. The system is designed for conflict. The idea is that the side with the most persuasive argument or evidence will win. That makes for great theory. The reality is somewhat different, of course. Fortune usually favors the side with the greatest firepower. When it comes to the triggering of asset forfeiture, the system is structured so that it's you *versus* the U.S. government, the richest and most powerful government the world has ever known. The odds aren't exactly in your favor.

The important thing to remember is that the government is always your adversary. This is a hard thing for honest citizens to get used to. Here's an example: Would you want someone from the IRS to help you com-

> In effect, here's the nation's chief law enforcement officer telling his people to go out and steal from the rich in order to meet budget targets.

plete your tax return? Probably not. This would be akin to having the fox guard the henhouse.

I've got a client who once made the mistake of trying to trust the government. It's a rather sad story. This client of mine is a movie producer in Los Angeles. He has made about 20 movies and has been rather successful. But that success was nothing compared to the joy he and his wife felt when they learned she was pregnant with their first child. They were bursting with pride.

Then tragedy struck. His wife had a miscarriage around the eighth month of the pregnancy. They were devastated. They bickered a great deal in the dark days following their loss. Each blamed the other. One night their arguing became so heated they decided to dial 911. They wanted someone—anyone—to come and help mediate their problems and calm things down. They thought dialing 911 was the best way to diffuse the situation and solve the problem.

This was a big mistake. Police quickly responded to the call, but treated the situation as a domestic dispute. They suspected the husband had assaulted the wife and placed him under arrest. My client and his wife were horrified. My client was carted off to jail. It didn't take very long before the courts realized the case was not one of domestic violence. My client was soon released, and the charges against him dropped. But he was still left with an arrest record. At the time, my client was bidding for a huge movie project. The story of his arrest hit the newspapers. The bad publicity killed his chances for the project.

I can happily tell you that my client and his wife later got back on track. But they also learned not to trust the government. When my client dialed 911, he thought he was calling in a friend. Instead, he became an enemy of the state.

THE ASSAULT ON YOUR RIGHTS

Let's get right to the point. If you have property, you are a target. The government views your homes, your boats, and your bank accounts as a means of financing its bureaucracy. All it has to do is *connect* you to some sort of criminal activity so it can trigger its asset forfeiture laws and seize your property. Are you really at risk? Billy Munnerlyn didn't think so until he had his plane, and with it his business, pulled out from under him by overzealous federal agents. Judy Enright didn't think so when she thought those pretty feathers from her backyard would make a great addition to her painting. And Donald Scott's widow didn't think so when she shrieked in terror at what she thought was a break-in, and Scott was killed as he confronted the intruders with his handgun.

The operation of the asset forfeiture law is structured to allow for these outrageous cases to occur with alarming frequency. Here is a summary of the law's key provisions so you'll understand just how strong it is:

- **Even the kitchen sink.** Officials can seize a person's property without notice and without hearing. The property can be anything you own: land, cars, boats, bank accounts, stocks. Because the government has no obligation to warn you about the seizure, the process is one of the government taking first, and letting *you* ask questions later.

- **Guilty until proven innocent.** The focus is on the property, not you. It doesn't matter how innocent you are. The government deems the property tainted. It might not even charge you with a crime, but the government will definitely ignore you when you protest your innocence.

- **Hearsay counts.** The government needs only the slightest bit of evidence to assert the property was involved with a crime. The police can act on hearsay, innuendoes, paid informants—even the testimony from people whose interests are adverse to yours. In other words, police can act on the lies of your enemies.

- **Beware the taint.** The degree of involvement can be very thin. A mere drop of water can poison the well. Let's say a customer gives you some cash and you put it in the bank. If that cash was used in a drug deal, your *entire* bank account is deemed to be tainted, because money is not fungible. It matters little whether you knew of the cash's dubious origins.

- **The government has leverage.** Once seized, the burden shifts to the owner to prove the property's innocence. This means fighting all the powers of the state. Even worse, it means weighing the value of the property against the possible risk of self-incrimination. That's an extraordinarily strong piece of leverage for the government.

- **Double jeopardy.** If you are convicted of a crime and must pay a fine and go to jail, you still don't get your property back. Double jeopardy is *allowed* in asset forfeiture law. A man from Minneapolis convicted for selling seven dirty books and videos was fined $100,000 and sentenced to six years in jail. But the punishment didn't stop there. The government also seized 10 pieces of commercial real estate, 31 of his businesses, and $9 million.

- **Seize the fort for the fly.** Proportionality isn't an issue. The amount the government seizes doesn't have to have any relation to the value of the alleged crime. I just gave you a good example of this. I strongly doubt seven dirty books and videos are worth 10 pieces of commercial real estate, 31 businesses, and $9 million.

A Chilling Scenario

Consider this: If an honest businessman's bank account contains even one dollar of tainted money, then asset forfeiture laws consider that the entire bank account is associated with a criminal activity and the account is seized. Now let's say this honest businessman wants to fight the government to get his money back. "Be our guest," the government agents will say. "Of course, you'll have to prove you are innocent at the risk of having us charge you with some sort of an offense. Do you really want to do that to yourself? Is fighting to get this money back really worth placing your personal freedom at risk?" This is the heavy-handed leverage the government has at its disposal after it seizes your cash. This is how the government is using honest people as sources of revenue.

This is clearly a system gone haywire. It gives the government unbridled, unchecked weapons to steal from hardworking, decent, honest people. And the U.S. legal system offers you nothing you can do to control this abuse. But you do have options in the offshore world.

The Offshore Shield

The offshore world can be your fortress against your government adversary. You've seen how moving assets offshore can protect you from exposure to frivolous litigation and reduce, perhaps even remove, the burden of taxes. Moving offshore can also protect your assets from abusive seizures. And it can accomplish this important objective without breaking the law.

There are six different steps you should follow in setting up your offshore shield—and make no mistake about it, shielding yourself is the key. That's why I call these six steps the SHIELD strategy. The six steps—Sanctuary, Hiding, Intelligence, Education, Legal System, and Diversion—form the acronym SHIELD. They can be your personal strategy to protect yourself from the government's asset forfeiture power.

"S" Is for Sanctuary

We start with your offshore destination. There are scores of offshore money havens out there. If you're concerned about asset forfeiture, the thing to do is to pick a country that will be extremely reluctant to buckle under to U.S. pressure. You need to find a country where the U.S. government can't use its leverage to take your money without first giving you plenty of notice about what it intends to do.

I recommend you consider these three: Nevis, Nauru, or the Netherlands Antilles. These are the three Ns I mentioned to you in an earlier chapter. The three Ns are three amigos that ensure your property is inviolate from a potentially threatening domestic legal system. They are a safe haven for assets because they're not party to any

> **You need to find a country where the U.S. government can't use its leverage to take your money without first giving you plenty of notice about what it intends to do.**

treaties that empower the U.S. government to seize assets without due process and due notice. They also have no civil asset forfeiture rules as onerous as those in the United States, and therefore they protect your property from attacks by judgment creditors.

"H" Is for Hiding

Out of sight is out of mind. The government won't go looking for assets it doesn't know you have, so you can do yourself a tremendous favor by hiding your assets. Don't be obvious. Never flaunt your wealth. Buying yourself a $200,000 Rolls-Royce or a palatial mansion in the most expensive neighborhood in town could draw unwanted attention you might later come to regret.

Along this line, the offshore world also offers the opportunity to use layering to distance yourself from assets. As I've explained, layering involves registering the title to your property with offshore trustees and corporations. Remember, the greater you can distance yourself from your property, the better you can keep your affairs private and your assets hidden.

"I" Is for Intelligence

Intelligence is the key to any conflict. You have to know what your enemy is up to. You need to know how strong he is and where he is located. That goes double when you're up against the feds. Like a CIA operative researching a covert action, you should establish a flow of information about what powers the government has regarding asset forfeiture.

Start by locating sources that will tell you where and when the government is seizing property. You can do this over the Internet, where several Web sites are dedicated to monitoring government use and abuse of the forfeiture power. One such site is www.fear.org, which is run by a group called Forfeiture Endangers American Rights (FEAR). You can also use the Internet to collect news stories from around the United States. This is called setting up an e-mail clippings service. If you don't know how to do this, call your Internet service provider and ask how.

You can also join organizations, such as FEAR, which are devoted to eradicating this invasive law. The better your intelligence, the better equipped you are to shield yourself from government attack.

"E" Is for Education

Go beyond merely tracking the latest bits of news on forfeiture. Become knowledgeable on the topic. Read books and attend seminars to educate yourself as much as possible about asset forfeiture. Laws can change quickly. All it takes is a new interpretation from the courts. Understand the basics of forfeiture so you can track any significant changes to the law.

You'll whither and die if you don't ingest the latest information on forfeiture. The law might be based on principles dating back to Old Testament times, but the modern law of forfeiture practiced in the United States is just being created. Politicians love to dream up new ways to expand the forfeiture laws so they can promote themselves as tough on crime. Prosecutors continue to twist the law in new ways so it can apply in far-reaching situations. Remember, it wasn't always legal for New York City police to steal cars simply on the allegations that the drivers were drunk.

"L" Is for Legal System

The more you distance yourself from trouble, the safer you're likely to be. As we've seen from our earlier examples, the government targets a lot of innocent people. If you don't have a lawyer, you should get one. Try to find someone who knows about asset forfeiture law. Then go over your affairs with this lawyer and determine whether your property is at risk. Ask this lawyer to help you master your understanding of the law. You want your lawyer to help you identify and understand all areas that could make you a target. You'll likely be shocked at the variety of activities that, despite your innocence, can open up a world of hurt.

Insider trading is an example. Be careful where your stock tips come from. Now, you're probably thinking to yourself that you haven't done any insider trading. As far as you're concerned, you're clean as a whistle. But can you trust your stockbroker? If your broker is giving you advice based on inside information, you could be the unwitting beneficiary of an illegal activity. If you're making money, that might not sound so bad. You'll think differently when federal agents seize your brokerage account because they claim you're participating in insider trading securities fraud.

Another thing to watch out for is cash. Dealing in cash certainly has its advantages. Privacy seekers like cash because it doesn't leave a paper trail. But the problem with cash is that it raises suspicion.

Let me tell you about the case of Willy Jones, a landscaper from Tennessee. Willy decided to fly to Dallas to buy some shrubs. He took a great deal of cash with him

Apparently, drug residue sticks to cash like glue. So when you deal in cash, you run the risk of coming into contact with money that is literally tainted with this substance.

because he thinks he can get better deals that way. At the airport, he also paid for his plane ticket in cash. This was a big mistake because, as an African American male who paid for a plane ticket to Texas by cash, he apparently fit the profile of a drug courier. The ticket agent got suspicious and called the DEA. Officers arrested Willy, searched him, and found $9,600 in cash on him. Of course, this was Willy's shrub money, not drug money!

It took two years before the courts realized the incident was a misunderstanding and Willy got his money back. (Don't forget that under the law of asset forfeiture, Willy was presumed guilty before he could prove his innocence.)

One more point about this case. DEA officers claimed there was drug residue on the cash in Willy's possession. The judge later found as fact that 90 percent of *all* cash circulating in the United States contains some form of drug residue. Apparently, drug residue sticks to cash like glue. So when you deal in cash, you run the risk of coming into contact with money that is literally tainted with this substance. You don't want to run the risk of being associated in any way with drug money.

This also means that you should choose your relationships very, very carefully. Not only do you want to avoid contact with drug money, you certainly want to avoid contact with anyone who has a history in the drug trade. Never forget that asset forfeiture law lets the government trigger guilt by association.

"D" Is for Diversion

D-Day will forever be remembered as one of the greatest surprise attacks in military history. When you think about it, it was amazing the Allies were able to amass an army of thousands of men a mere 25 miles from the French coast without the Germans ever suspecting a landing would take place at Normandy. One of the things that helped the United States surprise the Germans was a clever diversion. The U.S. Army set up a dummy army, complete with fake tanks and guns, which looked from the air like the real thing. This clever strategy diverted the German's attention from Normandy.

The offshore world offers you the opportunity to create your own diversion using the layering technique of registering your assets offshore—say, setting up your own offshore bank. Individuals are not readily associated with the ownership of a bank. Therefore, your government adversary will shift its attentions elsewhere.

The diversion strategy is particularly important for your liquid assets. You must preserve your cash and marketable securities at all costs. If the government targets you, the first thing it will try to do is find your liquid assets. The government knows you'll need access to money in order to pay for the lawyers who will fight the forfeiture. The government strikes you in the pocketbook in order to prevent you from putting up a fight.

Fortunately, layering is a particularly effective means of fighting forfeiture of your liquid assets. The government will repeatedly bump into dead ends every time it tries to track your assets down if you properly organize your ownership of them. And even if the government thinks it has finally located the whereabouts of your assets, your property should remain untouchable because the offshore money haven you've chosen will protect your confidentiality before it helps the U.S. government.

You see, the U.S. government has no power to give orders to bankers in other countries. Just think what bankers in our three N havens, Nevis, Nauru, and the Netherlands Antilles, would do if Uncle Sam asked them to fork over your cash.

I call the diversion strategy the "SOS system": Structure, Options, Strategy. Structure your affairs to give yourself the maximum number of options to conceal your identity and to divert government attention using the best possible strategy. If you want to protect yourself from asset forfeiture, send out an SOS!

FEAR OF THE FUTURE

One of the most frightening things about the U.S. government's asset forfeiture system is that the rest of the world is looking to it as a model. The United Nations has a policy of helping member states by directing them to models of administrative excellence. For example, the UN suggests that the government of France is a model state when it comes to bureaucracy. For anyone who has ever tried to deal with French bureaucracy, that conclusion is indeed bizarre, but this is what the UN suggests. And guess which country the UN suggests the rest of the world should look to when thinking about adopting asset forfeiture rules? The good ol' United States of America. What a dubious honor, and what a horrific prospect.

The good news is that some of our politicians have recognized the danger. The U.S. Congress passed a bill authored by House Judiciary Committee Chairman Henry Hyde (R-IL) that curtails the federal government's abuse of asset forfeiture. As he championed the bill, Hyde reported that 80 percent of those whose property is seized by the federal government have never been formally charged with any crime! The final House vote in favor of Mr. Hyde's Civil Asset Forfeiture Reform Bill was 375 to 48, a wonderful victory. Federal agencies have already responded. U.S. border inspectors in San Diego, California, have stopped confiscating thousands of cars from innocent owners who were unaware that their passengers lacked the legal status to enter this country. Before passage of the new law, INS officials at California's six border crossings estimated that they confiscated at least 1,000 cars per month. Since August 2000, when the law went into effect, that number has dropped to fewer than 60. Nevertheless, asset forfeitures continue. The possible applications are endless, especially when you remember that asset forfeiture functions not just at the federal level of government but at the state and municipal levels, too. The visions of the future can be frightening:

- You are accused of having bribed building inspectors during the construction of a building. It is conceivable that the municipality will seize your entire building because local prosecutors say you have participated in a criminal exercise.

- The computer you innocently bought turns out to contain pirated software. How are you to know that the version of Windows that came with your new PC wasn't legally authorized? Software piracy is a big and far too common problem these days. The government could decide to seize your computer on the pretext it contains pirated software and you are in possession of stolen property.

- If you have a new satellite system, you might find yourself with unauthorized access to a certain television channel. The government won't care whether this access is the result of ignorance on your part. The government is seizing computers that belong to hackers. If the government decides you're receiving illegal TV signals, what's to stop them from seizing your television and satellite equipment?

- If you have a lot of computers in your workplace, it can be hard to control what your employees do with them. You might be ultimately responsible for illegal actions on your employees' part. There have been lots of instances where employees have used their high-speed Internet connections and computers at work to download and save illegal pornography. Asset forfeiture is predicated on guilt by association. It's total and it's sweeping. If the authorities suspect that even one computer in your workplace is being used to store illegal images, all of your computers may be seized.

- The threat might not even come from within your own office. Hackers steal user names and passwords all the time. You might have your home or business computers seized simply because someone who is engaging in illegal activity claims to be you. The authorities might even seize your home, your bank accounts, your car, and your business while they're at it, and leave you to prove them wrong.

- Sometimes you see a basket of coupons near the cash register at the supermarket. The checkout clerk lets you scan those coupons and claim the discount even though you didn't clip the coupons yourself. What if the company publishing the coupons decides to take legal action against the supermarket for improperly and repeatedly using the same coupon? Would this make you a co-conspirator with the store in a scheme to defraud the company that publishes the coupons? Just imagine what the government could do if it claimed the immediate right to raid your pantry and seize all the goods obtained through fraud.

- Let's say you tape a show using your VCR. Have you ever heard the warnings sportscasters give about reproduction of the game being forbidden? Does this mean some men in dark glasses are going to pound down your door to seize your VCR, television, and collection of videotaped Broncos games? It doesn't seem that far-fetched when you remember the government will seize 10 pieces of commercial real estate, 31 businesses, and $9 million because of seven dirty books and videos.

In fact, the mechanics of asset forfeiture have become so cumbersome that the U.S. Marshals Service has commissioned Bid4Assets, an online Internet marketing service, to handle the cumbersome details. In one recent online auction of assets seized in Detroit, the company (which employs 35 people and boasts a worldwide clientele of over 32,000 registered bidders) auctioned property that included a 71-unit apartment tower, several luxury automobiles, a helicopter, ranch property in Hawaii and Montana, and an inner-city grocery where police say heroin had been sold (even though charges against the owners of the grocery had been dropped).

Asset forfeiture is a real law. It's more than just a plan to put drug dealers and money launderers out of business. It's a scheme to make money for the government. You are a target. Shield your assets in the offshore world. Protect your assets before the government comes to take them.

CHAPTER 9

EIGHT STEPS TO
OFFSHORE SUCCESS

Offshore money havens are no longer a luxury reserved for the ultrarich. Within today's global economic system, they are the prime financial option for anyone whose assets total $200,000 or more. That includes tens of thousands of Americans—all of whom want protection from lawsuits, tax protection, continuous profits, and financial privacy.

Why do you think so many investors—large, small, and in-between—are moving toward this global business approach? Why have they decided to compete (and win) at the offshore game?

In part, the offshore boom results from a wide array of technological advancements. Thanks to sophisticated telecommunications and computerized banking services worldwide, people can make, spend, win, lose, and transfer money faster than ever before. A conscientious investor may, for instance, assess the value of currency in any nation on a given morning, decide when it has

193

reached a danger point, and complete a cash-out program on all liquid investments held in that country by the following afternoon! This fast-paced movement of funds has made offshore investment very appealing to growing numbers of domestic businesspeople and entrepreneurs.

But there is an even more profound reason for the trend toward offshore investment, and that's the changing profile of today's financial players. Regardless of their individual differences, the economic winners of the 1990s and into the next century share a common view of the global marketplace. They see it as a wide-open environment from which to pick and choose the most lucrative investment options. They will have taken what I perceive to be the most important step in attaining genuine financial independence: learning to see the world without national borders. That gives them an almost limitless profit-making arena.

If you take only one message from this book, I hope it will be the enormity of your potential investment sphere. You no longer need to restrict your financial activity to the traditional Swiss bank account or to a paltry selection of onshore tax shelters.

Conventional investment vehicles (such as bonds, commodities, and securities), established in traditional brokerage accounts in your own name, have become relics of another era. The offshore world offers lucrative ventures and access to the same markets with all the trimmings. You just need to broaden your own investment horizon.

Experience has shown me that, for many reasons, Americans tend to see the world as a neatly divided assortment of cultures, countries, and currencies. We think of East as East, and West as West, and only at the United Nations do the twain meet. I can't tell you how many times I've consulted with extremely successful professionals and entrepreneurs from around the country, all of whom want to add offshore options to their financial portfolio. Nevertheless, their personal sense of economic nationalism limits their ability to reap the benefits of the offshore solution.

They pay a high price for this limited vision. They miss the benefits inherent in the international option. From those who have avoided offshore activity altogether, I most often hear about profit margins that are far less than satisfactory. From those who have severely restricted foreign investments, I learn of stymied venture activity and meager earnings. In each instance I find myself thinking of the more assertive investors (from the United States and around the world) who have entered the offshore arena. It is these enlightened investors who are constantly taking part in creative new ventures and sharpening their global edge.

THE BIG MYTH ABOUT OFFSHORE BUSINESS

Despite its proven benefits, the offshore option still lacks a level of public credibility. For too many people, the phrase "offshore banking investment" conjures up the image presented in John Grisham's novel *The Firm* and in the movie by the same name, starring Tom Cruise and Gene Hackman. The story is about a Memphis law firm that uses offshore money havens as places to keep and launder money belonging to the Chicago mob. The story makes for a great thriller, but distorts the truth about the offshore world by reinforcing the media stereotype of offshore banking as a haven for money laundering, drug trafficking, arms smuggling, insider-trading schemes, and tax evasion. Every television network, newspaper, and weekly news magazine in the country has run stories on illicit foreign financial ventures. After all, these complex intrigues make for attention-grabbing headlines.

Admittedly, there is some truth behind the hype. Illegal activity has occurred, and it continues to happen.

Although this criminal element accounts for only a small fraction of the total offshore investment community, it has managed to tarnish the reputation of an entirely legitimate financial option. Why? Because the global market is so inviting and so well tailored to unregulated profit, it has easily fallen prey to those with less than honorable intentions.

That said, the overwhelming impact of the negative press overshadows the reality. The offshore world is not the preserve of the Mafia. It is instead populated by some of the world's most important—and legitimate—corporations. Dow Chemical has an offshore presence. American Express is offshore. So are McDonald's, Nike, Wal-Mart, and DuPont. This list is endless. I know, because I have inspected SEC public filings, where offshore activities are described in detail.

Besides, some parts of the offshore world aren't kind to criminals. The most famous case would be that of Ferdinand Marcos, the late dictator who once ruled the Philippines. In December 1997 the Supreme Court of Switzerland ruled that two Swiss banks must return the $500 million the dictator looted from his country before he was thrown out of office in 1996. Switzerland, stung by the blizzard of media reports about its role as a banking center for the Nazis, welcomed the court decision.

In September 1997 Switzerland returned $2.7 million to Mali, one of the poorest countries in the world. Swiss authorities first seized the funds back in 1991 after

> **While the offshore world is a place where honest people can legally keep their money with full privacy and minimum tax, dictators and crooks are not as welcome as popular fiction suggests.**

dictator Gen. Moussa Traore was overthrown in a coup. The Swiss government also gave Mali legal assistance to make its claim for the return of Gen. Traore's loot.

Switzerland has frozen $4.3 million in bank accounts belonging to Mobutu Sese Seko, a dictator who plundered the Congo during a 30-year reign. The Swiss have also frozen accounts containing cash allegedly stolen by former Pakistani premier Benazir Bhutto. Switzerland also passed a law in April 1997 that requires bankers and other money managers to report suspected money laundering to authorities and freeze the assets in question.

So, while the offshore world is a place where honest people can legally keep their money with full privacy and minimum tax, dictators and crooks are not as welcome as popular fiction suggests, and as the Swiss experience shows. The rationale is simple: Bad business attracts more bad business. The offshore world is not the wild fantasy portrayed in *The Firm*. It's a legitimate, legal tool you can use to protect yourself and your assets.

EIGHT STEPS TO OFFSHORE SUCCESS

If you are taking the time to read this book, you're probably serious about an offshore financial involvement. Many of you may have already experienced the international arena; others are undoubtedly considering a first venture.

In either case, I would like to offer you some basic advice. There is nothing particularly unusual about these eight steps to success in the offshore world marketplace. In fact, you may have heard similar advice from other consultants.

However, there is one big difference. I've been on the front lines of the offshore investment expansion for 27 years. The following steps are based on my firsthand experience with real people. Working on the front lines has prepared me to offer you advice tempered by reality, not far-fetched academic theories.

Over the years, I've watched a lot of investors enter the world of offshore finance. While many of them have become tremendously successful in the process, I've seen some failures, too. In my view, each of those failures can be traced to an unwillingness or an inability to follow these basic steps.

Step One: Decide If an Offshore Financial Move Is Right for You

Not everyone is cut out for international finance. There are people who simply don't want to do business in a foreign country. Even among those who do like the global market, there are decisive differences. Some are satisfied when they are "invisibly" involved in an offshore investment. Others aren't happy until they get right in the middle of it: taking frequent trips abroad and juggling the challenges of offshore business relations for themselves. So the first step to successfully entering the offshore arena is careful self-assessment. Know your own level of interest and comfort. I advocate an informed and assertive approach.

This may be the time to point out how strongly I disagree with those experts who urge American investors to learn cross-cultural business skills in order to go global. The fact is, most successful U.S. businesspeople already have extensive cross-cultural experience. Anyone who lives in Manhattan and handles transactions in Los Angeles, New Orleans, Houston, or even Chicago has it. The United States really consists of many different cultures functioning together as a single country. So the challenge, as I see it, is one of expanding professional skills that already exist.

In short, going offshore is committing to an entirely new way of making money. It's expanding your investment perspective, and capitalizing on financial opportunities whenever and wherever they occur. Before you get involved, be sure you're really attracted to this very contemporary approach to personal investment.

Step Two: Develop a Strategy

Once you've decided that offshore action is for you, you must begin to develop a feasible financial strategy. You can't hope to make money, save taxes, or protect your privacy by merely stumbling around in the offshore marketplace. You must know what you're doing.

So take the time to ask yourself: What do you want from, say, a silent partnership in Tokyo? From your private brass-plate bank in the Caribbean? From an import/export firm in the Pacific? Each of these offshore ventures can be extremely profitable, but each is a distinct business activity with very specific demands and benefits. Developing a strategy involves serious consideration of your needs, your goals, and your future.

Every successful businessperson or investor that I've met has known the value of strategic thinking. This boils down to coming up with a well-designed plan of action and sticking to it.

Let's consider the strategy of international investor George Soros. Among the world's most celebrated financial wizards, Soros is best known for the nearly $1 billion that he made in the space of just a few days of currency speculation in 1992. By betting correctly on the collapse of the British pound, Soros made one of the biggest profits ever registered in the global market. That distinction alone makes him a man worth watching. A Hungarian Jewish refugee who is said to currently manage more than \$11 billion in assets, Soros has developed a complete theory on how to get rich in the international market. His general concept of "reflexivity" is very abstract. In a nutshell, it teaches investors to be ever on the lookout for "boom/bust sequences." Soros thinks you can make money when you correctly pinpoint a social imbalance that will precipitate radical change within a financial market.

We all can't be a George Soros, but we can emulate him by devising specific tactics that will make it possible for us to carry out our own strategies. In order to meet his particular objective, Soros trades and invests in very targeted markets and areas at very specific times. That obviously works for him. If *your* overall aim is, let's say, to lessen your tax load, then you, like Soros, must think of appropriate ways in which to carry out *your* strategy. These will be your tactics.

My advice is that those tactics should first of all embody the golden rule of financial investment: Diversification. Each individual offshore venture can satisfy only so many economic needs. I strongly discourage anyone from imagining that there is a single international investment, acquisition, or new business concept that can legally address all your financial needs. That's why the best international investors have assets strategically working around the world, functioning in different ways in different places.

Step Three: Select an Experienced Offshore Adviser

Realizing the need for a practical strategy, you must now consider the services of a first-class financial expert. While shopping for an adviser, remember that a number of professional qualities characterize a good consultant:

- **Superior financial skills.** You need someone who can develop an optimal strategy tailored especially to your needs. Don't accept a "one-size-fits-all" approach to offshore investment. Look for an adviser who is willing and able to help you design the plan that's right for you. Any reputable consultant should be well versed in handling a wide variety of foreign exchange matters, including preparing proper documentation and setting offshore operating parameters. Your consultant must be someone who can help with the implementation of *your* personal business strategy, not just the one he or she is *used* to implementing.

- **Excellent knowledge of offshore international investment alternatives.** A qualified adviser will offer various investment vehicles and will encourage you to compare them before making a final choice. Every investment has its own complexity and each requires careful consideration. You should be able to count on your consultant for help in balancing out the various accounting, tax, and legal issues involved in all your options.

- **A wide network of international contacts.** Avoid fly-by-night operations. By and large, international financial consultants are honest and reliable, but there are a few scam artists who make it their business to identify inexperienced investors. A good way to know if you've met a real professional is to ask

> A qualified adviser will offer various investment vehicles and will encourage you to compare them before making a final choice.

about his international business network. You want to look for an adviser who is well connected to people and institutions abroad. Those contacts are your insurance that an offshore venture will be implemented legally and on the best possible terms for you. If your consultant has a solid reputation throughout the offshore business establishment, he or she will want to protect it by seeing to it that you are treated right.

- **An in-depth understanding of the offshore market, and the staff to efficiently execute all transactions.** Establishing an offshore operation and conducting transactions in another country often involves close and regular interaction with government officials. You need to work with an adviser who understands the intricacies involved in your preferred offshore location. What's more, your adviser should offer you an experienced and efficient staff, capable of serving as backup for your project. Also, be sure the adviser you select has the communication technology to execute complicated transactions quickly and accurately.

Once you have selected an offshore adviser who meets these criteria, it's time to reassess your strategy—this time with his or her input. By working through the plan you've designed for yourself, you can benefit from your adviser's feedback and guidance. Although you probably have a good sense for what's right for you, don't be stubborn about taking your professional consultant's advice. After all, that's what you're paying for. Let your adviser help you refine and hone your offshore game plan.

Step Four: Put All the Proper Systems in Place

After you've clarified your priorities, mapped out your strategy, and identified a good adviser, it's time to put your systems in place. Before you attempt to negotiate your first deal, be sure you're prepared to do business the way it's done offshore. That means setting up a sound organizational structure to manage your international investments and/or operations. You need good people and the right equipment. That may sound like an obvious step, but you'd be surprised at how many new investors forget to take it.

You should now select your key people: an accountant, an attorney, and a clerical assistant. Depending upon the nature and scope of your particular strategy, you may want to hire them on a per-hour (or freelance) basis, rather than as full-time employees. This is an area in which a professional consultant can offer some experienced advice.

You will also need the right equipment. With a personal computer, Internet access, a couple of phone lines, a fax machine, and a photocopier, you can operate out of your home or office anytime, day or night.

An integral part of proper systems management is written confirmation of everything. To help you in this area, here are three basic tips on written communications:

- **Keep your writing simple.** Experience has shown me that basic, straightforward letters and memos are the key to successful business writing.

- **Make sure individuals' professional titles translate correctly.** Since the same position may vary around the world, getting the right title is essential.

- **Clarify all written items having to do with money amounts**. Be sure that currency differences and rate exchanges are taken into account.

Step Five: Create the Right Image

In my opinion, your business image is one of the most important factors in the successful consummation of offshore ventures. From my years of working and living in Los Angeles, one of the media capitals of the world, I am repeatedly reminded of the value in projecting a strong, clear image, and the benefits of keeping that image in front of those you want to impress favorably. This continues to be the case in Vancouver, my former home. Though it's a lot smaller than Los Angeles, it's also an important media city. Many Hollywood studios shoot their movies here, taking advantage of the low Canadian dollar, dramatic scenery, and the highly skilled workforce.

For offshore investors, the importance of image should direct everything from the design of your business cards to the wording of all printed material you use to outline your offerings, products, or services. Anything you produce to advance your financial activities should reflect the image you want to project.

You must establish your image before you go offshore. For example, your new offshore financial entity may offer banking services. Therefore, your bank will require a name, a logo, stationery, a services brochure, and various types of banking forms. The image you want to project will direct all these specific choices.

You can create and promote a very serious, cautious, financially conservative image by working with basic muted colors (like gray and brown). By the same token, you can generate a more relaxed, contemporary, and slightly adventurous impression by using pastel colors (like sky blue and sand). It's up to you. Both have their benefits and drawbacks. Remember that no choice will appeal to every prospective customer in every nation. So carefully think through your prime

You must establish your image before you go offshore.

markets and direct your choices toward their concerns and priorities.

The key is careful coordination. Make sure all your printed material is coordinated in some way. This makes it easier for investors, depositors, shareholders, and customers to identify your service or product. Consistency is a must in business because it conveys stability.

Finally, here are some ideas about advertising, which is critical to image making. Advertising is the direct approach to the people whose involvement you want. As such, it must send a message about your business image. Intelligent advertising will help establish your offshore business and, over time, will make it grow.

Let me quote from one of the masters of business advertising, Ted Nicholas: "It is not an oversimplification to say that nearly every ad, regardless of its degree of sophistication, follows the Attention-Interest-Desire-Action formula." That's exactly what you should keep in mind when you advertise. First, your ad must grab your potential client's attention, next create interest and arouse a real desire to act, and then explain how to take that action.

Check with your consultant about all advertising, particularly about this Attention-Interest-Desire-Action formula. Will it produce results? Are there marketing experts who would be willing to review your materials and offer their professional criticism? You should receive this kind of support and guidance from your adviser. Again, that's why you've commissioned his or her services. So don't be shy about asking for help.

Step Six: Do Your Homework

Going offshore is not like taking a vacation. Even for the most adventuresome at heart, it is not a time for playing things by ear. To be successful overseas—even if you never leave the United States—you need to learn something about the place where you're investing your money.

To be realistic, the extent of your "homework" should be tied to your level of personal contact with the foreign locale. If your entire plan is to purchase stock at a brokerage firm that handles foreign investments, your information needs are clearly minimal. If, on the other hand, you plan to conduct business with South Korean textile manufacturers, you'd be smart to spend time learning what is and isn't acceptable behavior in their part of the world.

According to Stanford University's Richard Pascale, too many people think that a cocktail conversation with a few world travelers will prepare them for even the most in-depth offshore involvement. As he points out, "Real effort is more like 30 hours of intensive study."

When it comes to this homework phase, I'm a firm believer in the value of small books and regular magazines. Clients who have been to my office often remark on my personal business library. They are sometimes amazed by my general encyclopedias, my collections on various international business subjects, and the scores of volumes on everything from international marketing to the history of world economic growth.

Of course, my work demands that I keep abreast of a wide range of international and global developments. You don't need to tackle that kind of reading load. Nevertheless, I do suggest that you consider building a basic collection that will help you understand the exciting changes that are constantly taking place in the offshore market.

Frankly, there are far too many books on the market that are just hype and do nothing more than feed existing fears and misconceptions. Don't be suckered into the belief that you must read everything that's published on the subject. Instead, take a conservative

approach to building your library. After all, the offshore market will be around forever. You have time to
become a master at it.

If you do decide to build a basic international investment bookshelf, the following tips may prove helpful:

- **General reference.** Every investor should have
  at least one book on general investment. It should
  cover some of the essentials, like the do's and
  don'ts of personal financial planning. Make sure
  that any general reference books you buy were
  written after the tax reform of 1986 and the tax
  legislation passed into law in 1990 and 1993,
  because anything published before that is out of
  date. You may also want to buy an investment glos-
  sary guide, such as the *Dictionary of Finance and
  Investment Terms* published by Barron's.

- **Books about offshore funds.** Offshore funds
  are investment funds based in tax havens or
  low-tax areas. As the *Financial Times* notes,
  "They are able to invest in a broader range of
  instruments than onshore domestic investment
  companies. It is this flexibility . . . [that] is their
  main attraction for investors." Because they are
  a cornerstone to offshore investment, I recommend that you get a basic background text about
  how they work, such as *How to Start Your Own
  Offshore Investment Fund.* I also recommend
  that before you invest in any fund, you send for
  and study its prospectus.

- **Books about hard assets.** With inflation always
  lurking around the corner, you may want to have a
  couple of books on real estate and gold. One well-
  recommended guide is Adam Starchild's *Portable
  Wealth: The Complete Guide to Precious Metals
  Investment.*

Step Seven: Know the Rules and Practices

Before you finalize the design of any international business plan, check out the legal requirements of your host country concerning local participation. It's no longer possible to just set up a business anywhere in the world, run it entirely with your own staff, and earn its full profit for yourself.

Growing nationalism and economic protectionism abroad have changed the nature of offshore ventures. Today many foreign governments have strict laws governing the percentage of required native workforce and mandatory contributions to various national development goals. Don't be caught off guard: Know the laws of any country before you move beyond the thinking phase.

In short, other countries are raising the stakes for entrance into their economy. If the potential profit is substantial, it may be worth the price. But if foreign governments become too demanding, they can begin to extinguish the allure of any site.

Before getting involved in an offshore center, try to meet people who have done business in that country. If that's not possible, then try meeting people with other experiences in (and connections to) the area. Even if that's difficult, I suggest that you keep trying until you find at least one person who's willing to offer limited social and professional support. You may dislike this sort of networking, but you'll ultimately be glad to know someone you can call on for advice on matters as minor as currency exchange or as major as government involvement in business operations.

These mentors can serve another essential purpose. They can provide you with names of people in the foreign location who, in turn, will refer you to others who will direct you to more contacts. And knowing people is the name of the game in international finance. Everyone likes a personal touch. That is especially true in other countries, where social customs tend to emphasize personal associations and reputation.

As a second phase in this networking strategy, I urge you to hire a reliable representative in the foreign center where you plan to conduct business. In some countries this is a legal requirement. Even where it is not, experts agree that you should pretend it is. The local representative should be native to the country.

Some people think they can just go out and place an ad in a foreign newspaper and they'll be deluged with resumes. It's not that simple. First of all, the cost of advertising is prohibitive. A small ad in a national Japanese-language newspaper can cost upwards of $20,000 per insertion. Secondly, the demand for talent far exceeds the supply.

Once you do locate an agent, keep two things in mind. First, if you don't click with a prospective representative, move on right away. It will only become more difficult to make a change later on. If you do decide to replace your representative, be careful not to offend him because his negative comments about you can have serious consequences. Second, don't count on your representative for everything. Few offshore operations can be initiated and successfully completed entirely by proxy. An agent can help, but at some point you will probably need to get directly involved.

Step Eight: Make Sure You Can Get Your Money Out

If you work with a professional financial consultant, you are unlikely to face this nightmare. However, if you try to handle an entire offshore venture alone, you can run into terrible trouble when it comes time to cash-out and return home. Some countries make it very easy to invest in, but very difficult to get out of, their economy.

The best insurance against this problem is to know ahead of time exactly what the conditions are for transferring your involvement back into U.S. currency. How can your stocks be sold? How can your franchise or distributor agreement be signed over to another investor? Can you dissolve your local partnership at any time with the understanding that your share of the profits to date will be liquidated and made payable?

Have all conditions of transfer and dissolution formally agreed upon in writing. Keep one copy in your foreign business site and another here in the United States. That way, in the event of any problem, you will have a legally binding agreement to show the exact nature of your investment arrangement.

Know, too, that Uncle Sam will lay claim to his share of every dollar earned abroad and brought back to this country. So don't plan to repatriate funds unless you're willing to pay taxes on them.

PUTTING IT ALL TOGETHER

These eight basic steps are only a beginning. They can provide you with the minimum you will need to know for even the simplest international investment venture. Perhaps the most important of all the suggestions is the value of a professional consultant. If you connect with the right person, he or she will help guide you through all the rest. Particularly in the beginning, when most aspects of any offshore project justifiably overwhelm you, a seasoned expert can offer professional assistance and reassurance. As you become more experienced, you may be able to initiate and implement some business deals without commissioning further expert advice.

International investment and business is a financial grab bag. Most of it is exciting. Much of it is lucrative. Some of it is risky. There are benefits and disadvantages to every kind of offshore venture. It's your responsibility to know what your options are and to understand the perks and pitfalls that are attached to each. In the process, you will prepare yourself to recognize the offshore involvement that is best for you and your financial priorities.

CHAPTER 10

WHERE TO GO,
WHERE NOT TO GO

G iven the sheer number of offshore money havens, it's not surprising the first question many of my clients ask is which one they should select. There are dozens of possibilities, so my answer is not always the same. No single place is best for everyone. The haven I recommend depends on a client's goal. Some havens are better suited for privacy seekers; some cater only to the superrich. This chapter will give you some basic information about the 40 offshore money havens I believe either stand out above the rest or show signs of future promise. It will also explain some of the things that distinguish havens.

Let me start by making the point that the secret-numbered Swiss bank account is a remnant from the financial past. Using one in today's intensely competitive and highly unpredictable economy is like riding a bike on a superhighway. The vehicle we should use always depends on need. And while no one would take a bike on the freeway, too many investors rely on a Swiss account when a much more versatile option exists: off-shore money havens.

People often ask me if they can really protect their money, earn a profit, and pay fewer taxes by using the off-shore option. I always say yes—as long as they are careful in selecting their offshore business venue. International money havens actually do exist, and in light of the worsening U.S. economy and the tightening of U.S. tax rules, they are fast becoming the preferred choice for smart investors.

Several years ago, a study called Service Banking was prepared for the prestigious London-based Institute of Bankers. In reviewing it, I came across an insightful observation and jotted it down because it contained the essence of the offshore rationale:

> Like water finding its own level, entrepreneurial business, when constrained in one place, will emerge in another. When restrictions in one place become too burdensome, too discouraging and perhaps too punitive, the businessman will look elsewhere . . . as one door closes, another opens.

Over the years, I've seen the truth of this observation borne out time after time, in life as well as in business. If you don't like a situation, change it. Whether it's your relationship with your spouse, your employees, or your dwelling, change it if it isn't working out.

Accordingly, there is no reason to tolerate the current situation in Switzerland. As it becomes subject to international agreements, and its famous secrecy laws dissolve under international political pressure, other places pick up the slack. Some who used to use Switzerland now go to Austria, while others prefer the British Virgin Islands (BVI). The point is this: Every investor can find what he needs, if he's just willing to look far enough.

One of the reasons I was compelled to write this book is that more and more of my clients have expressed alarm and concern over the uncertain economic situation in the United States. They also understand that in times of swift economic change, flexibility and liquidity are crucial requirements. When you factor in the bureaucratic red tape that has become part of all financial dealings within this country—as well as the low rates of return on investments, the heavy burden of taxation, and a general negative social environment—the offshore option is hard to overlook.

HOW THE OFFSHORE HAVENS CAME ABOUT

The world's first offshore bankers were Florentine merchants, royal treasurers, and brilliant bankers. They helped make Florence one of the world's most economically advanced centers. The mechanisms and strategies they originated have, of course, changed over the centuries. The goals, however, always remain the same.

In contemporary times, offshore money havens were originally established by onshore banks and corporations. Why? Because they felt hemmed in by archaic laws, regulations, and statutes. For example, Citicorp (one of the largest American-owned banks in the United States) was one of the first to set up offshore operations. It wasn't too long before 64 percent of its net income was being generated by offshore sources.

Some of the pioneering centers have evolved into first-class financial and economic headquarters. Since the early 1970s these centers have initiated policies deliberately designed to attract international trade by minimizing tax obligations and reducing (or entirely eliminating) other restrictions on business operations. The result is that economic activity within these centers is specifically geared to the special global needs of outside businesses and investors.

Typically, these centers are small states with tiny populations. To date, more than 200 of them exist throughout the world. Since 1985 the number has grown almost exponentially. Each one of them is a unique off-shore haven deliberately intended to attract very particular investors with very specific needs. Singapore, for example, was designed to serve the Asian dollar market. Today it's one of the most prosperous money havens in the world on a per-capita basis. Bahrain was developed to process the Middle East's offshore financial needs, especially those of Saudi Arabia.

Offshore havens have become an established part of the international intermediate economy. They operate as "brokers" of a sort for global business and finance. Remember, large banks, corporations, and even government agencies from around the world initiated all of this. Since every government in the world needs to obtain money on the international market, they, too, use money havens as convenient transaction points. The Bahamas became one of the biggest offshore havens because it serves the purposes of various government entities, from finance ministries to intelligence agencies.

THE SCHEMES TO CLOSE TAX HAVENS DOWN

Fifteen years ago, there were 450 offshore investment funds, but the free will of the marketplace and the ingenuity of small nations wishing for a piece of the world's economic pie quickly rocketed that number to 6,000. It didn't take long for the larger, established nations to sit up and take notice. And thus began an international campaign against "harmful tax competition" spearheaded by the Paris-based Organisation for Economic Co-operation and Development (OECD) and echoed by the Financial Stability Forum (FSF) and the Financial

> Offshore havens have become an established
> part of the international intermediate
> economy. They operate as "brokers" of a sort
> for global business and finance.

Action Task Force (FATF). FATF had actually been established by OECD in 1989 to marshal its forces against the laundering of money from illegal (primarily drug) activities.

Efforts to rein in the offshore financial centers started as polite attempts to persuade them to reform their tax systems and improve transparency. The efforts quickly escalated into blistering attacks and threatened sanctions against any emerging country with its own ideas about financial sovereignty. In June 2000 the OECD decided to wield the big club—identifying 35 international jurisdictions as "tax havens" and ordering them to reform by July 31, 2001 . . . or else.

These "tainted nations" included Andorra, Anguilla, Antigua, Aruba, the Bahamas, Bahrain, Barbados, Belize, the British Virgin Islands, the Cook Islands, Dominica, Gibraltar, Grenada, Guernsey/Sark/Alderney, the Isle of Man, Jersey, Liberia, Liechtenstein, the Maldives, the Marshall Islands, Monaco, Montserrat, Nauru, the Netherlands Antilles, Niue, Panama, St. Kitts and Nevis, St. Lucia, St. Vincent and the Grenadines, Seychelles, Tonga, the Turks and Caicos and Caicos Islands, the U.S. Virgin Islands, Vanuatu, and Western Samoa.

Meanwhile, Bermuda, the Cayman Islands, Cyprus, Malta, Mauritius, and San Marino were able to avoid inclusion on the list by pledging to eliminate their "harmful" tax practices by 2005 and to adhere to the yet undefined standards for transparency, exchange of information, and fair tax competition. Other countries resisted, using their own organizations to implore the OECD to clarify its demands. Moreover, the tax havens were incensed by what they saw as the OECD's linking of the legal interpretations of tax evasion (viewed by many as mere tax competition between nations) and money laundering by criminal syndicates.

The OECD response was to issue a second "blacklist" of 15 nations that it said had proven "insufficiently cooperative" in discouraging money laundering—and of maintaining bank secrecy even in the face of criminal investigations. This new list included the Bahamas, the Cayman Islands, the Cook Islands, Dominica, Israel, Lebanon, Liechtenstein, the Marshall Islands, Nauru, Niue, Panama, the Philippines, Russia, St. Kitts and Nevis, and St. Vincent and the Grenadines. But the list was highly political as Britain protected its offshore dependencies from scrutiny and France's protectorate, Monaco, also evaded the citation.

What followed was a flurry of charges and countercharges between the OECD and the tax haven nations. Enter U.S. Treasury Secretary Paul O'Neill. In May 2001 O'Neill announced that Washington and the new Bush administration believed the OECD blacklists and threatened sanctions showed too little respect to the small countries where offshore financial services are thriving. "The United States does not support efforts to dictate to any country what its own tax rates or tax system should be," said O'Neill, "and will not participate in any initiative to harmonize world tax systems." As we go to press with this fourth edition, all efforts of the world's rich democracies to sanction smaller tax haven countries have ground to a halt.

Understandably, officials in the tax haven countries are elated by this new turn of events. Joshua Sears, the Bahamas' ambassador to the United States said, "We always felt the initiative was biased. We think it undermines the rule of law and seriously impinges on a country's ability to manage its own fiscal affairs." And Lionel Hurst, ambassador from Antigua and Barbuda to Washington, remarked, "We thought this was the appropriate American response to this European idea."

What this all means is that offshore havens remain an accepted financial fact. Even more important, they are still seen as legitimate vehicles through which individual investors can take advantage of the offshore option. It's simply a matter of applying the basic financial principles of profit, tax protection, and privacy.

When I work with my clients I try to ensure that they are served by the money haven that is right for them. I help them customize and tailor a program in an offshore haven that meets their personal criteria based on their needs. As a consultant, I look forward to the discussions that help shape their final offshore money haven choice.

THE SCHNEIDER CRITERIA

Some havens pride themselves on their lack of red tape. Others are rolling in it. Some havens prefer to cater to the needs of the superrich and require investors to deposit a substantial amount of assets offshore before welcoming them with open arms.

Similarly, some havens charge significant user fees not only for establishing the offshore arrangement, but also the annual upkeep. It could cost as much as $20,000 a year to maintain an offshore investment in Bermuda.

That said, it is possible for a haven to come too cheaply. If it's too easy to set up an investment there, maybe this is a signal the haven suffers from a reputation problem.

A mere $700 lets you set up an offshore corporation with no questions asked in Panama, for instance. All you need is a heartbeat and a wallet. You can only imagine what sort of a person Panama attracts. The place itself suffers from the *"mañana"* system. In Panama, work requested for completion today often doesn't get completed until *mañana* ("tomorrow").

Overall, I can tell you that my favorite offshore money havens are the British Virgin Islands and my three Ns: Nauru, Nevis, and the Netherlands Antilles. These four locations have ironclad secrecy rules and a reputation of making it difficult for U.S. authorities to access private information.

Show Me the Money!

I've intensely studied 40 countries and put together a table (see table 10–1) that looks at several of the factors to consider when selecting your offshore haven. I've tried to sum up price as concisely as I can. This isn't always easy because pricing systems vary from haven to haven. For example, you can set up an offshore trust in the Isle of Man for about $3,000, but this fee doesn't include the cost of obtaining advice from your U.S.–based legal adviser. Your legal fees will vary depending on your lawyer's experience and expertise. The legal fees associated with setting up a trust in the Isle of Man, for example, can range between $5,000 and $50,000.

And remember that I said consulting a lawyer is an absolute necessity. Never forget that using an offshore program is all about using legal methods to reduce your exposure to legal difficulties, not increase them. Buy yourself solutions, not problems.

TABLE 10-1

| | Time Zone | | | |
	PST	EST	GMT	Main Languages
Andorra	+9	+6	+1	Spanish, French
Anguilla	+4	+1	−4	English
Antigua and Barbuda	+4	+1	−4	English
Aruba	+4	+1	−4	Dutch, English, Spanish
Austria	+9	+6	+1	German
Bahamas	+3	0	−5	English
Bahrain	+11	+8	+3	Arabic, English
Barbados	+4	+1	−4	English
Belize	+4	−1	−6	English, Creole, Spanish
Bermuda	+4	−1	−4	English
British Virgin Islands	+12	+9	+4	English
Cayman Islands	+3	0	−5	English
Cook Islands	−2	−5	−10	English
Costa Rica	+2	−1	−6	Spanish
Cyprus	+10	+7	+2	Greek, Turkish
Fiji	+20	+17	+12	English
Gibraltar	+9	+6	+1	English
Grenada	+4	+1	−4	English
Guernsey	+8	+5	0	English
Hong Kong	+16	+13	+8	Cantonese, English
Ireland	+8	+5	0	English
Isle of Man	+8	+5	0	English
Jersey	+8	+5	0	English
Labuan	+16	+13	+8	Malaysian, English
Liechtenstein	+9	+6	+1	German
Luxembourg	+9	+6	+1	French, German
Mauritius	+12	+9	+4	English
Monaco	+9	+6	+1	French
Nauru	+20	+17	+12	English
Netherlands Antilles	+9	+6	−4	Dutch
Nevis	+4	+1	−4	English
Panama	+3	0	−5	Spanish
Samoa	+9	+6	−1	Samoan, English
San Marino	+9	+6	+1	Italian
Seychelles	+12	+9	+14	English
Singapore	+16	+13	+8	Mandarin, Malay
St. Vincent	+4	+1	−4	English
Switzerland	+9	+6	+1	German, French, Italian
Turks and Caicos	+3	0	−5	English
Vanuatu	+19	+16	+11	English
Vatican	+9	+6	+1	Italian

Legal System	Privacy Rating	Travelability	Entry Cost	Annual Cost
civil	AA	treacherous	$1,200	$5,000
common	A	comfortable	$1,050	$500
common	A	comfortable	n/a	n/a
civil	AAA	comfortable	n/a	n/a
civil	AAA	comfortable	n/a	n/a
common	AA	comfortable	$ 2,500	$2,500
civil	A	exhausting	n/a	n/a
common	AA	comfortable	$2,200	$1,100
common	AAA	comfortable	$1,000	$400
common	AA	comfortable	$3,000	$3,000
common	AA	comfortable	$1,300	$300
common	A	comfortable	n/a	n/a
common	AA	exhausting	$2,750	$1,500
civil	AA	comfortable	n/a	n/a
common	A	comfortable	$6,000	$1,200
common	AA	comfortable	n/a	n/a
common	AA	comfortable	$700	$500
common	AA	comfortable	n/a	n/a
common	AA	tiring	$2,000	$1,000
common	A	comfortable	$1,500	$2,500
common	A	comfortable	$600	$900
common	AA	tiring	$3,000	$2,000
common	AA	tiring	$1,000	$1,000
common	AA	tiring	$1,500	n/a
civil	A	comfortable	$3,500	$3,000
civil	A	comfortable	$30,000	$7,000
common	AA	exhausting	minimal	minimal
civil	A	comfortable	$5,000	lots
common	AAA	tiring	n/a	n/a
civil	AAA	comfortable	n/a	n/a
common	AAA	comfortable	$50	$500
civil	A	comfortable	cheap	n/a
common	A	tiring	$800	$300
civil	A	tiring	n/a	n/a
civil	AA	exhausting	$1,100	$1,400
common	A	tiring	$460	$460
common	AA	comfortable	$1,100	$437
civil	A	comfortable	$5,000	n/a
common	AAA	comfortable	$3,000	$1,500
common/civil	AAA	exhausting	$2,000	$1,200
civil	A	comfortable	n/a	n/a

The game isn't over simply because you've paid the setup fee that gets your offshore program running. You then have to pay an annual fee to ensure your offshore account is looked after properly. This fee could include the annual cost of hiring a local firm to keep an eye on your account. It could also include government levies and licensing fees. And you must factor in the annual cost of keeping a U.S.–based lawyer on retainer. Remember that you will want to have a U.S. lawyer keep tabs on your off-shore property and ensure that all your offshore arrangements comply with the law. That's how you prevent unwelcome visits from the IRS.

Sometimes you can negotiate your annual fees in advance. Talk this over with your advisers. At the end of the day, the thing to remember is that you should only put your money in places you can afford. If your annual fees quickly gobble up your offshore nest egg, there's not much point in moving your money offshore.

Watch out for offshore providers who charge fees based on your ability to pay. I call this the "Dewey, Cheetam, and Howe" billing system (repeat that slowly and you'll get the point).

Fees based on the size of your offshore account might seem attractive when your account balance is relatively low. But once you're hooked on the system and your bank balance begins to climb, you might see your annual fee climb to double or triple the original amount. Some trustee firms have the ability to change their fees at will written into their trustee agreements. Watch out.

Legal System

There are basically two types of legal systems in the off-shore world: the common law system and the civil law system. The common law system is the one Americans are used to. Common law traces its roots back to

England in the Middle Ages. The English figured out that a good way to create a consistent and reliable legal system was to rely on precedents. In other words, if one judge decided a property case one way, it followed that all following similar property cases should be decided in the same way. The body of these legal precedents has come to be known as the common law. It's a very flexible system because it permits judges to quickly adapt to change. Politicians can drag their heels when it comes to writing new laws. A judge confronted with an unprecedented case doesn't have that luxury. He has to deal with the facts and reach some sort of a decision.

Even though the United States broke away from Great Britain in 1776, our founding fathers decided to keep the common law system. As a result, there are great parallels between the American and the British legal systems. This is of immense importance when looking for an offshore money haven. If you choose a former or present British colony, such as the British Virgin Islands, your U.S. lawyer will understand much of that haven's law.

For example, if you remember my explanation about trusts, you'll remember that they were invented in England. So if you want to set up an international trust, it is advisable to set it up in a common-law money haven where trust law is better understood.

The civil law system dates back to the sixth century. The Roman Empire was governed by a confusing mishmash of laws that varied from province to province. So a Roman emperor named Justinian decided to bundle up all those diverse laws into a single, unified code. That way, no matter where you went in the empire, the definitions of "contract" or "property" would be the same. Justinian's "civil code" is today the foundation on which most European nations base their laws.

For Americans, the civil law tradition can be a little awkward. Here's an example: We all know from television and the movies that when the cops arrest you, they say

> **It probably won't be long before every suit filed in the United States is searchable and readable on the Internet.**

you have the right to remain silent. When you are on trial, you can choose to remain silent and the jury isn't allowed to interpret your silence as an admission of your guilt. That's an old common law tradition.

Trials run very differently under civil law. Under that tradition, the judge can decide to consider your silence as an indication of your guilt. The judge asks most of the questions and expects you to answer. You are guilty until proven innocent.

I'm just using criminal law as an example. Obviously, you're not going to pick your offshore money haven based on what will happen to you if you get arrested. But this example illustrates the differences in legal thinking between common law and civil law. You'll probably want to locate yourself in a haven that most resembles home. U.S. and British courts are arguably the most sophisticated in the world. Locating yourself in a former or present British colony gives you access to that same level of sophistication, and offers you a comfort level born of relative familiarity.

If you do find yourself embroiled in a legal dispute, you will want it handled someplace where the laws are compatible with those in the United States. Consider, for example, what can happen if a U.S. company and an Irish company find themselves in dispute. Since both jurisdictions use common law, the odds are both the American lawyers and the Irish lawyers will better understand the issues. Settlement is more likely because lawyers from each side will understand the other's point of view.

There's another point to consider, though. You might not always want a haven equipped with sophisticated

Anglo-American courts. Don't forget that every suit filed in U.S. court is assigned a document number. More and more, documents from those cases are becoming available online. It probably won't be long before every suit filed in the United States is searchable and readable on the Internet. This is problematic when you consider all the private details that can become public in a legal dispute such as a divorce. You might want to base yourself in a location where the courts will be unsophisticated and the intimate details of your life won't be so readily available online.

Language

It goes without saying that since you speak English (or so I assume, since you're reading this book in that language), you are probably most interested in basing yourself in an English-speaking jurisdiction. Truth be told, this is not as big a problem as it seems because there are few places in the financial world where English is not understood.

Basing yourself in a non-English-speaking location (where the documents that create your company are written in some other language), however, can be a means of protecting your privacy. Your adversaries could be thrown off the trail if the documents that describe your company are based in Cyprus and drafted in Greek using the Cyrillic alphabet.

But at the end of the day, my clients are pretty clear on this point: They're nuts for English and usually want their offshore programs located in jurisdictions where English is at least understood, if not the official language.

Time Zone

This is another important criteria for people. You might not want to have to deal with the inconvenience of calling a trustee in the middle of the night. All too often, I've heard about clients of mine spending the whole night in their offices waiting for a call from their Swiss bankers, only to learn later the person they were looking for is away on vacation. I highly recommend you pick a jurisdiction that is at least close to, if not in, one of the six North American time zones.

Ease of Access

As a rule, I strongly suggest you pick a haven that you can reach within at least five hours. Mauritius might be an interesting place, but the flight to Cape Town from the United States can take 14 hours. Then, the flight from Cape Town to Mauritius, of which there are only two a week, takes another five hours. Unless you have a particular reason to locate your offshore arrangements on the other side of the globe, you shouldn't choose a haven where your travel costs will be several times the annual maintenance cost of your structure.

PRIVACY RATING

On the chart, I've assigned grades of A, AA, and AAA to each haven to give you my quick impression of which will best protect your privacy. I've considered not only the privacy laws of each location, but also whether each haven makes active efforts to enforce those laws and enhance them. Almost every haven guarantees privacy, but this usually comes with the warning that the haven will open up your books if there are grounds to suspect you of any criminal activity. This is the result of much pressure from the U.S. government, which is doing all it can to pry into the affairs of Americans maintaining financial structures offshore.

THE OFFSHORE INVESTOR'S GUIDE

The following guide is not meant to serve as a complete list of all offshore havens. Rather, it is a list of the financial centers that I consider most important for today's U.S. investor. Again, I caution against using the list as an absolute measure of a location's desirability. It is always best to hire a professional consultant who can balance the benefits of a specific location against your very individual needs.

Andorra

Andorra is an intriguing little country nestled in the Pyrenees Mountains between Spain and France. It's very hard to get to. Not only do you have to fly to Europe first, you also must drive the 8,000-foot high d'Envalira Pass to get to this tiny enclave. Franks and Catalans who were fighting the Moorish occupation of Spain founded the "modern" state in the Middle Ages. Although the country has been officially independent since 1278, the governments of France and Spain today jointly administer it. Catalan is the official language, but French and Spanish are widely spoken.

Today Andorra exists not to keep foreign invaders away, but to welcome them with open arms. European tourists flock there each year to enjoy duty-free shopping. The residency laws, which used to require presence in the

The company's president must also be either an Andorran national or a foreigner with 20 years' residence, and the main office of the company must be based in Andorra.

country for 20 years, have recently been loosened to welcome more foreigners fleeing their heavily taxed homelands. In November 1996 a new law called the "Law on Passive Residence Permits" was approved by the Andorran parliament. This set up a program that allows individuals to make Andorra their permanent residence. Indeed, 70 percent of the country's 66,000 residents come from abroad (usually Spain). There is no taxation in Andorra, though this has been a controversial local issue. (There was an attempt to introduce taxation in 1984, but it failed.)

Andorra is more of a residency haven than a place to establish an international business presence. The country was completely closed to foreign capital until 1983, when it finally permitted some foreigners to invest in the country. Even then, Andorra still demands that foreign companies have local control. Only Andorran nationals or foreigners who have lived in the country for 20 years can hold a majority of a company's shares. This includes beneficial shareholders. The company's president must also be either an Andorran national or a foreigner with 20 years' residence, and the main office of the company must be based in Andorra. It costs about $1,200 to set up a company there—though this fee does not include the company president's annual salary.

I like Andorra because I think the easy residence regulations are a great idea. While the local company laws are unfavorable to foreigners, this can be of little concern because you could still base your offshore program in other locations. This is an interesting concept.

Anguilla

Anguilla is a tiny island of about 60 square miles with a population of 9,000, located east of the British Virgin

Islands and Puerto Rico. The average temperature is a comfortable 82°F, and the language spoken is English.

I can usually highly recommend British colonies to Americans as money havens, but my experience with Anguilla has been somewhat different. I find the attitude of the government and the professionals in Anguilla to be more receptive to European, Asian, and Canadian clients than Americans.

I also have some concerns about the secrecy laws in Anguilla. The law on the books threatens offenders with a fine of up to $50,000 and one year in jail for breaching client secrecy. Banks in breach automatically face the maximum fine. Trouble is, I don't recall ever reading about a case where someone has gone to jail for breaking the secrecy law. Perhaps due to its efforts to shake its shady reputation for phony banks, the Anguilla government has readily assisted the FBI and IRS agents in tracking down U.S. lawbreakers.

Even though the island uses an English common law, the island's legal system seems to operate on hits and misses, not the consistency one would expect from a more experienced and reliable haven. And you can count this country out if you're considering setting up an offshore bank. The government isn't equipped for bank supervision.

The island has adopted a new computerized registration system called ACORN (Anguilla's Commercial On-line Registration Network) that allows you to set up offshore companies using the Internet. The system is designed to allow incorporations 24 hours a day, seven days a week, 365 days a year. This was probably necessary in order to lure back some of the business Anguilla was losing to other offshore havens. However, Anguilla has publicly balked at the OECD's efforts. Victor Banks, the country's minister of finance, economic development, investment, and commerce, has stated, "Our view is that the OECD shouldn't unilaterally police the rest of the world. We don't want a new colonial environment where we are told what to do."

In summary, my recommendation is that you take a wait-and-see attitude before plunging into Anguilla. The island's infrastructure might improve and become more accommodating to Americans. But for now, my opinion is that Anguilla's laws and services haven't reached the fiber and character of other British colonies, such as the Cayman Islands.

Antigua and Barbuda

These two islands lie about 140 miles southeast of Puerto Rico. Antigua occupies 108 square miles and is home to more than 60,000 people. Barbuda is much more thinly populated, with less than 2,000 people living on its 75 square miles. About 20,000 people live in the bustling capital of St. John's.

Antigua achieved independence from Great Britain on November 1, 1981. English remains the official language, and the islands continue to use English common law.

Antigua offers the usual catalog of offshore entities, including international business corporations (IBCs), captive insurance firms, and offshore banks. Banks require at least $1 million in paid-up capital. IBCs receive a 50-year holiday on both capital gains and income taxes.

Responding to the OECD and its efforts to curb money laundering, the government recently revoked the licenses of 21 offshore banks and provided significant assistance to the United States on both fraud and money-laundering cases.

I get a lot of questions about Antigua and Barbuda, especially since the islands started selling licenses for Internet casinos. I don't have a lot of positive things to say about Antigua, and this foray into online gambling has only served to reinforce my negative views. It seems to me the islands are using online gaming as a means to prop up an otherwise weak performance in the offshore world. I'm very cautious about recommending these licenses, which cost $75,000 a year. The U.S. Congress continues to try to regulate Internet gambling, even though most recent attempts have failed. As a result, Internet gambling sites have doubled in the past year to more than 1,400 (with 850 located in Antigua), accounting for millions of U.S. dollars leaving the country.

This foray into gaming gives Antigua and Barbuda an ominous air of questionable outside influence. I'd avoid the islands for now.

Aruba

I find this haven extraordinary. Aruba has connections to other Dutch colonies in the West Indies, but unlike Curaçao or St. Maarten, Aruba enjoys the unique status of being fully independent of the Netherlands. English and Spanish are spoken everywhere, although the official language is Dutch.

The Aruba government is very flexible and, since the early 1980s, has been concerned with developing alternative sources of revenue. For several decades it survived and prospered due to the presence of one of the world's largest oil refineries. When that refinery closed in 1985, the government decided to concentrate on tourism and international financial services.

Due to its longtime status as a center for oil, Aruba has a highly developed infrastructure. This, combined with government flexibility and a willingness to attract

Aruba boasts ironclad secrecy. I can think of no cases of breach in my experience.

investors, makes Aruba a fine choice for anyone interested in establishing an offshore corporation in a friendly and strategically located center.

The island is equipped with excellent communications equipment, and its population of 80,000 is well educated and multilingual. This is a great place to establish an international presence.

Aruba boasts ironclad secrecy. I can think of no cases of breach in my experience. The country has no double taxation treaties with the United States, so you don't have to worry about the IRS knocking on Aruba's door to inquire about your finances there.

Because of its ties to Holland, Aruba follows the continental or civil law system. This means the country is not really equipped for trusts and most of the other innovative entities available in common law jurisdictions. It's also not a place to base your own offshore bank.

What it does offer, and something I highly recommend, is the Aruba exempt corporation. This is a fully tax-exempt company that is very easy to maintain. Secrecy can be maintained through the use of nominee shareholders, and there is no requirement to file annual accounts with the government. Shareholder meetings can be held anywhere in the world, and no minutes need be kept. A registered agent in Aruba is required, but this is hardly a problem given the range of professional management firms available.

I also have to add that Aruba is an excellent vacation spot. It's located just 12 miles off the coast of Venezuela. The climate is incredible. I would highly recommend you consider it for any Caribbean vacation.

Austria

This mountainous country, located south of Germany, east of Switzerland, and north of Italy, is one of my favorite European money havens. I like to tell people that Austria is in that wonderful part of the world that seems to have created the concept of money. The integrity of the Austrians is 1,000 percent. The professionalism and the expertise are top-notch. While the first language in this country of eight million is German, almost all professionals speak and understand English.

That said, Austria is not a location to consider if you're looking for a more exotic offshore environment. Austria's legal system is based on the continental or civil law system, so trusts aren't really used or understood there. But Austria's investment professionals are simply top rate. If you're looking for a place to connect with expert portfolio advisers, Austria is an excellent choice. The secrecy laws are rock solid. Austrians set up bank accounts using pseudonyms.

Austria taxes domestic corporations and charges a withholding tax on some forms of dividend income. Yet it is possible to avoid those taxes by creating an Austria-based holding company. If more than 25 percent of that company's assets are based outside of Austria, the company pays no withholding or corporate taxes.

While I would give it a low rating when it comes to creating novel offshore arrangements and structures, I give it my highest rating as a location to keep your money safe. The banks there generally have very attractive interest rates. Austria is also a great place to establish a holding company for your investments.

Bahamas

A stable democracy since 1729 and an established international money haven, the Bahamas has become both a popular Caribbean money haven and a popular vacation spot. The Bahamas constitutes an independent state within the British Commonwealth. Comprising more than 700 islands scattered over 100,000 square miles of heavenly blue seas and with a total land area of about 4,000 square miles, the Bahamas extends from 60 miles east of Florida to just north of Haiti. The population is about 350,000, with most people living on New Providence Island, where the capital, Nassau, is located. English is the official language.

New Providence is just a 35-minute plane flight from Miami. Americans love it—particularly yachtsmen, who enjoy a pleasurable cruise over to the islands for mixing business with some island fun. Traveling there is made even easier because the currency trades in parity with the U.S. dollar. This is an interesting point. One way of gaining privacy without sacrificing the stability of the U.S. dollar is to accumulate Bahamian banknotes.

The Bahamas uses the common law system. While the country's company law used to be rather archaic, it has recently modernized it and provided for the creation of modern IBCs. Now you can incorporate a company there in as little as an hour. Bahamian IBCs can use corporate directors (allowing you to add layers of secrecy to your arrangements), and the government keeps no official record of the identities of shareholders and directors. There are now approximately 100,000 such IBCs, as well as 580 mutual funds registered there. The Bahamas has also overhauled its trust legislation and provided for the creation of flexible, modern trusts. Another recent development is new securities legislation. The Bahamas International Stock Exchange is up and running. Overall financial services are second only to tourism in producing revenue for the islands, with more than 400 banks from 36 countries licensed to do business.

The Bahamas has some drawbacks. The bank market is fairly well saturated at this point. In fact, owning your own bank is nearly impossible because the government rarely issues a bank license to individuals or small companies. Even if you do qualify for bank ownership, a hefty minimum capital is required. As a result, this may be a poor offshore site for the single investor or small consortium. And banking secrecy laws were recently lifted to fight money laundering. Now banks must report deposits greater than $100,000 to the Bahamas government. That said, none of this banking data is reportable to the IRS because the Bahamas, which has no income tax, doesn't consider tax evasion to be a crime. Indeed, apart from a two cents per gallon tax on gasoline, the island hasn't charged a single penny in income, corporation, capital gains, remittance, estate, or inheritance tax since 1717. There is such a thing as paradise!

Overall, I give the Bahamas a thumbs-up as a location to base an IBC or other modern offshore entity. You'll probably have to look elsewhere if you're looking for a bank, however.

Above all, the Bahamas is a great place to be. Paradise Island is a popular place to have some fun and to gamble. The premier resort is the Ocean Club, and I highly recommend it.

Bahrain

Bahrain deserves mention because it has become a serious and established offshore money haven with investors from the Middle East. The country itself is an independent state made up of some 33 islands about 15 miles off the coast of Saudi Arabia. Arabic is the official language, but English is widely spoken.

The government of Bahrain originally lived off petro dollars. In the early 1980s, when the emir realized his country would sooner or later run out of oil, he decided to secure a future for his 600,000 people by setting his country up as an offshore money haven for wealthy Arab investors, particularly those from the OPEC countries. There is no tax on income of any kind, including salaries, capital gains, estates, interest income, dividends, or royalties. There is also no sales tax. Because of its Middle Eastern focus, Bahrain doesn't offer many of the exotic entities that interest North American or European investors, such as asset protection trusts or captive insurance companies. The country screens potential investors closely and is an expensive place to do business.

There are also a lot of political issues in dealing with Bahrain. The country officially boycotts Israel. Nearby Iran claims the islands and is thought to have supported a failed 1981 coup by Shiite Muslim guerrillas.

In short, I would give Bahrain high marks for those who live in the Middle East and a low application rating for Americans looking for a haven.

Barbados

Political stability is a major benefit to anyone considering financial ventures in Barbados. Without racial friction, military rule, or serious labor problems, it operates as a parliamentary government located a few hundred miles off the northern coast of South America.

It is 21 miles long and 14 miles wide (166 square miles in total) and has about 256,000 residents. It is a wonderful vacation spot due to the balmy trade winds that blow year-round and the sunshine that brightens every day. The Hilton Hotel there is exquisite. And one thing I absolutely love about Barbados is that there are no mosquitoes. This is a wonderful place for an island getaway.

Communication systems are top-of-the-line throughout Barbados. For example, it has a satellite system that allows for international data transfer. It also offers the

Caribbean's best roads and highways. As an added plus, the official and spoken language is English.

Barbados has recently embarked on a program to upgrade its image. It has simplified many of its regulations and incorporation procedures. It has also lowered its paid-in capital requirement for a bank license. It is truly on a course of improvement. This new attitude combined with its beauty make Barbados one of the better places to conduct your offshore transactions. The government's regulatory legislation does a good job of protecting investors. Overall, however, the regulatory environment tends to be heavy on the red tape, and this makes Barbados unpopular with entrepreneurs. My sense is that there is not a lot of room for investors who are interested in setting up trusts, offshore banks, or other exotic entities.

There is no written secrecy law in Barbados, but confidentiality can be achieved through the use of an IBC. There is an official income tax rate of 2.5 percent for IBCs, investment companies, and offshore banks, but the government allows tax exemptions for all dividends, royalties, interest payments, and management fees paid to nonresidents or other IBCs. There is an excellent pool of experienced professionals available to help you set up and administer IBCs.

An important thing to note is that all bank accounts are open to government scrutiny, and the Barbadian government does share information with tax collectors, including the IRS, from other countries.

Barbados is popular with Canadians. The Canada-Barbados tax treaty permits some amazing tax benefits to be gained (see appendix 2 for more details).

To sum it all up, Barbados is a good place to establish an IBC, but is better suited to the larger investor or the company looking to establish an international presence than the smaller investor looking for affordable privacy and asset protection.

Belize

Belize, a former British colony on the east coast of Central America that achieved full independence in 1981, has grown into an excellent and popular offshore money haven. It is about 174 miles long and 68 miles wide and has 240,000 inhabitants. About 25 percent of the population lives in the capital, Belmopan. The people speak English and Spanish.

Belize's exclusion from earlier editions of my book angered a number of readers who wrote and telephoned me to tell me of their positive experiences there. I've since reevaluated the country and found it worthy of mention. In fact, I think there are a lot of reasons why the offshore investor should consider Belize.

One thing I really like is the country's economic citizenship program. You can become an instant citizen of Belize simply by paying a $35,000 fee. This cash-and-carry citizenship gives you access to a visa network that guarantees you entry to most British Commonwealth jurisdictions.

As a former British colony, Belize uses common law and has adopted most of the offshore business entities available in other common law jurisdictions.

The company has a fairly good IBC law based on the widely regarded British Virgin Islands legislation. Belize corporations can be set up to ensure maximum secrecy and minimum reporting requirements. The Belize Trusts Act of 1992 is very well regarded—some even consider it the world's best. This trust law offers a high level of asset protection and can be set up quickly and affordably.

With respect to offshore banking, Belize makes for an excellent location. It is perfectly situated and has an excellent reputation in the financial community. The government is honest and organized, and its banking supervision is strong enough to preserve Belize's reputation.

The government is honest and organized, and its banking supervision is strong enough to preserve Belize's reputation.

Acquiring a banking license from the Belize government would definitely be a good move, though an expensive one; a banking license costs about $20,000 a year. The company has tough secrecy laws and acted quickly to strengthen them after a 1992 incident in which some private information was leaked. I think any country that acts to strengthen a secrecy law should be applauded.

The drawback to this Central American nation is that it is still rather primitive compared to Caribbean nations. There are no luxury hotels in Belize, at least nothing like a Four Seasons or a Hilton. This isn't really the place for people who want to travel in style. Another problem is that the infrastructure of Belize isn't really up to par with the rest of the world. For example, the occasional open sewer in downtown Belmopan can add an unpleasant odor to the air. I know one businessman who described the phone system there as two tin cans connected by a string.

There's a bizarre irony about Belize, too. The government seems to be honest and forthright, yet according to insurance experts, Belize has the largest collection of U.S. stolen car parts in the world.

On the whole, I'm impressed with the efforts the Belize government is making to streamline the country's financial services sector. Belize is one of the more affordable places to set up an IBC or an international trust. The country is presently working on new legislation that will allow for the creation of mutual funds. Belize is poised to become a major player in the offshore community, and I give it a full recommendation.

Bermuda

Bermuda is the oldest self-governing state in the British Commonwealth. Located less than one thousand miles southeast of New York City and six hundred miles east of North Carolina, it is a small country consisting of 150 islands with a total area of less than twenty-five square miles. Communication and air facilities are excellent.

Bermuda is a true tax haven: There is no income tax, corporation tax, capital gains tax, or withholding tax imposed by the local government. This makes it a hot spot for investors whose main concern is tax protection.

Nothing, of course, is perfect. When it comes to this island cluster, the major drawback is its stuffiness. Bermuda is only for the carriage trade because of local capital requirement laws. Bermuda will require substantial capital amounts to establish a corporation or insurance company, perhaps a major stumbling block for some investors. For instance, the minimum paid-in capital needed to form an insurance company is $125,000, and some Bermudan attorneys actually suggest a minimum of $250,000 to ensure incorporation. In addition, a proposal to introduce offshore banking was recently defeated by the houses of government.

Politically, Bermuda has been plagued by periodic unrest—including the assassination of a newly appointed governor in the 1970s. Tourism has traditionally accounted for a good part of the island's economy, but since the mid-1980s its popularity as a vacation spot has plummeted. The problem is primarily economic: The island's currency is pegged to the U.S. dollar and 85 percent of its tourists are U.S. citizens. However, most American vacationers are looking for getaways that offer a better exchange rate.

From almost every perspective, Bermuda is not a place to establish an inexpensive offshore presence. Besides, Bermuda is quite dependent upon the U.S. economy. Bermuda has recently acknowledged that it will

"cooperate" in any way with the United States and OECD
to uphold anti–money laundering procedures and will
cooperate fully with the U.S. IRS on tax investigations
involving U.S. taxpayers.

British Virgin Islands

I have been to the British Virgin Islands (BVI) many
times and have established quite a few companies and
trusts there. I think so highly of the BVI that I have even
recommended it as a center for my own family's interests.
The BVI is one of the most innovative former British
colonies when it comes to developing offshore programs.
The government there is very quick to respond to
requests and suggestions from professionals in the financial services industry. The BVI government is also quick
to copy any good ideas that pop up in other jurisdictions.
A recent example of this is a new Partnership Act that
took effect in 1996. This is the top flight of money havens.

The BVI is very careful about weeding out bad ele-
ments. The country doesn't want to have any association
with crooks or tax evaders. To that end, the BVI passed
the Proceeds of Criminal Conduct Act in 1997. The law
targets drug lords, insider traders, those committing
fraud, money launderers, and other criminals.

The BVI has a well-regulated mutual fund industry
and is an excellent safe haven for an offshore mutual fund.
As of 2001, more than 1,600 mutual funds were registered
representing total assets in excess of $60 billion. It oper-
ates under the English legal system, its currency is the
U.S. dollar, it has no exchange controls, offshore mutual
funds are statutorily exempt from all forms of BVI taxation, and the license fees for registering them are fixed
and nominal (presently averaging about $15,000).

The country's infrastructure offers everything an
international business company would expect: state-of-

the-art communications, an excellent range of trust
companies, law firms and financial advisers, and beautiful hotels. I specifically adore the Peter Island Resort,
which is a 15-minute boat ride from the country's capital, Road Town, on Tortola Island. There's nothing better
than hopping on a small boat, cruising into town for
some business, then cruising back to Peter Island for
more relaxation and pleasure.

That said, I do find the banking system somewhat
marginal and unsophisticated. It is not as preferable a
place to deposit money as Austria. Another problem with
the BVI is its popularity. About 1,000 new IBCs are
created in the BVI *each week!* By the end of 2000, there
were 350,000 IBCs registered in the BVI. That means
that it's quite a chore to come up with a company name
that hasn't already been used there.

All in all, if you're looking for an innovative offshore
arrangement, I give the BVI my strongest recommendation.

Cayman Islands

The glory days are over for the Cayman Islands. I once
put the Caymans in the top tier of money havens. The
Caymans' government pioneered innovative offshore legislation, and made it immensely easy to set up bank
accounts and companies there with a minimum amount
of red tape.

But over the last decade, the Caymans have thrown
their once ironclad secrecy rules out the window. In 1990
the United States and the Caymans signed a treaty that
allows U.S. agents to peek at the once-secret records of
Cayman Islands banks.

In the 1970s and 1980s, reliable secrecy laws, no
taxes, and excellent communications and business infrastructure helped the Caymans establish a reputation as
the "Switzerland of the Caribbean." Here's an abbreviated

"who's who" of the 45,000 companies, 570 banks, and 2,200 mutual funds that have set up shop in the Caymans: Detroit Edison Company, Marine Midland Banks, Mellon Bank Company, United Energy Resources, Conagra, Kansas City Power and Light Company, McDonnell Douglas Corporation, Archer Daniels Midland Company, Amerada Hess Corporation, Houston Natural Gas Corporation, Wells Fargo . . . this list could continue for pages. In just the past two years, capitalization in the Cayman Islands has risen to about $22 billion.

But even though the vast majority of the business being done in the Caymans is legitimate, the Islands have not been able to shake a reputation as being a haven for crooks. Perhaps this shady image of the Caymans is fostered by fictional stories, such as the movie *The Firm*, starring Tom Cruise and based on the John Grisham novel of the same name. More likely this image comes from the real-life stories of four banks closed by Caymans regulators since 1993.

In 1999 a Cayman Islands banker named John Mathewson cooperated with U.S. agents in a massive crackdown on tax evasion. As part of his own plea bargain in U.S. courts, Mathewson turned over once-secret computer files of about 1,500 clients of Guardian Bank & Trust (Cayman) Ltd., which he owned and ran before the Caymans government shut it down. This secret banking information is now being used as evidence against Americans charged with income tax evasion.

The U.S. government has been pleasantly surprised by the degree to which the Cayman Islanders now cooperate

The U.S. government has been pleasantly surprised by the degree to which the Cayman Islanders now cooperate with U.S. agents.

with U.S. agents. In a *Los Angeles Times* article published in 1999, Michael Anderson, head of the FBI's money-laundering section, marveled at how "the Caymans have had kind of a change in attitude" regarding U.S. criminal investigations. This was especially apparent in the case of Kenneth Taves, of Malibu, California. In January 2001 Taves pleaded guilty to bilking more than $37.5 million from 900,000 credit card holders all over the world by falsely billing them for access to several pornographic Web sites he operated. Taves initiated his scheme by purchasing lists of more than three million valid MasterCard and Visa numbers from Charter Pacific Bank in Agoura Hills, California. The Caymans seemed to fall over backwards in order to help U.S. investigators in the Taves case. The Islands government has shut down the bank Taves used, Euro Bank Corp., and arrested two Euro Bank employees on suspicion of money laundering. And another Cayman Islands banker swore out an affidavit detailing some of the previously secret banking information about Taves and his wife.

The Caymans are anxious to shake their bad reputation. Cayman Islanders are very shy about welcoming new business. They demand extensive references from you. They also want detailed explanations as to why you want to do business in the Caymans and where your money comes from. The reputation the Caymans might once have had—that of a no-questions-asked place to do business—is very much a thing of the past. Instead, they have adopted a strong, "know-the-client" mentality designed to prevent and keep the Islands out of trouble. This intensified after the OECD blacklist. And although the nation maintains a zero-tax policy, it has committed to the exchange of "information of tax matters" and advised service providers that aggressively marketed services based exclusively on the Islands' confidentiality or secrecy are not in the "national interest."

This is a rather sad state of affairs. The Caymans were once one of my favorite stop-off places. Not only did the Cayman Islands invent some innovative offshore structures, it was a fun place to visit. It's a great vacation spot, especially if you like water and beach sports. I've always liked the Hyatt Regency, which has amazing service and a great staff. The Cayman Islanders themselves are wonderful people and are especially kind to Americans (provided, of course, you're not under suspicion for money laundering or fraud).

Even in their heyday, the Caymans were too expensive for use by small- to medium-size investors. Bank charters and licenses are available only to long-established companies with a paid-in capital of at least $500,000.

Since there's no guarantee of secrecy in the Caymans anymore, the high cost of doing business in the Islands is just not worth it. I recommend that you avoid it.

Cook Islands

Out in the South Pacific are a group of islands whose climate is very similar to Hawaii's. These 15 islands, called the Cook Islands, became an independent state in 1965. Located near New Zealand, Fiji, and Tahiti, the Cooks have a population of about 26,000 English-speaking people. The atolls and volcanic islands feature low-income and corporation taxes.

The capital, Rarotonga, has an average annual temperature of 81°F. Telephone communications are excellent, based on 20 satellite circuits. The Cooks also have a fully operational international airport with service to the United States through Tahiti on Air New Zealand.

The Cooks have strong links to New Zealand and use the same currency (although the original currency was like a work of art, with pagan gods riding canoes through the sea and Polynesian goddesses atop sharks over waves).

I have been there about five times and, to be honest, can't remember ever having a good night's sleep there. It seems I've either been besieged by mosquitoes, buzzed by low-flying airplanes, or barged in upon by hotel managers waking me up at 5 A.M. for exercises.

I have to say the Cooks are as unaccommodating a tax haven as they are a place to get some rest. The Cooks got into the haven business in 1982. But the islands didn't attract any real interest until Ronald Rudman and Barry Engel encouraged the Cooks government to pass asset protection trusts legislation. The new trust law improved protection from lawsuits. The problem was that this new trust regime didn't set up any checks or balances. The Cooks government had no idea whom these trusts were protecting; theoretically, bank robbers could even leave their ill-gotten gains there without fear of civil liability.

The result has been that the Cooks are very much a second-tier haven. There are a few trust companies left on the islands, but I would quickly recommend the Cayman Islands, the British Virgin Islands, Belize, or Nevis before I'd recommend the Cooks.

Costa Rica

I've been to Costa Rica a number of times and I can't wait to go back. I think it is the Rio de Janeiro of Central America. It's clean, modern, always warm, relatively inexpensive, and just three hours from Miami by plane. My wife is after me to buy a place there, but I don't know how to speak Spanish yet.

The legal profession in Costa Rica is quite sophisticated, and the number of banks is numerous and modern.

The government there has adopted a nimble attitude to the offshore business with its low taxes and strong secrecy laws, and is constantly on the lookout for ways it can attract new ventures. Where Costa Rica has experienced a real boom is in the number of *pensionates,* or retirees, who have decided to relocate there to enjoy the country's warm climate, low cost of living, and excellent medical facilities. The Costa Rican government has modified residency laws making it very easy for moderately wealthy Americans and Canadians to move there. It's a wonderful place.

Costa Rica has a population of 3.5 million people. It uses civil law, so many of the offshore structures that interest Americans, such as trusts, aren't readily available. That said, I remind you that Costa Rica is near Belize, a common law jurisdiction offering excellent trust legislation and other exotic offshore structures. I often suggest to investors that they set up their offshore program in Belize, then establish residency in Costa Rica.

Cyprus

This Mediterranean island has become a popular offshore money haven with Eastern Europeans. Russians particularly like it because Greek-speaking Cyprus uses the same Cyrillic alphabet that is used in Russia. It is also common for sophisticated Russian businessmen to know some Greek. Russians feel at home in Cyprus.

But it is a system of tax treaties that makes this Mediterranean nation really popular with investors from the newly liberated Eastern-bloc countries. Under these treaties, Eastern Europeans can extract dividends, royalties, interest, and management fees from their accounts in Cyprus for next to nothing in taxes.

The Cypriot legal system is based on common law. The island was formerly a British colony, the United Kingdom having acquired the territory after the old Ottoman Empire failed to repay a British loan. Cyprus has been independent since 1960.

This island nation has had its problems in the past. The country is divided into two sections. Greeks, making up about 80 percent of the population, occupy the southern half of the island. Turks and Caicos, about 20 percent, live in the north. Cyprus was divided after Greek officers orchestrated a coup in 1974, then threatened to join Cyprus to Greece. Turkish troops invaded the north to block the threatened annexation. The resulting division reflects a standoff that has existed ever since.

The Greek-speaking portion of the island is relatively stable and offers competitive advantages as a money haven. For one thing, it does not have a terribly complex regime for starting new businesses, particularly shipping firms and insurance companies. It is not yet a party to the international Mutual Legal Assistance Treaty (MLAT), so the question of whether Cyprus will some day crack down on money laundering is still on the table. It will likely join the MLAT family in order to establish itself as a reputable European nation. The Greek government in the south has applied for membership in the European Union, but this application isn't likely to get anywhere until the Turkish government in the north endorses the application.

I give Cyprus a positive recommendation for European investors or U.S. investors looking to benefit from the tax treaty.

Fiji

Even though it has not officially declared itself an offshore money haven, Fiji is one of my favorite offshore localities.

Its advantages are obvious. It is strategically located in the heart of the South Pacific and is as important to that region as Miami is to the entire Caribbean. Fiji hosts a major international airport that supports 747 Jumbo Jets and has direct international air connections to Los Angeles, London, New York, Australia—virtually every place in the world.

Fiji consists of 332 islands and islets covering an area slightly smaller than New Jersey. The population is 820,000, with about 150,000 of those people in the capital of Suva. Fiji is a former British colony. It attained independence on October 10, 1970. English is the official language.

Despite its wonderful location, Fiji remains a tourist attraction as yet undiscovered by the Western world. Jean Michel Cousteau, son of the famous oceanographer Jacques Cousteau, has set up a luxurious retreat on the island of Vanua Levu. Nearby, Anthony Robbins of infomercial fame has established a beautiful resort called Namale. I have stayed at both and can tell you they are truly wonderful.

At present, the Fijian dollar is deflated, making everything in the country a true bargain, much the same way the U.S. dollar goes farther in Mexico or Canada. Everything costs less: from health care to plane fares, from electronic goods to factory labor.

Fiji's first step into the offshore area has been to pass a residency law in July 1998, similar to that of Costa Rica and Andorra, which allows foreigners to gain full-time residential status. It's easy to qualify. All you need to do is pay a small registration fee and purchase real estate in Fiji worth at least $30,000.

Permanent residency status is popular with investors who want to take advantage of the country's cheap labor costs. Tax holidays have been available to foreigners establishing new factories. A large portion of Fiji's manufacturing business involves the garment trade.

On the horizon, Fiji will adopt an offshore regime that will borrow from the best of the ABC countries—

Austria, the Bahamas, and the Cayman Islands—while avoiding the problems of the Cook Islands and Anguilla.

Gibraltar

I've only been to Gibraltar twice, but I can unequivocally say this British outpost near the southern tip of Spain is a microcosm of London. Of course, unlike London, this tiny colony of only 2.25 square miles and 30,000 people offers a full range of offshore benefits, including tax breaks, privacy protections, and investment entities such as tax-exempt corporations. Presently, there are 21 banks with deposits of £2.38 billion and assets of £5.5 billion in the local currency. There are many qualified professionals available to handle the offshore business. Gibraltar's strong reaction to the OECD proposals and threatened sanctions came from chief minister Peter Caruana: "The moral positions of such organizations are pretty tenuous. We will not submit to a regime that applies only to off-shore centres."

Gibraltar is a favorite destination for European investors, but is shunned by British investors because it is still part of the British Crown. It can be reached by daily flights from London.

I find doing business there to be a slow process. An offshore company can be set up within two weeks, but it can take as much as two months before the tax-exemption certificate is processed.

U.S. investors looking for a British-style haven might do better to look at one of the Channel Islands or one of the British colonies in the Caribbean.

Residency requirements are stringent and are not beneficial to tax minimizers. Applicants must have annual incomes of at least £45,000 pounds a year, purchase property in Gibraltar, and pay at least £10,000 a year in tax. Gibraltar has been a British colony since 1704. Spain still claims this rock, which rises 1,300 feet above the Mediterranean. Spain used to limit access to the colony in protest of British rule, but reopened the border in 1985.

Gibraltar is a great location for Anglophiles and European investors, but is rather remote for Americans. U.S. investors looking for a British-style haven might do better to look at one of the Channel Islands or one of the British colonies in the Caribbean.

Grenada

This wonderful Caribbean island, certainly best known for the American invasion in the early 1980s, has had an on-again off-again love affair with offshore banking. I began working with Grenada in the late 1980s. I established a number of private banks there, as well as countless insurance companies and offshore holding corporations. At the time, the island had a rather arcane company law that made doing business there a veritable nightmare.

It wasn't until the mid-1990s that a new government came to power in Grenada and gave the country the vision it needed to develop into a full-service offshore banking center. The change for the better came following persistent pressuring from Anslem Clouden, a noted barrister and solicitor in the island's capital, St. George's. Anslem, perhaps due to his taste for fine New York suits, worked hard to convince the government that the island's standard of living would derive a great boost from more offshore business.

Anslem's vision worked. Today Grenada is a flourishing offshore banking center with full-fledged legislation based on Bahamian and BVI laws. This wonderful legislative framework makes it a serious contender for the establishment of offshore banks. The only quibble I have with Grenada is that the island's annual banking license fee of $20,000 is too expensive. But given the island's active pursuit of offshore business, I believe they will lower that fee in order to grow the banking business. In response to the OECD's efforts to sanction Grenada, Elvin Nimrod, the country's minister of foreign affairs, told reporters, "We're told we have to end our dependence on sugar, bananas, or tourism, but when we try to move into financial services we find ourselves under attack."

Grenada is a great place to visit, by the way—even if you're not a U.S. marine or medical student. It features white, sandy beaches, a stunning central mountain range, and gray, warm water. Its currency, based on the eastern Caribbean dollar, is a bargain at 37 cents to the U.S. dollar. You get a lot for your money. When in St. George's I usually stay at the Ramada Renaissance resort.

Oliver North recently spoke at one of my offshore wealth summits. He was one of the commanders in charge of the invasion ordered by Ronald Reagan after a Castro-friendly regime began building a large airstrip on the island. It's also ironic to say that the island is today wonderfully served by the Port Salines International Airport only five miles from St. George's. It receives direct daily flights from Miami and one a week from New York.

I recommend Grenada to those searching to set up an offshore company, but you should take a wait-and-see approach if you want to set up your own offshore bank there.

Guernsey

Guernsey is a well-evolved offshore money haven very popular with Europeans. It is a small island of about 25 square miles and 55,000 inhabitants just off the coast of France in the Bay of St. Malo. The island is part of the ancient Duchy of Normandy, which means it is not formally part of the United Kingdom. It is this independence from Great Britain, which Guernsey has enjoyed for some 700 years, that makes the island a popular destination for British citizens fleeing their country's crushing tax rates.

Of its many innovations, one I find particularly interesting is the cell corporation. This is a company that segregates liability among several cells. It's a very clever idea and many other money havens have borrowed the concept. The idea comes with one caveat, however. The cell concept has not been tested in court, and it remains to be seen whether it will form part of the common law. So at this early stage, it's still too exotic for me to recommend it to any but the most adventuresome of experimenters.

Guernsey taxes only that portion of an individual's income that is collected within its territory. Such territorial taxation is the norm throughout the Channel Islands and other British protectorates.

Generally speaking, while I admire Guernsey for its innovation, I find it hard to recommend to American investors. It's simply too far away and very awkward to get to. You'll recall that I generally prefer havens you can travel to within five hours. Its long history as a tax haven has provided it with a great depth of financial experience, but this expertise doesn't come affordably and is often too expensive for American investors.

Hong Kong

Hong Kong was once one of the great free market centers of the world. It has long been a mandatory shopping destination for anyone traveling through Southeast Asia. I often used it as a stop-off point in the early 1980s when I was traveling to and from the South Pacific.

Hong Kong's storied past as a money haven and international port left the city chock-full of excellent management companies. British expatriates and experts from around the world were attracted to this bustling city. It was a prime place to do business. If you liked New York City, you had to love Hong Kong because it was just like the Big Apple, only without the price tags. A competent and connected businessman could live a life of tremendous profit and luxury in the Hong Kong of old.

Of course, Hong Kong's D-Day was July 1, 1997. Great Britain's 99-year lease on the colony expired and the Communist government of the People's Republic of China resumed control. A sense of fear shook the incredible optimism previously felt by Hong Kong's movers and shakers, and many businesspeople pulled their money out. Some 250 large companies redomiciled their head offices to Bermuda from Hong Kong in the period prior to the Chinese handover. Another 40 companies switched their head offices to the Cayman Islands.

The Communists have promised not to interfere with Hong Kong's free market economy for at least 50 years, but it seems that Hong Kong now operates with a harness. A businessperson can't do anything there without wondering whether the Chinese government will approve. This former British colony, which was once the source of many ingenious business entities, has now lost that spirit of innovation. It is not a place to invent new offshore strategies. You don't want to get too creative or exotic there because you can never be certain how the Beijing government will react.

For these reasons, I would discourage the use of Hong Kong as a base of operations and as a place to establish an offshore company. But the financial expertise is still there, and investors looking for opportunities in Asia could find Hong Kong to be an excellent place to hire off-site managers. Even after the takeover, Hong Kong still offers an excellent roster of accounting services, banks, and professionals well versed in Asian markets, languages, and traditions. What's more, the meltdown of the Asian economies in late 1997 has made many of these services extremely affordable.

Ireland

Ireland has developed into quite a credible offshore money haven and international financial center. It appeals to a large, wealthy clientele who are prepared to establish formidable structures, such as international banks, brokerage houses, insurance companies, and offshore corporations. The Irish government encourages investment by providing several tax advantages, especially for projects that generate lots of local employment. There are already some 6,000 companies operating in Ireland's offshore investment program, including Merrill Lynch, XL, Deutsche Bank/Morgan Grenfell, Société Générale, Sumitomo Bank, ABN AMRO, NatWest, Chase Manhattan, AIG, Citibank, IBM, BIL, and Grand Metropolitan.

One of the great advantages of Ireland is the tax treaty that exists between the Emerald Isle and the United States. This treaty allows royalties and license fees to be paid to Irish companies free of U.S. withholding taxes, provided the beneficial owners of the Irish companies are Irish. This arrangement is particularly advantageous for authors, artists, publishing companies, and any other company that is seeking to minimize taxes on the money made from intellectual property. This has also made Ireland very popular with computer software and high-tech firms.

Ireland has also become an expatriate haven for many Irish Americans wishing to reestablish ties with their ancestral home. The new U.S. law that precludes Americans from renouncing their citizenship makes a special exemption for Americans returning to their countries of origin. Ireland itself is eager to welcome Americans home. If your parents or grandparents were Irish citizens, and if you are willing to invest $1 million in Ireland, you can become an instant citizen. Packaging heirs Robert and Kenneth Dart have done it. So has oil-fortune heir Mark Getty.

Isle of Man

I like to call the Isle of Man the Caymans of the British Isles. Like the Channel Islands, it is not part of the United Kingdom and is therefore a popular tax haven for British residents seeking to avoid the tax man. The Isle of Man's independent parliament, called Tynwald, has operated for 1,000 years. The island occupies 227 square miles in the Irish Sea between England and Northern Ireland. The population is 72,000.

The Tynwald parliament began its successful experiment as a money haven in the 1960s. Since then, the Manx government has continued to be extremely responsive to the requests of private lawyers.

The Isle of Man will never shut the door to a good idea, particularly one that addresses and solves particular problems. An example is the purpose trust. These were invented in Bermuda and were intended to help protect large corporations involved in huge financial transactions. The Bermudan purpose trust, which had large minimum capital requirements, was thought to be

> **I think the Manx legislation does a much better job than the Cook Islands, and is better equipped to withstand legal challenges.**

the preserve of the deep-pocketed multinational corporation. But the Manx government decided to create purpose trusts for small-time investors. I like to joke that while Bermuda might be a haven for the blue bloods, the Isle of Man is a haven for the blue collars.

The Manx government has also created legislation for excellent asset protection trusts, but has done away with nonresident companies. I think the Manx legislation does a much better job than the Cook Islands, and is better equipped to withstand legal challenges.

One of the more interesting things happening on the Isle of Man lately has been its film industry. The Manx government offers direct equity investments of up to 65 percent of a film's budget, plus grants of up to £350,000 to film producers, provided at least part of the movie is shot on the Isle and 20 percent of the budget is spent with local service providers.

With 60 banks and current assets of more than £25 billion, the Isle of Man is an innovative leader in the offshore money haven scene. And presently the financial services of banking, insurance, and asset management account for 42 percent of the Isle's income. When confronted with the actions against tax havens proposed by the OECD, John Cashen, chief financial officer to the Manx Treasury, responded, "Our commitment is qualified. We are prepared to change certain of our regimes provided there is an international level playing field, but we're not going to proceed unless others do." The government further reacted to the OECD proposals with its own preemptive strike, slashing the corporate levy to 10 percent over the next few years, and dropping the top income tax rate to 15 percent.

While it's a little out of the way for U.S. investors, the Isle of Man is an attractive possibility for Americans interested in a European base of operations. Thumbs up!

Jersey

Much of what I said about Guernsey applies to Jersey, another of the three Channel Islands. Jersey has everything Guernsey has, only more of it: more people, more flights, more banks, more trust companies, and more offshore companies. There are minor differences in each haven's company laws. In a nutshell, Jersey's law is a little more up to date and less restrictive about the types of business a company can undertake.

Jersey is one of the world's busiest tax havens (with more than £100 billion in assets), catering mostly to large international firms, as well as British and European companies and individuals. Jersey itself is a booming home base for offshore mutual funds.

One black mark on Jersey's record has been recent revelations of money laundering. This will hurt the reputations of those involved with the islands and could lead to a regulatory crackdown. Jersey was one of the first nations to develop formal plans to adhere to OECD policies, including reforms forcing businesses to name board directors and removing the zero-tax on nonresident companies making it equal to that applied to residents. However, all has been put on hold for now. As it is, the island's company law requires the disclosure of beneficial ownership, a measure that removes some privacy.

Labuan

This tiny island of only 92 square miles lies near Malaysia off the northwest coast of Borneo, facing the South China Sea. It is quite remote—Manila is 800 miles distant, Bangkok is 1,875 miles away, and Singapore is 875 miles. Suffice to say, Labuan is a gross violation of my five-hour rule.

The name "Labuan" comes from the Malaysian word for an "anchorage," and the island is known for its safe harbor. The country, once a British colony, gained its independence in 1963. But in 1984 it gave up independence to become a federal territory of Malaysia. Since 1990 it has been working to become a safe harbor not only for ships, but also foreign investors.

Labuan is a free port with no sales tax, surtax, or excise and import taxes. Its principal source of government revenue comes from duties charged on petroleum products. The government of Labuan is heavily promoting its efforts to become an offshore center. A modern business complex has recently opened, which includes office space, a hospital, an international school, airport terminal, and communications system upgrade.

Because of its location, the main economic focus in this territory of 26,500 people is to attract business from Southeast Asian centers, such as Hong Kong, Singapore, Thailand, the Philippines, Indonesia, Brunei, and Kuala Lumpur. The island has suffered greatly from the Asian economic meltdown, although Labuan still managed to attract 213 new offshore companies in 1998, an increase of 13 percent over the previous year. Labuan is also home to 63 offshore banks, 40 offshore insurance companies, and 20 trust companies. All of the top 10 banks in the world have a presence in Labuan.

To attract new business and stimulate its local economy, Labuan changed its international company legislation on September 1, 1998. It now allows offshore companies to own local Labuanese companies. Time will tell whether many Americans will flock to Labuan to capitalize on this opportunity. Labuan is best considered only by U.S. investors with a serious interest in Asia.

Liechtenstein

This tiny little state, 16 miles long and less than four miles wide, is wedged in a visually stunning mountain valley near Switzerland. It is about an hour's drive from Zurich. Liechtenstein has a population of about 31,000, of whom 5,000 live in the capital, Vaduz. This "modern" country dates back to 1712, when a Viennese prince, John Adam Andrew of Liechtenstein, bought two territories left over from the old Holy Roman Empire.

Liechtenstein offers the European advantage. Service providers on the Continent are exceptionally polite and gracious. They do everything in their power to please you, which is something exceptionally welcome in the push-and-shove world of business. Liechtenstein's financial community is exceedingly accommodating. The banks and trust companies operating there assume from the beginning that their clients want to lower their tax bills without attracting the notice or attention of their governments. Liechtenstein follows the Swiss tradition: The instant you show up at the teller's window, it is implicit that all of your funds will be handled discreetly and confidentially, as well as invested wisely, and that no tax collector will ever touch your funds. This low-tax principality now has incorporated more than 80,000 "letter box companies" in addition to its venerable old banks.

That said, the governing legislation in Liechtenstein is very dense and is certainly not for the fainthearted. The legal system is a mishmash of civil law borrowed from Austria, Switzerland, and Germany. Liechtenstein moves very slowly to update its business entities with ideas from more inventive jurisdictions, such as the Channel Islands or the Isle of Man. For example, Liechtenstein still clings to a business entity called the Anstalt. This was once a novel idea in that it disguised ownership and protected privacy. The problem is that lately, the IRS has decided that if it suspects you have an

Anstalt in Liechtenstein, you will be presumed to owe tax from Anstalt income until you can prove you don't own the Anstalt. Sound complicated? It is, and I strongly advise you to avoid complicated situations.

Another problem with Liechtenstein is that it is tremendously expensive. It is one of the world's oldest and best tax havens. This reputation doesn't come cheap.

Liechtenstein has extremely strict bank secrecy laws. All customer contact with banks, whether by telephone, in person, by fax, or by letter, is dealt with under an agreed password. No bank statements mention the account holder's name. However, the government has responded to international concerns over money laundering by establishing a Financial Intelligence Unit to investigate any inquiries from foreign governments. Furthermore, bankers are now required to ascertain the identity of any owners for accounts established by a Liechtenstein-licensed trustee. Switzerland might be famous in the rest of the world for its banks. But one European financier told me that Liechtenstein is still where the Swiss go when they want to protect their money. In fact, most of Liechtenstein's offshore business is really conducted in offices based in Zurich.

Unfortunately, for small to midsize U.S. investors, this charming but minuscule principality has little to offer. Like some of the other money havens I've already covered, its users tend to be very wealthy individuals, large international corporations, and multinational banking institutions.

However, if you love forests or like to ski, and you have a lot of money to spend, this could be a viable option for you. As the *Washington Post* noted in a report, "Liechtenstein has everything a traveler needs for a European vacation—flowing rivers and dark forests, a bustling capital city and quaint farms, castles on the hills, mountains and lush valleys, good food, one superb hotel, Old Masters paintings, vineyards galore, fine wines, a benign prince, famous Winter Olympics competitors, friendly natives—all in an area the size of the District of Columbia."

To enjoy Liechtenstein, you need to like rubbing elbows with Europeans. Because Liechtenstein is located on the Continent, it caters mostly to European business. One reflection of this orientation is the official language: German. So for most U.S. investors, Liechtenstein's attractions are outweighed by its practical drawbacks and antiquated laws.

Luxembourg

I have yet to do business in Luxembourg and feel like I've gotten my money's worth. This multilingual Grand Duchy surrounded by France, Germany, and Belgium was once an appealing alternative to Switzerland, but it is still reeling from the scandal involving the Bank of Credit and Commerce International (BCCI).

This haven is used for two activities. First, it's often used as a base for offshore mutual funds. Second, it's often used as way to skirt around North American securities regulators. Under an international agreement between securities regulators, companies listed on the Luxembourg Stock Exchange can be sold to U.S. investors. Given Luxembourg's less-than-onerous securities regulations, this European country offers a way credibility-seeking promoters can get into North America through the back door.

Prior to 1991, Luxembourg was an interesting banking haven with ironclad secrecy rules. Capital requirements were lenient, making it a good, convenient place to set up an offshore bank. But then the big BCCI scandal hit, leaving the Luxembourg banking community with a huge black eye. Banking regulations were tightened. Luxembourg's banks didn't want the rest of the world to think they were all tarnished with crime and corruption.

I've found that in providing bank licenses, Luxembourg gives clear preference to large international companies. This precludes Luxembourg from smaller investors hoping to set up their own offshore banks. Language is also an issue. While English is widely spoken in Luxembourg, the official language is French, and German is a second language.

Another concern is the freeing up of capital movements and exchange controls that came with the European Union of 1992. This is increasing competition for banking customers and is leading countries to clamp down on tax avoidance strategies by requiring banks to divulge details about their customers' accounts.

For all these reasons, I advise even my most privacy-conscious clients to stay closer to home, and to choose a money haven that operates in their own language.

Mauritius

Mauritius is an English- and French-speaking island located in the Indian Ocean some 1,250 miles off the east coast of Africa. It has beautiful weather, with temperatures ranging from 70 to 85°F all year round. The population numbers about 1.1 million. Already some 14,000 offshore companies have been registered in Mauritius. A great deal of those were formed in the months leading up to July 1, 1998, when Mauritius passed a new law subjecting all offshore companies created thereafter to a 15 percent tax rate. Offshore companies formed prior to July 1 remain tax-exempt, and trusts are allowed secrecy for both settlors and beneficiaries. Mauritius used to be an inexpensive and simple place to set up and operate an offshore company, but this may change as investors try to buy companies created prior to July 1, 1998, instead of forming new ones.

> **Another downside to Mauritius is that it
> is very remote for North Americans. For
> Americans, Mauritius is well beyond my five-
> hour rule.**

Another downside to Mauritius is that it is very
remote for North Americans. By plane, it is 11 hours from
London, 10 hours from Paris or Frankfurt, 4 hours from
Johannesburg, and 6 hours from New Delhi. So for
Americans, Mauritius is well beyond my five-hour rule.

But this distance could be turned into a positive. If
you're looking for a good, contingency nest-egg haven that
is remote and secluded, Mauritius is an excellent candi-
date. This island is way, way, way beyond the reach of
most pursuers.

Monaco

Monaco is an expensive place. How expensive? The last
time I was there, the bill for my breakfast was $85. I don't
think I need to go any farther to underscore how much it
would cost to get things done there. This is clearly a
haven reserved for the mega–blue bloods.

Financial activities constitute one-third of the
national income, and Monaco now has an estimated
200,000 overseas bank accounts. To qualify to set up an
offshore program in Monaco, you must set up your own
corporation and hire high-price Monegasque locals to
run it. To ensure you're serious about your commitment
to doing business in Monaco, the principality requires
you to at least rent an apartment there. The minimum
monthly rate on even the smallest apartment will cost
you at least $10,000. And what do you get for $10,000? I

stopped by to visit one such flat. It measured 10 feet by 10 feet.

Monaco is particularly popular with Italians since it is such a short drive from the border. They like to load up the "boot" of their cars with cash and bring it over the border to the haven.

Monaco had a dubious reputation in the past. Writer Somerset Maugham once quipped that Monaco was a "sunny place for shady people." In recent years, Monaco has worked hard to clean up its act. Residency visas are issued only after lengthy investigations.

The famous opera singer Luciano Pavarotti made headlines with his use of Monaco. He thought it a convenient and legal place to avoid Italian income taxes. But the Italian government took him to court and convicted him of tax evasion because he didn't spend enough time there. He's appealing the ruling.

Maybe a world-famous opera star can try to use a high-ticket jurisdiction such as Monaco. But it's too ridiculously expensive for me to recommend it to you. And if you do travel to Monaco, you might want to remember to bring your own breakfast.

Nauru

Of all the havens in the world, one of my favorites is the tiny republic of Nauru, located in the middle of the west-central Pacific Ocean. While I have to say Nauru doesn't boast Fiji's beautiful beaches or the Cayman Islands' azure skies, the capability of the Nauruans to accommodate offshore business has been unsurpassed. Nauru's government has consciously set out to create a center that would meet the financial needs of international investors.

For starters, it's the least expensive jurisdiction in the world in which to license your own bank, and at present has registered more than 400 offshore banks. And

Nauru has one of the lowest capital requirements for banks of all credible jurisdictions.

Nauru does not require public disclosure of any records for holding companies conducting financial transactions in the small island nation. In addition, Nauru imposes no taxes on income or capital, which means that it is not party to any double taxation treaties. As of 1997, there is no provision for the exchange of information with other countries. With no taxes on inheritance, property, or real estate acquisitions, it is truly a money haven.

I have been there 10 times and always come away amazed at the range of entertainment I enjoy during my visits. If you go, stay at the Menen Hotel near the capital, Yaran. You'll stay a week—not because you want to, but because there's only one weekly flight onto the island. Unless you can get your work done during the 20 minutes each Tuesday the plane is on the runway at Nauru airport, you'll be on the island until the next Tuesday. But believe me, the climate is warm, and you will find things to do.

The island is sparsely populated, with fewer than 10,000 people living on its 8.2 square miles. English is widely spoken and used for most government and commercial purposes. Because the government provides a free education for every one of its citizens, Nauru has a 99 percent literacy rate. And with a per capita income of more than $20,000 (one of the highest in the world), it is fairly affluent. Its government was established in 1968 as a republic, and it is now an associate member of the British Commonwealth.

Nauru has international phone links, telex service, and mail service that rank high on the money haven scale of amenities. Its national airline, Air Nauru, offers jet service between Nauru and Hong Kong, the Philippines, Australia, Japan, Guam, and Samoa. The Australian dollar is its currency. Nauru has no exchange control restrictions.

The island's biggest company is the Nauru Phosphate Corp., but phosphate reserves are close to exhaustion. Early phosphate mining projects ecologically devastated the island. Australia, Great Britain, and New Zealand recently pumped up the economy by paying Nauru an out-of-court settlement of $133 million for environmental damage stemming from the mining. Looking to its post-phosphate future, Nauru is developing shipping, air services, and tax haven industries to keep the economy alive. The government does a professional job in assisting entrepreneurs in the registration of holding and trading corporations, and in obtaining banking, trust, and insurance licenses.

I give Nauru a clear thumbs-up as a base for your offshore operations.

Netherlands Antilles

The last time I went to the Netherlands Antilles, I chartered a small airplane and hopped to and from five of the many islands that make up this beautiful Caribbean getaway. When I wasn't boating or water-skiing in the heat, which averaged 80°F, I took some time to learn about the elaborate range of services the islands offer. It was amazing that so much was available in what would seem to be the middle of nowhere.

The Antilles, as they are commonly known, offer island-seeking and part-time wealth preservationists a virtual paradise. Located at the crossroads of key shipping and airline routes, these Caribbean islands combine wonderful, top-of-the-line international communications with trained personnel and easy access.

The Antilles are a particularly efficient jurisdiction. They may not be as popular as they used to be, but the infrastructure that served them so well in the late 1980s and early 1990s is still in place. There are several excellent trust companies there and the islands have registration of nearly 21,000 IBCs. After the OECD issued its blacklists, the government of the Antilles enacted legislation requiring gems and real estate dealers to report suspicious activity to the Netherlands Antilles Reporting Center, and issued guidelines for detecting money laundering to all banks. The Antilles continues to be one of my favorite jurisdictions for secrecy.

The Netherlands Antilles includes the Leeward Islands of Curaçao and Bonaire, which are 35 miles north of Venezuela, and the Windward Islands, which include St. Maarten, which are 144 miles east of Puerto Rico.

The total population is 200,000 and the main language is Dutch, though English and Spanish are widely spoken and understood. The islands have been self-governing members of the United Kingdom of the Netherlands since 1954. The legal system is based on the Dutch one.

The Netherlands Antilles is the nicest of the countries that make up my three Ns. (The other two, you'll remember, are Nevis and Nauru). Whether I go for business or for pleasure, I never regret the trip. I give the Netherlands Antilles my highest recommendation, especially for investors who place a premium on personal privacy.

Nevis

Nevis is an odd little country, yet one I highly recommend as an offshore haven. Two of the oddest growth phenomena of the past 10 years have been the Internet boom and the explosion of interest in Nevis as an offshore haven. Both have shot from next to nothing to becoming something huge almost overnight.

Two friends of mine, Vincent Hubbard and Mario Novello, invented Nevis as an offshore haven. For as long as I remember, they ran Liberian Services in Monrovia, Liberia, and set up tens of thousands of companies there. They were eventually run out of the country because of a

civil war. So they put together a massive Noah's Ark operation and moved their offices out of Africa and across the
ocean to Charlestown, Nevis.

This tiny island forms part of a tense federation with
its neighbor, St. Kitts. Nevis held a referendum in August
1998 on whether the island should secede from the union,
but the two-thirds vote required for secession was not
obtained. Despite its strained relations with St. Kitts,
Nevis is considered politically stable.

Nevis has embraced the money haven concept with
open arms. Indeed, it has become the copycat haven of the
Caribbean. The legislature latches on to the best laws of
any credible country and adopts them as policy in Nevis.
The Nevis legislature works at warp speed and offers the
best of anything you can think of in the offshore world:
purpose trust legislation, limited liability corporations,
asset protection trusts, bank licensing, and so on. It's a
top-notch haven.

The incorporation system in Nevis is one of the simplest in the world. There is very little in the way of vet-
ting requirements and no restrictions on who can own a
company. And because it is relatively new, there's still an
abundance of names available in the corporate registry.
Companies pay no tax, and Nevis has virtually no reporting requirements, making it a perfect place for the privacy seeker.

Its Caribbean location makes it relatively easy to get to
within five hours—and the Nevis government boasts of its
recent success in keeping Charlestown airfield clear of goats!

The hotels are beautiful, the climate and the beaches
fantastic. I love this place. Thumbs up all the way.

Panama

Unfortunately, I do not feel as favorable about Panama
as I do about Nevis. Simply put, I dislike Panama and
advise you to avoid it at all costs. I have not had one

**All and all, Panama is a poor choice, and I
advise you to avoid it.**

experience or heard one report about the competence or
integrity of any financial transactions that take place in
Panama City. It seems to be a pirate's womb.

Though some English is spoken, the main language
is Spanish, and the law follows Spanish civil law traditions. This is not a jurisdiction that is very conducive to
Anglo-American common law transactions. The banking
law is awkward and the supporting infrastructure is
unreliable at best. Communications are poor, and the
country is politically unstable.

All and all, Panama is a poor choice, and I advise you
to avoid it.

Samoa

Samoa used to be known as Western Samoa, but it has
recently dropped the "Western." It became independent of
New Zealand in 1962. It maintains the parliamentary
government, common law, and English language it inherited from New Zealand. Samoa is located in the South
Pacific, just northeast of Australia and Fiji. The population is 200,000.

Samoa became a serious offshore location in the late
1980s. The country's legislation borrows heavily from the
British Virgin Islands. Samoa allows for the creation of
tax-exempt companies and international trusts. There is
no income tax or capital gains tax in Samoa.

Samoa continues to update its legislative regime. In
1998 it changed its company law to allow for the creation of

companies limited by guarantee and hybrid (limited shares and guarantee) firms, and eased redomiciling procedures. There are a couple serious drawbacks to Samoa. First, its South Pacific location is a serious violation of the five-hour rule for Americans. And second, in 1998 it adopted some regulator-to-regulator data exchanges under a new "know-your-customer" rule. This could cause problems for privacy seekers. I take a neutral position on Samoa. Consider it only if there's a serious need for you to establish yourself in that distant part of the world.

San Marino

San Marino isn't ordinarily thought of as a money haven, but it is an interesting little place. And I stress the word "little," since it's nothing more than a hill in the middle of Italy. The main industry seems to be tourist stalls selling San Marino stamps and postcards.

But this is an ancient, independent country. It is named after a humble stonecutter named Marino, who centuries ago founded a small religious community on top of Mount Titano. In time, this community became a bit more organized. The republic was officially founded 1,700 years ago on September 3, 301.

San Marino's love of freedom has endured ever since. Now this country, which is one of the world's smallest, is looking at using technology to increase international trade and carve out a niche for itself as a service center for international investors.

I can't really recommend San Marino yet because the country has yet to get itself organized as a haven. But I've got my eye on it. San Marino is strategically located in the middle of Italy and is not far from the former Eastern-bloc nations. If it so chooses, it could become an important center.

Seychelles

Seychelles has the dubious distinction of once being the ultimate offshore haven. This is because Seychelles once promised to provide extradition-free residency to murderers in return for a $1 million fee. It didn't matter who you were or how heinous your crime. Paying your $1 million was your stay-out-of-jail card. Needless to say, Seychelles changed things after—surprise, surprise— the islands became overrun with Mafia types.

Seychelles is a collection of 118 islands in the middle of the Indian Ocean. The islands lie near the equator, so the weather is warm all year. France colonized Seychelles in 1770. It was occupied by the British in 1811, then granted independence in 1976. The islands offer one of the most pristine environments in the world and, besides Mafia hit men, is home to the world's largest nut: the coco-de-mer.

The government hopes the environment will result in a booming tourism trade and is offering generous tax breaks to foreign investors willing to develop resorts. The government says it is currently looking for someone to develop a yacht marina and an 18-hole golf course. There is also an international trade zone created to allow offshore companies to do local business. An example of this would be a tuna plant, owned by Heinz Group, that sells produce locally. Beyond that, Seychelles offers the usual roster of offshore services, including offshore bank licenses, international corporations, and arrangements designed to minimize or eliminate taxes.

Perhaps due to its distant location and dubious reputation, Seychelles hasn't attracted much of a Western following. Any of the business entities available in Seychelles are also available elsewhere, so I suggest American investors consider havens closer to home.

Singapore

Singapore is incredibly British. And given the brilliant aptitudes former and current British colonies have shown for the money haven business, that's a good thing.

Singapore, which has been an independent republic since 1965, is a very credible money haven. What Austria is to Europe, Singapore is to Asia. It's home to a variety of banks and specializes in deposit taking and offshore company management.

Singapore boasts a great number of companies that will administer firms registered in other money havens. That's something to consider if you want to base your offshore operations in a less accessible Asian money haven but also want to visit a clean, modern country when you have to do some business in person.

Citibank of the United States operates in Singapore. I've always found it interesting to note that the Citibank office in Singapore provides a huge array of services that are not available from the New York office. Visa International and MasterCard International have based their regional headquarters in Singapore due to its excellent reputation and stability.

The people of Singapore are remarkably honest and law abiding. It's illegal to chew gum in the subway there. Nick Leeson, the rogue trader who brought down Barings Bank through illegal options trading, was prosecuted and jailed there. And Singapore attracted big headlines in the United States after Michael Fay, a U.S. teenager living in

> **Singapore is a very conservative jurisdiction, and it isn't given to quick changes. In that sense, it is the opposite of Nevis.**

Singapore with his parents, was caned as a punishment for vandalizing a car.

Singapore is a very conservative jurisdiction, and it isn't given to quick changes. In that sense, it is the opposite of Nevis. Recent legislation and regulations require financial institutions to report suspicious transactions and identify customers in large currency transactions. Generally, however, you won't find Singapore changing its laws quickly to compete with other offshore jurisdictions. Then again, Singapore doesn't exactly need the business. I give it a strong recommendation as a place to keep a bank account or hire a firm to administer an offshore company.

St. Vincent

St. Vincent is a picturesque group of 17 islands in the Windward region of the Caribbean. Yachtsmen absolutely love it. St. Vincent, once part of a second tier of money havens, decided in 1976 that it would aggressively pursue status as a first-class haven. The island introduced a program of zero-tax IBCs in 1977 using laws drafted by Swiss consultants.

St. Vincent puts a premium on secrecy. Unlike many jurisdictions, which are under pressure from U.S. investigators to ease secrecy laws, St. Vincent actually increased the scope of its confidentiality legislation with the Confidential Relationships Preservation (International Finance) Act of 1996. This goes even farther than the Cayman Islands secrecy law. Under the new St. Vincent law, the government there takes the position that financial privacy is a basic right. Period. The only exception to the law is that it grants St. Vincent police officers the right to inspect documents that might contain evidence of crimes against St. Vincent. With reference to the OECD, Conrad Sayers, foreign minister of St. Vincent and the Grenadines, issued the following statement: "We're disappointed that we've met such opposition from powerful countries that should be our partners in development."

There is a bizarre quirk to St. Vincent's company law. The zero-tax IBCs offered by the country require the payment of annual fees. Yet St. Vincent also offers a program whereby companies deemed "nonresident" don't have to pay an annual fee and don't have to pay tax on income from foreign sources. If you're considering St. Vincent as the site of your haven, make inquiries to see whether your plans will allow for the creation of a nonresident corporation.

Switzerland

Switzerland is one of the oldest money havens in the world. It invented the concept prior to World War II by creating a place German Jews could protect their savings from the Nazis. But where Switzerland was once one of the best money havens in the world, it has now fallen to the second tier through what I call the "Swiss cheesination" of its banking secrecy law. The U.S. government has successfully pressured the Swiss into relaxing their once-famous secrecy laws, and this makes Switzerland a questionable choice for the true privacy seeker.

Nearly 6.5 million people call the 16,000 square miles that constitute Switzerland their home. According to some estimates, there is one bank for every 1,400 citizens in this visually stunning Alpine financial center.

Although its longtime reputation as a stable banking capital has helped it maintain a strong position in world finance, this country, known as the "heart of Europe," is now more like the grand old dame of offshore finance. Her best days are behind her, but she still has 250 years of earned dignity.

There are reasons that Switzerland has its reputation for banking expertise. For one, the Swiss have served as Europe's bankers since as far back as the Middle Ages. More important, as one Swiss investor once told me at a conference in Geneva, "The single most important aspect that makes us different from other bankers is that we see the world without borders where money is concerned." In other words, as bankers and financiers, the Swiss were probably one of the first to see the value of the offshore concept.

Because Switzerland is bounded by so many large countries, including France, Italy, and Germany, it has been forced to see the world in a certain way. The Swiss have also been able to turn a geographic circumstance into a prized asset. Their famous neutrality has made it possible for them to attract money in search of protection and privacy.

Today's offshore market owes a lot to the Swiss. However, like so much else, all things must pass. I think that its days as the number one offshore money haven have come and gone. Although Switzerland still plays a key role in international finance, recent economic changes in the world and the emergence of new centers with stricter secrecy laws have made Switzerland a haven only for those who are in no hurry to move their money. Switzerland has become too overregulated and too expensive to serve U.S. investors in any meaningful way. Interest rates are low and service charges are high. Don't expect to make money there.

You may want to put some small percentage of your assets into Swiss francs due to the ongoing stability of that currency. Otherwise I recommend that you stay away from Switzerland as an offshore haven. Its ties to the U.S. government are too strong for anyone who wants to create a certain distance from Uncle Sam. Since so many of the big Swiss banks want to operate in the United States, they must cooperate with American authorities. That effectively makes Switzerland an unsafe center.

Turks and Caicos

The Turks and Caicos Islands are a great place and, like Costa Rica, a wonderful retirement haven for Americans and Canadians. They're easy to travel to and they offer an abundance of services. Earlier in the decade, it looked like the islands were setting themselves up to be as aggressive as Nevis in pursuing modern and innovative offshore strategies. In the end, it seems that Nevis has upstaged them—they've fallen off the radar screens of money haven enthusiasts. Don't ignore them, however. In addition to being a great place to base your offshore corporation or trust, they are also a wonderful place to live. The temperature varies between 83°F in summer and 77°F in winter.

About 15,000 people live in the Turks and Caicos, a group of 40 islands spread over 193 square miles almost 600 miles southeast of Miami. The main language is English, and the capital is Cockburn Town. The islands are still a colony of Great Britain.

The Turks and Caicos are a popular location for trusts, particularly since new legislation provides for the creation of asset protection trusts. The law pegs the limitation period at three years. Any civil action launched against you after that period is not enforceable against your trust property. That makes asset protection trusts here a great tool for principalists, those who prefer to see their accusers prove they were insolvent at the time they set up the trust.

In addition to the new trusts law, the Turks and Caicos have recently passed legislation that sets up mortgage guarantee reinsurance companies, regulates local company managers and agents, and speeds up the creation of small mutual funds. The colony recently hired KPMG to recommend improvements that will attract more business.

Quite simply, the Turks and Caicos is a haven on the move. It might have been overshadowed by Nevis, but I encourage you to shine a light on some of the possibilities available there.

Vanuatu

After Nauru, this is my second favorite location for offshore banks. The nearly 100 South Pacific islands collectively known as the nation of Vanuatu have recently gained status in investment appeal. They are considered a desirable money haven and have earned the confidence of investors throughout the world.

As Reuters News Service put it, "Normally sleepy Vanuatu, its islands fringed with coral and coconut palms, has no personal tax, no local exchange controls, no capital gains or profit tax, no company tax, and offers complete secrecy."

For 17 years Vanuatu worked to build its status as a financially beneficial tax and money haven. As one wire service reported, "Today over 1,200 companies, including major banks and law and accounting firms that represent billions of dollars, are incorporated in the small South Pacific island-state." Most of these companies are from Australia, New Zealand, Hong Kong, Taiwan, Singapore, and Indonesia.

Although located far in the Pacific, Vanuatu is developing into one of the most interesting money havens in the world. Because it's close to Australia and New Zealand, it is a place to consider when setting up your offshore program. OECD officials have been very hard on Vanuatu in recent years, accusing it, Nauru, the Cook Islands, and Samoa with having a "heavy concentration of financial activity related to Russian-organized crime." The government in this island paradise has responded by asking the British government to assist in an investigation of possible Russian connections. I've been there a couple of times. The place to stay is the Intercontinental, which is located conveniently near Port Vila. Make sure you take full advantage of the jet skis.

Vatican

This tiny enclave surrounded by Rome is usually thought of only as the home of the pope and the Roman Catholic Church. But it is important to note that it is a fully independent state, formally known as the Holy See. The Vatican officially became independent of Italy on February 11, 1929. The pope used to have holdings throughout the Italian peninsula until the modern state of Italy was born in 1861. The Holy See continued to claim parts of Italy until 1929, when a formal truce launched a period of peaceful coexistence.

The Vatican occupies only 0.17 square miles, making it the smallest independent state in the world. So why look at this tiny religious state as a business location? Because the Vatican Bank, which is also known as the Institute for Religious Works, is famous for its secrecy and has a network of corresponding banks and agencies throughout the world. The Institute made headlines in the summer of 1999 after Martin Frankel engineered a fraud that removed hundreds of millions of dollars from Vatican coffers.

The Vatican deserves mention as a place to do business, though its reputation has certainly taken a beating at the hands of Martin Frankel.

MAKING YOUR CHOICE

At minimum, you should look for an offshore center that offers the following: secrecy, privacy, reputation, quality of regulation, entry requirements, movement of funds, and jurisdictional ties to the United States.

In addition, you'll want to look for a haven that offers government concessions, few or no taxes, easy access, smooth entry, political stability, absence of currency restrictions or controls, banking secrecy, a common language (preferably English), trained personnel, excellent telecommunications, and a positive attitude toward Americans. The jurisdictions I've just described offer a full spectrum of some of the best-known centers based on the criteria I developed to rate money havens throughout the world.

As you sit down to analyze your offshore options, it's important to clarify the financial benefits that mean most to you. It's just as essential to go about your research in a methodical way. If you're not the kind of person who wants to do that, then hire a professional consultant to do it for you. But comparison-shop the various services and limitations that are associated with different foreign money havens. It's only when you can compare your needs with the benefits of several offshore sites that you can confidently select the spot that's right for you.

Does it sound like too much to hope for? It's not. Remember, you will be entering the international arena, where entire governments are organized around policies aimed at attracting foreign investment. They want your business, and they'll do a lot to get it. So start asking!

CHAPTER 11

INVESTORS ON FILE

O n average, I talk with 12 offshore benefit seekers a week. That translates into 600 or more new clients every year. I've been a consultant for more than 27 years. So to date I've worked with more than 15,000 people who are now involved with offshore money havens.

Some of these people are extremely well informed and convinced about the benefits of offshore banking even before we shake hands for the first time. In fact, I'm amazed by how aware many investors are of offshore financial planning. Maybe their growing sophistication is just one more reflection of the dwindling profit opportunities available in the domestic marketplace.

Many clients come to me with more than just business ideas. They want a complete lifestyle change. Sometimes they want a new career; sometimes they just want to retire. They want to take drastic steps to overhaul their lives.

Of course, many people contact me with only a hazy sense of the offshore experience they desire. Occasionally, they tell me they've seen or skimmed through one of my books. Maybe they've heard about me from a friend or business associate.

Other times they come to me with elaborate plans already formulated in their minds. I've had complicated charts of offshore trusts, corporations, and bank accounts handed to me on napkins. It's amazing what the creative mind can do while sitting at a restaurant table.

The people who visit me aren't all hard-headed businesspeople, however. Some are like a family I recently met. A father and his five grown children came up to visit me from Oregon. These weren't tough-nosed sharks, but soft-spoken individuals looking for a stronger voice when it comes to protecting their assets. They wanted to build a shield that would prevent governments and creditors from taking all their cash and limiting their possibilities of future growth.

Whatever the research my prospective clients have done prior to our initial meeting, all these clients have the same things in common. In talking about the prospect of globalizing their assets, they communicate a combination of anxiety and hope—anxiety over a leap into the unknown, and hope for some level of economic freedom. In particular, freedom from the tax man.

Not all these conversations end with a signed agreement. But I have established enough offshore arrangements for individuals, partnerships, small consortiums, and mid-size companies to know that a lot of people are making a lot of money and avoiding a lot of taxes in complete privacy.

Too often, I think, people imagine all offshore investors are glamorous kingpins of the underworld, famous Greek tycoons, or crowned heads from Europe. Certainly, there are offshore programs owned and operated by these types of characters. But the majority of my clients are much more down to earth. They live and work in virtually every part of the United States. Some come from wealthy families in which being an experimenter is second nature. Others are self-made businesspeople and career professionals. There are doctors, politicians, university professors, and ministers. There are also used-car dealers, building contractors, real estate agents, and plumbers.

And in every case, it's lifestyle and personality that ultimately determine the specific nature of their offshore plan. For example, a professional couple in their mid-30s may set very modest economic goals: a bigger home in a better part of the city, a guaranteed education for their two kids at one of the country's leading universities, and the assurance of a comfortable retirement. Offshore banking is tailor-made to meet those objectives.

Meanwhile, an aggressive and experienced businessman in his late 40s may approach the offshore arena as the means to a diversified investment program that earns megaprofits in Asia, Europe, Latin America, and Canada—all at the same time. Private bank ownership can handle that assignment, too.

For me, the true enjoyment comes in knowing that I've helped someone enhance his or her life. That's my main motivation. I want to help people carry out their dreams. I want to show them the means toward realizing their aspirations. I understand their aspirations because, like everyone else, I'm moving toward my own dreams and goals. The empathy I have for my clients comes from my own life experiences.

Earlier I told you the story of Federico Solas. Many of my clients have read about him in earlier editions of my books. His tremendous business sense has been an inspiration to many and has sparked countless entrepreneurs to go global. I'd like to share some more of my clients' stories with you. Telling you a good story about one of my clients might inspire you to take offshore action, too.

When you read through the following client profiles, maybe you'll see a bit of yourself. If not, contact me at my office in Vancouver, British Columbia (see page 335 for phone number). I'd like to hear from you because, just maybe, yours is the one offshore game plan that I still haven't heard!

THERE'S NO SUCH THING AS RETIREMENT

I first met Peter Masterson through a phone call he made to my office in 1997. He'd been researching offshore investment opportunities for about a year when he read one of the earlier editions of this book. After several conferences in which we discussed his hopes for his future, Peter decided that he was ready and willing to take the plunge. He was a retired Air Force officer who had been in civil engineering, and although he was familiar with finances and managing projects, budgets, and the like, he was certainly not a financier. But he was smart and eager, and caught on quickly to the idea of establishing his own offshore banking center.

Peter's approach was actually pretty low-key. As a retired federal employee, he had the security of a steady retirement income, and he had no particular preference as to where he wanted his bank to be located. He had traveled the world, seen pretty much all of it, and wanted to base his decision in logic and good business practices. I suggested Nauru. Even now, Peter's never been there—saying he's already seen enough of remote islands in the Central Pacific. But what he does like about Nauru is that it is small, operates a relatively limited number of banks, and doesn't come in for a lot of scrutiny. So there's a certain amount of privacy available there that you just can't find in other larger, more touristy spots. He says he also likes the fact that a very substantial portion of

Nauru's national income comes from being an international banking center. That way, he says, they're not as likely to roll over to the demands of other larger, more powerful nations. With that in mind, he's been watching the actions of the OECD very carefully as they try to rein in the world's smaller banking centers.

"The OECD's blacklists are not about laundering money, stamping out drugs, or saving our children," he told me. "They're all about taxes. But I'm not worried about them because, as a nun once said in an old movie, 'When one door slams shut, a window opens.' So as fast as the OECD changes things, other opportunities will come along.

"Mainly I'm glad to see President Bush's position on the OECD. He comes from a business background, and he really understands—certainly more than his predecessor did—that people should not be depending upon the government for their livelihoods. If they are physically able, they should be willing to work for it—to earn it themselves—and then prosper."

I think he's absolutely right. There will always be opportunities for people who want a good return on their hard-earned money and who are willing to take a slight risk to get there. No matter how any government or international organization tries to control economies, the fact is that nothing works except the free market. How does Peter make this work for himself? Primarily, he contacts other retired Air Force officers through their national organizations, giving them the opportunity to

> **There will always be opportunities for people who want a good return on their hard-earned money and who are willing to take a slight risk to get there.**

deposit large and small amounts of capital in his offshore bank and thus reap interest rates they could never find in the United States. Six times a year he also writes and distributes a financial newsletter to clients and potential clients. Working less than half-time from his home office, and profiting from a very strong word of mouth, this supposedly "retired" bank owner steadily brings in earnings that ensure his own financial future and that of his family.

THE BIG BONANZA

Imagine this: A man in his mid-40s—dressed in a navy blue suit, striped shirt buttoned all the way up with no tie, hair combed straight back, and wearing dark glasses (inside a hotel)—walks up to me at one of my seminars with a check in his hand. The check is made out to my firm in the amount of $40,000. Clipped to it is a handwritten note: "I need a bank. You select the place. Call me when all the papers have been prepared." The phone number on the note has a New York City area code.

This is a true story. The client's name is Don Brenner, and in the years since that initial encounter, I have become one of his many admirers. Not, I might add, because of his personal charm. Don is not a charming guy. But he is a brilliant guy. And he typifies a new breed of offshore investor. They're lean and a little mean and they waste no time in getting down to business. What they lack in conversational savior faire, they more than make up for in brains and gumption.

I was surprised to find out that Don was an attorney. He didn't have that graceful, patrician air you get with a lot of high-powered Manhattan lawyers. He was fast talking and a bit pushy. When I returned to my office after the seminar, I called him. I was not about to make the decisions he had asked me to make without knowing anything about his particular offshore concerns.

He did not seem happy to get the call. "I thought the note was clear enough," he said. "I don't know where to buy a bank. That's your business, isn't it? Pick the best spot and get me one." I pursued the matter a bit further by asking, in general, why he wanted the bank. "To make deals," he said. "To make a killing. Isn't that why everybody wants one?"

And that rock-bottom explanation of the offshore banking motive still tops my list for hitting the nail right on the head.

I selected Vanuatu for Don's offshore center. Simply titled the First Bank of Vanuatu, it has become one of the fastest-growing facilities in the area. Naturally, it offers all the basic services you'd find in any offshore facility. But that's only the start. Don most avidly uses the bank as a kind of intermediary between himself and a wide array of international investors looking for U.S. financial involvement.

Don himself may not be all that knowledgeable about cross-cultural, transnational business negotiations, but he has put together a team of people who are. Together, they nurture close and ongoing associations primarily with Japanese and Arabian investors who want to start, acquire, or merge with a U.S.–owned company.

Most of my clients use their offshore banks to get involved in global business opportunities. And they're well rewarded for their effort. Don likes to work the other way around. He uses his bank to structure deals with foreigners who are trying to get into the U.S. marketplace. He charges a hefty fee for making the proper introductions, handling the delicate stage of negotiations, and drawing up the final business contracts.

Even more important, the First Bank of Vanuatu aims to create a role for itself in the ongoing international partnerships that result from the initial deals. In a sense, the bank brings major global players together and makes itself a third member of the profitable business triads that get established.

Not many investors can wheel and deal like Don Brenner. Not many would want to try. He spends all his time running a very diversified investment program, and his profits show it. He is now retired from banking and has entered real estate development, but before retirement, Don's bottom line surpassed $25 million. Don played a high-risk game, which is not to everyone's liking. But his enormous success bears out what I've been saying all along: When you're involved in offshore banking, the sky's your only limit.

A SILICON VALLEY SUCCESS

William Roesser was already a very successful man when I met him 15 years ago. He was an established leader in high-technology research and industry development. He had worked for some of the biggest names in Silicon Valley, sometimes as a staff executive and other times as an independent consultant. He told me quite matter-of-factly that he charged handsomely for his time and still never had any of it to spare. In fact, our first meeting was over lunch in San Francisco. Bill invited me there because a flight to my offices involved more downtime than he could afford.

As a private investor, Bill had also done quite well for himself. His computer savvy played a big role in that success. By feeding stock market information into his own software program design, he could predict with uncanny accuracy the companies that would do well over the coming months. His prerequisites for an attractive stock option were strict: a six-month forecast had to show at least a five-to-one profit advantage. And even then he was skeptical. "But at that point," he says, "I will seriously consider it."

Halfway through that afternoon's appetizer, it became clear that offshore banking was not a new concept for Bill. For some time he had been researching it as an investment technique. First and foremost, he told me, he was drawn to its flexibility. A hard-core high-tech whiz, Bill wanted the freedom to control a truly diversified international investment plan from his comfortable home office in Palo Alto.

He also liked the privacy guarantees that come with careful offshore finance. Again, his computer background had taught him the extent to which personal information is gathered, stored, and even exchanged between software data banks. His investments were entirely legitimate, but he liked the idea of circumventing what he considered excessive government and private industry investigation.

Five weeks to the day after our first meeting, Bill received formal title to Independent Commerce, his offshore bank in Vanuatu. In the beginning, he worked closely with an investment management firm that was based in Canada. With their help, he diversified his portfolio to include investments in the Far and Middle East, West Germany, Latin America, and Australia. Technically, of course, all these investments were owned and managed by Independent Commerce. So Bill's privacy was guaranteed.

I saw Bill later at one of my two-day seminars. He had come, he said, to explore the idea of expanding his offshore business. He was quite satisfied with the results of his international investment program; he had earned a two-year profit of just over $1 million. Now he was interested in attracting a wider spectrum of international depositors and borrowers.

My suggestion was that he keep Independent Commerce as his offshore investment arm and open a second foreign bank (perhaps in the Caribbean) to operate as a more active banking services facility. That way, he could more easily keep track of where his profits were being generated. And he could spread out his financial independence, enjoying top-notch banking benefits at two foreign financial centers instead of just one.

He wanted to know what kind of profit he could expect on the second facility. Immediately, I remembered our initial meeting and his strict rule about a five-to-one profit advantage. "Better than five to one," I smiled. "Well, then," he replied, "I'll seriously consider it."

OFFSHORE MOUNTAIN MAN

One of the most intriguing clients I've had in a long time is Chuck Davis. My first contact with him came over the phone. He called me out of the blue, asking if he could come in to talk about a venture capital idea he had in the works. We settled on an appointment for the next day.

When Chuck walked in, he looked like he had stepped right off a Marlboro Man billboard. He was tall and thin, and dressed top to bottom in faded denim. He wore boots and his beaded and bone wristbands were some of the most beautiful Indian artwork I'd ever seen. In every way, Chuck radiated masculinity. He was confident but fairly soft-spoken. He knew what he wanted from our meeting but was totally at ease in working through his agenda.

As it turned out, Chuck was only in town for a week. He lived and worked in Anchorage, Alaska. Originally trained as an engineer, he had been working for the past three years for a company, owned and operated by the Inuits, as a consultant on alternative energy development. Along with two other associates, he had been commissioned to design cost-effective solar-powered architectural plans for family residences and small business offices.

Together, the three partners were now interested in forming their own company, which would market very similar plans throughout the uppermost Northwest. The problem was simple and common: insufficient venture capital. They just didn't have enough cash on hand to commission a marketing firm and follow through on a professional promotional campaign. Interestingly, Chuck had heard about offshore banking from one of the tribal officials who had established a bank himself through my firm a number of years ago.

He suggested that Chuck use an offshore bank to generate part of the necessary money, and then use it to help borrow the rest from various international sources. Although Chuck's long-term aim was quite unique, his offshore banking plan was rather basic. He wanted to own a bank as a way of funding his own onshore business projects. The profits earned from depositors, borrowers, and assorted offshore business transactions would constitute the venture capital base that he needed to get them off the ground.

I suggested that, from the start, Chuck should know what he wanted to do with his newly established Vanuatu Citizens' Bank. I suggested he work with an experienced international advertising consultant who could help select appropriate publications for ads to let potential depositors know about the facility's attractive interest rates and specialized international banking services.

In truth, there was nothing so amazing about Chuck's bank. It offered precisely the kind of customer-oriented amenities that have become closely associated with most offshore banks. But Chuck and his partners did something that most other banks don't do: They put some real time, effort, and money into a very professional advertising campaign.

The results were impressive. When I last talked with Chuck, it was by phone. He had been shut in by 12 feet of fresh snow, but he was as pleased as he could be. Citizens'

Bank had on account deposits of more than $6 million, and his newly titled design firm (Solar Homes Unlimited) had already marketed over a hundred residential and office floor plans. With a little creativity and the confidence to try what other people might only dream about, he and his partners had made the first phase of their professional dream come true. Undoubtedly, the profits they will continue to earn should help propel them into an exciting second phase.

A MAIL-ORDER MILLIONAIRE

One of the global market's great allures is its ability to turn small but solid business ideas into big success stories. Edith Metcalfe's story is a perfect example of this phenomenon.

A hard-driving but soft-spoken single mother with two teenage sons, Edith lives in Indianapolis. Shortly after divorcing her husband in 1992, she developed the idea for a small mail-order distribution company. At the time, she was desperately trying to think of some way to compensate for too little child support and too much grief at her midlevel management job in the auto industry. Edith's business concept was actually quite simple. She wanted to find and develop affordable items that would make everyday life a little easier for people. She assembled an eclectic product line—everything from hypoallergenic cosmetics to auto care gadgets—and she tried to interest direct-mail catalog distributors in promoting them.

Edith had a good idea, but she soon learned that the catalog business is a pretty closed industry. There are a few giants out there, and they dominate the mail-order market, while lots of tiny companies scurry around trying to get their toe in the door. Edith wanted (and needed) to make some real money and, despite her creativity and tenacity, she knew she was never going to earn it within the U.S. marketplace.

I met her at one of my seminars. Initially, she seemed almost embarrassed to tell me about her predicament, but after she'd finally described the whole scenario, I was certain that an offshore game plan could help her. After several meetings, and a fair amount of support, she was convinced, too. The first step was a private bank license, which I secured for her in the British Virgin Islands. Edith took virtually every cent she had and transferred it into the bank. "This money was going to be a first-year's college tuition for both my kids," she told me as we made arrangements for the transfer of funds. And I could tell that Edith was scared to death.

Things turned out well, though. Initially limited by Edith's relatively meager resources, the Freedom Bank of the British Virgin Islands didn't have much. But it had enough to get started. Using her bank as an official financial intermediary, Edith approached two well-established mail-order catalog publishers in Western Europe. She offered them an appealing proposal: Would they be interested in creating a catalog for distribution throughout the nations of the former Eastern bloc? In exchange for including her products in their mailing, the Freedom Bank would be happy to cover partial publication costs on the premier issue—enough to ensure that the mailer would be a beautifully designed, full-color home-shopping guide.

The publishers agreed to try one issue, and within six months it was obvious that Edith's idea was golden. Finally free to investigate Western goods, Eastern European consumers were more than eager to buy. By the end of the first year, her bank was realizing a profit in the low six figures. This money allowed Edith to do two things. First, she could stop worrying about basic expenses. It no longer mattered so much whether her ex-husband made each month's payment. She could take care

> The global market is fast paced. If you wait,
> if you hesitate for too long, you usually lose
> out to someone with the gumption to step
> forward first.

of herself and her kids on her own. Second, Edith finally
had a little bit of investment money—and, believe me, she
didn't let much grass grow under her feet. She took a hefty
percentage of that capital and established her own catalog company. By advertising in a number of international
money magazines, she was able to solicit a wealth of products from manufacturers all over the world. By incurring
the entire cost, Edith earned the entire profit. Business
has been growing steadily for several years.

I got a Christmas card from Edith a couple of years
ago. In it was a One Number Card that allows me to call
her toll-free at her Indiana home office. It was not just an
ordinary telephone calling card. It had an elaborate modern art design printed on the front. Her greeting said:
"Here's a new product in my line, a series of special-order,
fine-art telephone calling cards. We're marketing them as
a promotional tool for small businesses and freelancers.
They're selling like hotcakes." She also scribbled a P.S. at
the bottom: "Aren't these offshore profits amazing?"

Edith is like many bright, deserving women entrepreneurs. For years, she bought into the notion that hard
work and diligence would reap their just rewards. She
finally realized that, too often, they do not. The global
market is fast paced. If you wait, if you hesitate for too
long, you usually lose out to someone with the gumption
to step forward first. That can be intimidating—especially for women who have been socialized to wait their
turn. Edith is an example of just how well women can
actually do offshore. All you need is the courage to try.

THE INVENTOR'S APPROACH

Clayton Louis Young did not fall quickly in love with the offshore option. Looking back, I think that's because it struck him as too clever a way around U.S. banking regulation. "You have to understand," he said, "African-Americans have only just begun to gain financial entry into this country. Somehow, it doesn't feel right to walk out the back door of a banking system that funded my education for six years."

Basically, Clayton is an inventor. After receiving an MBA from Morehouse University in 1980, he had worked nearly three years for a New York–based import-export firm. The job never suited him, he told me, but it gave him the chance to monitor a steady flow of electronic imports. Fascinated by the idea of designing identical products that could be produced less expensively right here in the United States, he eventually quit and opened his own business.

It was initially a small operation. His girlfriend ran the front office, and a crew of five women worked in back, assembling parts for his electronics line. He developed and marketed his inventions—products like a portable ionizer (designed to clean the air and generate negative ions within a six-foot radius), a handheld hologram camera (capable of producing three-dimensional images), and a digital thermometer.

When I met him, the business was four years old, and Clayton was doing well. Still, he had a major problem: aggressive competition. Almost every time he developed a new item, his company ran into legal trouble. He had been sued three times by manufacturers who claimed unfair product duplication. Other times, he had initiated legal action against competitors.

Regardless of who sued whom, Clayton said, he had been through one too many court battles in which access to his financial records was awarded to another manufacturer. "That means my entire business operation is laid bare for long and drawn-out legal review," he explained.

Although most rulings had been in his favor, Clayton was tired of fighting the war. He wanted an escape from constant regulatory intrusion, and knew he wasn't going to find it in the domestic banking scene.

We talked first about the benefits of maintaining bank accounts offshore in someone else's private foreign bank. I assured him that simply by transferring his company's checking account to an overseas facility, he would gain significant protection. Nevertheless, I encouraged him to consider a private purchase.

One of the great allures to offshore banking is "intellectual product" protection. In other words, for inventors like Clayton, the international arena offers a way around copyright red tape and bureaucracy. Each time Clayton sought to copyright a new formula or product, he had to disclose it to the U.S. Copyright Office. In the process, his million-dollar concepts were made part of the public domain and became vulnerable to reformulation and subsequent competition.

By owning his own offshore bank, Clayton could convert his product designs into "financial information." Technically, they might be called "exhibits to an agreement between scientist and formula owner." Of course, each formula's owner would be the offshore bank, strategically located in a jurisdiction where bank secrecy laws prevent reporting to any foreign investigator, including the U.S. court system.

It took almost three months, but Clayton finally called to say he was ready to proceed with a purchase. I could hear a level of resignation in his voice. I tried to reassure him that a bank in the Mariana Islands would offer him a level of professional privacy and product protection that he deserved. Then, without much more conversation, we hung up.

Much later, I had lunch with Clayton. I told him, as I had before, how different he seemed from the man who made that phone call two years ago. In that sense, he is a lot like many of my clients. They start out unsure of what internationalization can do, but they're willing to test the waters.

His bank, like theirs, has been the springboard to important introductions. In fact, his ionizer is now the rage in Germany—all because one of his bank's customers got to know him and decided to test market his electronic line in Berlin. "That should put an extra million in my pocket this year," he told me. And then he laughed, "Not bad for a kid from Harlem, is it?"

Mr. Elegance

My work introduces me to a lot of sophisticated people, but when it comes to sheer personal elegance, they all take a back seat to Carson Slater. With his chiseled features and deep voice, he is the picture of old California gentry. He's suave and charming, and no matter what the circumstances, he makes the right move. To my way of thinking, he is refinement personified.

Carson is not a self-made man. His family has been a respected part of Los Angeles's high society for several generations. His grandfather amassed a fortune in agribusiness. His father was a doctor. His mother was actively involved in various cultural and charitable institutions throughout the city.

A graduate of an Ivy League architectural school, Carson had run his life just as you might expect. He had married a woman from an equally respected family. They had two sons and a daughter, all of them grown and involved in their own lives. Years before I met him, he had left his own thriving architectural firm in order to devote all of his time to managing his and his wife's assets. He did, however, sit on the board of two major corporations.

Shortly after one of my firm's two-day seminars, Carson called the office to let me know that he had been there and had enjoyed the workshops. He was also interested in meeting privately about his own international options. Naturally, I invited him to my office, but he suggested instead that we have lunch at his club. "You might enjoy a quick steam bath before," he said, "and this way, we can feel comfortable about talking as long as we like." The invitation was casual, like everything about Carson Slater, but I suspect he does quite a lot of serious business over these "casual" lunches at the club.

I enjoyed that first meeting. I especially enjoyed watching the ease with which Carson talked about investment diversification. It was a familiar subject for him, I could tell. Off the cuff, he mentioned regular columns and specific articles from a wide array of financial publications. He obviously read all the right newspapers, and made it his business to stay abreast of the newest trends and profit-making strategies.

It was also clear that Carson was extremely well traveled. He talked about Japan as confidently as most people talk about their hometowns. He was unshakably convinced that he wanted to pursue investment opportunities throughout the Far East. He was intrigued by the role a private offshore bank might play in that pursuit.

Although his interests were specifically geared to Japan, I urged him to consider Vanuatu as an appropriate foreign jurisdiction. I knew it would be easy to establish operations there. Furthermore, it is particularly respected by U.S. bankers, and I thought that would be important to Carson, given his extensive network of contacts. Finally, Vanuatu is a fine vacation spot—perfect for someone who makes it a habit to mix business with pleasure.

Within a month, Fidelity International Bank and Trust opened for business. At first, Carson ran the bank truly as a private institution. It handled only his financial transactions. His many checking and savings accounts were immediately transferred. And a number of stocks (domestic and international) were quickly purchased in the bank's name.

Unlike most of my clients, Carson decided to roll up his sleeves and handpick his own island representative. He ran a classified ad in one international publication and received enough responses to schedule six interviews. After meeting all the applicants, he chose a British gentleman who had been a London stockbroker for 18 years. His knowledge of offshore banking was extensive. He lived in Vanuatu and knew local officials on a first-name basis. He had replied to Carson's ad because he liked the idea of a low-key involvement in a diversified investment plan. The match was perfect.

Occasionally, I get a call from Carson. Always the gentleman, he typically mentions having read about me in this magazine or that. Usually, he's calling for a referral. That's one of Carson's many strong points: He likes to keep up on who's who in every aspect of financial planning. He never boasts about the success of his offshore venture. In fact, I almost have to drag information out of him.

At last report, his portfolio had expanded to include a number of Asian market involvements. He had also added several friends, associates, and social connections to his client roster. A few of them were utilizing the bank for just checking and savings accounts. Most were taking advantage of the attractively low interest rates Fidelity can offer on business loans.

It's also interesting that Carson's focus has somewhat shifted away from Japan. Australia seems to intrigue him the most these days. In fact, he has recently used the bank to purchase a hefty percentage of two mineral resource plants deep in the outback. Maybe it's time for another bank purchase.

DRS. LASMAN AND LASMAN

When Judith Lasman graduated from orthodontic school in 1983, she could have joined any number of prestigious practices in Miami Beach. Instead, she joined her father in the small family dentistry practice he had established many years before.

From the way Dr. Bernard Lasman described his office, it was hardly the high-tech environment we now associate with medical care. It had two exam rooms, a waiting area, and the same receptionist he'd hired 37 years ago. "But it's comfortable and it's familiar," he told me. "You have to remember, a lot of my patients have been coming to me since they were kids."

Judith had read my first book, she said, while she was still in school. By the time we met, she had been in practice with her dad for two years. She had saved some money and had convinced him to save some, too. She was interested in talking about a bank purchase partnership. Essentially, she wanted two things from the venture. First, to liberate her own finances from excessive taxation. Like most medical and dental professionals in this country, she was in the 30 percent tax bracket, and needed relief. "My other concern is Dad's retirement," she said.

It seems Bernie had taken care of just about everyone but himself. He had spent a good deal of his career treating low-income families for very low fees. He had also been offering volunteer services through the same synagogue for more than 20 years. His accounts were a mess. In fact, some of his patients had owed him money for untold lengths of time. In short, he had ignored the realities of financial planning and now found himself over 60 without the security he wanted. "I don't want a luxurious old age, mind you," he kept insisting, "but I think Judy's right. I need to take some action."

What intrigued me most about this client team was the fact that they had such different offshore objectives. Judith obviously planned on a lucrative career and wanted to protect a substantial income from the long reach of the IRS. Bernie just wanted to retire in a comfortable fashion. I remember thinking, after we concluded that first meeting, how ironic it was that they should need to move assets offshore in order to achieve those objectives. But then, that is the economic reality of our time.

I suggested that they attend an upcoming seminar I had scheduled for Miami. They did, and shortly afterward, they contacted me with a firm okay on the bank charter and license purchase. They chose Nauru as their offshore base. I helped locate a management firm to handle the operational end of the business. They purchased a fax machine for their office so they could rapidly send and receive pertinent information. The entire package cost them less than $35,000, and it formed the basis for a banking and investment plan that changed both their lives.

Drs. Lasman and Lasman started the International Bank of Nauru. And after six years of operation, Judith tells me that she has already earned close to $250,000— tax-free—through a series of investments.

She has focused most of her attention on commodities: gold bullion, silver, and various gems. When we last spoke, she was still instructing her management firm to handle most acquisitions and sales. But she had begun to dabble a bit in diamonds. In fact, she had taken a trip to South Africa just to meet a dealer who was offering a number of unusual cuts.

And how's Bernie? He's great! He's changed a lot, though. Like many people who walk in the offshore door, he's glimpsed a different world on the other side. He's still in practice with his daughter, but their office has been transformed. They moved last year to a new building in downtown Miami. It's larger and has more state-of-the-art equipment. Bernie has cut his patient load almost in half. He sees only the people who have been coming to him for years. All new patients are referred to Judith, or to a third partner who joined their practice some years ago.

Bernie's offshore involvements have stayed fairly conservative. He has investments in Canada and Australia. He also joined Judith in the purchase of a Miami mini-mall—in the bank's name, of course. In short, Bernie's retirement is secure. Moreover, it will be a lot more comfortable than he ever imagined. And what about his volunteer work? "Oh, I still do that," he chuckles. "We rich guys have to do what we can, you know."

THE POWER OF EXPERIENCE

I can tell story after story about my clients. They are people who have caught sight of an economic opening and walked right into it. I can describe all their idiosyncrasies—the personal traits and tendencies that motivated them toward assertive international investment. I can do that because I've made it my business to know my clients. They form the basis of my business, and I admire almost all of them. For me, they are the pioneers, the global adventurers who are making tomorrow's world a reality today. They are the people who will be interviewed and profiled in economic journals 20 years from now for having taken a daring plunge at the right time.

There is only one thing that distinguishes these people from you. They have already made the first move toward protecting assets, avoiding unnecessary taxes, and securing privacy. As you've learned, it wasn't easy for all of them to make that move. It may not be easy for you. But I truly believe that unless you do it, you'll never know what it is to be financially free.

CHAPTER 12

GETTING AMNESTY: HOW TO SQUARE PAST IRREGULARITIES WITH THE AUTHORITIES

In the 27 years since I started advising people about the offshore process, I've come into contact with many clients who have gotten into trouble because they have followed incompetent or unprofessional advice.

Take the case of John Mathewson. This 71-year-old construction magnate from Chicago fancied himself a hotshot Cayman Islands banker. His Guardian Bank & Trust was shut down and collapsed by Cayman Islands regulators in 1994. Mathewson cooperated with U.S. authorities in the summer of 1999 and pleaded guilty to money laundering. Now, due to his incompetent advice, some 2,000 American clients of Mathewson could soon receive an unwelcome visit from an IRS agent.

Some advisers who claim to be offshore experts understand only a single process, such as setting up trusts. These are one-trick ponies who offer the same solution to every problem. For example, a common pitfall, often promoted by so-called experts like Mathewson, is to set up a foreign corporation owned by nominee shareholders or holders of bearer shares. This strategy is what Mathewson recommended to his 2,000 clients now under an unwelcome spotlight. The IRS disregards nominee shareholders and bearer-share ownership for the purposes of determining ownership and control of foreign corporations. Thus the IRS is now pursuing Mathewson's clients for allegedly lying on their tax returns by failing to disclose the existence of their foreign accounts and corporations.

Everyone's situation is unique and the offshore world offers a myriad of solutions. You have to choose your adviser carefully in order to make sure he or she points you to the best offshore path to follow.

Another common occurrence is for entrepreneurs to rush off and set up their own structures. Having acted without the proper advice, they find themselves sitting on a structure that creates more problems than it is supposed to solve. I see this all the time, and I can understand how it happens. Entrepreneurs tend to prefer quick, decisive action. They get it in their minds that they want an offshore program, and they make it happen. Unfortunately, they usually do it without proper planning.

First, let me say that I do not mean to criticize anyone for having tried to set up their own offshore program. At least you've tried. One of the hardest issues you can face is making that decision to leap offshore. Second, if you have gone off on your own and gotten yourself into trouble, I want to tell you that there is no need to panic.

In my experience, I've learned that there is no problem that cannot be fixed—provided you are willing to fix it. The only real mistake you can make is to ignore a problem situation. Letting problems fester will only make things worse in the long run. Square problems now and you'll have nothing to fear for the future.

In all previous editions of my books on the offshore
world, I've constantly focused on what people *should* do
in order to be certain they've set up offshore arrangements that are legal. In a nutshell, I want it to be
absolutely clear that you should consult a lawyer before
making any move. Your lawyer must be convinced your
offshore arrangement will follow U.S. law, will withstand
an audit by the IRS, and will protect you in the case of a
civil action.

Of course, this advice is of little help to people who
have already taken the offshore plunge. If you have
already established an offshore program and are reading this book for further research, I think the odds are
better than 50 percent that you have been acting on bad
advice. This is particularly the case where you've based
your arrangement on advice you received from the
haven itself.

Have you squared your program with a U.S.–based
adviser who specializes in offshore transactions and
arrangements? If not, there are a lot of pitfalls that can
get you in trouble.

I'll give you a common example. A lot of people venture offshore with a pile of cash, open a foreign account,
then think they've set up a secret nest egg that need not
be reported to the authorities. Not always true. You *must*
report all foreign accounts under your control with
assets of $10,000 or more. In fact, Schedule B of the pres-
ent IRS 1040 form (Interest and Ordinary Dividends)

> But remember that reporting the existence
> of your offshore accounts doesn't immediately
> mean your offshore savings will trigger tax
> liability.

requires you to list such funds and the country in which they are being held.

Did you know that? Are you reporting these accounts? I know that news is bound to upset some privacy seekers and tax minimizers. But remember that reporting the existence of your offshore accounts doesn't immediately mean your offshore savings will trigger tax liability.

This is why you need to speak with an offshore specialist. You need advice on how you can feel comfortable that your offshore arrangement won't result in a surprise visit from an IRS agent, or even worse, you being arrested for tax evasion. What's more, if it turns out you have unwittingly set up an illegal arrangement, you'll need to hire an experienced professional to help you correct your mistake. Don't do it yourself. Admitting mistakes, while absolutely necessary, must be done with great care. Experienced professionals can show you how to put the best face on your problems and minimize adversity.

The government even has mechanisms that allow for this, but doesn't like to publicize them. I'm about to tell you what they are.

COMMON PROBLEMS

I often run into four common problems. Each one can be solved, so there's no need to panic or stick your head in the sand if any of these four scenarios sounds familiar.

1. The foreign account. Several years ago you traveled overseas and set up a foreign bank account. You put some money in it and these funds have generated some interest income. You think this is great because the IRS doesn't know about it. What's more, you think you do not have to tell the IRS about it. Wrong. You are indeed required to report this foreign account. If this is your situation, don't worry because you are not alone. This situation accounts for about 90 percent of the problems I come across.

2. The "souvenir" corporation. You took a trip to the Cayman Islands a few years back and thought it would be novel to return home with an offshore company as a souvenir. Maybe you had heard about a Caymans corporation and thought it would be useful for your business. Maybe you thought a secret corporation would simply be a fun thing to have as a memento of your journey. Trouble is, even if you do nothing with it, acquiring an offshore corporation does trigger some reporting consequences. You have to complete certain IRS forms, and this should be attended to.

3. Importing and exporting cash. Sometimes people leave the country with more than $10,000 in cash or monetary instruments. These days $10,000 isn't that much money, especially if you're traveling to an expensive part of the world where cash is better understood than credit cards or travelers checks. If you didn't report this cash transfer to customs agents, you've broken federal law. Can you fix that? Yes. And believe me when I say you *will* *want* to fix this situation. You never, ever, want to get yourself in a situation where the federal government thinks you are secretly hauling large amounts of cash out of the country.

4. Unfiled returns. And finally, a lot of people who come to see me are such ardent tax minimizers that they've stopped filing tax returns. While I can understand their frustration and I sympathize with their desire to deny the IRS any knowledge about their affairs, the plain and simple fact is that the law requires you to file. Since moving offshore could attract the attention of the government, you do not want to be in a position where the government can pursue you. You want to move offshore with a clean record, and that means filing all returns for all missing years. This can be done.

All of these problems are fixable. I know this because I've helped countless clients fix them. So let's look at how it's done.

HOW TO DEAL WITH GOVERNMENT

The first thing to remember is that the government doesn't want to throw you in jail. Prosecutors and jailers are more interested in getting violent offenders off the streets than hauling you off to jail because you forgot to fill in a 1040 or didn't know or understand some obscure provision of the tax code. Jail is the government's bargaining chip. What they're really after is for you to pay your rightful and legal tax bill.

Besides, in order to prove a criminal case, prosecutors have to establish your criminal state of mind beyond a reasonable doubt. In other words, they have to prove that you had a calculated intent to defraud or rob the government. In most tax cases, this high degree of criminal intent is absent. What usually happens is that taxpayers honestly believe they have arranged their affairs legally. A court could still find that the taxpayer's arrangement goes against the spirit or the letter of the tax law, but the court can't convict the taxpayer of criminal tax evasion where the taxpayer honestly thought his arrangements were legal.

The bottom line is this: Correct your mistakes early in the game, and the government is not going to send you to jail.

Fixing Problem Number One: The Foreign Account

In my 27 years of experience advising people how to move offshore and set up offshore structures, never once have I come across anyone who has been prosecuted for filing forms late or after the fact. And this is all you have to do in order to set yourself right with the government. The government just needs to know if you collected any interest income off that foreign bank account.

The process is incredibly simple. First you have to get the form relevant to foreign accounts. This is U.S. Treasury Department Form 90-22.1 (see "Reporting Requirements," page 352). Next you will need to contact an accountant or enrolled agent and have them complete this form for you. You'll need to fill in one form for each tax year in which you've held the foreign bank account.

Hiring an accountant or enrolled agent to work on this problem for you is an absolute must. This is because the professional can deal directly with the IRS without making any admission of liability on your part. Once the forms are ready, have the professional type up a simple letter explaining the circumstances.

If it turns out that you owe some tax on the foreign bank account interest you've collected, your professional will calculate the amount due, plus all applicable penalties. It's not often you'll hear me advising you to pay tax, but this is definitely one of the appropriate times. I can help you set up structures that can legally minimize or eliminate taxes in the future, but there is nothing I can do about the past. You never want to get

into a fight with the IRS over money you already owe
Uncle Sam.

Fixing Problem Number Two:
The "Souvenir" Corporation

This situation is a lot more common than you might
think, and there is a way to prevent your souvenir corporation from becoming a bad memory.

Even dormant corporations must report to the IRS.
There is even a relevant form that addresses dormant corporations: Form 5471, Schedule O. It doesn't matter
whether you've ever used that corporation or not. What
does matter is whether you intend to keep it. You have
either of two choices: You can fill in the form and keep the
company, or you can ignore the form and kill the corporation. You don't have the option of doing nothing or sticking
your head in the sand. So decide whether to "fill it or kill it."

If you do decide to keep the corporation, there is a
place on the form where you can describe your corporation as "nonactive."

The situation is more difficult if the corporation has
resulted in producing some income. This could cause you
some serious problems. In that instance, you must immediately contact an accountant to discuss how you should
properly treat this income.

Fixing Problem Number Three:
Importing and Exporting Cash

This situation is a little more difficult. As you might have
guessed from problems one and two, the solution involves
filling in another form. In this case, you need to file a
Form 4790.

You'll want to enclose a letter with the form explaining why you're filing it late. Here's an example of what you might want to say:

Commissioner of Customs
Washington, D.C.

Dear Sir:

Please find enclosed a completed Form 4790 on cash and monetary instruments.

I inadvertently removed $10,000 out of the country without completing this form on the date of my departure.

At the time, I wasn't aware of the necessity for me to complete this form. Since learning of this oversight, I have completed this form with all due haste and am sending it to you at the earliest possible time so that I can be in full compliance with the law.

I apologize for this oversight and any inconvenience it might have caused.

Fixing Problem Number Four: Unfiled Tax Returns

This situation is the trickiest of all, and if handled incorrectly, can result in serious trouble. But at the end of the day, always remember that the government is more interested in collecting its money than throwing you in jail. You won't be the first person to file late tax returns, and you won't be the last.

The procedure that applies to your situation depends on your reasons for not having filed. The available procedures are a little too complex to sum up here briefly. But the basic mechanism is that you file tax returns for all the missing years. In other words, this means you fill in the forms for the missing years, just as if you were completing them prior to the April 15 due date of the relevant year.

If you pay all tax due plus any penalties, the government should walk away happy.

CONTAINMENT

Overriding all of these situations is a need to behave properly. And in order to contain future problems, the important thing to remember is that when it comes to taxes and dealings with government, behaving properly means behaving innocently. You want to structure your affairs so that no one can isolate something you've done wrong and use it against you as a criminal action.

If ever you stumble across a situation where you appear to have broken the law, you must immediately confront the issue so you can control it as much as possible. Collect all the relevant facts, and put the best possible face on the information. You may be required to share your story with your spouse, peers, and employer—though only if they absolutely need to know. Make the case to those people that you didn't intend to break the law. You want to create a network of support that sees and understands how you could have made the oversight that landed you in trouble.

There is a reason for this. If ever you have a falling out with your spouse, your peers, or your employer, you don't want any of these people running off and telling tales about how you intentionally played fast and loose with the tax code. Instead, you want there to be a pervasive view that you were always a well-meaning person who simply made an honest mistake.

Most people are tax illiterate, and given the complexity of the tax code, most people can understand how mistakes can be made. To be fully compliant with the Internal Revenue Code and understand all of its ins and outs, your accountant would have to spend every day giving you a kindergarten class on how the system works. There is simply no quick way to develop a clear and concise understanding of the Internal Revenue Code. It's easy to run astray of that legislative monstrosity. If you get in trouble, don't get arrogant and claim the IRS has failed to understand your brilliant tax-minimizing scheme.

DOING BATTLE WITH THE IRS

In my previous editions, this was the section in which I would evaluate your odds of being audited by the IRS. And for years they've been pretty scant. In 1999 the mantle of "lowest state in which you were likely to be audited" passed from Ohio (at 0.22 percent of all Buckeye households) to a region of northern Florida, where only 14 out of every 10,000 households were audited for a staggeringly low 0.14 percent. Nationally, audits in 1999 were only 0.20 percent, or 20 in every 10,000 households. Moreover, civil suits filed by the IRS against recalcitrant taxpayers dropped from 2,519 in 1992 to 641 in 1999. The reasons for these declines were many, including a decade-long slide in staffing at the IRS, antiquated computers, and legislation passed in 1998, which gave IRS agents new customer-service responsibilities that pulled them away from enforcement. In fact, last year the IRS literally "wrote off" $2.5 billion in taxes owed. Among the highest rates of noncompliance were our own federal employees—with the highest delinquency rates occurring at the Inter-American Foundation (concerned with the development of Latin America and the Caribbean) at 9.8 percent noncompliance among employees. Meanwhile, employees at the Treasury Department had a noncompliance rate of 1.9 percent , and IRS employees themselves had a delinquency rate of 4.7 percent!

But all of that is changing. As mentioned earlier, an integral part of President Bush's tax reform plan includes a major bolstering of the IRS, including more manpower and resources to go after delinquent taxes. More agents, more audits, and more enforcement. Now the message is if you mess with the IRS, you will be more likely to go to jail. If you are an American, you're tempting suicide if you try to evade taxes. This new policy of "inescapability" includes prison terms of up to two years for a tax loss of $90,000. Nobody should risk two years in prison for $90,000.

Slim though the odds might still be, what do you do if you get that horrifying form letter from the IRS notifying you that Uncle Sam wants to put you under the audit microscope? Your first instinct might be to panic. Don't. Instead, focus your energies on preparing your case. Organize your files. Collect all your receipts and make sure you can document all your tax decisions. Where you've made judgment calls on some expenses, jot down some arguments that explain why you made those decisions.

Here's something to remember: The IRS is so understaffed that it will not have the manpower to challenge everything on your return. You might be nervous about some medical bills you claimed, but feel very confident about that *Wall Street Journal* subscription you declared as a business expense for your home office. As it turns out, the IRS may decide to challenge your home office expenses instead of your medical bills. So, it may well turn out that the IRS tries to pin you down on the expenses you feel you can best document and justify.

Do not cave in immediately. Do not complete a Form 870, which is basically a document of surrender. The IRS might try to tell you that giving in will save you the has-

> **If you are an American, you're tempting suicide if you try to evade taxes.**

sle of preparing for the audit. But it also means that the extra tax you owe becomes due immediately. It also means you forgo your right to challenge the IRS's action in tax court.

Remember that it will be up to the IRS to prove your decisions were incorrect. Force the IRS to make its case, and prepare to counter the IRS official's thoughts with vigorous replies. If you've done a good job documenting your every move, you should be able to respond to all queries. Don't plan on being rude or difficult; just don't give in without putting up a fair, honorable fight. Don't be intimidated. The auditing process is a one-on-one, adversarial process with you on one side and Uncle Sam on the other. Force the IRS to prove it's right and you're wrong.

It helps to realize that the audit process is not so much an investigation as it is a negotiation. Your tax return was like your first offer to the IRS. The government's audit notice was like its counteroffer. The audit itself could result in you hammering out a deal. Neither side has to declare total victory. The IRS might be happy if it can squeeze a couple hundred dollars out of you. You might be a principalist and find yourself pleased enough just to force the IRS to go through the process. Even if the IRS determines you do owe some tax, you might come out of the audit owing less than the government tried to collect.

Depending on the sum of money involved, you might want to hire an accountant or a lawyer (maybe even both) to help you prepare. This is obviously an economic decision more than a legal one. If the IRS is after thousands of dollars or is auditing you for incredibly complex reasons, you will want to get some professional advice to match wits with the IRS officials. And there are a few situations where hiring a lawyer is absolutely necessary. If there is any possibility the IRS wants to charge you with criminal tax evasion, you should hire a defense lawyer immediately. It's one thing to haggle with the IRS over a few hundred dollars in tax. It's another to risk jail.

Now, what happens if you put up a good fight, but the government still thinks you owe them? If this is the case, you will receive a report from the IRS within a week of your audit. This decision is not final. It is an administrative determination that can be appealed. If the IRS does not want to reconsider, you can take the government to tax court. Be very careful of the timing, because you only have 90 days from the date you receive the audit report to protest the IRS decision in tax court.

There are two branches of the tax court: one for big claims and one for small ones. The rules for each level are different, but in essence the small court is set up to decide cases quickly, whereas the big court is designed to hear the more complicated disputes. Go to court and fight. Tax cases are rarely all-or-nothing affairs. Even if the taxpayer "loses," in that the judge rules in the government's favor, the odds are still good the judge will find the taxpayer owes the government less money than the IRS claimed.

In short, there is only one reason for you to be afraid of an audit. This is if you cheat. If you fear you are going to be audited because you have committed tax fraud, put this book down and call a lawyer immediately.

If you've ever thought about cheating on your tax return, think again. Cheating costs more than you save. In a worst-case scenario, you could even go to jail. But even if you don't, the penalties you will face, the legal bills you will incur in protecting yourself, and the loss of reputation you could suffer all outweigh the gains you would have made from cheating. It's just not an option.

CHAPTER 13

GETTING STARTED
THE EASY WAY

I cringe when I hear about offshore consultants who promote only one aspect of moving offshore. Some specialize in setting up trusts, others specialize in setting up offshore corporations. There is so much more to the offshore world that the same solution won't always address the same problem. The Internal Revenue Code and U.S. securities laws aren't written with a single theme in mind. The notion a single sugar pill could magically immunize an individual from the breach or application of those laws is ridiculous. I see this with a lot of offshore consultants. They like to apply the same approach to every problem, giving no thought to the consequences. I've heard one consultant promise that obtaining an offshore credit card and banking debit card will solve *all* tax problems—and charge his clients $700 for this piece of information and assistance in filling out the credit card application. This is silly, and it doesn't work.

In addition to these consultants, there are stacks of what I call "cookbooks" out there (better known as "crookbooks"). These tell you how to set up an offshore international business corporation (IBC) or how to set up an offshore trust fund simply by following the steps and filling out the forms. This approach doesn't help you at all. Unless you speak with an expert, how would you even know that a particular offshore company or trust is the answer to your particular question? Those who write these crookbooks are motivated by profits from book sales, not concern for clients. You get what you pay for. Buy a $19.95 book, and all you get is $19.95 worth of advice.

The bottom line is you *must* have a sincere chat with someone who understands your situation. I have more than a quarter century of experience in the area of off-shore planning. This experience has taught me that one solution doesn't skin all cats. In this book I've told you about 40 different money havens. Each one of those havens has different laws regarding offshore companies, trusts, banks, and other investment vehicles, not to mention residency and tax regulations and now citizenship. Even then, the laws of these money havens are in constant flux. Some jurisdictions, such as Nevis, change their laws quickly so they can compete for more offshore business. Other havens, such as Liechtenstein, are slow to change as they've grown top-heavy with blue-blood clients. You need to deal with an expert to know not only what type of offshore structure you should consider, but also in which jurisdiction you should base this structure. There's a myriad of options out there, and the options differ for each client's situation.

I often get clients who come to me very unsure about the offshore world. I'll listen to their stories and talk about their needs. If they still seem uncertain about proceeding, I'll send them away to think some more. You have to be ready. If you're not up to the offshore challenge, if you're not the sort of person I've described as an International Man, there's no point in going offshore. Only decisive action stands between you and lucrative opportunities. If you've taken the time to read this book, then you must be fairly serious about entering the offshore world. If you're like most readers, you've probably moved from one chapter to the next, calculating the investment profits you could earn outside the United States. You're undoubtedly attracted to the idea of genuine financial privacy. Like everyone, you'd like to reduce your taxes.

Still, there's a definite difference between admiring the concept of offshore financial activity and actually taking part in it. Don't get me wrong: Offshore "fans" have their place. In fact, over the past several years, they have become a major force in the growth of global banking and business. They buy books, subscribe to newsletters, attend workshops, and, in general, contribute to the popularity of a burgeoning offshore world.

It's the offshore participants, however, who transform enthusiasm into profit. There's nothing magical about making money offshore. You simply need to take the proper steps. As I've argued in previous chapters, you must separate yourself from your assets and then strategically place funds in the foreign markets most likely to generate a sizable return. Then, as international financial dynamics change, you can move your money around, always making sure that it works for you in the most profitable places.

> There's nothing magical about making money offshore. You simply need to take the proper steps.

My major aim in writing this book is to help you decide what's right for you. Will you be happiest pledging your allegiance to the offshore fan club? Or would you prefer to take the plunge into an actual international involvement? I've tried to give you the facts you'll need to make that decision. I've also tried to acknowledge the psychological considerations that come into play when you consider a personal role in global finance.

Ultimately, though, it is up to you. Taking into account all that I've said, and tossing in whatever you may have picked up from other reliable sources along the way, you must decide the next move for yourself. If you think it through and decide that foreign moneymaking doesn't suit you, I hope you'll consider this book a worthwhile investment in your financial education.

If, however, you feel that you're ready to get started, then the rest of this chapter will point you in the right direction.

REVIEWING YOUR OPTIONS

In presenting my argument for offshore investment, I've covered a number of offshore options. There are lots of ways to make and save money within the domestic economy. That goes double when you're operating internationally. In fact, it's easy to conceive of a profit-making venture that is legal and feasibly implemented somewhere in the world. The key is what I call "tax neutral" offshore planning. As discussed earlier, this means establishing an offshore presence—and letting the IRS know about it. In this way, you can still garner the benefits of offshore holdings while paying taxes on the profits.

The point is, there are various ways to operate beyond your country's borders. I suggest that you learn a bit about the ones that really interest you. I would not encourage you to become an expert on every conceivable offshore investment option. You'll only exhaust yourself by trying, and still not get the job done.

To help you outline some of your choices, let's review the six most popular ways in which Americans get financially involved offshore. Consider the benefits as well as the drawbacks associated with each of these investment strategies, and then begin developing a game plan that complements you and your portfolio objectives.

Option Number One: Foreign Trusts

Until the late 1970s, foreign trusts were an extremely popular form of offshore financial involvement. Before the federal government implemented the Tax Reform Act of 1976, they offered a creative form of tax avoidance and simultaneously allowed people to take long-term care of their heirs. Unfortunately, foreign trusts have run into a lot of trouble over the past several years, and no longer provide the wide range of benefits that once attracted so many people to them.

Under the old law, a U.S. citizen could create an irrevocable foreign trust that was taxed in basically the same manner as a nonresident alien would be. To put it simply, American investors could use foreign trusts to indefinitely defer taxes on their assets—until distributions were actually made to their beneficiaries. And even when the distributions were made, they were taxed without any interest or penalty to offset the advantages of many years of tax-free accumulation.

But even in the old days, foreign trusts were imperfect. For example, the grantor of the trust had to place all trust property beyond his control for his entire lifetime. Furthermore, neither the grantor nor the grantor's spouse could be a beneficiary. Still, these offshore "wills" were an appealing option for investors with substantial assets and a concern for the welfare of family members after their death.

Today, even those fundamental benefits have been scaled back in certain circumstances. As part of the Tax Reform Act, Congress enacted several provisions designed to penalize the use of foreign trusts. Under them:

- The grantor of such a trust (with more than one U.S. beneficiary) continues to be taxed on the foreign trust's income for the rest of the grantor's lifetime, as though he or she still owned all the trust's assets.

- Upon distribution of those assets, a nondeductible 6 percent per year interest charge is imposed on taxes due under "throwback" rules. If there has been a lengthy accumulation period, the tax plus the interest can sometimes wipe out the entire amount originally envisioned as a gift to the beneficiaries.

- If the trust is ultimately distributed to U.S. beneficiaries, then all accumulated capital gain is converted into ordinary income, and is sometimes taxed at a higher rate than the beneficiaries' income tax bracket would suggest.

As a result of these legislative changes, most Americans no longer stand to derive significant tax benefits from transferring property to a foreign trust. Trusts are still fairly popular, but I would say that in today's market, given their limited benefit standing alone, they should be avoided. They have no economic purpose, and with the possibility of even more restrictive tax legislation down the line, it just doesn't seem worth the bother. In a sense, the foreign trust concept is just another example of how Uncle Sam makes it his business to get you, one way or another.

Option Number Two: Foreign Annuities, Endowments, and Private Annuities

Annuities and endowment policies are most easily understood as special types of savings deposits with some specific features guaranteed by the issuing insurance company. Foreign annuities can be either lump sum or periodic savings deposits, and they guarantee an income for the rest of the depositor's (or named beneficiary's) lifetime. The income level will vary based on the owner's age, the deposit size and frequency, and when the income payments begin. They're a fairly common approach to offshore investment, and for good reason. If the international currency exchange rate is in your favor, they can allow you to make a handsome profit.

Swiss banks have become particularly well known for handling these foreign annuities, and during times when the Swiss franc exchanges favorably with the U.S. dollar, a guarantee-level franc annuity income can produce increasing dollar income. For example, if you had purchased a single-payment, immediate-income Swiss franc annuity worth $10,000 in 1970, it would have been worth more than $17,000 by 1976.

Americans are investing in these insurance annuities for the following reasons:

- To protect their purchasing power against the falling U.S. dollar
- To partake of the safety and security of Swiss insurance companies
- To protect themselves against possible future government attacks on retirement plans as well as the potential failure of pension plans
- To assure themselves of the liquidity and offshore protection in the event of a market collapse or financial panic in the United States
- To seize the opportunity of investing globally

Endowment policies add life insurance protection and dividends to annuities, and are also available in single deposit, periodic deposit, and increasing deposit forms. An example of the single deposit form might go like this: For a 45-year-old man making a single 100,000 Swiss franc deposit payment, the cash account value would grow to 252,107 francs by age 65. The immediate death benefit to his beneficiary would be 159,058 francs at age 45, and would rise to equal the cash value by the time he reached age 65.

The drawbacks to foreign annuities and endowments are, I think, obvious. First, their appeal is inseparably tied to international currency exchange rates. So long as the dollar compares negatively with the currency in which you happen to hold your annuity, you're safe. But as the exchange balance fluctuates, you are vulnerable to profit loss and, perhaps, even capital devaluation.

Another problem with annuities is that they make their profit very slowly. In the case illustrated previously, it took six years for $10,000 to grow to $17,000! That's very sluggish activity when you begin to compare that with the return on other investments. This same criticism applies to endowments.

Again, the example above shows a 4.75 percent annual rate of dividend compounding. Most offshore ventures offer much more impressive profit potential. However, if you know what you're doing, have a good consultant work with you, and take the time to monitor the market for impending adjustments in the international currency exchange rates, I think that annuities and endowments can be reliable investments. They're a conservative choice, and as such, they don't involve a great deal of risk.

Private annuities offer additional benefits for offshore investors. They offer the ability to custom design an investment program while at the same time have the gain or income accumulate free of tax until payments are made. There are no reporting requirements for private accounts until distributions are made.

Option Number Three: A Foreign Bank Account

You can move toward faster and larger profits by opening a checking or savings account with a foreign bank. For starters, an offshore account allows you to rest assured that your money is being held by a financially stronger and better managed institution than you could ever find here in the United States. In part, that's because your offshore bank must maintain a higher ratio of liquid assets to accumulated debts.

An offshore account will also let you avoid the high service costs that have become part and parcel of domestic banking. And you'll benefit from the international banking environment, where regulations are kept to a minimum and customer service is made the top priority. We have already covered the specific benefits that come with an offshore bank account. Just for review:

- Foreign banks offer a very attractive interest rate—typically several points above what you could find onshore. Remember, too, that the longer you keep the money on deposit, the more interest you earn.

- Checks written from a foreign account allow you to enjoy "float time," usually three or four weeks between the writing of a check and its arrival at the offshore bank for clearing. During that period, you will continue to earn interest on the money in your account.

- "Twin accounts" let you combine the benefits of a current checking account with the profits of a high-interest deposit account. You keep most of your money in the bank for high-interest earnings, but maintain a small balance for everyday withdrawal.

- Offshore banks also offer fiduciary accounts that allow you to direct the bank to make proxy investments for you. The record shows that your bank acted on its own behalf, but all profits earned on the investment are paid to you. However, they're not tax-free because they were earned outside the United States.

Are there problems with having one (or more) of these offshore accounts? No, but there are limitations to what they can do for you.

I should also mention offshore debit cards. Yes, just like the ones you use here in North America when you shop at the grocery store. You know how they operate. You put your debit card (a regular-sized plastic card) through the merchant's electronic verifier and you punch in your personal identification number (PIN).

If your account is approved, your bank account is immediately debited by the amount you have purchased or withdrawn.

The beauty of the card is that it is convenient and very popular with banks. Also, it allows a certain level of freedom since these cards can be used throughout the world. The new Maestro card issued by MasterCard is a global debit card and will probably overtake Visa as the number one card for global transactions. As one financial analyst put it, "No money in your account, no transaction." This up-and-coming tool can be issued by your offshore bank, with all purchases debited to your offshore bank account. (For more detailed information on foreign accounts, refer to appendix 1.)

One important note—foreign bank accounts valued over $10,000 must be reported to the US Treasury Department. (See "Reporting Regulations," page 352.)

Option Number Four:
Private International Corporations

If you like the idea of actually running a foreign business, you might want to own your own private international corporation. You might want to establish a manufacturing business and make your million-dollar invention concept a reality. Believe me, it's been done by people no more experienced at international business than you.

If you're less confident about what you'd like to do with your business, you can finalize the incorporation and allow the corporation to function simply as your broker in the international marketplace. It can invest in stocks, commodities, CDs, real estate, and foreign currencies. It can import and export, and serve as a holding company to protect patents and trademarks.

You can also choose a professional offshore management firm to operate your new corporation. If you don't know how to identify such a firm, talk with any reputable offshore consultant. He's likely to refer you to a number of Hong Kong and Vancouver firms—any one of which will impress you with a wide range of investment and administrative services.

There's not a lot to be said against the private international corporation concept. Particularly if you can manage to buy a company that's already been licensed and approved for operation, it can be an affordable way to establish an offshore involvement. These prepackaged, "turnkey" situations are not easy to find, but they're worth pursuing. A good financial consultant can sometimes help you locate a business that's named and ready to go.

Remember, offshore corporations are not IRS-proof. They must be reported as a controlled foreign corporation.

Option Number Five:
Offshore Asset-Protection Trusts

In chapter 7, I explained at great length the nature of
offshore asset-protection trusts (APT). This type of trust
is so important that I want to briefly revisit it. First of
all, it is one of the best asset protection strategies. This
single offshore venture can provide you with an unpar-
alleled level of tax protection and financial invisibility.
The very purpose of an APT is to place both legal and
physical obstacles in the way of creditors. It puts your
assets substantially beyond the reach of any U.S. court,
and severely limits anyone's ability to enforce a money
judgment against you.

One of the keys to a successful foreign trust is the
selection of a friendly host country. By that I mean you
should establish your trust in an offshore jurisdiction
that, first and foremost, maintains stringent laws
against enforcing foreign judgments. It's also critical
that your preferred foreign site has nothing equivalent
to the U.S. "statute of frauds." In other words, you want
to be sure that if you were to physically transfer your
assets to the offshore center and then place them in
trust there, courts and creditors here in the United
States would be unable to claim fraudulent intent. Why?
Because the laws that govern the creation of trusts in
your chosen offshore center do not recognize such fraud.

A basic offshore APT can be set up with anyone as the
direct beneficiary—including you as the creator of the
trust. However, for maximum protection, it's better to
choose someone else for that role. (Otherwise you could be
seen to have too much of a beneficial interest in the trust
and its activities.) Just like domestic trusts, all offshore
APTs have a "trustee," someone to administer the trust
and hold its assets for the benefit of the beneficiaries.

Establishing an offshore APT is not a terribly complex
or lengthy undertaking, but it does require expert legal

advice from a trust attorney. You'll remember some of the cases I pointed out earlier that show how APTs can lead to disaster if not properly created or used. There are a number of special features that should be included in the trust agreement. One is an antiduress provision. This allows the offshore trustee to simply disregard a U.S. court order stipulating that the creator of the APT or the trustee turn over the trust's assets to your creditors. Another important clause is called "transfer of situs." This clause allows the APT's trustees to change the legal locale of the trust. For example, if some type of action is to be taken against the creator of the trust, the APT trustees can move the trust and its assets from the British Virgin Islands to a bank in the Bahamas. This forces the creditor back to square one. And this can be done again and again.

Finally, because it is generally required that you transfer title or ownership to the property to the offshore jurisdiction before you actually establish a trust there, the offshore APT is usually best for holding liquid assets: cash, stocks, bonds, and certificates of deposit. In addition, assets transferred to a simple APT should generally be those not needed for your daily living or business needs. As always, I recommend that you work with an experienced adviser or consultant in designing and setting the terms of your offshore APT.

Option Number Six:
The Private Offshore Bank

If you want the benefits associated with all five options outlined above, and several more, then consider the creation of your own private international or offshore bank. In my opinion, it is the single most complete and profitable move you can make into the offshore arena.

For starters, your own bank will provide all the advantages of a foreign checking and savings account at

no charge, because you'll be your own customer. All your
transactions can be handled in the bank's name, so your
financial privacy is guaranteed.

Like all businesses, your bank will aim to make an
impressive profit. So it will probably attract customers
via various international publications and the Internet.
As the customers come in, they will figuratively pass
through a revolving door and become money with which
your bank offers loans to international borrowers. Within
a matter of months, the interest generated by those loans
will form the basis of a handsome bottom line.

Your bank can increase its profit by expanding services. For example, once you get enough depositors, you
can begin issuing letters of credit and financial guarantees. You can offer back-to-back loans. You can also provide venture capital loans at whatever interest rate the
free market will allow—sometimes as much as 10 percentage points above the comparable domestic rate.

Private international banks offer you as much
investment flexibility as you desire. If you tend to be
cautious in your portfolio management, you can use
your private bank as a discreet international broker.
Essentially, it can be a one-person operation. Using its
name rather than your own, you can purchase low-risk
stocks and commodities from around the world and
watch your profits gradually build without tax. If you're
a more adventuresome investor, you can use the bank to
structure high-stakes business partnerships and ventures on virtually every continent. You can turn your
bank into a full-scale operation, with an experienced
staff of employees to monitor your numerous international involvements.

Ownership of the bank may be structured to overcome most IRS and tax traps. For more detailed information, consult my book, *How to Own Your Own Private
International Bank* (Prima Publishing, 1998).

DON'T DO IT YOURSELF

If you decide that the offshore bank concept is for you, then you immediately face a critically important choice. Do you want to try to handle the entire transaction on your own? Or would you prefer to work with a company that can manage the process for you?

Frankly, most people are intimidated by the prospect of so much research and so many international business maneuvers. I think they're wise to feel that intimidation. There's nothing more foolish than biting off more than you can chew, especially when there are qualified professional teams that can help you.

You need months just to research the various offshore jurisdictions and their particular strengths and weaknesses. Even if you feel certain that you've identified the right place, several overseas visits will also be required in order to meet with island officials and process the necessary paperwork.

As you consider all this, remember that if you spend a lot of time setting up your offshore bank, you will pay a price in lost investment opportunity. They say that time is money, and I certainly agree. When you're looking at offshore profit strategies, every minute counts.

To ensure that your bank's legal framework is well conceived, I suggest that you work with a reputable attorney based in your preferred offshore center. This way, you can sidestep involvement with any U.S. officials or agents, but also rest assured that someone with appropriate expertise is looking out for your interests.

If you don't know anyone who can refer you to a good lawyer in the area, you'll need to conduct still another phase of meticulous research. I suggest that you thoroughly check professional references. On occasion, U.S. investors have found themselves with a costly legal bill and no offshore bank charter or license to show for it. The legal acquisition of an offshore bank is not an extremely complicated matter, but it does require specific knowledge and skill.

Be prepared for a lengthy application process. For example, under your guidance, the attorney can begin drafting your bank charter. That process alone is likely to take several weeks, since these articles of incorporation and banking bylaws constitute the backbone of your arrangement. The charter should literally spell out the reasons why you have decided to establish the bank, and it must specify all the financial activities that you intend to conduct.

Since you're establishing a new bank, your lawyer will also need to run a check on the bank's proposed name. Far more often than you might think, investors choose a name only to discover that someone else is operating under the same title. In that case, the entire procedure must begin again, but with another name.

Usually, the host government approves a well-drafted charter, but you must submit it for official review. This, too, takes time. If your foreign attorney is well connected within his jurisdiction, you can expect legal authorization within several weeks. If he is not, the process could take several months.

It is common for an independent investor to be sent back to the drawing board. In other words, a foreign government may demand that you recast your entire charter. It's possible, in fact, that you may be denied an operating license altogether. At that point, you're back to square one, and you must look for another offshore jurisdiction.

The bottom line: Don't do it yourself. Go the safer way.

Far more often than you might think, investors choose a name only to discover that someone else is operating under the same title.

THE SCHNEIDER APPROACH

For those of you who want to avoid the hassle of doing all the work yourself as well as avoiding the pitfalls of going out on your own, here is good news. You can hire a qualified consultant or attorney to do all the work for you. You need someone with the expertise to cover all the steps I mentioned above. For sources, you can contact your local bar association or my office in Vancouver. I am always ready to give referrals.

Although I have reduced my consulting time as far as offshore banking is concerned, I do accept a limited number of new clients. What I usually do is help my clients cut down on the months of research and legwork required to establish a bank. I also arrange for an international bank management firm to handle the specific operations of your offshore program.

Frankly, I put a strong emphasis on the availability of such international management because few things can have a greater impact on the ultimate success of a bank than a quality management service. Most of my clients have no firsthand international banking experience. So my recommendation is that they hire a top-notch management team upon whom they can rely for key administrative functions and skilled investment advice. Your management company can also give you foreign exchange privileges and access to wholesale capital markets.

As your consultant, I can eliminate the risk of offshore operation in disadvantageous jurisdictions and secure private banking facilities in island environments supportive of private bank operation. My clients can select from jurisdictions that:

- Impose no income tax, no capital gains tax, no death tax, no stamp duty, no estate duty, and no gift duty.
- Require no previous banking experience on the part of the controlling owner.

- Offer, on a case-by-case basis, an exemption from customary paid-in capital requirements (often totaling $200,000 or more).
- Charge an extremely low annual license renewal fee (sometimes as low as $3,000).
- Allow for bank ownership by nominees or in the form of bearer shares owned by a holding company. Such arrangements help preserve the total anonymity of the actual bank owner.
- Guarantee the strictest bank secrecy law, including a guarantee that information pertaining to past or present banking transactions will never be disclosed; and maintain excellent banking legislation.

SHALL WE MEET?

This has been a book about the profit, privacy, and tax protection available to you through offshore money havens. In this edition of my book, I have tried to review the current state of the U.S. economy. I have also offered a bit of insight into the global economy—those mysterious dynamics by which even countries with opposing political orientations rely on one another financially and face a future of escalating interdependence.

I hope I've managed to fully warn you about the poor financial outlook for our domestic economy. Our national debt keeps growing, while those who owe us money find themselves increasingly unable to meet their commitments. Inflation looms as a constant threat. Even our biggest corporations are often unable to compete effectively with their foreign counterparts. In short, the future is bleak for U.S. investors who confine their financial activity to domestic ventures.

By contrast, I hope I've succeeded in showing you that an offshore involvement will offer benefits that will brighten your economic future. There's more money to be made today than there has ever been. And it's there for a song. But you have to know the tune. Offshore involvement is part of tomorrow's most successful investment strategy. It's the vision of a bright economic future. Best of all, it's legally and affordably available to you today.

So think about it, but don't think too long. Every day, the government closes a few more doors to international profit potential. My advice is to get out there and get started while the laws still allow you to discreetly make a lot of non-taxable money. When I look at the people who have read my books and the clients who have explored investment in the offshore arena, I can tell you that they are all markedly better off today than they were before we met.

When you're ready to get started, let me hear from you. I'd like to be involved in developing your offshore game plan. I think my experience will allow me to offer some worthwhile pointers. I know I could learn from you, by watching you create the international investment package that best suits you and your priorities. So give me a call. Let's get together because, who knows? It could be the start of a great friendship. You can contact me at:

Jerome Schneider
Premier Corporate Services, Ltd.
1185 West Georgia Street, Suite 902
Vancouver, BC, Canada V6E 4E6

Telephone: (604) 682-4000 or (800) 453-2553
Fax: (604) 682-7700

E-mail: info@premiercompanies.net
Web site: www.offshorewealth.com

APPENDIX 1

HOW TO OPEN
A FOREIGN BANK ACCOUNT

Suggest to the average American that he or she might benefit by owning a foreign bank account and you'll more than likely get a questioning look and a response such as, "Why on earth would I want to do that?"

Americans, in my opinion, tend to have an extremely parochial attitude when it comes to their money—and they also tend to have an almost unnatural suspicion of foreign banking activities. After all, the media has exposed them to an unending series of foreign banking tales involving political shenanigans, financial fiascoes, and criminal capers.

Yet the simple fact is most Americans could benefit by owning a foreign bank account. Already, foreign banking—or, as it is more popularly known today, "offshore banking"—has become an important tool for thousands of legitimate and highly successful businesses and individuals.

In practice, a foreign bank account gives the prudent investor the opportunity to synchronize the benefits of various banking activities and blend them into a unique profit-making and tax-saving financial strategy. For the careful and conscientious investor, it is one of the most practical ways of expanding the realm of financial opportunity, because it is one of the most creative ways to diversify assets.

Accounts held in offshore banks are rarely subject to our state and federal laws and regulations. Offshore banks can also offer a wide range of services well beyond the legal ability of domestic banks. Through aggressive use of these services, investors can increase their profits, reduce their tax burdens, and raise capital at lower interest rates—all without the restrictive maze of red tape often encountered in the United States.

A foreign bank account is probably the easiest option to choose, but it may not be the best option. Foreign accounts have no tax protection. All interest one receives must be reported to the IRS. Furthermore, if your account's value exceeds $10,000, the mere existence of the account must be disclosed to the IRS. Failure to adhere to these regulations is a federal offense. That said, a foreign bank account is still a good idea.

SECTION ONE: WHY OPEN A FOREIGN BANK ACCOUNT?

There are a number of legitimate reasons for opening a personal bank account in a foreign country; foremost among them is the fact that maintaining a foreign bank account carries a greater degree of freedom, security, and opportunity than would be possible in the United States. Depending on the depth of one's portfolio, one's penchant for adventurous investing, or one's strategic financial needs, a foreign bank account can provide a varying degree of advantages and conveniences.

Following are some of the principal reasons why an ever-increasing number of savvy U.S. investors are opening one or more foreign bank accounts for themselves. (These are by no means all the reasons, and you may well find additional personal motivations for banking offshore.)

Privacy

Americans who have accumulated any kind of retained wealth are finding it more and more difficult to hold on to their assets. Other people, as well as the federal and state governments, are becoming increasingly nosy about the financial affairs of individual Americans—and the courts are helping them.

The best solution to this ever-increasing assault on your financial well-being is to do your banking in a country safe from the prying eyes of government agents, creditors, competitors, relatives, ex-spouses, and others who might want to appropriate your wealth. In our hyper-litigious society, it's nice to know that your money is in a country where your enemies can't touch it.

Many countries specialize in guaranteeing bank secrecy. Some offshore havens have bank secrecy laws so strict that it is a crime for a bank employee to disclose any information about a bank account to any person other than the owner of the account.

Unfortunately, as some countries have strengthened their secrecy laws, the United States has virtually eliminated bank secrecy. Any transaction involving more than $10,000 must be reported to the U.S. Treasury. Records of transactions involving less than this amount can be subpoenaed by the IRS, litigants in a lawsuit, or anyone else with a real or imagined need to pierce your secrecy.

Thus if you want to maintain real financial privacy, you have little choice but to look offshore, where your bank accounts are protected, rather than opened by the governments and the courts.

Currency Controls

Despite the fact that more than 80 percent of the nations of the world impose some form of currency control, few U.S. citizens have actually experienced the discomfort of living in a country that severely restricts their ability to move their money outside their own borders. However, with annual budget deficits running at $200 billion and with trade imbalances growing steadily larger, the United States may be the next country to clamp a lid on the outward movement of dollars. In fact, we may have already seen the beginning of a trend—under current law, Americans must now complete a customs declaration when taking more than $10,000 overseas.

Thus it only makes good financial sense to move at least a portion of your assets into a foreign country while you still can. Such a move also protects you against the possibility that the U.S. government, at some point in the future, may confiscate a portion of the wealth of its citizens—most likely under the guise of combating drug trafficking or dealing with the underground economy. Citizens living under totalitarian regimes in Latin America and the Middle East have already experienced the trauma such actions can bring—and they would be the first to advise you to move at least a portion of your assets offshore.

Higher Return on Investment

If a foreign bank will give you a better interest rate on your invested money than a U.S. bank, there is little reason to keep your money here. Many foreign banks can offer better interest rates because they're unregulated and can make more lucrative investments with their depositors' funds.

However, dealing with an unregulated bank carries risk. This includes poor consumer protection. For example, one of my faculty members, Donald MacPherson, represents a client who sent a deposit to John Mathewson's bank in the Cayman Islands. The amount represented $1 million, the client's life savings. The $1 million was sent to Mathewson's bank just before the bank and trust were closed by the Cayman Islands monitoring authority. MacPherson had no luck trying to retrieve these funds from Mathewson. Mac then went to the Cayman Islands government for action and received no response. He is now in court trying to receive the funds. On the plus side, foreign banks operate in countries that don't place a premium on lavish offices, high rents, and excessive executive salaries. Thus they are able to pass these savings on to you in the form of higher deposit rates.

Taxes are another important consideration. By maintaining assets in an offshore jurisdiction, the prudent American investor gains tremendous opportunities to realize capital gains—and, by keeping those gains offshore, he or she can also avoid paying taxes on the profits. Many foreign financial centers have earned an international reputation as legal tax havens—and many investors find that the tax benefits of offshore investment activity greatly enhance their financial performance.

Diversification

You would never put all your assets into one investment—it's inherently too risky. Yet most people do all their banking in one country. No one knows what the future will bring. If you hope to hedge your financial security against the unforeseen, it's best to hold your assets in bank accounts in more than one nation.

Have Fun While You Earn

Wouldn't it be nice to vacation in a tropical paradise while doing your banking? Many Americans do. Many of the world's offshore banking centers are located in the world's best vacation spots.

SECTION TWO: DIFFERENT TYPES OF FOREIGN BANK ACCOUNTS

There can be no doubt about the advantages of banking in a foreign country—advantages such as privacy, freedom, diversification, and enhanced investment opportunities. In addition, the American who banks in an offshore locale also enjoys more flexibility in the selection of accounts that can be maintained. The following are just a few of the types of accounts that are offered by most foreign banks.

A Current Account

This is the most common type of foreign bank account—and the one that gives you the most flexibility in managing your funds. It allows you to withdraw all or part of your account balance at any time. Most current accounts pay interest on your balance, though some do not. Many current accounts can be maintained in U.S. dollars, or they can be held in a host of foreign currencies; some offer "multicurrency" privileges, meaning you can deposit or withdraw funds in your choice of currencies.

Most current accounts provide you with checking privileges, and some foreign banks provide you with a check card (the most popular of which is the Eurocard), which permits you to write checks anywhere up to a certain amount. You usually receive a statement of your account's activity semiannually.

Regardless of the complexity of your international business, you should have at least one current account.

Deposit Account

A deposit account is a savings account in a foreign country. The account will pay you interest, but the rate of interest will vary according to the currency in which the account is denominated and the length of time for which the money is deposited. Generally, the longer the money is deposited, the higher the interest rate. Most deposit accounts require a minimum deposit of $5,000 or more.

Deposit accounts are not as liquid as current accounts, and you may be prevented from withdrawing your money for a period of time. As with a current account, you will receive a semiannual statement of the account's activity.

Numbered Account

Switzerland, Belgium, Luxembourg, and Mexico all provide numbered accounts. A numbered account is an account identified by a number, rather than by a name. To that extent, it provides a certain amount of protection and privacy, especially if bank records or passbooks are lost, stolen, or obtained under duress.

It's important to remember what a numbered account is not: A numbered account doesn't mean that no one at the bank knows who the real owner of the account is. It just means that the junior people at the bank, who handle the transactions, don't know your identity.

Safekeeping Accounts

A safekeeping account is one in which you deposit such things as bonds, stocks, and other valuables. The bank will clip the coupons, redeem the bonds, and do whatever needs to be done with the valuables entrusted to them. The bank will charge you for the service, something in the range of 0.015 percent of the market value of the securities or other assets they are safekeeping.

Commodities Account

Some of the larger foreign banks have geared themselves up to trade in commodities on your behalf. (This is a prime example of the freedom foreign banks have to operate, as contrasted to the restrictions imposed on U.S. banks.) They're set up to give you the latest commodities prices, and to let you buy and sell commodities over the phone.

Managed Accounts

Many of the larger foreign banks also offer a variety of managed accounts, wherein you entrust your money to the bank's investment advisers and they choose the types of investments, based on your objectives and investment goals. Managed accounts are offered for stocks, currencies, debt instruments, commodities, or combinations. Again, the bank charges for this service, with fees usually based on a percentage of the funds under management.

A bit of caution about managed accounts applies here. The same rules of prudence that you would adhere to in selecting a U.S. stockbroker should definitely apply to selecting an overseas manager for your portfolio of stocks and investments. You're not likely to have the NASD, SEC, or any other regulatory agencies disclose the overseas manager's disciplinary history, since managed accounts fall under offshore banking. Therefore choose your manager carefully. Be careful about commission, receiving monthly statements, and not being sold financial products that are not readily tradable on a stock exchange. For example, a lot of Swiss banks sell unusual securities that cannot be readily traded.

The previous list represents only the tip of the iceberg. There are countless types of accounts and services—including such familiar American-style amenities as automated tellers and Visa and MasterCard accounts—that foreign banks can provide for you. And the number of such services is growing annually.

SECTION THREE: HOW TO OPEN A FOREIGN BANK ACCOUNT

Before you can actually open one of the accounts we've just discussed, you must take some time to select both a foreign country and a foreign bank for your account. (An evaluation of some of the major offshore financial centers is featured in chapter 10, and a list of many of the leading overseas banks is provided in appendix 3.)

If you plan to visit the country in which you'll be banking, you should check out a number of banks. Insist on meeting with a director of each bank you visit. If they won't meet with you, don't give them your business. Whether you visit or can only correspond by mail, here are some of the criteria you should consider when selecting a bank:

- Does it provide the banking services you require? For example, if you need to earn interest on your current account, and also require a check card, keep searching until you find a bank that will provide both services. One of the best sources of leads is the *Rand McNally International Banker's Directory*.

- How large is the bank? There are trade-offs here. A larger, more established bank may offer greater security than a smaller bank, but at a price—the larger bank may pay a lower interest rate and charge you higher fees for its services.

- How secure is your investment? Deposit insurance is not nearly as prevalent overseas as it is in the United States. If you require that your account be insured, you should inquire specifically as to the types of accounts that are insured and the investment limitations. Local insurance regulations can be confusing. For example, most Swiss banks do not provide insurance, but some Swiss cantonal (i.e., regional) banks do. Be aware, too, that the absence of deposit insurance can actually be an advantage since banks must employ prudent investment and business practices in order to successfully compete and remain in business. In the United States, banks can be inefficient and poorly managed and can follow imprudent investment strategies because they know the government will rectify their mistakes.

- How easily will you be able to communicate with your bank? There's no problem here if you plan on doing all your overseas banking in person. However, if you'll need to communicate with bank officials by mail, it's important to establish whether the officials will communicate with you in English. Even if they do, some offshore banking centers are so remote that mail, courier, and even telephone communications are tenuous. There's nothing more frustrating than needing to conduct a banking transaction and not being able to get through to your bank.

Once you've narrowed down the possibilities, the next step (assuming you won't be visiting the bank) is to send each bank a short, typed letter. The letter should state that you are interested in opening a certain type of account. You should ask about the following:

- The fees that the bank charges—both to open and to maintain an account.
- The minimum balance required to maintain an account.
- The currencies in which an account can be maintained, and the ease or difficulty of switching from one currency to another.
- The extent to which the account will be insured, and who will insure it.

Ask about how the bank will communicate with you, and you with it. Some banks will provide you with a telex code, which will allow you to give the bank instructions and conduct normal banking business without revealing your identity. The use of the code also assures the bank that it is dealing with you and not someone who wants your money.

You also may wish to ask about any other services the bank provides, such as a check card, credit cards, safe deposit boxes, etc.

The first thing you'll receive from most banks in response to your letter is an account application form (see page 437) and signature cards, similar to the forms needed to open an account in the United States. Some banks may also require letters of reference. Be wary of this—the more information you have to reveal, the lower your level of confidentiality. If you plan on opening a corporate account (one whose owner is a corporation), you may have to provide proof that the corporation is in existence and minutes of resolutions from the board of directors authorizing the account.

You may wish to consider keeping an account in a fictitious name. Before you do, you should inquire into the laws of the country in which you'll be banking. Many countries prohibit accounts with fictitious names, even those countries with strong bank secrecy laws.

You may also wish to open an account for a minor. Before you do, check with the bank to determine their local rules regarding an adult maintaining an account for a minor.

Since almost every bank requires a minimum deposit to open an account, you'll have to send money with the application form and the signature cards. The guidance for the initial deposit is the same for any subsequent transmittal of funds. Wire transfers are the best way to do it—they are more secure than sending checks or money orders through the mail, and there is a minimal loss of interest (your local bank will, however, charge you for the wire). The overseas bank should provide you with wire transfer instructions.

If you use the mail to send checks, have the checks made out to you, endorsed: "For deposit only at Bank for the account of _____." Whenever you mail funds, the mail should be preceded by a fax transmission, alerting the bank that a deposit is in the mail, and stating the amount of the deposit and any further instructions you deem helpful to the bank's personnel. (Note: If you send more than $10,000 overseas, your bank is required under the Bank Secrecy Act to report the transaction to the U.S. Treasury. Under current law, they are not required to report a wire transfer, regardless of the amount.)

If you are opening a managed account of any kind, the bank may also require you to grant it a power of attorney over the assets in the account. If so, make sure the power of attorney is specific and offers protections for both you and the bank. (A sample power of attorney form can be found on page 438.)

SECTION FOUR: SOME SUGGESTIONS ON HANDLING YOUR ACCOUNT

There are as many different particular investment needs as there are investors, so it is impossible to tell you exactly how to handle your foreign bank account. However, here are some general tips that should apply in almost every instance:

- Start conservative. If you've never had an overseas bank account, start out by being a conservative investor. I suggest starting out with an account denominated in U.S. dollars. Place only a fraction of the amount you have available for savings in an overseas account until you ascertain you are comfortable with the concept, the country, and the bank. If, after six months or so, you're comfortable, you can add to the account or open a different account. I advise against such activities as commodities accounts until you have your feet on the ground and are comfortable with your overseas banker.

- Diversify. Once you're comfortable overseas, you should consider diversifying your overseas holdings. This may result in your spreading out the countries in which you do your banking, or at least diversifying the currencies in which you invest. There is one downside to diversification—the more you have in any account, the higher the rate of interest you'll usually earn, and diversifying obviously reduces your account size. Thus, it's important to diversify in such a way that your effective rate of interest is reduced as little as possible.

- Consider a managed account. If you are unfamiliar with the foreign investment markets and unaccustomed to dealing in foreign currencies, you may want to consider opening a managed, or discretionary, account—one where your banker is given the authority to invest your funds on your behalf. Of course, your banker will charge you for the service, but you will get the benefit of his expertise.

You should never open a discretionary account by mail. It is essential that you get to know your funds manager and that he gets to know you. Only after you're comfortable with his investment philosophy and background should you entrust any funds to him.

If your investment philosophy is conservative in nature, a Swiss managed account may be for you. The Swiss reputation for conservatism is well earned (though recent changes in Swiss attitudes toward secrecy have diminished the appeal of Swiss bank accounts).

SECTION FIVE: TRANSFERRING MONEY ANONYMOUSLY

Moving money around the world anonymously can be a boon to privacy and convenience. There are many ways to do it, but there are three ways not to do it. Over the years, each of these notorious methods has acquired its own special name.

1. The Richard Nixon Method. Former U.S. President Richard M. Nixon's Committee to Re-elect the President (CREEP) actually encouraged various large American businesses to use offshore companies to donate anonymous cash for the campaign.

CREEP's fund-raising was headed by U.S. Commerce Secretary Maurice Stans and Attorney General John Mitchell. Stans and Mitchell naturally preferred cash-in-hand contributions because there could be no processed checks to connect the campaign to its sometimes highly suspect sponsors. Anonymous cash also concealed the near-blackmail efforts CREEP used to solicit donations.

For example, CREEP put the squeeze on George Spater, then-chair and CEO of American Airlines, for $100,000 in cash. Spater was then faced with the task of finding a way to divert corporate funds without alerting the company's internal auditors. So he simply arranged to have a Lebanese corporation called Amarco submit a phony invoice for a commission allegedly earned on the sale of airplane parts to a Mideast airline.

American Airlines paid the invoice. Amarco deposited the money in its Swiss bank account, and then wired it to its U.S. dollar account in New York. After it arrived, Amarco's agent withdrew the $100,000 in cash and handed it to Spater, who dutifully handed it over to Stans and Mitchell.

American Airlines' auditors never questioned the transaction. And if the whole tawdry story of the Nixon fund-raising effort had not come out in the aftermath of Watergate, the true nature of this transaction would have remained a secret to this day.

2. The Oliver North Method. In the mid-1980s, the Reagan administration wanted to support the Nicaraguan Contra rebels who were fighting a jungle insurgency against the country's leftist Sandinista government. But an amendment passed by the U.S. Congress specifically outlawed sending any U.S. government funds to aid the Contras.

Stripped to its essentials, the administration's problem was identical to the one faced by George Spater: How to move money from here to there in such a way that its origins could not be traced? The solution: They used a Panamanian offshore company called Lake Resources.

The architect of this particular scheme was Marine Lt. Col. Oliver North, then a National Security aide to the Reagan White House. With his partners—Air Force Gen. Richard Secord and businessman Albert Hakim—North bought 2,000 high-tech American antitank missiles from the CIA for $12 million. North then sold these missiles to

Iran for $30 million. (North considered the sale as harmless to U.S. interests because he knew the missiles would be used in Iran's ongoing war with Iraq.)

Iran paid the money into Lake Resources' Swiss bank account, which sent the profits on to the Contras. Because the offshore company was not subject to U.S. tax scrutiny, this transaction would also never have come to light had it not been uncovered by politically motivated snooping.

3. The CIA Method. In 1947 U.S. President Harry Truman signed the National Security Act that created the CIA. It wasn't long before a pressing need arose to transfer funds from here to there in a way that could not be traced.

In 1953 the United States sought to overthrow Iran's Mossadegh regime and put the shah back on the Peacock Throne. But the Eisenhower administration could scarcely ask Congress to appropriate money for such a venture. To secretly funnel U.S. funds anywhere in the world, the CIA eventually created a vast network of private offshore corporations—many of which are controlled by former military and ex-CIA personnel.

Such companies helped obscure the origins of the funds used in President Kennedy's well-documented attempts to assassinate Cuba's Fidel Castro and Ronald Reagan's attempts to get rid of Libya's Mu'ammar Qaddafi.

The most famous of the CIA's clandestine offshore ventures was Air America, the Southeast Asian airline that functioned as a front for all manner of intelligence-related matters during the Vietnam War era.

The U.S. government isn't alone in its use of offshore banks and companies. Most other governments do the same thing for the same reasons. During the Cold War, governments on both sides of the Iron Curtain used hundreds of offshore banks and companies for just this reason.

As you can see from the three methods I've outlined, I cannot recommend a way to transfer money anonymously. Whatever you do, you must always follow reporting requirements.

SECTION SIX: REPORTING REQUIREMENTS

You may have noticed on your Form 1040 personal income tax return the following question: "Did you have at any time during the taxable year a financial interest in or signature authority over a bank, securities, or other financial account in a foreign country?"

If the answer is yes, and you have $10,000 or more in a foreign account (or a foreign credit card account with a limit of $10,000 or more), you must file Form 90-22.1 by June 30 of the year following any year in which you had the account. (A copy of the form can be conveniently downloaded from the IRS Web site at www.irs.gov/forms_pubs/forms.html.) There is a stiff fine—and the possibility of criminal prosecution—for failure to file this form. The form cannot be obtained from the IRS by your creditors or by opponents in a lawsuit.

If you physically transport more than $10,000 outside of the United States, you'll have to fill out an appropriate customs declaration. There is nothing, in and of itself, illegal about moving money outside of the United States—you violate the law only if you fail to declare it. The declaration requirement applies if you mail, ship, or carry bearer securities, traveler's checks, or cash.

SECTION SEVEN: A BRIEF REVIEW OF OVERSEAS BANKING CENTERS

Here is a list of some countries that want to do business with foreigners. Each of these countries has done something to make itself attractive to overseas investors. The list is by no means complete, and it changes rapidly.

Austria

Located in central Europe, Austria has a reputation as one of the most politically and financially stable countries in Europe. Austrian bank accounts are freely convertible from one currency to another, which makes them attractive. Austrian bankers also have a strong commitment to privacy, yet Austrian bank accounts are seldom viewed with the same suspicion that might be engendered by an account in other jurisdictions. Austria's bank secrecy law is very strict in that it is a crime for any Austrian bank official to reveal information on an account without authority. However, they will reveal information to a foreign government in the context of a criminal investigation or an investigation regarding tax evasion.

Bahamas

Now an independent nation in the northern Caribbean, the Bahamas has made itself into one of the premier offshore banking centers of the world. Bahamian banks are modern and efficient, and communications with the United States and the rest of the world are excellent. The country is also a tax haven and attracts all aspects of international business as well as banking. Adjuncts of all kinds are available, in any currency. There are no foreign exchange controls. The Bahamas has a strong bank secrecy law. However, it is newly independent and has a vocal left-wing minority, and cannot be considered as politically stable as other countries.

Bermuda

Of all the tax and banking havens in close proximity to the United States, Bermuda is the oldest and has the best reputation. Located 570 miles southeast of Cape Hatteras, it is conveniently located for most U.S. investors, and it boasts excellent banking and communications facilities. Bermuda has no exchange controls; accounts may be kept in any currency; and no taxes are imposed on interest earned by nonresidents.

Cayman Islands

Located due south of Cuba, these three little islands have one major industry: international banking. This is no fluke; the government does everything it can to nurture the industry. Funds may be transported out of the Caymans free of any reporting requirement, and accounts can be maintained in any currency. Travel, hotel, and communications services are excellent. The Caymans also have what may be the strongest bank secrecy law in the world. However, even the Caymans have recently had to knuckle under to pressure from the U.S. government, and local banks will cooperate with U.S. criminal and tax investigations. It is relatively easy for a nonresident to form a bank in the Caymans. Consequently, you should exercise extra caution when choosing a bank located in the Caymans.

Channel Islands

The Channel Islands are eight small islands in the English Channel, the most important of which are Jersey and Guernsey. Except for defense and foreign policy, the Channel Islands are independent from Great Britain. Over the years, Channel Islands banks have developed an excellent reputation for secrecy and probity in the handling of offshore investors' business. As a result, it is the principal offshore financial center for British citizens.

There is no taxation of interest paid to foreigners and no exchange controls, and accounts may be maintained in any currency.

Singapore

Singapore is an island nation on the eastern edge of the Malay Peninsula. It has been independent since 1965, and it is politically and economically stable, as well as being one of the busiest ports in the Pacific. The government has worked hard to make Singapore an international banking center. Communications are excellent. There are no taxes on interest earned by nonresidents, and it is relatively easy to open an account in any currency.

Other Locations

There are approximately 45 other jurisdictions around the world that bill themselves as offshore financial centers or banking havens. However, many of these centers are remote, lack adequate support facilities, or have flaws in their banking or tax laws that could affect your privacy or your rate of investment return. That does not necessarily mean you should avoid banks in these jurisdictions when shopping for a location for your foreign bank account. However, it does mean that you should exercise additional caution, making sure the bank is well managed and offers the services, experience, and security you are seeking.

APPENDIX 2

HOW TO USE TAX HAVENS LEGALLY FROM CANADA

On a recent visit to Canada, a manufacturer told me it was impossible for him to be profitable in his business at current Canadian tax rates—and that the situation was getting worse. His concern—and that of so many other businesspeople—is that the tax bite leaves insufficient cash for reinvestment. I've heard similar tales of concern before, and all too often they end up with a comment such as: "If only we could use tax havens like the Americans in your book do."

The truth is that Canadians can use tax havens legally and profitably, as you'll read in this appendix. You'll discover exactly how it can be done, including facts on the exciting potential that exists to save on taxes. Here and there, the details may get a little legalistic and boring, but you'll have all the technical information you need to be assured that tax havens do work for Canadians. What's more, you'll learn about the many exciting ways to put these legalistic details into fun and profitable practice.

For example, merely creating a foreign sales and marketing subsidiary for your Canadian company can reduce the tax rate from 45 percent to 2.5 percent! On a profit of $750,000, after paying the tax haven country only $18,750 in taxes, there is a $731,250 profit that can be remitted to Canada—without paying any Canadian taxes.

For a variety of reasons, Canadians now earning $100,000 or more annually can profit greatly by creating foreign-based tax-reduction devices: sophisticated legal arrangements that can also double as successful asset-protection mechanisms. The bigger tax bite means those whose income places them in the upper reaches of Canada's middle class—lawyers, doctors, dentists, airline pilots, professionals in general—should seriously consider "going offshore" as a means of generating immediate tax savings. Reductions of as much as half of an individual's total annual income tax bill are possible!

Is Tax "Avoidance" Legal?

To the uninitiated, the exotic phrase "tax haven" may evoke a mental picture of some far-off corner of the world, populated with secretive millionaires who spend their days sipping daiquiris on the beach, their cash secure in numbered Swiss bank accounts. Not so. As we have seen, tax havens are no longer the exclusive playground of the ultrarich. Canadians can play. In fact, those of a bit more than average means ($100,000-plus in annual income) can now at least partially escape the clutches of Revenue Canada (RC) by joining the modern financial jet set.

As federal government powers continue to expand, swallowing individual human rights, the national deficit and income taxes grow apace. Intelligent individuals seek protection for their hard-earned income and assets. While the tabloid media love to tattle about celebrity "tax evaders," a very important point is ignored: Tax evasion is illegal. Tax avoidance is not. This is a crucial distinction lost on many people.

Because of the potential for tax avoidance, tax havens should be of great interest to the international investor—yet too few Canadians of wealth understand and use them properly. Some disregard tax havens as hiding holes for dirty money, which is certainly not a legitimate use. Others think tax havens are only for banking money after you have earned it. Not true either. Canada's wealthiest families and largest corporations have been using tax havens profitably for a long time—and you can, too.

Your money grows much faster if you include a tax haven in your planning, and almost any international investor can create an opportunity to use one. It is the purely domestic investor, confined by uninformed choice to one country, who fails to benefit from the many available international tax savings.

Most often, people tend to make the move offshore one step at a time. They open an offshore bank or brokerage account, then consider an offshore trust, and finally begin thinking about engaging in offshore business activities. A better approach for most wealthy individuals is to look at an overall offshore strategy—one that employs trusts, bank accounts, business operations, and/or other activities to provide real protection for personal assets, as well as both corporate and individual tax savings. To give you an idea of the possibilities, the remainder of this appendix will provide an overview of the various types of offshore structures available for use by Canadians.

OWNING YOUR OWN OFFSHORE BANK

Suppose you don't want to simply open a foreign bank account. Suppose you want to bank offshore, but you

want more control of your money. One option is ownership of an offshore bank.

Owning a bank is a lot easier in many countries than
it is in Canada. Some countries cater to individual foreigners who want to own banks, streamlining chartering
rules and making the cost affordable (approximately
$40,000). A privately owned bank can take deposits, make
loans, issue letters of credit, and invest money—just like
the major players.

And here's the best part for Canadian taxpayers:
Offshore banking income is not presently taxed until it is
paid to the owners. If you set up the bank in the right
country, your taxes will be low in your home country.
Careful investing and use of tax treaties should eliminate
or reduce taxes from other countries.

To qualify for the income tax exception, however,
your bank must conduct real business. This means you
have to solicit business from independent parties. You
have to get deposits and make loans. If the parties
involved are not independent of the bank's owners, RC
likely will say it is simply an offshore investment corporation and not a bank, and will tax the shareholders on
the corporation's income.

To start a foreign bank properly, you need professional advice to select the right country for incorporation
and to find six employees who will work for your bank
full-time, which is required under Canadian tax law. One
of the real advantages of an offshore bank is that you do
not need a walk-in retail operation, like your neighborhood bank. Most offshore banking transactions are done
through modern electronic communications. The occasional client who wants to visit the bank will be satisfied
with an office that looks like any other professional office.

If you are serious about operating an offshore
bank—and if you seek help from someone who is fully
informed on the international banking situation—you
might find that your own private offshore bank is the
ultimate opportunity.

THE TAX BITE

Upper-income Canadians are driven to seek new tax-reduction methods because of a constantly increasing tax bite on individual income (in excess of 50 percent in some cases) and on corporations (now as high as 45 percent). The effective combined federal/provincial personal tax rate in Ontario, for example, is 52.35 percent this year. The elimination of the $100,000 capital-gains tax exemption, which took effect with the 1995 federal budget, spurred thousands more beleaguered upper-income taxpayers to consider ways and means to escape what rapidly became confiscation, rather than just mere taxation.

Still another incentive for moving business abroad is the possibility of the reimposition of federal or provincial estate taxes. Although the federal estate tax was abolished in 1971, several provinces continued these taxes until the last one was repealed by Quebec in 1986. Now, however, there is talk of imposing new death taxes—especially in Ontario.

ATTRACTIONS ABROAD

As if you need more reason to be disturbed about the trend of government, just compare the outrageously high Canadian income taxes with those imposed in many foreign countries, where rates for the same income and corporate taxes are in the low single digits. Prudent Canadians can take advantage of this wide international tax disparity by establishing an offshore tax shelter that can easily double disposable after-tax income. This feat can be accomplished in full compliance with federal law and the tax code so that RC cannot mount a successful challenge—although, based on recent history, RC may well go after anything it considers to be an "overly aggressive tax strategy."

In addition, various proposals for further tax law changes are pending, although it is interesting to note that changes proposed in February 1994 were revised again in June 1994, before even being presented to Parliament. What is clear from these new proposals, however, is that future Canadian law will tend to follow American law, with the use of tax havens for individuals being limited, but no restrictions being imposed to prevent corporations from using tax havens for their legitimate business. Thus whatever form the law finally takes when adopted, opportunities will continue to exist for offshore business-related activity.

TO PROTECT WHAT YOU HAVE

Another reason Canadian taxpayers are eyeing other parts of the world is the increasing problem of individual personal asset protection.

Professional malpractice suits, nasty divorce proceedings, legislative and judicial imposition of no-fault personal liability on corporate officers and directors—these are now common occurrences of everyday life. Any active business or professional person can suddenly find himself or herself held responsible for unforeseen obligations flowing from a company's environmental pollution, bank failures, dissatisfied clients, or just a disgruntled employee. Premiums for professional malpractice insurance have gone through the roof.

In this unpredictable climate, astute people are forced to find new ways to protect their personal assets. Legal offshore mechanisms, called "asset protection trusts," are available to do just that. (Note: The proposed new changes in Canadian tax law will not affect asset protection trusts for individuals, as they are generally tax neutral.)

A NEED FOR CAUTION

The objective of an offshore tax haven is the legal reduction of your tax obligations.

Keep in mind: It will do you no good to suffer the bother of extensively restructuring your personal economic life only to find yourself embroiled in years of complex and expensive court battles with RC—or worse, finding yourself facing criminal charges for tax evasion or a variety of other possible tax crimes.

Reasonable caution places a premium on following the right path by relying on competent expert advice. Cutting corners can only mean you and your financial advisers could be headed for deep trouble.

For example, one of the easiest methods to avoid taxes is to transfer your cash to a bank in the United States, then simply fail to declare the interest paid to you when you file your income tax forms. There is only one major problem with this: It is against the law. Of course, since U.S. banks issue no tax receipts to nonresident alien account holders, it is all but impossible for Canadian authorities to discover your nice little scheme. But if they do—watch out. They usually do find out because an underpaid secretary or a spouse in a divorce case decides to tell them.

DON'T DO ILLEGALLY WHAT YOU CAN DO LEGALLY

The most dangerous attitude one can adopt when dealing with the establishment of offshore business arrangements is the cavalier approach. This is the idea that white-collar crimes are somehow less serious than violent crimes, such as bank robbery; or the notion that the federal government is less concerned about tax or financial offenses than other civil wrongs. The truth is, the chances of getting away with fudging on Canadian domestic tax laws—even as they apply offshore—are minimal at best. There are many court cases to prove this point. And don't think geographic distance offers sure protection for those who want to bend the law by going offshore. During the last 15 years, Canada has rapidly expanded its tax-treaty relations—bilateral and multilateral—aimed at stifling both tax avoidance and tax evasion. Canada now has more than 60 mutual tax agreements in force (or under negotiation) with foreign governments. Canadian courts display a stiff attitude toward tax scofflaws, and the judicial long arm reaches across oceans. For example, the Canadian Supreme Court held (in *Robert Spencer v. R*, 85 DTC 5446) that the former manager of the Freeport branch of the Canadian Royal Bank could be forced to give testimony at a tax-evasion trial in Canada, even though doing so would be a breach of Bahamian bank secrecy laws.

New and powerful laws aimed at tax avoidance practices have aided the federal government and RC's vigorous international tax enforcement efforts. For example:

- Laws were changed to extend the statute of limitations on government questioning of certain offshore tax transactions from three to six years.

- RC was given greatly increased powers to obtain "foreign-based information or documents" about a Canadian citizen's business activities abroad.

- Elaborate, detailed annual corporate reporting requirements were imposed on "intercompany transactions" between Canadians and any offshore affiliated entities. Failure to report, or false statements concerning such transactions, can result in fines of up to $24,000.

Revenue Canada keeps an eagle eye on the tax-shelter industry and tracks the offshore business activity of individual Canadians as best it can. RC spokesperson

Luce Morin means it when she says, "This department is concerned about any kind of tax shelter."

Whether RC, employing its own informational sources, finds out about offshore activity or not, reporting requirements concerning foreign investments place personal responsibility squarely on taxpayers to reveal what they are doing abroad, or suffer the legal consequences if they get caught.

In spite of these tough federal tax-enforcement policies and an array of laws with sharp teeth, there are still many lawful opportunities for offshore financial activities designed to minimize the impact of Canada's high tax rates. Offshore tax havens are legal. In selective circumstances, there are useful ways in which nonresident-owned international investment and business structures can serve you by substantially reducing your exposure to Canada's high taxes.

THE CANADIAN TAX SYSTEM

The tax system of Canada is comprehensive and, as I have pointed out, imposes burdensome tax rates on the income of individuals (over 50 percent) and corporations (up to 45 percent).

Canada taxes the worldwide income of its residents—citizens and resident aliens alike—who are resident in Canada at any time during the year. Residents include individuals, corporations, and trusts. Nonresidents are also taxed on income from employment, business, and certain capital assets located in Canada. Canadian citizens employed abroad, even for extended periods of time, have been held liable for domestic income taxes, though double taxation credits are permitted when taxes are paid abroad. Any person who spends 183 days or more in Canada in a year is deemed to be a resident for income tax purposes.

From the 1997 taxation year, Canadians face additional disclosure requirements for offshore property and offshore investments valued at $100,000 or more. These new reporting rules seem to have intimidated the Hong Kong Chinese who immigrated to Canada in droves since 1988. For the most part, the rules appear to be straightforward and do not invite additional scrutiny, nor remove any of the tax benefits.

TAX SHELTERS UNDER SIEGE

Parliament, even when under Conservative control, has had a record in recent years of cracking down on tax shelters, particularly those operating domestically. Its actions include the 1988 adoption of the infamous "General Anti-Avoidance Rule."

This radical rule gives RC the discretionary retroactive power to revisit and recharacterize for increased taxation purposes any business transaction that RC interprets as having no "bona fide purpose," other than to effect a tax savings. This places squarely on business the burden of demonstrating a "bona fide purpose" (other than tax savings) in order to obtain that savings. And, as you might imagine, there have been more than a few court cases contesting the rule's application, scope, and still unsettled meaning. That this draconian rule even exists should give you an accurate idea of the essence—and the direction—of federal tax policy.

Strangely enough, the federal anti-tax shelter attitude generally has not extended to offshore tax entities, still governed for the most part by the Foreign Affiliate System statute, which has been law since 1972. As you will see, this law allows plenty of room for legitimate international tax planning designed to minimize domestic taxes by using Canadian-foreign affiliate company profit sharing and dividend distributions.

IS THERE AN OFFSHORE TAX SHELTER FOR YOU?

No one, probably including RC, knows for sure how many Canadians now have established—or are in the process of setting up—some form of offshore tax shelter.

However, there is definitely a rush of offshore-bound taxpayers, as indicated by booming attendance at tax-haven seminars, sales of books on the subject, and the number of foreign bankers suddenly arriving here seeking Canadian business. Every increase in the tax rates means another layer of upper-income taxpayers finds it affordable to recoup their tax losses by setting up an offshore tax-savings mechanism. Where that should be done, as we will discuss, is a matter of choice. There are several excellent foreign locations to consider.

Among the foreign jurisdictions that are popular tax-shelter destinations for Canadians are Barbados, the Cayman Islands, and the Turks and Caicos—all Caribbean favorites. European choices include Ireland, the Netherlands, and the Channel Islands. All of these foreign bailiwicks have exceptionally low tax rates on corporate and personal income earned by foreign nationals, as well as other attractions to make them economically feasible for offshore Canadian operations.

One thing should be understood: Going offshore is not cheap. Start-up and annual operating costs can be considerable, depending on the form of shelter employed. Before you decide on an offshore plan, these costs must be realistically calculated against tax savings and other expenses—including the possible need to defend your tax shelter against attack by RC. However, if you can cut your taxes by half, that should finance much of your initial cost; after that, the net results will be like receiving an annual bonus. So this isn't something to measure in absolute dollars spent, but in percentage of savings—at which point it becomes extremely profitable.

TAX HAVEN OR "SHAM"?

Before you start planning how to spend the increased income that will start rolling in from your offshore tax haven, you should understand four very basic rules of the game laid down by Canadian law—and strictly enforced by RC. These rules apply to all offshore tax shelters— both corporations and trusts—and are aimed at abuse of such operations.

1. Residence. A corporation or a trust, even though created in a foreign country under that country's laws, whose effective management is in Canada, will be taxed on its entire income and capital gains as if it were a resident of Canada.

This means actual control and management must be located within the foreign country, and all legal formalities must be observed. You are not prevented as a Canadian citizen from being a shareholder, officer, or director of an offshore company, but proving foreign control, on paper and in fact, is essential.

2. Artificiality. There must be a demonstrably credible reason for the operations of the corporation or trust in the foreign country, other than mere tax avoidance. If there isn't one, Revenue Canada will hold it to be a sham and tax it as a Canadian resident. This means there must be a legitimate purpose, a functioning business, a board of directors, an office and staff, and all the other trappings of corporate life.

When there is a legitimate business purpose, there will be no Canadian taxes on any income from a corporation based in a tax-haven country until it is actually paid to the Canadian resident in the form of salary or dividends. There is no penalty for accumulation of capital in the foreign company, and no rules that require capital distribution.

This means that until the Canadian owner needs money for his or her use, or until they sell the foreign business, taxes on these earnings can be deferred indefinitely, even for decades. Owners who want the money right away can be paid dividends, on which the Canadian tax is 36 percent, well below the income tax rate of 50 percent plus.

It is worth underscoring that if a Canadian corporation has a foreign affiliate company in a country where Canada has a reciprocal tax agreement (nearly 60 nations are now listed by RC), any dividends paid out of the affiliate's exempt surplus (essentially meaning profits from current income) will be tax-free if paid in Canada to a corporate shareholder.

For example, an Irish foreign affiliate manufacturing for export to the United Kingdom—and enjoying a tax holiday under liberal Irish business-incentive laws—or a Barbadian, Cypriot, or Jamaican foreign affiliate qualifying under the domestic tax-incentive laws of those nations can easily generate surplus dividends not taxable in Canada to a Canadian corporate shareholder. This is a major and very profitable tax savings in many instances.

Dividends paid by a tax-haven affiliate company to a Canadian corporate shareholder are treated as exempt surplus and are tax-free to the Canadian company—a major boon for tax planning and tax reduction. Interest and royalties paid between two such affiliated companies are also tax-free. For example, loan interest paid by a U.S. affiliate to a Canadian company is subject to a 15 percent gross tax, but the same U.S. payment routed through a Netherlands affiliate corporation to its Canadian affiliate company would be tax-free. It is worth noting that Canada does not tax foreign affiliates that are, in fact, holding companies.

3. Foreign Accrual Property Income. In order to regulate offshore financial activity by individual Canadians, the federal government in 1976 promulgated the Foreign Accrual Property Income—known fondly to RC and accountants as FAPI. The FAPI bottom line requires reporting on income tax forms any "foreign accrual property income," especially "passive" income from offshore investments of any kind. This is so even if the income is not transferred back to Canada, even if the money only accumulates abroad in a foreign trust or corporate account. Depending on the applicable provision of law, such foreign income may or may not be taxable; but regardless of any tax liability, every dollar of it must be reported.

Personal foreign accrual property income not only must be reported, but certain types of FAPI (as defined by law) from a Canadian-controlled foreign corporate affiliate, and from certain specified foreign trusts, is currently taxable to Canadian shareholders or trust beneficiaries, whether or not that income is actually remitted to Canada. This covers Canadian investors, regardless of how many shares they own, who have passive interests in offshore investment corporations. While the entire actual net profit of the offshore investment company is not taxed proportionally to each shareholder, there is a complicated RC formula that apportions annual tax liability. Together with annual FAPI reporting requirements, this annual offshore investment tax has dampened Canadian enthusiasm for foreign ventures devoted solely to producing investment income.

4. Intercompany Pricing. There can be no overpricing charged by a foreign parent company—for example, for exporting goods from a Canadian subsidiary for international sales. (Tax-haven companies created solely for importing into Canada were subjected to full Canadian taxes beginning in 1972.) Overpricing has been a popular, but illegal, tactic used in an attempt to shift capital from parent companies in high-tax Canada to the low-tax offshore affiliate. RC has gone to court repeatedly to challenge such schemes, albeit with mixed results.

In cases of offshore trading in which a Canadian-affiliated tax-haven company transfers goods between two other countries, RC authorities always watch very closely and often conduct annual audits. Even if the tax-haven company survives the RC residency and sham tests, it may fail the intercompany pricing regulations, especially if Canada is involved in one leg of the shipping triangle as an importer or exporter. Of course, when Canada is "out of the loop," as when an affiliate in the Channel Islands is shipping Scottish woolens to Europe, such pricing regulations don't apply and neither do the taxes.

All this may sound discouraging, but it can be done! Here's how.

USING FOREIGN TAX HAVENS—LEGITIMATELY

Simply stated, a tax haven is any country whose laws, regulations, traditions, and (usually) international treaty arrangements make it possible for any person or corporation, domestic or foreign, to reduce their overall tax burden. This general definition, however, covers many types of tax havens, and it is important to understand the differences.

"No-Tax" Havens

These are countries with no personal or corporate income, capital gains, or wealth (capital) taxes, where you can easily incorporate and/or form a trust. The governments of these countries do earn some revenue from corporations and they may impose small fees on documents of incorporation, a charge on the value of corporate shares, and annual registration fees. Primary examples are Caribbean countries such as Bermuda, the Bahamas, and the Cayman Islands.

Consider, for example, the Cayman Islands tax structure. There are no taxes levied except stamp taxes on certain transactions and import duties. Nonresidents who form exempted corporations automatically qualify for and receive a government guarantee of no taxes for 20 years; trusts are given a 50-year, no-tax guarantee.

The process of incorporation is quick, simple, and relatively inexpensive. It can be done in a matter of hours at the office of the Registrar of Companies in George Town, the capital city located on Grand Cayman Island, only 475 air miles from Miami International Airport. There is a registration fee and an annual operating fee thereafter. Start-up costs can run as low as $2,500, with a yearly operating cost of about $1,000. Establishing a trust can cost as little as $2,000. The Cayman Islands' corporation and trust statutes allow a wide range of business activities, stock issues, and great flexibility in actual operation.

The Cayman Islands are noted for laws strongly protecting corporate and bank privacy, with stiff penalties—including fines and/or prison—for anyone, including government officials, who violates the law.

In every respect, experience shows the Cayman Islands are superior because of future no-tax security, low costs, easy incorporation and operation, flexibility of business structure, privacy, immigration, and proximity to North and South American business markets.

It is obvious why the Caymans are a favorite location for Canadians to establish offshore trusts and investment corporations. The problem is, most Canadians getting involved in the Cayman Islands, or any other no-tax haven touting secrecy, don't get professional advice. Instead, they fly to the islands and buy into a scheme based on secrecy and lies. Then if their newfound Cayman friends overcharge or make unexplained withdrawals from their capital, there is always the blackmailer's threat of "you can't sue us because then your secret corporation will be revealed on court records, and you'll go to jail in Canada for tax fraud." Trusting strangers to keep your secrets is a very foolhardy way to proceed, especially when everything can be done legally and profitably with proper professional advice.

Here's how you could use a financial base in the Caymans: Let's say you have $3 million you wish to invest. Being a reasonable person, you want to avoid Canadian taxes on the income produced by your investment, and also avoid the application of the infamous FAPI rules.

First, you need a nonresident friend or relative to act as manager of your offshore investment corporation, which will be registered in George Town. You can't do it yourself or it might be called a sham. You transfer the $3 million to an offshore Cayman-registered trust, also administered by your friend, probably in the same George Town office. That money is invested in Canadian Treasury bills or public company stocks, and the interest income this produces can be paid to your children tax-free. At current interest rates, that translates into a savings of about $100,000 a year.

Given such savings potential, this tax-haven structure—a Cayman corporation and a trust—is worth a try. However, it may be expensive to establish and will probably be challenged by RC because it wasn't set up with professional advice using an interplay of Canadian law and double-taxation treaties with appropriate haven countries (such treaties do exist with Ireland, the Netherlands, and Barbados—three of the most useful tax havens for Canadians). Besides, it's not really necessary. By using treaties and professional advice, you can create a completely legitimate tax-haven structure that does not require dishonesty and secrecy for its functioning.

"No-Tax-on-Foreign-Income" Havens

These countries do impose income taxes, both on individuals and corporations, but only on income earned within the country, not abroad. The laws here exempt from tax any income earned from foreign sources involving no local business activities, apart from simple "housekeeping" matters. For example, there is often no tax on income derived from the export of local manufactured goods.

The no-tax-on-foreign-income havens break down into two groups, those that:

1. Allow a corporation to do business both internally and externally, taxing only the income coming from internal sources.

2. Require a company to choose at incorporation whether it will do business locally, with consequent tax liabilities, or whether it will do only foreign business, and thus be exempt from taxation.

Primary examples in these two categories are Panama, Liberia, Jersey, Guernsey, the Isle of Man, and Gibraltar.

"Low-Tax" Havens

These countries impose some taxes on all corporate income, wherever earned worldwide. However, most have international double-taxation agreements with high-tax countries such as Canada that may reduce the withholding tax imposed on income earned in the high-tax countries by the local corporations. Cyprus is a primary example. Barbados, about which I'll say more later, is another low-tax country popular with Canadian businesspeople.

"Special Tax" Havens

These countries impose all or most of the usual taxes, but either allow valuable tax concessions, write-offs, or "holidays" to special types of companies they wish to encourage (such as a total tax exemption for shipping companies, movie-production companies, or financial institutions), or they allow special types of corporate organization, such as the flexible corporate arrangements offered by Liechtenstein. The Netherlands and Ireland are particularly good examples of nations that offer major tax concessions to selected foreign businesses.

Ireland: Special Opportunities for Canadians

Just as with Barbados, the Republic of Ireland can also be used as the location of an offshore corporate affiliate, giving you commercial access to the 340 million people who live within the boundaries of the European Union. Ireland has many useful features, especially for manufacturing subsidiaries, but also sometimes for holding companies, to collect royalties and interest under various tax-saving treaty arrangements.

Using Ireland as an affiliate base is one way to lock in low labor costs and a 20-year tax holiday in the process. In some cases, you can even get free government money to fund your start-up costs. Irish labor costs are only 60 to 70 percent of Canadian wage levels; there is a 10 percent ceiling on corporate taxes, and cash grants are available to lure foreign business investors.

Since the 1970s, the Irish government has pursued an aggressive foreign investment program. To encourage foreign entrepreneurs to set up businesses, the government created the Irish Development Authority (IDA). To qualify for IDA incentives, a company must be engaged either in manufacturing or in international services. The latter category includes computer or software services, offices for insurance companies, and financial and other primary services.

Recently, the Irish parliament passed a law extending, through the year 2010, the maximum corporate tax rate of 10 percent on foreign investments. Thus Canadian companies investing now can look forward to 15 years of tax relief. The government cash grants can take the form either of reimbursement for the entire first year's payroll for a labor-intensive business, such as software development, or capital grants for factories or other more capital-intensive operations.

In addition to the IDA package, Ireland offers other programs. One of them is the Shannon Free Zone program. Incentives are similar to those of the IDA, with taxes held to 10 percent and capital grants available. Companies are required to locate near Shannon Airport. The Shannon Free Zone operation is administered separately from the IDA.

Ireland offers many advantages compared to rival centers such as Luxembourg and the Channel Islands, including lower wage and housing costs, a skilled and abundant labor force, and good communications with other European business centers.

Another Irish program is the International Financial Services Center (IFSC), a special zone in Dublin for financial services companies such as mutual funds, insurance companies, and banks. One of the IFSC's attractions has been the possibility for cash-rich firms to place their surplus cash in investment funds, which are then managed in Dublin by specialist companies. Profits are taxed at the 10 percent rate and can be repatriated without further tax liabilities due to Ireland's double-taxation treaties.

The Barbados Offshore Corporation

A simpler approach than the Irish manufacturing subsidiary is to create an offshore corporation in a tax haven such as Barbados. Done properly, this can be one of the most effective tax-saving devices for a Canadian business.

The offshore corporation is best suited to the needs of Canadian business owners who wish to do good business, as well as lower their taxes and increase profits.

But foreign corporations—as we have seen, and as RC demands—must be more than a mere "sham." A full-scale company, complete with working offices, staff, international fax and telecommunications facilities, bank accounts, a registered agent, a board of directors, a local attorney, and an accountant, is expensive. However, it will be more than worth it when weighed against the easily measurable tax savings.

Members of your board of directors—usually associates of the local tax specialists who help you form the company—will be paid about $2,500 a year. There will be annual taxes to pay and reports to be filed with the local government and with Canada.

As the Canadian owner, you will want to visit your company offices once or twice a year, a pleasant enough activity if you locate your business in one of the tropical venues specializing in such corporate arrangements. January is an excellent month to visit.

How will it work? Let's say you are a Canadian manufacturer exporting $5 million in products around the world each year. Because you are a legitimate business with established foreign transactions, your Canadian company can incorporate an offshore affiliate in, say, Barbados. Like Canada, Barbados is a member of the Commonwealth and, very unlike Canada, is a place where international companies pay only 2.5 percent corporate income tax.

There are fewer than three quarters of a million people living on this pleasant, tropical 166-square-mile island, where the mean temperature hovers between 76 and 80°F year-round.

Your adviser can set up your affiliate with offices in the capital, Bridgetown (population 8,000), a city with eight major international banks, including branches of the Royal Bank of Canada and the Canadian Imperial Bank of Commerce, as well as Chase Manhattan and Barclays. Regular air service is offered by Air Canada, British Airways, and American Airlines, among others.

Your Bridgetown affiliate will handle all foreign sales and international marketing for your Canadian company, charging for its services a 15 percent markup on the value of the goods it sells, or about $750,000 a year, at your current export levels.

What you have done is legally transfer your Canada profits to your offshore affiliate where taxes are much lower—2.5 percent versus 45 percent! After gladly paying only $18,750 in Barbados local corporate income taxes, the rest of the money, $731,250, can be sent back to Canada as a dividend from exempt surplus income and paid to the parent company tax-free!

Until the parent company shareholders need the money for their own use, or until they sell the business, Canadian taxes on the income can be deferred indefinitely. If the shareholders want payment immediately, it can be paid out as dividends—and taxed by Canada at the rate of 36 percent, well below the personal income tax rate of 50 percent-plus.

Investment Potential

The Barbados affiliate could also serve as an investment arm for your parent company, actively making international investments.

All the earned income from such investments—dividends, interest, and capital gains—will go to your Bridgetown affiliate and be taxed at the 2.5 percent rate. Investment profits can also be sent to the parent company, tax-free. In order to follow this course successfully, meeting the requirements laid down by RC, all corporate investment decisions must originate with your Bridgetown money manager, who runs your affiliate on a daily basis. It cannot be you dictating every move by phone from Montreal or Ottawa. As an added consideration, those with experience say that in order to be successful in using foreign affiliates for investment purposes, a minimum of $1 million in initial capital is needed to start, although many have been profitable and successful on less.

In theory this all sounds grand, but there are practical problems associated with an offshore corporation. First of all, just as in establishing a domestic corporation, legal formalities must be strictly observed when you incorporate abroad; RC will check this carefully. You will need a local legal counsel who knows the law and understands your business and tax objectives. Corporations everywhere are rule-bound creatures requiring separate books and records, meetings, minutes, and corporate authorizing resolutions that make them less flexible than many other arrangements. However, you can pay for a whole lot of record keeping with the tax money you can save.

In the right circumstances, Barbados can also become a base for your private offshore bank or other financial corporation, since rendering a financial service is just as much a product under the tax code as is a physical manufacturing operation.

ASSET PROTECTION TRUSTS: A VALUABLE STRATEGY FOR INDIVIDUALS

Although most tax-haven plans involve business corporations, the asset protection trust is one strategy that every individual with assets should be using.

When tax havens are mentioned, knowledgeable people think of foreign offshore trusts. There is good reason.

The trust is an established and proven fixture in the use of tax havens and offshore financial planning. One way to place your assets beyond the reach of potential litigation plaintiffs, creditors, and their lawyers is the creation of an offshore asset-protection trust located in a foreign country where the law favors such goals.

Even though an offshore trust, especially under RC's FAPI rules, may not mean greatly reduced taxes these days, some of the biggest benefits of offshore trusts are the nontax benefits. To many Canadians, these benefits are far more valuable than any potential tax savings. Nontax benefits of offshore trusts include not only the protection of assets from creditors, but privacy, estate planning, and international investing and diversification benefits as well.

Many wealthy Canadians today have at least one financial foe they fear more than RC: a plaintiff's lawyer. Business and professional people see a legal system out of control and courts willing to give others' assets to a sympathetic plaintiff. One mistake, or even one unfortunate accident, can take away the fruits of life's labors. And insurance companies often cannot or will not cover an entire claim.

Because of this, many successful professionals and business owners are putting a higher priority on asset preservation than on tax avoidance. A foreign trust is one key to preserving assets from creditors.

Fair-Weather Financial Planning

One of the most important considerations about foreign asset-protection trusts is anticipation of future problems. In order to avoid allegations of fraud, tax planners insist such trusts should be established well before problems with creditors, an irate spouse, or a court judgment develop—at least two years prior is recommended. This arrangement will only work if it is planned and created at a time of financial calm, not in a personal asset crisis.

If the foreign asset-protection trust is established only days or weeks before you are sued or forced into bankruptcy (or especially afterward), the act of transferring your assets to a foreign trust will subject you and your assets to strict fraudulent-conveyance laws, which strongly favor creditors. In such an instance, a court can declare the trust an illegal sham designed to conceal or remove assets from creditors and therefore void. If your assets are still within the court's jurisdiction, conveying title to a foreign trustee won't protect them from domestic attachment.

Financial Privacy

The country in which the trust and trustee are located should be one with strong financial privacy laws. The ideal countries for asset-preservation trusts are usually tax havens such as the Cayman Islands, Jersey, the Channel Islands, and the Cook Islands, among others. In these places, trustees are not required to divulge information about assets held by the trust, and cannot be forced by Canadian courts to turn over those assets to Canadian creditors unless and until those creditors go through the host country's judicial system.

You generally should transfer only cash and intangible assets (e.g., bonds, stocks, etc.) to the trust. Portable assets, such as gold coins or diamonds, can also be used. You should not transfer title to real estate or a business located in Canada. This does nothing to keep the assets away from Canadian creditors, and could make the trust subject to the jurisdiction of a Canadian court; that is, by holding title to assets within the country, the trust would be deemed to be doing business in Canada.

An offshore asset-protection trust will not affect your tax return. You will be the grantor who creates the trust by transferring your selected assets to it. The beneficiaries likely will include your family members but will not include yourself. The foreign trustee will follow your instructions on how trust assets should be invested and disbursed. You will notice very little difference in how you operate—unless you suddenly are faced with creditors who want your assets.

Under FAPI rules, you must disclose the existence of the trust on your federal tax return, but creditors must get a court to order you to reveal your tax return—and that takes time. If they do discover the trust's offshore location and file a collection suit in that country, foreign laws are likely to be hostile to nonresident creditors, and the trustee can shift the trust and its assets to another country and another trustee. Then creditors must begin the process all over again. Many of these foreign jurisdictions do not recognize Canadian or any nondomestic court orders, and a creditor must completely retry the original claim that gave rise to a Canadian judgment. It won't be long before the creditor will want to talk with you directly about settling the dispute.

Unlike a corporate charter and bylaws, the actual language of a trust agreement is not registered with government authorities in most countries. However, some tax-haven countries require registering trust agreements, so you must consider whether this is helpful or harmful in choosing a locale for your trust. In most cases, the terms of the agreement are between you and the trustee unless a dispute forces one of you to bring the trust agreement into court. Many beneficiaries have never even seen the trust agreements.

The Trust Advantage

Trusts can have a distinct privacy advantage over corporations.

In every country, at least one person involved in organizing the corporation must be listed on the public record, along with the name and address of the corporation. In most countries, the directors must also be listed. In a few maximum-privacy tax-haven countries, only the organizing lawyer is listed—but even that reference gives privacy invaders a starting point from which to work against you.

With a trust, however, you are usually required to register nothing but its existence—and often not even that fact. The trust agreement and the parties involved do not have to be disclosed, and there is little or nothing on the public record. In privacy-conscious countries, the trustee is allowed to reveal information about the trust only in very limited circumstances.

The country chosen for such a trust must have local trust experts who understand fully and can assist you in your objectives. The foreign local attorney who creates your trust unquestionably must know the applicable law and tax consequences.

Once established, the offshore asset-protection trust in its basic form can consist of as little as a trust account in an international bank located in the foreign country. Many well-established multinational Canadian banks can provide trustees for such arrangements and are experienced in such matters—but you might want to consider using a non-Canadian bank. With today's instant communications and international banking facilities, it is as convenient to hold assets and accounts overseas as it is in another Canadian city. Most international banks offer Canadian and U.S. dollar–denominated accounts, which often offer better interest rates than Canadian institutions.

Asset Protection Trust Costs

Because a foreign jurisdiction is its situs, the cost of creating an asset protection trust abroad usually is more than $15,000 initially, plus several thousand dollars in annual maintenance fees. As a rule, unless the assets you seek to shield are worth more than $2 million, the trust may not be a practical device—although *Business Week* magazine estimated in 1990 that "a net worth of $500,000" or more could be enough to justify a foreign asset-protection trust.

Depending on the country of choice, the settlor of a foreign asset-protection trust can gain many advantages, including the exercise of far greater control over assets and income from the trust than permitted under domestic law.

The trust can provide privacy, confidentiality, and reduced domestic reporting requirements in Canada. The trust can also help in avoidance of domestic taxes and probate in case death taxes are reimposed, and it offers increased flexibility in conducting affairs in case of disability, in transferring assets, in international investing, or in avoiding possible domestic currency controls. A foreign asset-protection trust can also substitute for or supplement costly professional liability insurance, or even a prenuptial agreement as protection for your heirs and their inheritance.

Trust Creation Abroad

The structure of foreign asset-protection trusts is not very different from that of a Canadian trust. The settlor creates the trust and transfers title to his assets to the trust, to be administered by a trustee according to the terms of the trust declaration. Usually, the trustee is a bank in the offshore jurisdiction chosen. Beneficiaries can vary according to the settlor's estate-planning objectives, and the settlor himself may be a beneficiary, although not the primary one.

Many foreign jurisdictions also permit appointment of a trust "protector," who, as the title indicates, oversees the operation of the trust to ensure its objectives are being met and the local law is followed. A protector does not manage the trust but can veto actions in some few cases.

The greatest worry about a foreign asset-protection trust often is the distance between you, your assets, and the people who manage them. While your assets do not have to be transferred physically to the foreign country in which the trust exists, circumstances may dictate such a precautionary transfer. Without such a physical transfer, a Canadian court could decide to disregard the trust and take possession of the assets.

If you are considering a foreign asset-protection trust, you should find out whether the foreign jurisdiction's laws are favorable and clear, and if they truly do offer the protection you seek. Examine the economic and political stability of the country, the reputation of its judicial system, the local tax laws, the business climate, language barriers, and available communications and financial facilities.

Several offshore financial centers have developed legislation hospitable to foreign-owned asset-protection trusts, among them the Caribbean-area nations of the Cayman Islands, the Bahamas, Belize, and the Turks and Caicos Islands; the Cook Islands near New Zealand; and Cyprus and Gibraltar in the Mediterranean.

Most of these countries have laws preventing foreign creditors from attacking trust assets as long as two years have passed since the date of the trust creation, so there is a good reason to set up your trust as soon as possible.

GET STARTED NOW

Tax havens are a very complex subject, but the hours you spend studying their use will probably pay you more per hour than the hours you spend directly earning an income—an unfortunate commentary on the confiscatory taxation policies of most governments.

Just stop and think for a moment how much faster your money can grow if you are not paying out an average of 40 percent to a taxing government somewhere. And the sooner you start, the sooner you begin saving that money. With proper professional advice, you can enjoy these benefits almost immediately.

APPENDIX 3

OFFSHORE BANKS

ANGUILLA

BARCLAY'S BANK PLC
P.O. Box 140
The Valley, Anguilla
Telephone: (1-264) 497-2301
Fax: (1-264) 497-2980
Telex: 0391-9310 BARDCO LA
Cable: BARDC
Web site: www.barclays.uk/anguilla
E-mail: barcang@anguillanet.com
Branch: Head Office in London, UK
Contact Manager: David Solomon
Branch Management: Derek Pinard

CARIBBEAN COMMERCIAL BANK
P.O. Box 23
The Valley, Anguilla
Telephone: (1-264) 497-2571
Fax: (1-264) 497-3570
Telex: 9306 CARITRUST LA
E-mail: ccbaxa@anguillanet.com
Type: Investment bank established 1976

Principal Correspondents USD: Bank of America; Miami: National
   Association; Charlotte, NC: Bank of America NA; New York City,
   NY: Bank of New York
Member: The Caribbean Association of Indigenous Banks
Manager of Account Operations: Leslie Richardson
President, Managing Director: Preston B. Bryan

HANSA BANK & TRUST COMPANY, LTD.
The Hansa Bank Building (TV1 O2P)
P.O. Box 213 (TV1 02P)
The Valley, Anguilla
Telephone: (1-264) 497-3800
Fax: (1-264) 497-3801
Web site: www.hansa.net
E-mail: hansa@attglobal.net
Type: Private bank/investment bank merchant established 1984
Ownership: Lynwood S. Bell (100%)
Managing Director: Malcolm Hope-Ross (E-mail:
   Malcolm_Hopeross@counsel.ai)
General Manager: Lynwood Bell

NATIONAL BANK OF ANGUILLA, LTD.
P.O. Box 44
The Valley, Anguilla
Telephone: (1-264) 497-2101
Fax: (1-264) 497-3310
Telex: 0391-9305
Cable: NABAXA LA
Web site: www.skyviews.com/nba
E-mail: nbabankl@anguillanet.com
Member: The Caribbean Association of Indigenous Banks
Type: Commercial bank established 1985
Principal Correspondents: Toronto, Canada: Royal Bank of Canada;
   Roseau, Dominica: National Commercial Bank of Dominica;
   London, UK: National Westminster Bank; USD: Bank of
   America NA, San Fernando
Managing Operator: L. Icilma Vanterpool

SCOTIABANK ANGUILLA, LTD.
P.O. Box 250
The Valley, Anguilla
Telephone: (1-264) 497-3333
Fax: (1-264) 497-3344
S.W.I.F.T. address: NOSC AI AI
Telex: 9333
Ownership: Scotia International Limited Nassau, Bahamas (100%)
Established: 1995
Branch Manager: Walter MacCalman

ARUBA

ABN AMRO BANK, NV
Caya Gilberto F Betico, Croes 89
P.O. Box 391
Oranjestad, Curacao, Aruba
Telephone: (297-8) 21515
Fax: (297-8) 35877
S.W.I.F.T. address: ABNA AW AX
Web site: www.abnamro.nl
E-mail: www.abnamro.com/email
Head Office in Amsterdam, Netherlands
One of top 20 banks worldwide
Branch Manager: J. W. H. van den Bosch

ARUBA BANK, NV
Caya G F Betico, Croes 41
P.O. Box 192
Oranjestad, Curacao, Aruba
Telephone: (297) 821550
Fax: (297) 829152
Telex: 5103 ABANK, 5040 ABANK
Web site: www. arubabank.com
E-mail: customersupport@arubabank.com or info@arubabank.com
Type: Commercial bank established 1936
Member: Aruba Bankers Association
Ownership: Foundation John G. Eman
Managing Director and CEO: I. D. Simon
Branch Manager: E-mail general inquiries to Yolanda Wolter

FIRST NATIONAL BANK OF ARUBA
Caya Gilberto F Betico, Croes 67
P.O. Box 184
Oranjestad, Aruba
Telephone: (297) 833221/4
Fax: (297) 821756
Telex: 5034 FNBAR AW
Web site: www.rbtt.com/first_aruba.htm
E-mail: firstcr@setarnet.aw
Type: Commercial bank established 1987
Ownership: SFT (76%), JR Croes (24%)
Managing Director: Edwin L. Tromp
Branch Manager: Charles Rung

INTERBANK ARUBA, NV
Caya G F Betico, Croes 38
P.O. Box 96
Oranjestad, Curacao, Aruba

Telephone: (297) 831080
Fax: (297) 824058
Telex: 5224 INTER AW
Web site: www.interbankaruba.com
E-mail: idurand@interbankaruba.com
Type: Commercial and retail bank established 1982
Ownership: Mansur Trading Company, NV, Oranjestad (100%)
Managing Director: Irving A. Durand

AUSTRIA

ANGLO IRISH BANK (AUSTRIA) AKTIENGESELL SCHAFT

Rathausstrasse 20, P.O. Box 306
Vienna (A-1010), Austria
Telephone: (43-1) 406 61 61
Fax: (43-1) 405 81 42
Telex: 114911 AIBA
S.W.I.F.T. address: ANGLO AT WW
Web site: www.angloirishbank.at
E-mail: Use Web site link
Type: Joint stock bank established 1890
Principal Correspondents: Dusseldorf: Comerzbank; London: HSBC
    Bank PLC; USD: Chase Manhattan Bank, NYC
Member: Austrian Bankers Association; Forex Club–Austria; Vienna
    Stock Exchange–Vienna
Ownership: Royal Trust Co., Ltd.–Toronto, Ontario, Canada (100%)
Managing Director: Gerhard Leopold
Chairman: Terence A. Carroll

BANK AUSTRIA AG

Am Hof 2
Vienna (A-1030), Austria
Telephone: (43-1) 71191/ext. 6512, 6521
Fax: (43-1) 71191/ext. 6155
Telex: 115561 BACA A
Web site: www.bankaustria.com
Type: Commercial/savings bank established as Osterreichische
    Landerbank AG 1880; merged 1991
Ownership: AVZ (35.06%), Republic of Austria (14.09%), institutional
    investors (28.03%), widespread stockholders (21.02%)
Member: Haupt Verband der Osterreichischen, Sparkassen; Verband
    Osterreichischer Banken and Bankiers, Vienna;
    ABECOR–Brussels
Services: Broad spectrum of retail banking services such as savings,

credit cards, loans, financial planning, international banking, electronic banking
Chairman of Managing Board: Gerhard Randa

BANK FOR ARBEIT AND WIRTSCHAFT AKTIENGESELLSCHAFT

Seitzergasse 2-4, P.O. Box 171 (1101)
Vienna (A-1011), Austria
Telephone: (43-1) 534530
Fax: (43-1) 53453 /2840
Telex: 115311 BAWAG A
Cable: BAWAGBANK WEIN
Web site: www.bawag.com
E-mail: #GS001.org.bawag
Type: Joint stock and commercial bank established 1947
Member: Verband Osterreichischer Banken und Bankiers–Vienna
Ownership: Austrian Federation of Trade Unions (52.7%);
    Bayerische Landesbank Girozentrale, Munich, Germany (45.7)%
Principal Correspondents: Bank Brussels Lambert and KBC Bank in
    Brussels, Belgium; Credit Suisse, First Boston, and UBS in
    Zurich, Switzerland; Deutsche Bank in Frankfurt, Germany;
    Bayerische Landesbank Girozentrale in Munich, Germany;
    Banque Francaise de Credit Cooperatif in Paris
Services: Commercial business loans, mortgage lending, invest-
    ments, lending to other banks, leasing services, insurance
Management Chairman: Helmut Elsner

CENTRO INTERNATIONALE HANDELSBANK AKTIENGESELLSCHAFT

Tegetthoffstrasse 1
Vienna (A-1015), Austria
P.O. Box 272
Telephone: (43-1) 515200
Fax: (43-1) 5134396
Telex: 136990 SERIE
Cable: CENTROBANK VIENNA
Web site: www.centrobank.com
E-mail: general@centrobank.com
Type: Commercial and merchant bank established 1971
Ownership: Kleinwort Benson Ltd. (10.46%)
Member: Austrian Bankers Association–Vienna
General Manager: Dr. Gerhard Vogt
Management Executive: Andrzel Dutkiewicz

CITIBANK INTERNATIONAL PLC

Lothringerstrasse 7, P.O. Box 90
A-1015 Vienna, Austria
Telephone: (43-1) 717170

Fax: (43-1) 7139206
Telex: 01 12105 CITI A
S.W.I.F.T. address: CITI AT WX
Web site: www.citibank.com or www.citicorp.com
Type: Commercial bank established 1959
Member: Vergand Osterreichischer Banken and Bankiers–Vienna
Holding Company: Citibank Overseas Investment
    Corporation–Wilmington, DE, US (100%)
Principal Correspondents: Frankfurt Am Main: Citibank, NA;
    Johannesburg: Citibank, NA.
Managing Director: A. Walter Hollmer

CREDITANSTALT AG
Schottengasse 6, P.O. Box 72
Vienna (A-1010), Austria
Telephone: (43-1) 531312
Fax: (43-1) 53131/47566
Telex: 115561 baca
S.W.I.F.T. address: CABU AT WW
Cable: CREDIT
Web site: www.creditanstalt.co.at
E-mail: ipc@creditanstalt.co.at
Type: Commercial/joint stock company bank established 1855
Services: Commercial and investment banking services to clients in
    Austria and abroad with an emphasis on providing banking,
    finance, and services for Austria's trade industries
General Manager: Dr. Alarich Fenyves
Relationship Managers for Non-Residents: Christian Ivanovsky,
    Monika Steffny, Eva Zach

DIE ERSTE OSTERREICHISCHE
SPARKASSEN AG (FIRST AUSTRIAN BANK)
Graben 21, P.O. Box 182
Vienna (A-1010), Austria
Telephone: (43-1) 53100-0
Fax: (43-1) 533 100-2272
Telex: 132 591 erste, 133 006 erste
S.W.I.F.T. address: GIBA AT WW
Web site: www.erste-bank.com
E-mail: Use Web site link
Type: Private; Commercial/joint stock company bank established 1819
Ownership: Erste-Holding (AUS) , 43.37%; Free Float, 31.1.%;
    Strategic Partners, 16.47%; Savings Bank, 9.06%
Member: Hauptverband der Osterreichischen Sparkassen–Vienna
Moody's rating (1995): bank deposits–A1/P-1; financial strength–B+
Services: Full range of domestic and international banking services
    such as retail, commercial, and investment banking
Chairman of Managing Board: Andreas Treichl

BAHAMAS

BANK OF THE BAHAMAS, LTD.
50 Shirley Street, P.O. Box N-7118
Nassau, New Providence Island, Bahamas
Telephone: (1-242) 326-2560
Fax: (1-242) 325-2762
Fax to Managing Director: P. M. Allen-Dean
Telex: 20141 BBL
Cable: BAHAMONT
Type: Commercial bank established 1970
Principal Correspondents: London: Bank of Montreal; Montreal:
    Bank of Montreal; USD: Chase Manhattan Bank, New York City
Ownership: Bahamian Government (80%)
Managing Director: Pauline M. Allen-Dean
Chairman: Hugh G. Sands

BANKAMERICA TRUST AND BANKING
CORPORATION (BAHAMAS), LTD.
BankAmerica House
East Bay Street, P.O. Box N-3024
Nassau, New Providence Island, Bahamas
Telephone: (1-242) 356-8540
Fax: (1-242) 328-7145
Fax to Investment Manager
Telex: 20-159 BATNASL
Cable: BATNASL
Type: Trust and banking company
Web site: bankofamerica.com
Principal Correspondents: Antwerp: Bank of Antwerp NA; Toronto:
    Bank of America, Canada
Subsidiary of BankAmerica Corporation–San Francisco, CA, US
Management: David G. MacKenzie

BANKBOSTON TRUST COMPANY, LTD.
Charlotte House, Charlotte Street
P.O. Box N-3930
Nassau, New Providence Island, Bahamas
Telephone: (1-242) 322-8531
Fax: (1-242) 328-2750
Telex: 20189 BOSTRUST
Cable: BOSTRUST
S.W.I.F.T. address: FNBB BS NX
Web site: www.bankboston.com or www.fleet.com
Branch bank, holding company: Bank of Boston
    Corporation–Boston, MA, US
Managing Director: Joycelyn E. Rahming, AVP

BANKERS TRUST COMPANY
Claughton House
P.O. Box N-3247
Nassau, New Providence Island, Bahamas
Telephone: (1-242) 325-4108
Telex: 20262
Web site: www.deutsche-bank.com
Branch of New York (Manhattan), NY, US

BARCLAY'S BANK PLC
Bay Street
P.O. Box N-8350
Nassau, New Providence Island, Bahamas
Telephone: (1-242) 356-8000 or (1-242) 356-8021
Fax: (1-242) 328-7979 or (1-242) 323-3591
Telex: 20149 BARCLADOM BS
Web site: www.bahamas.barclays.co.uk
E-mail: bbplcbah@batelnet.bs or use Web site link
Branch of bank in London, UK
Branch Manager: Bob Griffiths, Senior Manager Offshore Banking
Bahamas Director: Ms. Sharon Brown

CITITRUST (BAHAMAS), LTD.
Thompson Boulevard, Oakes Field
P.O. Box N-1576
Nassau, New Providence Island, Bahamas
Telephone: (1-242) 302-8787
Fax: (1-242) 302-8699
Telex: 20420
Cable: CITITRUST
Web site: www.citibank.com
E-mail: mike.fields@citicorp.com
Type: Joint stock bank established 1960
Subsidiary of Citibank NA, New York City (Manhattan), NY, US
President: David A. Tremblay
Vice President of Technology: Mike Fields (address general inquiries)

LLOYDS TSB BANK & TRUST (BAHAMAS), LTD.
King and George Streets
P.O. Box N-1262
Nassau, New Providence Island, Bahamas
Telephone: (1-242) 302-3000
Fax: (1-242) 322-8719
Telex: 20107 BOLAM
Cable: LONMONT NASSAU
S.W.I.F.T. address: LLOYD BSNS
Type: Commercial bank
Web site: www.lloydstsb-offshore.com

E-mail: Use Web site link
Ownership: Lloyds Bank PLC–London, UK
Principal Correspondents: Bank of Montreal, Canada; Schroder
    Munchmeyer Hengst & Co, Frankfurt, Germany
Relationship Branch Manager: Chris Adderly
Senior Manager: James B. Galbraith Morgan
Principal Manager and Director: David G. Nicoll

SCOTIABANK (BAHAMAS) LTD.

Scotiabank Building
Rawson Square
Box N-7518
Nassau, New Providence Island, Bahamas
Telephone: (1-242) 356-1400
Fax: (1-242) 322-7989
Telex: 20187
S.W.I.F.T. address: NOSCBSNS
Web site: www.scotiabank.com
E-mail: scotiacb@batelnet.bs
Branch of Bank of Nova Scotia–Toronto, Ontario, Canada
General Administrator: Lynn Bastian
Manager: Anthony C. Allen

SG HAMBROS BANK & TRUST (BAHAMAS) LIMITED

West Bay Street, P.O. Box N 7788-7788
Nassau, New Providence Island, Bahamas
Telephone: (1-242) 302-5000
Fax: (1-242) 326-6709
Cable: ENOPEE
Telex: 20111
Web site: www.sghambros.com
E-mail: betty.roberts@sghambros.com
Type: Offshore bank established 1981
Member: Association of International Banks and Trust Companies
    in the Bahamas
Managing Director: Betty Roberts
Deputy Head & COO: Olivier Gougeon

THE ROYAL BANK OF SCOTLAND INTERNATIONAL (NASSAU)

Bahamas Financial Center, 3rd Floor
Shirley & Charlotte Streets
Box N-3045
Nassau, New Providence Island, Bahamas
Telephone: (1-242) 322-4643
Fax: (1-242) 325-7559

Telex: 20142
BIC Address: RBOS BS N1
Web site: www.rbsint.com
E-mail: rbscot@bahamas.net.bs
Principal Correspondents: Chase Manhattan Bank, London and
    New York
Type: International private bank established 1950
Managing Director: C. Gibbs
Chairman: James D. Paton

BARBADOS

BARCLAY'S BANK PLC
Bridgetown Business Center
Broad Street
P.O. Box 301
Bridgetown, St. Michael, Barbados
Telephone: (1-246) 431-5151
Fax: (1-246) 431-0691
Telex: 2348 BARCLADOM WB
Cable: BARCLADOM
Web site: www.barclays.com
E-mail: barcbobc@sunbeach.net
Branch of London, UK
Manager: K. L. Lewis
Branch Manager: Wendy Harrison

BAYSHORE BANK & TRUST
(BARBADOS) CORPORATION
Lauriston House, Lower Collymore Rock Drive
P.O. Box 1132, Bridgetown, Barbados
Tel: (1-246) 430-5348
Fax: (1-246) 430-5335
Services: Chartered bank provides comprehensive wealth
    management, fiduciary, and trustee services
E-mail: dlittlewood@bayshore-international.com
President & Chief Executive Officer: Dalia Littlewood

CENTRAL BANK OF BARBADOS
Spry Street
P.O. Box 1016
Bridgetown, St. Michael, Barbados
Telephone: (1-246) 436-6870
Fax: (1-246) 427-9559

S.W.I.F.T. address: CBAB BB BB
Web site: www.centralbank.org.bb
E-mail: cbb.libr@caribsurf.com
Board Chairperson and Governor: Marion Williams

THE CHASE MANHATTAN BANK, NA
Neil and Broad Streets, P.O. Box 699
Bridgetown, Barbados
Telephone: 809-6-1100
Telex: WB269 CHASEBANK
S.W.I.F.T. address: BARC BB BB
Web site: www.chase.com
Branch of New York (Manhattan), NY, US
Manager: David Da Costa

DGM BANK & TRUST, INC.
International Trading Centre, 3rd Floor
Warrens, St. Michael, Barbados
Telephone: (1-246) 425-4940
Fax: (1-246) 425-4944
Web site: www.altabank.com
E-mail: question@altabank.com
HQ in Toronto
One of Canada's largest investment counselors, mutual fund
    managers (24 offshore mutual funds)

THE ROYAL BANK OF CANADA (BARBADOS), LTD.
Building #2, 2nd Floor
P.O. Box 986
Chelston Park, Collymore Road
Bridgetown, St. Michael, Barbados
Telephone: (1-246) 429-4923
Fax: (1-246) 429-4948
Telex: 2459 WB ROYSHORE
Web site: rbcprivatebanking.com or www.royalbank.com
E-mail: Use Web site link
Type: Offshore bank established 1981
Subsidiary of RBC Bahamas Limited–Nassau, Bahamas
Ownership: The Royal Bank of Canada–Montreal, Quebec, Canada
Principal Correspondents: Montreal–Royal Bank of Canada
Managing Director: Michael Moodie

SCOTIABANK
Broad Street
P.O. Box 202
Bridgetown, St. Michael, Barbados
Telephone: (1-246) 431-3100

Fax: (1-246) 228-8574
Telex: 2223
S.W.I.F.T. address: NOSC BBBB
Web site: www.scotiabank.com
E-mail: peter.vanschie@scotiabank.com
Branch of Bank of Nova Scotia–Toronto, Ontario, Canada
Vice President and General Manager: P. Van Schie
Branch Manager: Mr. Doug Cochrane (Fax: 1-246-426-0969)

BERMUDA

THE BANK OF BERMUDA, LTD.
Bank of Bermuda Building
6 Front Street
P.O. Box HM 11
Hamilton HM AX, Bermuda
Telephone: (1-441) 295-4000
Fax: (1-441) 295-7093
Telex: BA 3212
Cable: BANCO BERMUDA
S.W.I.F.T Address: BBDA BM HM
Web site: www.bankofbermuda.com
E-mail: Use Web site link
Type: Commercial bank established and incorporated 1890
Member: American Bankers Association
Services: Full-service banking including ATMs
As of June 30, 1998, total assets exceeded $10 billion
President and CEO: Henry B. Smith
Branch Manager: Cynthia Woods (Fax: 1-441-299-6573)

THE BANK OF NT BUTTERFIELD AND SON, LTD.
Bank of Butterfield Building
65 Front Street
P.O. Box HM 195
Hamilton HM AX, Bermuda
Telephone: (1-441) 295-1111
Fax: (1-441) 292-4365
Telex: 3211 FIELD BA
Cable: FIELD BERMUDA
Web site: www.bankofbutterfield.com
E-mail: contact@bntb.bm
Attention: Judy Khoo, Personal Banking
Type: Commercial bank established 1858 and incorporated 1904
As of June 30, 1997, total assets were nearly $4.5 billion

Member: American Bankers Association–Washington, D.C., US;
    Bank Marketing Association–Chicago, IL, US
President and CEO: M. Calum Johnston
Services: Full-service banking including ATMs, banking by
    computer/modem

BERMUDA COMMERCIAL BANK, LTD.
Bermuda Commercial Bank Building
44 Church Street
P.O. Box HM1748
Hamilton HM GX, Bermuda
Telephone: (1-441) 295-5678
Fax: (1-441) 295-8091
Telex: 3336 COMBK BA
Cable: COMBANK BERMUDA
S.W.I.F.T. Address: BPBK BM HM
Web site: www.bermuda-bcb.com
E-mail: enquiries@bcb.bm or bcbit1@ibl.bm (attention: Lynne Taylor,
    Corporate Client Liaison Officer, Telephone: (1-441-299-2856)
Incorporated in 1969 as Bermuda Provident Bank, Ltd. Name
    changed in 1984. Acquired by First Curacao International Bank
    (FCIB) in May 1993. Along with Merrill Lynch, established BCB
    Merrill Lynch Asset Management. Received a B/TBW-1 rating in
    1995 by Thomson Bank Watch of New York.
Managing Director: Barry Munholland

BRITISH VIRGIN ISLANDS

VP BANK (BVI), LTD.
3076 Sir Francis Drake's Highway
P.O. Box 3463
Road Town, Tortola, British Virgin Islands
Telephone: (1-284) 494-1100
Fax: (1-284) 494-1199
Web site: www.vpbankbvi.com
E-mail: info.bvi@vpbank.com or vpbank@caribsurf.com
Wholly owned subsidiary of the Verwaltungs-und Privat-Bank
    Aktiengesellschaft Vaduz, Liechtenstein
Services: Complete financial services including customized banking,
    accounts in all major convertible currencies, call and time
    deposits, money market funds and investment, foreign exchange
    trading, securities and precious metal trading, loans, custodian
    bank services, investment management services
Inquiries: Tino, Associate
Management: Urs Stiriman

CAYMAN ISLANDS

ALEXANDRIA BANCORP, LTD.
P.O. Box 2064
George Town, Grand Cayman
Cayman Islands, British West Indies
Telephone: (1-345) 945-1111
Fax: (1-345) 949-1122
E-mail: bancorp@candw.ky
Type: Trust company/offshore bank
Subsidiaries in Tortola, St. Thomas, and Curacao.
Services: Private banking, multicurrency accounts, trust
   administration, company formation and management, mutual
   and pension fund administration, investment management
Managing Director: Frank Flanagan
Trust Manager: David Dobson

ALTAJIR BANK
Sigma Building, Smith & Hospital Road
P.O. Box 691-GT
George Town, Grand Cayman
Cayman Islands, British West Indies
Telephone: (1-345) 949-5628
Fax: (1-345) 949-6339
Type: Offshore bank; small private stock bank established 1974
Principal Correspondents: Royal Bank of Scotland, London
Member: Cayman Island Bankers Association
Ownership: Altajir Establishment–Liechtenstein
Services: Personally tailored banking programs. A deposit taker for
   US dollar, sterling, and Canadian dollar accounts; small
   accounts welcome.
Deputy Manager: Lillian Burgos:
Managing Director: M. Rosaleen Corbin

ANSBACHER (CAYMAN), LTD.
Ansbacher House, Jennett Street
P.O. Box 887
George Town, Grand Cayman
Cayman Islands, British West Indies
Telephone: (1-345) 949-8655
Fax: (1-345) 949-7946
Telex: ANSBAC CP 4305
BIC Address: ANLI KY K1
E-mail: info@ansbacher.com.ky or use Web site link
Type: Commercial bank/trust company established 1971
Services: Private banking, trust and corporate services
Managing Director: J. Bryan Bothwell
Chairman: Hugh C. Hart

BANCO BILBAO VIZCAYA
Westwind Building
P.O. Box 1115
George Town, Grand Cayman
Cayman Islands, British West Indies
Telephone: (1-345) 949-7790
Fax: (1-345) 949-9086
Telex: 424706 BBVNYK
Wire: BIC BBVI KY K1
S.W.I.F.T. address: BBVA KYKY
Web site: www.bbva.es
E-mail: bbvgc@candw.ky
Branch: Head Office in Madrid, Spain
Attention: Branch Manager

BANCO BILBAO VIZCAYA ARGENTINA BRASIL SA
British American Centre, Building 3
2nd Floor, Jennett Street
P.O. Box 1112
George Town, Grand Cayman
Cayman Islands, British West Indies
Telephone: (1-345) 949-7690
Fax: (1-345) 949-7679
Telex: CP 4433
BIC Address: BFYB KYK1
E-mail: bbvgc@candw.ky
Branch bank of a major banking/financial services provider in
    Salvador, Brazil
Services: Full range of banking services available
Branch Manager: Andre Nesser

BANCO BRADESCO, SA
Caledonian House, 3rd Floor, Jennett Street
P.O. Box 30327 SMB
George Town, Grand Cayman
Cayman Islands, British West Indies
Telephone: (1-345) 945-1200
Fax: (1-345) 945-1430
Telex: 4264 BRADESCO CP
S.W.I.F.T. address: BBDE KY KY
E-mail: bradesco@candw.ky
Branch office of bank in Sao Paulo, Brazil
Services: Promoting and providing support to international
    trade-related financing
Branch Manager: Roberto Medeiros Paula
Contact: Joao Albino Winkelmann

BANCO COMERCIAL PORTUGUES SA
Scotia Building, 4th Floor, Cardinal Avenue
P.O. Box 31124
George Town, Grand Cayman
Cayman Islands, British West Indies
Telephone: (1-345) 949-8322
Fax: (1-345) 949-7743
Telex: 4283 ILEK
Web site: www.bcp.pt
E-mail: investors@bcp.pt
Local branch of largest commercial and international bank in
    Oporto, Portugal
Services: Comprehensive range of corporate services and private
    banking services, agency representation to international banks,
    company incorporation, and registered office services
Branch Manager: Maria Helena Carneiro

BANCO DO ESTADO DE SAO PAULO, SA
Transnational House, West Bay Road
P.O. Box 1811
George Town, Grand Cayman
Cayman Islands, British West Indies
Telephone: (1-345) 945-5144
Fax: (1-345) 945-5153
Telex: 4296 BANESGC CP
E-mail: banespa@candw.ky
Incorporated in Sao Paulo, Brazil; limited liability
Branch Management: Odiwaldo Julio Sancinetti

BANCO DO ESTADO DO RIO GRAND DO SUL, SA
British American Centre, First Home Tower
P.O. Box 31499 SMB
George Town, Grand Cayman
Cayman Islands, British West Indies
Telephone: (1-345) 949-6604
Fax: (1-345) 949-4834
Fax inquiries to: Marcelo Magalhages
Web site: www.banrisul.com.br
E-mail: Use Web site link
Services: Private banking, international trade-related transactions,
    asset management
General Manager: Alexandre Pedro Ronzi
SERVES BRAZILIAN CUSTOMERS ONLY

BANK OF BERMUDA (CAYMAN), LTD.
36C, Bermuda House, British American Centre

P.O. Box 513 GT
George Town, Grand Cayman
Cayman Islands, British West Indies
Telephone: (1-345) 949-9898 or direct line (1-345) 914-5126
Fax: (1-345) 949-7959
S.W.I.F.T. address: BBDA KY KX
Web site: www.bankofbermuda.com/office/cayman.htm
E-mail: KingBB@BankofBermuda.com
Type: Commercial bank/trust company established 1988
Services: Full range of banking services, including corporate banking
 services, cash management, checking accounts,
 computer/modem access to accounts
Manager: Billy King
Tel: (1-345) 914-5126
Fax: (1-345) 949-7959
Managing Director, Banking: Ray Iler
Managing Director: Allen J. Bernardo

BANK OF BUTTERFIELD INTERNATIONAL (CAYMAN), LTD.

Butterfield House, 68 Fort Street
P.O. Box 705
George Town, Grand Cayman
Cayman Islands, British West Indies
Telephone: (1-345) 949-7055
Fax: (1-345) 949-7004
Fax attention to New Accounts Department
Telex: 4263 BFIELD CP
Cable: CIFIELD GRAND CAYMAN
BIC Address: BNTB KY K1
Web site: www.bankofbutterfield.bm
E-mail: contact@bntb.bm
Type: Commercial bank established 1967
One of six clearing banks on the Cayman Islands
Branch of Bank of NT Butterfield and Sons, Ltd.–Bermuda
Services: Comprehensive range of personal and confidential services
 including trust, corporate and private banking; investment
 management
Managing Director: Conor J. O'Dea
Manager: Niall Brooks

BANKAMERICA, NATIONAL ASSOCIATION

Anchorage Centre, Harbour Drive
P.O. Box 1078
George Town, Grand Cayman
Cayman Islands, British West Indies
Telephone: (1-345) 949-7888

Fax: (1-345) 949-7883
Telex: CP 4234 BATCAYL
Cable: BATCAYL
Web site: bankofamerica.com
Services: Deposits, payments, loans, personal trust services for tax
    and estate planning, corporate services, investment programs
    and management, safe custody
Vice President: Keith Carter
Managing Director: Daniel Haase

BARCLAY'S BANK PLC
Cardinal Avenue
P.O. Box 68
George Town, Grand Cayman
Cayman Islands, British West Indies
Telephone: (1-345) 945-7820
Fax: (1-345) 945-2113
Telex: 4219 BARCLAYS CP
Cable: BARCLADON
Web site: www.barclays.com
E-mail: bbplccym@candw.ky
Part of Barclay's PLC Group; head office in London, UK
Services: Private banking, investment management, corporate
    management, trusts, registered office and bank agencies
Offshore Corporate Manager: Gordon Rhodes

CALEDONIAN BANK AND TRUST, LTD.
Caledonian House, Ground Floor, Mary Street
P.O. Box 1043
George Town, Grand Cayman
Cayman Islands, British West Indies
Telephone: (1-345) 949-0050
Fax: (1-345) 949-8062
Web site: www.caledonian.com
E-mail: info@caledonian.com
Type: Category "A" licensed commercial bank and trust company;
    licensed mutual fund administrator and insurance manager
Services: Corporate, trust, and mutual fund administrative services;
    accounting services; registered office services
Branch Manager: Mr. Balan Muruagesu
Managing Director: David S. Sargison

CAYMAN INTERNATIONAL BANK &
TRUST COMPANY, LTD.
20 Jennett Street
P.O. Box 887
George Town, Grand Cayman

Cayman Islands, British West Indies
Telephone: (1-345) 949-8655
Fax: (1-345) 949-7946
Telex: CP 4305 ANSBAC C
Web site: www.ansbacher.com
E-mail: info@ansbacher.com.ky
Type: Bank and trust company established 1971
Ownership: Ansbacher (Cayman) Limited
Member: Cayman Island Bankers Association
Managing Director: J. Bryan Bothwell

CAYMAN NATIONAL BANK, LTD.
Cayman National Building, 200 Elgin Avenue
P.O. Box 1097
George Town, Grand Cayman
Cayman Islands, British West Indies
Telephone: (1-345) 949-4655
Fax: (1-345) 949-7506
Telex: 4313 CNBBANK CP
Cable: CAYNA TBNK
BIC Address: CNBT KY K1
Web site: www.caymans.com/~caymans/Cayman_National_Bank.html
E-mail: turtle1@caymans.com
Type: Commercial bank established 1974
Member: Cayman Islands Bankers Association
Ownership: Cayman National Corporation, Ltd.
President and Director: David J. McConney
Chairman and Director: Eric J. Crutchley

CIBC BANK AND TRUST COMPANY (CAYMAN), LTD.
Edward Street
P.O. Box 695 (Banking Division)
George Town, Grand Cayman
Cayman Islands, British West Indies
Telephone: (1-345) 949-8666
Fax: (1-345) 949-7904
Telex: 4222 CP
Cable: CANBANK
S.W.I.F.T. address: CIBC KY KY
Web site: www.cibcwm.com
E-mail: Use Web site link
Type: Commercial bank/trust company
Services: Representation/management of offshore banks; fiduciary
    services for managed banks; full retail banking such as term
    deposits, letters of credit, foreign exchange, checking and
    savings accounts; international trade; project finance
Ownership: Canadian Imperial Bank of Commerce, Toronto, Canada

General Manager: T. J. Crawford
Managing Director: C. Richmond

DELTA BANK AND TRUST COMPANY, GRAND CAYMAN

Genesis Building, 2nd Floor, Jennett Street
P.O. Box 706
George Town, Grand Cayman
Cayman Islands, British West Indies
Telephone: (1-345) 949-0437
Fax: (1-345) 949-9327
Telex: 6801462
Type: Trust company/offshore bank
Services: International private banking services, money market
      accounts, investment portfolio management
Branch Manager: Mr. Gaspar
General Manager: I. Henrique D. Campos

DEUTSCHE MORGAN GRENFELL (CAYMAN), LTD.

Elizabethan Square
P.O. Box 1984
George Town, Grand Cayman
Cayman Islands, British West Indies
Telephone: (1-345) 949-8244
Fax: (1-345) 949-8178
Telex: 4455 MG CYMN CP
S.W.I.F.T. address: DEUT KY KX
Web site: www.deutsche-bank-24.de
E-mail: info@db.com or use Web site link
A wholly owned subsidiary of the Deutsche Bank Group
Ownership: Morgan Grenfell & Company, London, UK
Services: Offshore administrative services for mutual funds; banking
      services for international corporate clients
Branch Manager: Mr. Jennings
Managing Director: R. P. Apsey

DEXTRA BANK AND TRUST CO., LTD.

Global House
North Church Street
P.O. Box 2004
George Town, Grand Cayman
Cayman Islands, British West Indies
Telephone: (1-345) 949-7844
Fax: (1-345) 949-2795
Telex: 4475 DEXTRA CP
Cable: DEXTRA
E-mail: dextra@candw.ky

Type: Discount bank and trust company incorporated in Switzerland
Member: Cayman Islands Bankers Association
Services: Investment and private banking, trustee services,
    estate planning/administration, company formation and
    administration
Executive Director: Alex Wood
Contact: Israel Behar

DRESDNER BANK LATEINAMERIKA AG

Anderson Square Building
P.O. Box 714
George Town, Grand Cayman
Cayman Islands, British West Indies
Telephone: (1-345) 949-8888
Fax: (1-345) 949-8899
S.W.I.F.T. address: DRES KY KX
Web site: www.dresdner-bank.com
E-mail: dbla.net
Head Office: Hamburg, Germany
Services: Trust services, investment management services,
    company formation and registration
Contact: Guenter Backer, Manager

IBJ WHITEHALL BANK AND TRUST COMPANY

Westwind Building, 3rd Floor
P.O. Box 1040
George Town, Grand Cayman
Cayman Islands, British West Indies
Telephone: (1-345) 949-2849
Fax: (1-345) 949-5409
Telex: 0293-4274
A subsidiary of the Industrial Bank of Japan–New York City, NY,
    US; affiliated with the Schroder Group
Services: Cash management services, US dollar clearing, interbank
    deposits
Resident Manager: Rory Healy

ITAU BANK, LTD.

Ansbacher House, 3rd Floor, Jennett Street
P.O. Box 10220 APO
George Town, Grand Cayman
Cayman Islands, British West Indies
Telephone: (1-345) 945-4175
Fax: (1-345) 945-4185
Telex: 4284 ITAUBK
Web site: www.itau.com

Incorporated in the Caymans in 1992 under class "B" unrestricted
  banking and trust license. A wholly owned subsidiary of Banco
  ITAU, SA–Brazil.
Services: Offshore commercial banking services
General Manager: Antonio Carlos Genoveze

LLOYDS BANK INTERNATIONAL (CAYMAN), LTD.
CIBC Financial Center, 3rd Floor
P.O. Box 694
George Town, Grand Cayman
Cayman Islands, British West Indies
Telephone: (1-345) 949-7854
Fax: (1-345) 949-0090
Cable: LONDONBANK
Web site: www.lloydstsb-offshore.com
E-mail: Use Web site link
Established: 1972
Principal Correspondents: London: Lloyds TSB Bank, PLC; USD:
  Bank of New York, New York City
Services: Full range of international trust and private banking
  services; investment portfolio management; company
  incorporation.
Member: Grand Cayman Islands Bankers Association
Contact: R. C. Barker, Manager

MERCURY BANK AND TRUST, LTD.
Caledonian House, 3rd Floor, Mary Street
P.O. Box 2431
George Town, Grand Cayman
Cayman Islands, British West Indies
Telephone: (1-345) 949-0800
Fax: (1-345) 949-0295
Telex: 0293 4331 MERBANK
BIC Address: MTRL KY K1
Web site: www.mercury.com
E-mail: offshore@mercury.com.mx
Member: Cayman Islands Bankers Association
Established 1986
Principal Correspondents: Georgetown: Royal Bank of Canada; New
  York City: BBVA Bancomer; Northern Trust International
  Banking Corporation, Standard Charter Bank
Services: Trusts, mutual fund administration, banking services,
  company formation
General Manager: Lucia Aranda
ONLY ACCEPTING NEW CLIENTS THROUGH EXISTING
  CLIENTS, BY REFERRAL.

MUTUAL SECURITY BANK (CAYMAN), LTD.
Caledonian House, 3rd Floor, Mary Street
P.O. Box 31120 SMB
Grand Cayman
Cayman Islands, British West Indies
Telephone: (1-345) 949-8002
Fax: (1-345) 949-4006
Telex: 4278 MSB
E-mail: ncbky@candw.ky
Services: Private banking for international private and corporate
    clients; formation and management of companies; small
    accounts welcome
General Manager: Mr. Iton
Contact: Karen Pachman

PT BANK BALI
Micro Commerce Centre #203A, North Sound Road
P.O. Box 31241 SMB
George Town, Grand Cayman
Cayman Islands, British West Indies
Telephone: (1-345) 945-2921
Fax: (1-345) 945-6532
Telex: 63692 BALIFX
Cable: BANK BALI JAKARTA IN
Head office in Jakarta, Indonesia
Services: Corporate finance, treasury services, commercial
    and syndication loans, investment fund management,
    guarantees
Branch Manager: Suyradi Pajio
Branch Management: Suherman Samiri

ROYAL BANK OF CANADA TRUST COMPANY (CAYMAN), LTD.
Cardinal Avenue
P.O. Box 1586
George Town, Grand Cayman
Cayman Islands, British West Indies
Telephone: (1-345) 949-9107
Fax: (1-345) 949-5777
Telex: 4424 ROYBANK CP
Cable: ROYALBANK
Web site: rbcprivatebanking.com
E-mail: Use Web site link
A local branch of Canada's largest bank
Services: Personal and commercial banking, trust, and investment
Managing Director: Steve Mackey

SCOTIABANK (CAYMAN ISLANDS) LTD.
Scotia Centre
Cardinal Avenue and Airport Industrial Park
P.O. Box 689
George Town, Grand Cayman
Cayman Islands, British West Indies
Telephone: (1-345) 949-7666
Fax: (1-345) 949-0020
Telex: 4330
S.W.I.F.T. address: NOSC KYKT
Web site: www.scotiabank.com
E-mail: scotiaca@candw.ky
Services: Complete range of personal, commercial, and corporate
    banking services for local and international clients
Serving Cayman for more than 25 years. Local branch of one of
    North America's largest financial institutions, headquartered in
    Toronto, Canada; parent bank operates in 44 countries through
    1,400 branches and offices
Ownership: BNS International Ltd. (100%)
Branch Manager, Managing Director: Alan Brodie

UNITED STATES TRUST COMPANY OF
NEW YORK
Edward Street
P.O. Box 694
George Town, Grand Cayman
Cayman Islands, British West Indies
Telephone: (1-345) 949-2127
Fax: (1-345) 949-7904
Telex: CP 254
Web site: www.ustrust.com
E-mail: bbrennan@ustrust.com or use Web site link
Holding Company: US Trust Corporation, New York, NY, US
Managing Director, Investment Management Services: William L.
    Brennan (E-mail: bbrennan@ustrust.com)
Branch Manager: Mr. Marshall
Branch Management: Douglas B. Gearhart

CHANNEL ISLANDS

BANK OF AMERICA (JERSEY), LTD.
Durell House, 28 New Street

P.O. Box 120 (JE4 8QE)
St. Helier, Jersey, Channel Islands
Telephone: (44-1534) 875471
Fax: (44-1534) 878546
Telex: 4192239 BAMERJG
Cable: BAMERJG
Web site: www.bankofamerica.com
Type: Joint stock
Subsidiary of Bank of America National Trust and Savings
    Association–San Francisco, CA, US
Manager: Mr. Anthony Robinson
Managing Director: Bob Gautier

BANK OF BUTTERFIELD INTERNATIONAL
Roseneath, The Grange
P.O. Box 153 (GY1 3AP)
St. Peter Port, Guernsey, Channel Islands
Telephone: (44-1481) 711521
Fax: (44-1481) 714533
Telex: 4191362 FIELDG
BIC Address: BNTB GG S1
Cable: ANZBANK
Web site: www.bankofbutterfield.com
Type: Joint stock
Member: Association of Guernsey Banks; International Bankers
    Association of Guernsey, St. Peter Port
Ownership: Australia and New Zealand Banking Group,
    Ltd.–Melbourne, Victoria, Australia
Managing Director & CEO: Robert S. Moore

BANKERS TRUST COMPANY
40, Esplanade (JE2 3QB)
West House, Peter Street
St. Helier, Jersey, Channel Islands
Telephone: (44-1534) 22500
Fax: (44-1534) 38907
Telex: 4192364 BTCJER G
Cable: BTCOJER
Branch of New York City (Manhattan), NY, US
Holding Company: Bankers Trust New York Corporation–New York
    City (Manhattan), NY, US
Contact: M. T. Frost, Manager

BARCLAY'S BANK PLC (GUERNSEY), LTD.
Le Marchant House
    P.O. Box 41
St. Peter Port, Guernsey GY1 3BE Channel Islands

Telephone: 44 (0) 1481 705 600
Fax: 44 (0) 1481 705 690
Telex: 4191671 BARCGU G
BIC address: BARC GGS1
Web site: www.offshore banking.barclay.co.uk
E-mail: guernsey@offshorebanking.barclays.com or
    kay.parnwell@barclays.co.uk
Local branch of Barclay's Bank–London, UK
Services: Full range including offshore banking services,
    multicurrency banking, international payment service, letters
    of credit, cash management, trade and international services,
    checking. Ability to order checkbooks, statements, and other
    information via e-mail
Branch Manager: Mr. Malcolm Le Cheminant
Branch Manager: K. Gregson

BARCLAY'S BANK PLC (JERSEY), LTD.
P.O. Box 191 (JE4 8RN)
29/31 The Esplanade
Georgetown, Jersey JE4 8RN Channel Islands
Telephone: (44-1534) 877990
Fax: (44-1534) 725311
Cable: BARFINCO JERSEY
Web site: www.internationalbanking.barclays.com
E-mail: jersey@offshorebanking.barclays.com or cssl@barclays.co.uk
Local branch of Barclay's Bank PLC, London, UK
Services: Full range including offshore banking services,
    multicurrency banking, international payment service, letters
    of credit, cash management, trade and international services,
    checking. Ability to order checkbooks, statements, and other
    information via e-mail.
General Manager: Nigel Smith

BARCLAY'S BANK PLC (JERSEY), LTD.
P.O. Box 784
Victoria Road
Georgetown, Jersey JE4 8ZS Channel Islands
Telephone: (44-1534) 880 550
Fax: (44-1534) 505 077
Web site: www.internationalbanking.barclays.com
E-mail: jersey@internationalbanking.barclays.com
Local branch of Barclay's Bank–London, UK
Services: Full range including offshore banking services,
    multicurrency banking, international payment service, letters
    of credit, cash management, trade and international services,
    checking. Ability to order checkbooks, statements, and other
    information via e-mail.
Senior Manager, Personal Banking International: Mike McQuaid

BARCLAY'S BANK PLC (JERSEY), LTD.
P.O. Box 8
13 Library Place
St. Helier, Jersey JE4 8NE Channel Islands
Telephone: (44-1534) 880550
Fax: (44-1534) 58662
Telex: 4192152 BARJSY G
Web site: www.internationalbanking.barclays.com
E-mail: jersey@offshorebanking.barclays.com or cssl@barclays.co.uk
Local branch of Barclay's Bank–London, UK
Services: Full range including offshore banking services, multicurrency banking, international payment service, letters of credit, cash management, trade and international services, checking. Ability to order checkbooks, statements, and other information via e-mail.
Manager and Island Director: Martin Scriven

BBVA PRIVANZA BANK (JERSEY), LTD.
2 Mulcaster Street
P.O. Box 569
St. Helier, Jersey, Channel Islands
Telephone: (44-1534) 511200
Fax: (44-1534) 511201
Telex: 4192042
S.W.I.F.T. address: BBVI JE SH
Web site: www.bbvprivanza.esoterica

CHASE BANK AND TRUST COMPANY (C.I.), LTD.
Chase House
Grenville Street, P.O. Box 289
St. Helier, Jersey JE4 8QH Channel Islands
Telephone: (44-1534) 626262
Fax: (44-1534) 626301
Telex: 4192209
S.W.I.F.T. address: CHAS JE SX
Cable: CHASJY
Web site: www.chase.com
Type: Commercial bank/joint stock bank established 1966
Member: Jersey Bankers Association, St. Helier
Holding Company: Chase Manhattan Overseas Banking Corporation–New York City, NY, US (100%)
Management Chairman: C. Lenz
Account Manager: Margaret Brennan

CITIBANK (C.I.), LTD.
P.O. Box 104
38 The Esplanade

St. Helier, Jersey, JE4 8QB Channel Islands
Telephone: (44-1534) 608000
Fax: (44-1534) 608190
Telex: 4192313 CITIJERSEY
Cable: CITI JERSEY
Web site: www.citibank.com
E-mail: info@citicorp.com
Type: Investment bank/joint stock bank established 1968
Holding Company: Citibank NA–New York (Manhattan), NY, US
Account Manager: Martin James
Managing Director: C. Jones

HSBC BANK PLC
28/34 Hill Street
P.O. Box 26
St. Helier, Jersey JE4 8NR Channel Islands
Telephone: (44-1534) 616100
Fax: (44-1534) 616222
Telex: 4192098
BIC Address: MIDL JE H1
Web site: www.offshore.hsbc.co.je
E-mail: midoffsh@itl.net or use Web site link
Type: Trust company, commercial and merchant bank established 1967
Ownership: Midland Bank PLC–London, UK
Managing Director: Philip George Hickman

HSBC MIDDLE EAST
One Grenville Street
P.O. Box 315
St. Helier, Jersey JE4 8UB Channel Islands
Telephone: (44-1534) 606512
Fax: (44-1534) 606149
Telex: 4192254 HCIJYG
Cable: 4192254
Web site: www.hsbc.com
Ownership: HSBC Holdings PLC (100%)
General Manager: Mr. Michael Curtis
Executive Director: C. J. M. Keirle

LLOYDS TSB BANK (JERSEY) LIMITED
Lloyds TSB House, 25 New St (JE4 8RZ)
P.O. Box 160 (JE4 8RG)
Telephone: (44-1534) 503000
Fax: (44-1534) 503047
Telex: 4192164
Web site: www.lloydstsb-offshore.com
E-mail: Use Web site link

Type: Retail bank/clearing house (non-US) established 1986
Member: Jersey Bankers' Association
Ownership: Lloyds TSB Group PLC London, UK (100%)
Director: Robert Thomas McGinnigle

LLOYDS TSB OFFSHORE PRIVATE BANKING (JERSEY)
New Business Centre
7 Bond Street
P.O. Box 195
St. Helier, Jersey JE4 8RS Channel Islands
Telephone: (44-1534) 604888
Fax: (44-1534) 604726
Telex: 888301 LOYDLNG
Web site: www.lloydstsb-offshore.com
E-mail: pvtbankingj@lloydstsb-offshore.com or use Web site link
Type: Trust company/joint stock bank established 1947
Subsidiary of Lloyds Bank PLC–London, UK
Principal Correspondents: London Lloyds Bank PLC
US clients contact Isle of Man Branch Fax: 01624638181, attention
    New Business Department
Directors: Peter Niven, Robert Thomas McGinnigle

NATIONAL WESTMINISTER BANK PLC
23 Broad Street, P.O. Box 20
St. Helier, Jersey JE4 OYX Channel Islands
Telephone: (44-1534) 282 828
Fax: (44-1534) 282 730
Fax to Records Department
BIC Address: NWBK JE S1
Type: Deposit taking and mortgage finance company
Ownership (Ultimate Holding Company): National Westminster
    Bank PLC, Coutts and Company Trust Holdings, Ltd.
Contact: P. Taylor, Manager

ROYAL BANK OF CANADA (CHANNEL ISLANDS) LIMITED
P.O. Box 48
Canada Court
St. Peter Port GY1 3BQ, Guernsey
Channel Islands, UK
Telephone: (44-1481) 723 021
Fax: (44-1481) 710 958
Web site: rbcprivatebanking.com
E-mail: Use Web site link
SVP, Regional Head of British Isles: Philip Brewster
Contact: Philip Dunn

ROYAL BANK OF CANADA (JERSEY), LTD.
P.O. Box 194
19–21 Broad Street
St. Helier, Jersey JE4 8RR Channel Islands
Telephone: (44-1534) 283000
Fax: (44-1534) 283801
Telex: 4192351
Cable: ROYL TRUST JERSEY, CI
S.W.I.F.T. address: ROYC JE SH
Web site: rbcprivatebanking.com or rbcprivatebanking.com
E-mail: info@royalbankci.com or use Web site link
Type: Offshore trust and merchant bank established 1962
A local branch of Canada's largest bank
Member: British Bankers' Association
Ownership: Royal Trustco, Ltd.–Toronto, Ontario, Canada (100%)
Services: Banking and deposit services, trust and company
    management, investment management, insurance services
Managing Director and Regional Head, British Isles:
    Philip Brewster

TSB BANK CHANNEL ISLANDS, LTD.
P.O. Box 597
St. Helier, Jersey JE4 8XW Channel Islands
Telephone: (44-1534) 503 909
Fax: (44-1534) 503 211
E-mail: tsbci@itl.net
Services: Offshore checking accounts, fixed deposit accounts,
    investment accounts, credit cards, personal loans
Contact: John Hutchins (Banking Services); Liz Wiscombe
    (Investment Services)

COOK ISLANDS

ANZ—AUSTRALIA AND NEW ZEALAND BANKING GROUP, LTD.
1st Floor, Dev Bank Building
P.O. Box 907
Avarua, Rarotonga, Cook Islands
Telephone: (682) 21750
Fax: (682) 21760
Telex: 62038 ANZBANK RG
Web site: www.anzbank.com
Branch of group headquartered in Melbourne, Australia

Established in the Cook Islands in 1988
Branch Manager: Paul Murphy

HONG KONG

AUSTRALIA AND NEW ZEALAND BANKING GROUP, LTD.
One Exchange Square Suites 3101-05
8 Connaught Place Central, Hong Kong
Telephone: (852) 2843 7111
Fax: (852) 2868 0089
Telex: 86019 ANZBHK HH
Web site: www.anzbank.com
E-mail: hkgmo.anz.com
Branch of bank in Melbourne, Victoria, Australia
Treasury Products Francis Lee (852 2843 7160)
General Manager: Peter Richardson
General Manager: David Morgan

BANK OF AMERICA (ASIA), LTD.
17/F Devon House, 979 King's Road, Hong Kong
G.P.O. Box 133
Telephone: (852) 2597 2888
Fax: (852) 2597 2500
Telex: 73471 BOFAAHK
Cable: BOFAAHL
S.W.I.F.T. address: BOFA HKAX
Web site: www.bankamerica.com.hk
E-mail: Asia_Retail03@BankAmerica.com
Type: Commercial bank established 1912
Ownership: BankAmerica Corporation–San Francisco, CA, US
Manager: M. Peter Hong

BANK OF CHINA
14/F Bank of China Tower, 1 Garden Road Central
G.P.O. Box 19, Hong Kong
Telephone: (852) 2826 6688
Fax: (852) 2810 5963
Telex: 73772 BK CHI HX
Cable: CHUNGKUO
Web site: www.bank-of-china.com
Branch of bank in Beijing, China, which was established in 1912
Services: General banking activities, deposits, credit cards,
    international banking, and finance activities
General Manager: Yang Zilin

THE BANK OF EAST ASIA, LTD.
10 Des Voeux Road Central
G.P.O. Box 31, Hong Kong
Telephone: (852) 2842 3200
Fax: (852) 2845 9333
Telex: 73017 BEASI HX
Cable: BANKEASIA
S.W.I.F.T. address: BEAS HK HH
Web site: www.hkbea.com
E-mail: Use Web page link
Type: Commercial bank/joint stock company established 1918
Member: The Hong Kong Association of Banks–Hong Kong
Services: Worldwide banking services including investments,
     property development and management, asset management,
     corporate formation and management
Senior Deputy Manager: Simon K. H. Sham

CHEKIANG FIRST BANK, LTD.
60 Gloucester Road, Wanchai and One Duddell Street, Central
G.P.O. Box 691, Hong Kong
Telephone: (852) 2922 1222
Fax: (852) 2866 9133
Telex: 73686 HX FIRST
Cable: HONFIRST
S.W.I.F.T. address: CFHK HK HH
Web site: www.cfb.com.hk
E-mail: vanessa@cfb.com.hk
Type: Commercial bank established 1950
Member: Hong Kong Association of Banks
Hong Kong ownership: The Dai-Ichi Kangyo Bank, Ltd.–Tokyo,
     Japan (100%)
Services: Comprehensive range of banking and related financial
     services, including trustee services
General Manager: Edward Yeung
Public Relations: Vanessa Wo, Cherry Law
Tel: (852) 292 1631; Fax: (852) 861 2284

CITICORP INTERNATIONAL, LTD.
47-48/F Citibank Tower, Citibank Plaza
3 Garden Road, Central
Hong Kong
Telephone: (852) 2868 6666
Fax: (852) 2508 0043
Telex: HX 73243 FNCB
BIC Address: CILI HK H1
Web site: www.citibank.com

Type: Merchant bank and licensed deposit-taking company
established 1970
Subsidiary of Citicorp International Group–Delaware, US; Member:
Association of International Bond Dealers
Contact: Antony Leung Kam Chung, Chairman

HONG KONG AND SHANGHAI BANKING (HSBC) CORPORATION, LTD.

One Queens Road Central
G.P.O. Box 64, Hong Kong
Telephone: (852) 2822 1111
Fax: (852) 2810 1112
Telex: 73201 HKBG HX
Cable: HONGBANK
Web site: www.asiapacific.hsbc.com
E-mail: Use Web site link
Type: Commercial bank established 1865
Member: Hong Kong Association of Banks, Hong Kong; British
Bankers Association–London, UK
Ownership: numerous shareholders, each with less than 1%
Chairman: David Eldon

THE HONGKONG CHINESE BANK, LTD.

Lippo Centre, 89 Queensway, Central
P.O. Box 194, Hong Kong
Telephone: (852) 2867 6833
Fax: (852) 2845 9221
Telex: 73749 HONCH HX
Cable: HONCHIBANK
S.W.I.F.T. address: HKCB HK HH
Web site: www.hkcb.com
Type: Commercial bank established 1954
Member: The Hong Kong Association of Banks–Hong Kong
Ownership: HKCB Bank Holding Company, a joint venture of Lippo
Group & China Resources Enterprises, Ltd. (100%)
Principal Correspondents: Melbourne, Australia: ANZ Banking
Group; Toronto, Canada: Royal Bank of Canada; Beijing, China:
Bank of China; Frankfurt, Germany: Bank of New York;
Frankfurt, Germany: Deutsche Bank; San Francisco, CA, US:
Union Bank of California NA
Managing Director and Chief Executive: Ranmond Wing-Hung Lee

KOOKMIN FINANCE ASIA, LTD. (H.K.)

19th Floor, Gloucester Tower
11 Peddler Street, Central
Hong Kong

Telephone: (852) 2530 3633
Fax: (852) 8269 6650
Telex: 68015
Web site: www.kookmin.ac.kr
E-mail: kangseok@kookmin-bank.com
Type: Merchant Bank
A wholly owned subsidiary of Kookmin Bank–Seoul, Korea
Services: Corporate banking, syndicated loans, lease financing, bond
    investment, bond trading, trade financing, project financing,
    money market operations
Managing Director: Hyung-Sa Oh

WELLS FARGO, NA
27th Floor, Edinburgh Tower, The Landmark
15 Queens Road, Central
P.O. Box 35
Hong Kong
Telephone: (852) 2315 9500
Fax: (852) 2721 0033
Telex: 61467 WFBHK HX
S.W.I.F.T. address: WFBI HI HB
Web site: www.wellsfargo.com
Head Office in San Francisco, CA, US

ISLE OF MAN

BANK OF SCOTLAND (I.O.M.), LTD.
Bank of Scotland House, Prospect Hill
P.O. Box 19 (IM99 1AT)
Douglas, Isle of Man
Telephone: (44-1624) 623 074
Fax: (44-1624) 625 677
Telex: 629677
Web site: www.bankofscotland.co.uk
E-mail: offshoreenquiries@bankofscotland.co.uk
Established: 1987
Local branch of Bank of Scotland; wholly owned by Bank of Scotland
Services: Private and business banking; checking, money market
    accounts, and other investments
Managing Director: David Doyle

BARCLAY'S BANK PLC
International Premier Banking
BARC IM D1

Eagle Court, 25 Circular Road (IM99 1WE)
P.O. Box 135
Telephone: (44-1624) 684 343
Fax: (44-1624) 684 313
Telex: 418139 BARIOM G
Wire: BIC BARC IM D1
Web site: www.internationalbanking.barclays.com
E-mail: iom@offshorebanking.barclays.com
Branch: Head Office in London, UK
Branch Management: E. Shallcross

BARCLAY'S BANK PLC (ISLE OF MAN), LTD.
International Personal Banking
Eagle Court, 25 Circular Road
P.O. Box 213
Douglas, Isle of Man IM99 1RH
Telephone: (44-1624) 684 444
Fax: (44-1624) 684 321
Telex: 418139 BARIOM G
Web site: www.internationalbanking.barclays.com
E-mail: iom@offshorebanking.barclays.com or malcom.whetnall@barclays.co.uk
General inquiries to: Customer Service
Local branch of Barclay's Bank–London, UK
Services: Full range of services including offshore banking services, multicurrency banking, international payment service, letters of credit, cash management, trade and international services, checking account, statements, and other information via e-mail
Senior Account Manager, Premier International: Malcom Whetnall

BARCLAY'S FINANCE COMPANY (ISLE OF MAN), LTD.
P.O. Box 9, Barclay's House, Victoria Street (IM99 1AJ)
Douglas, Isle of Man
Local branch of Barclay's Bank–London, UK
Telephone: (44-1624) 684 567
Fax: (44-1624) 684 593
Web site: www.barclays.com
E-mail: finco.iom@barclays.co.uk
Managing Director: P. O'Shea

BARCLAY'S OFFSHORE BANKING SERVICES
Queen Victoria House, Victoria Street (IM99 1DF)
P.O. Box 48
Douglas, Isle of Man
Telephone: (44-1624) 682 828
Fax: (44-1624) 620 905

Wire: BIC BPBL IM D1
BIC Address: BPBLIM D1
Web site: www.offshorebanking.barclays.com
E-mail: central.office@offshorebanking.barclays.com
Type: Trust company established 1959
Principal Correspondents: London, UK: Barclay's Bank
Managing Director: John Church
Chairman: B. H. Cooper
Island Director: J. F. Linehan
Director: E. R. Thomas
Fiduciary Services Director: Kevin Bromley
Compliance Director: Alan Harding
Managing Director: Colin Jones
Private Client Director: Alan Patrick

CAYMANX TRUST COMPANY, LTD.
34 Athol Street(IM4 1RD)
Douglas, Isle of Man, British Isles
Telephone: (44-1624) 646 900
Fax: (44-1624) 662 192
Web site: www.cnciom.com
E-mail: mail@cnciom.com
Type: Trust company established 1985
Holds a full banking license issued by the Isle of Man Financial
    Supervision Commission
A wholly owned subsidiary of Cayman National Corporation,
    Ltd.–Cayman Islands, British West Indies
Services: Private banking, trusts, company formation and incorpora-
    tion, investment management, credit cards
Managing Director: Eammon Harkin
Bank Manager: Barry Williams

LLOYD'S PRIVATE BANKING (ISLE OF MAN), LTD.
Victory House
P.O. Box 8, Prospect Hill (IM99 1AH)
Douglas, Isle of Man
Telephone: (44-1624) 638 200
Fax: (44-1624) 628 267
Telex: 626110 LOYTST G
Web site: www lloydstsb-offshore.com
E-mail: iompersbkg@lloydstsb-offshore.com
Manager: T. P. Wild

NORTHERN BANK (I.O.M.), LTD.
Sixty Circular Road
P.O. Box 113(IM99 1JN)
Douglas, Isle of Man

Telephone: (44-1624) 629106
Fax: (44-1624) 627508
BIC Address: NORB IM D1
Web site: www.nbonline.co.uk
E-mail: Use Web site link
Member: National Australia Bank Group
Ownership: Northern Bank Group–Belfast, UK
Services: Investment management, trust and company services,
    loans, deposit accounts, checking accounts, expatriate services
Managing Director: Alice Clarke

STANDARD BANK (I.O.M), LTD.
Standard Bank House
One Circular Road
P.O. Box 43 (IM1 1SB)
Douglas, Isle of Man
Telephone: (44-1624) 643 643
Fax: (44-1624) 643 800
Telex: 628665 SBIOM G
S.W.I.F.T. address: SBIC IMDX
Web site: www.sboff.com/contact
E-mail: sbiom@sboff.com
Type: Commercial bank owned by Standard Bank Investment
    Corp Ltd.–Johannesburg, South Africa
Managing Director: K. J. Foden

LIECHTENSTEIN

CENTRUM BANK
Heiligkreuz 8 (FL-9490)
P.O. Box 1168
Vaduz, Liechtenstein
Telephone: (423) 235-85-85
Fax: (423) 235-86-86, attention Werner L. Eberle, Commercial Agent
Direct telephone: (423) 235-85-81
Telex: 889203 CENT FL
S.W.I.F.T. address: CBKV LI 2X
Established 1993
Member: Liechtenstein Bankers Association
Ownerships: Dr. Peter Goop, Dr. Peter Marxer, Dr. Peter Marxer Jr.,
    Dr. Walter Kieber
Deputy Manager: J. Lenherr
Chairman: Dr. Peter Marxer

LGT BANK IN LIECHTENSTEIN AKTIENGE-SELLSCHAFT
Herrengasse 12
P.O. Box 85 FL-9490
Vaduz Furstentum, Liechtenstein
Telephone: (423) 235-11-22
Fax: (423) 235-15-22
Telex: 889222 BIL FL
Cable: BANK VADUZ
S.W.I.F.T. address: BLFL LI 2X
Web site: www.lgt.com
E-mail: AB4@lgt.com
Customer Service: I. A. D. Pompilii
Type: Commercial and merchant bank established 1920
Member: Liechtenstein Bankers Association and Swiss Bankers
    Association
Services: Domestic and international credit and lending services
    including mortgages, foreign exchange, money markets,
    securities dealings and administration, portfolio management,
    investment counseling
Ownership: Liechtenstein Global Trust (100%)
CEO Executive Board: Thomas Piske
Management Chairman: Heinz Nipp, President
Management: Dr. Konrad Bachinger
Manager: Mr. M. Fluri, telephone: (423) 235 13 78
Manager: Mr. M. Petriella, telephone: (423) 235 12 75

LIECHTENSTEINISCHE LANDESBANK AG
Stadtle 44
P.O. Box 384 (FL-9490)
Vaduz, Liechtenstein
Telephone: (423) 236-88-11
Fax: (423) 236-88-22
Telex: 889400
Cable: LANDESBANK
S.W.I.F.T. address: LILA LI 2X
Web site: www.llb.li
E-mail: llb@llb.li
Type: Universal bank established 1861
Member: Swiss Bankers Association, Liechtenstein Bankers
    Association
Services: Financial and custodial services, investment transactions,
    credit and lending, money markets and other investments,
    portfolio management
Ownership: Liechtenstein Government
Customer Service: Daniela Matzler (E-mail: daniela.maetzler@llb.li)
Management Chairman: Benno Buchel

NEUE BANK AG
Kirchstrasse 8 (FL-9490)
Vaduz, Liechtenstein
Telephone: (423) 236-0808
Fax: (423) 232-9260
Telex: 889444 NEUEF1
S.W.I.F.T. address: NBAN LI 22
Web site: www.neuebankag.li
E-mail: info@neuebankag.li

VERWALTUNGS-UND PRIVAT-BANK AKTIENGESELLSCHAFT
P.O. Box 885
Im Zentrum (FL-9490)
Vaduz, Liechtenstein
Telephone: (423) 235-66-55
Fax: (423) 235-65-00
Telex: 889200 VPB FL
Cable: PRIVATBANK
S.W.I.F.T. address: VPBV LI 2X
Web site: www.vpbank.com
E-mail: info.li@vpbank.com
Type: Commercial and merchant bank established 1956
Member: Liechtenstein Bankers Association, Swiss Bankers
    Association, Association of Swiss Stock Exchanges
Ownership: Several hundred shareholders, mainly in Liechtenstein
Services: Domestic and foreign lending, money market transactions,
    deposits, portfolio management, precious metals trading
General Manager: Adolf E. Real

LUXEMBOURG

ABN-AMRO BANK
46 Avenue J. F. Kennedy
P.O. Box 581 (L-2180)
Luxembourg-Kirchberg (L-1855), Luxembourg
Telephone: (352) 42-49-49-42
Fax: (352) 42-49-49-499
Telex: 60816 AABL LU
S.W.I.F.T. address: ABNA LULL
Web site: www.abnamro.lu
E-mail: info@abnamro.lu
Managing Director: Frits B. Deiters

BANQUE DE LUXEMBOURG, SA
14 Boulevard Royal
P.O. Box 2221 (L-1022)
Luxembourg City (L-2449), Luxembourg
Telephone: (352) 49 92 41
Fax: (352) 46 26 65
Telex: 2247 BLCEN LU
Cable: BLUXLULL
E-mail: catbl@bt.lu
Type: Private stock bank established 1937
Member: Association des Banques et Banquiers, Luxembourg
Ownership: Deutsche Bank Saar Aktiengesellschaft Saarbrücken,
    Germany (3.95%), Deutsche Bank Luxembourg, SA
    Luxembourg, (25%), Credit Industriel d'Alsace et de Lorraine
    Strasbourg, France (71.05%)
Chairman Executive Board: Mr. Robert Reckinger

BANQUE GENERALE DU LUXEMBOURG SA
50 Avenue J. F. Kennedy
P.O. Box 547 (L-2951)
Luxembourg City (L-1855), Luxembourg
Telephone: (352) 4242-1
Fax: (352) 4242 2579
Telex: 3401 BGL LU
Cable: GENERAL BANK LUXEMBOURG
S.W.I.F.T. address: BGLL LU LL
Web site: www.bgl.lu
E-mail: info@bgl.lu
Type: Commercial bank established 1919
Member: Association des Banques et Banquiers, Association des
    Banques et Banquiers Luxembourgeois, Luxembourg
Services: Checking and savings accounts, foreign exchange and
    depository transactions, security dealings, portfolio
    management, lending, investment advice
Ownership: Generale Bank, NV Brussels (52.64%); Luxembourg
    Public Ownership
Branch Management: Mark Hentgen

BNP PARIBAS LUXEMBOURG
10 A Boulevard Royal
P.O. Box 51 (2093)
Luxembourg City (L-2093), Luxembourg
Telephone: (352) 46461
Fax: (352) 46464141
Telex: 2253 PARIB LU
Cable: NATIOPAR-LUX
S.W.I.F.T. address: PARB LU LL

Type: Commercial bank established 1964
Member: Association des Banques et Banquiers, Luxembourg
Services: Checking and savings accounts, foreign exchange and
    deposit transactions, investment fund management, asset
    management, money market transactions, fiduciary
    representation
Ownership: Groupe Paribas–Paris, France
Principal Correspondents: Luxembourg, Luxembourg: Banque et
    Caisse d'Epargne de l'Etat, Luxembourg; Vienna, Austria:
    Creditanstalt; Brussels, Belgium: Artesia Bank; Toronto,
    Canada: Royal Bank of Canada; Zurich, Switzerland: UBS;
    Frankfurt, Germany: Paribas; Frankfurt, Germany:
    Schweizerischer Bankverein (Deutschland)
Executive Manager: Pierre Schneider

CHASE MANHATTAN BANK LUXEMBOURG SA
5 Rue Plaetis
P.O. Box 240 (L-2012)
Luxembourg City (L-2338), Luxembourg
Telephone: (352) 462685/1
Fax: (352) 224590
Telex: 1233 CHASE LU
Cable: CHAMANBANK LUXEMBOURG
BIC: CHAS LU B1
S.W.I.F.T. address: CHAS LU LX
Web site: www.chase.com
E-mail: Use Web site link
Type: Commercial/joint stock bank established 1973
Member: Association des Banques et Banquiers, International
    Bankers Club, American Bankers Club–Luxembourg
Ownership: Chase Manhattan Overseas Corporation (100%)
Principal Correspondents: Deutsche Bank SA, Brussels,
    Belgium; Chase Bank, Frankfurt, Germany; Banco Pastor,
    Madrid, Spain; Société Générale, Paris, France; Chase
    Manhattan Bank, London, United Kingdom; Chase
    Manhattan Bank, Tokyo, Japan; Chase Manhattan Bank,
    New York City
Managing Director: Walter S. Close

DEXIA BANQUE INTERNATIONALE A LUXEMBOURG
69 Route d'Esch (L-1470)
P.O. Box 2205 (L-2953)
Luxembourg City, Luxembourg
Telephone: (352) 4590-1
Fax: (352) 4590-2010
Telex: 3626 BIL LU

Cable: INTERNATIONBANK
S.W.I.F.T. address: BILL LU LL
Web site: www.dexia-bil.lu
E-mail: contact@dexia-bil.lu
Type: Commercial bank established 1856
Member: Association des Banques et Banquiers Luxembourg,
  Associated Banks of Europe–Brussels, Belgium
Services: Foreign exchange and money market transactions, portfolio
  management, precious metals trading, securities dealing, project
  and international trade financing, letters of credit, life
  insurance, loan syndication
Ownership: Dexia Public Finance Bank SA (23.12%), Dexia SA
  (10.62%), Minority Shareholders (.64%)
Principal Correspondents: Melbourne: National Australian Bank;
  Montreal: Bank of Montreal; Zurich: Cr. Suisse; London: Barclay's
  Bank; Tokyo: Bank of Tokyo-Mitsubishi; Stockholm:
  Skandinavisha Enskilda Bken; USD (New York City):
  Citibank NA
Rated by Moody's (1995): bank deposit rating: Aa3/P-1; financial
  strength rating: B. Luxembourg's oldest banking institution
  with right note of issue
Senior Vice President/Administrative Managing Director: Michel
  Henaut
National International Network: Donny Wagner, Camille Neiseler
Tel: (352) 4590-2007; Fax: (352) 4590-3816

KOOKMIN BANK LUXEMBOURG
11A, Boulevard du Prince Henri
Luxembourg City (L-1724), Luxembourg
Telephone: (352) 466555
Fax: (352) 466566
Telex: 60130 CNB LU
Web site: www.kookmin-bank.com
Type: Commercial bank established 1991
A wholly owned subsidiary of Kookmin Bank–Seoul, Korea
Services: Corporate banking, syndicated loans, lease financing, bond
  investment, bond trading, trade financing, project financing,
  money market operations
Managing Directors: Dae-Hoon Lee
Manager: Jae-Gyun Choi

NORDEA BANK SA
P.O. Box 562 (2015)
672, Rue de Neudorf, Findel
Luxembourg (2220), Luxembourg
Telephone: (352) 438 871
Fax: (352) 439 352

Telex: 1590 UBLUX LU
S.W.I.F.T. address: UNIB LULL
Web site: www.unibank.lu
E-mail: nordea@nordea.lu
Principal Correspondents: Deutsche Bank, Frankfurt; Unibank, London and New York City
Managing Director: Jhon Mortensen

PANAMA

ABN AMRO BANK, NV
Calle Manuel Maria Icaza 16
Apartado Postal 10147
Panama City 4RP Panama
Telephone: (507) 206-5700
Fax: (507) 269-0526
Telex: 2644/2218
S.W.I.F.T. address: ABNA PA PA
Web site: www.abnamro.com/panama
E-mail: abnamrobank@sinfo.com
Branch of bank in Amsterdam, Netherlands
Branch Manager: Milton B. Ayon Wong
General Manager: Stef Merck
Head Office Chairman: R. Hazelhoff

BANCO SANTA CRUZ, SA
Calle 51, Este, Campo Alegre, El Dorado
P.O. Box 6-4416 El Dorado
Panama City, Panama
Telephone: (507) 263-8477
Fax: (507) 263-8404
Telex: 29002613 BSCA PG
Cable: BANCRUZ PANAMA
Web site: www.bsc.com.bo
E-mail: jmoreno@mail.bsc.com.bo
Head Office: Santa Cruz, Bolivia
Principal Correspondents: Banco de la Provincia de Buenos Aires, Buenos Aires; Banco Santa Cruz SA, Santa Cruz; Corp Banca, Santiago; Banco Santander Central Hispano SA, Panama City; Banco Santa Cruz SA, Miami; Barclay's Bank, Miami
Manager: Percya Yceballof

CHASE MANHATTAN BANK
Edif Plaza Chase, Avenida Aquilino de la Guardia

Apartado Postal 9A-76
Panama City, Panama
Telephone: (507) 263-5877
Fax: (507) 263-6009
BIC Address: CHAS PA PI
Web site: www.chase.com
Branch of bank in New York City (Manhattan), NY, US
Branch Manager: Olegario Barrelier
Deputy General Manager: Jaime Silvera

FLEET NATIONAL BANK
Edif Banco de Boston, Via Espana 122
Apartado Postal 5368
Panama City 5, Panama
Telephone: (507) 265-6077
Fax: (507) 265-7400
Telex: 3232 BOSBANK PG
BIC Address: FNBB PA P1
Web site: www.fleet.com
E-mail: kboston@sinfo.net
Branch of bank in Boston, MA, US
Holding Company: Bank of Boston Corporation–Boston, MA, US
Branch Manager: Luis A. Navarro Linares

SCOTIABANK—THE BANK OF NOVA SCOTIA
Avenida Federico Boyd y Calle 51
Edif PH Scotia Plaza, Campo Alegre
Apartado Postal 7327
Panama City (5), Panama
Telephone: (507) 263-6255
Fax: (507) 263-8636
Telex: 2073/3266
S.W.I.F.T. address: NOSC PA PA
Web site: www.scotiabank.ca
E-mail: email@scotiabank.ca or scotiabk@sinfo.net
Commercial branch of bank in Toronto, Ontario, Canada
Manager: M. J. Gonzalez-Delgado
Manager: Mr. Terence S. McCoy

UBS—UNION BANK OF SWITZERLAND (PANAMA), INC.
Swiss Tower, Calle 53 Este, Marbella
P.O. Box 61 (9A)
Panama City, Panama
Telephone: (507) 206-7000
Fax: (507) 206-7100
Telex: 3166 USBPA PG

Cable: SWISBANK PG
S.W.I.F.T. address: UBSW PA PA
Web site: www.ubs.com
E-mail: http://www.ubs.ch/e/index/contact/contact.html
Fax inquiry to: Daisy de Lowe, Associate Director, or Gloria Garcia de Paredes, Associate Director
Type: Commercial bank established 1975
Member: Association Bancaria de Panama–Panama City
Ownership: Union Bank of Switzerland AG, Zurich, Switzerland
Principal Correspondents: Miami–Northern Trust International; New York–Irving Trust Company
General Management: Werner P. Luthi

SINGAPORE

ABN AMRO BANK, NV
63 Chulia Street
P.O. Box 493 (049479)
Singapore City (049514) Singapore
Telephone: (65) 231 8603
Fax: (65) 231 7508
Telex: RS 24396
Cable: BANCOLANDA
Web site: www.abnamro.com.sg
E-mail: sgconsumerbank@ap.abnamro.com
Type: Merchant bank
Branch of bank in Amsterdam, Netherlands
Branch Management: P. H. M. Van Amerongen

BANK ONE, NATIONAL ASSOCIATION
9 Raffles Place, #29-02 Republic Plaza
Singapore City (048619), Singapore
Telephone: (65) 438 2488
Fax: (65) 438-2070
S.W.I.F.T. address: FNBC SG SG
Web site: www.bankone.com/international
E-mail: Yew_Chong_Tan@em.fcnbd.com or use Web site link
Head Office: Chicago, Illinois, US

FLEETBOSTON FINANCIAL—SINGAPORE
150 Beach Road #07-00
Gateway West
Singapore 189720, Singapore

Telephone: (65) 296 2366
Fax: (65) 296 0998
Telex: 23689 BOSTNBK
Cable: BOSTONBANK
S.W.I.F.T. address: FNBB SG SG
Web site: www.fleet.com
E-mail for William Chung: wchung@bkb.com
Branch of bank in Boston, Massachusetts, US
Holding Company: Bank of Boston Corporation–Boston, MA, US
Branch Manager: Barry W. Lamont
Product Sales Manager and Trade & Cash Management, A/P:
    William Chung

KEPPEL TAT LEE BANK, LTD.
The Octagon, 105 Cecil Street, 1st Floor (069534)
Singapore City (069534) Singapore
Telephone: (65) 422-8259
Fax: (65) 221-6980
Telex: RS 21911 KEPBANK
Cable: KEPPELBANK
S.W.I.F.T. address: KEPB SG SG
Web site: www.keppelbank.com.sg
Type: Commercial bank established 1959
Member: Association of Banks in Singapore
Ownership: Temasek Holding (Private) Ltd. (45.25%); Keppel
    Corporation Ltd. (35.59%)
Principal Correspondents: Vienna, Austria: Creditanstalt;
    Melbourne, Australia: National Australia Bank; Brussels,
    Belgium: Bank Brussels Lambert; Toronto, Canada: Bank of
    Montreal; Beijing, China: Bank of China; Frankfurt, Germany:
    Commerzbank; Paris, France: Banque Nationale de Paris
Managing Director and CEO: Benedict Kwek Gim Song
Executive Director: Walter G. Coakley
Branch Manager: Ms. Fiona Tan

OVERSEA–CHINESE BANKING CORPORATION, LTD.
65 Chulia Street, #08-00, OCBC Centre
P.O. Box 548
Singapore City (049513) Singapore
Telephone: (65) 535-7222
Fax: (65) 533-7955
Telex: RS 21209 OVERSEA
Cable: OVERSEA
S.W.I.F.T. address: OCBC SGSG
Web site: www.ocbc.com.sg
E-mail: info@ocbc.com.sg or use Web site link

Type: Commercial bank established 1932
Ownership: OBS Nominees (Private) Ltd. (12.03%); Raffles
    Nominees (Private) Ltd. (10.11%)
Member: Association of Banks in Singapore
Principal Correspondents: Sydney, Australia: Westpac Banking Corp;
    Montreal, Canada: Bank of Montreal; Toronto, Canada: Toronto-
    Dominion Bank; Zurich, Switzerland: UBS; Munich, Germany:
    HypoVereinsbank
Board Chairman: Lee Seng Wee
Vice Chairman and CEO: Alex Siu-Kee Au

OVERSEAS UNION BANK, LTD.
One Raffles Place, OUB Center
Singapore City (048616) Singapore
Telephone: (65) 533 8686
Fax: (65) 533-2293
Telex: RS 24475 OVERSBK
Cable: OVERSUNION SINGAPORE
Web site: www.oub.com.sg
E-mail: Use Web site link
Type: Commercial bank established 1947
Member: Association of Banks in Singapore
Ownership: Wah Hin & Co. (Pte) Ltd. (15.75%); DBS Nominees (Pte)
    Ltd. (13.45%); Overseas Union Enterprise Ltd. (9.38%); Raffles
    Nominees (Pte) Ltd. (7.95%); Oversea–Chinese Bank Nominees
    (Pte) Ltd. (5.33%)
Principal Correspondents: Brussels, Belgium: Bank Brussels
    Lambert; Brussels, Belgium: Générale Bank; Zurich,
    Switzerland: Credit Suisse First Boston; Beijing, China: Ag
    Bank of China; Beijing, China: Industrial & Commercial
    Bank of China
Director and Chief Operating Officer, Singapore: Gracy Choo

SCOTIABANK—BANK OF NOVA SCOTIA
10 Collyer Quay, #15-01
#15-01 Ocean Building
Singapore City (049315) Singapore
Telephone: (65) 535-8688
Fax: (65) 532-2240
Telex: RS 22177 SCOSING
S.W.I.F.T. address: NOSCSGSG
Web site: www.scotiabank.ca
E-mail: bns_sg@scotiacapital.com
Branch of bank in Toronto, Ontario, Canada
Managing Director: Glenn W. D. Martin
Country Head, Vice President, and Manager, Singapore Branch: Ms.
    W. S. Seong Koon

SWITZERLAND

ABN AMRO BANK (SWITZERLAND) LTD.
12 Quai Général-Guisan
P.O. Box 3026
Geneva CH-1211/3, Switzerland
Telephone: (41-22) 819-7777
Fax: (41-22) 311-7209
Telex: 412 626 ABNG CH
S.W.I.F.T. address: ABNA CH 22 2A
Web site: www.abnamro.com
E-mail: Use Web site link
Ownership: ABN AMRO Bank, NV–Amsterdam, Netherlands
Address inquiries to: Enrique Gastpare, Branch Manager
Branch Manager: Boudwijn J. de Hoop Scheffer

BANCO BILBAO VIZCAYA ARGENTARIA
Neumuhleauqi 6
P.O. Box 7530
Zurich (CH-8023), Switzerland
Telephone: (41-1) 268-9111
Fax: (41-1) 268-9391
Telex: 814550 BBCH
Web site: www.bbva.es
Branch: Head Office in Madrid, Spain

BANK HOFMANN AG ZURICH
Talstrasse 27
P.O. Box 8022
Zurich CH-8001, Switzerland
Telephone: (41-1) 217-51-11
Fax: (41-1) 211-73-68
Telex: 813485 BHK CH
Cable: HOFMANNBANK
S.W.I.F.T. address: HOFM CH 22
Web site: www.bankhofmann.ch
E-mail: bankhofmann@hofmann.ch or bank@hofmann.ch
Type: Commercial and stock exchange bank established 1897
Member: Swiss Bankers' Association–Basel; Zurich Stock
        Exchange–Zurich
Ownership: Leu Holding AG–Zug, Switzerland (100%)
Principal Correspondents: London–HSBC Bank PLC; USD, New
        York–Credit Suisse, First Boston Corporation
Chairman: Dr. William Wirth
CEO Branch Manager: Markus R. Todtli

THE CHASE MANHATTAN BANK
63 rue du Rhone
P.O. Box 476 (CH-1204)
Geneva (CH-1211/3), Switzerland
Telephone: (41-22) 735-3640
Fax: (41-22) 736-24-30
Telex: 413 400 CHAS CH
Cable: CHAMANBANK
S.W.I.F.T. address: CHAS CH GX
Web site: www.chase.com
E-mail: sam.fiore@chase.com or use Web site link
Type: Commercial bank established 1969
Member: Swiss Bankers' Association–Basel; Association of Foreign
    Banks in Switzerland–Zurich
Holding Company: Chase Manhattan Overseas Banking Corporation
Management Chairman: Robert D. Hunter
Vice President: Mr. Sam Fiore
General Manager: William M. Rowan

CITIBANK, NA
16 Quai General Guisan
P.O. Box 162
CH-1204 Geneva, Switzerland
Telephone: (41-22) 20-55-11
Fax: (41-22) 28-85-17
Telex: 823920
Cable: CITIBANK
Web site: www.citibank.com
Branch of bank in New York City (Manhattan), NY, US

HABIB BANK AG ZURICH
Weinbergstrasse 59
P.O. Box 4931
CH-8022 Zurich, Switzerland
Telephone: (41-1) 269 4500
Fax: (41-1) 269 4535
Telex: 815151 HBZZ CH
Cable: HABIBBANK ZURICH
S.W.I.F.T. address: HBZUCH ZZ
Web site: www.habibbank.com
E-mail: webmaster@habibbank.com or use Web site link
Type: Commercial bank established 1967
Member: Swiss Bankers' Association–Basel; Association of Foreign
    Banks in Switzerland–Zurich
Ownership: Habib Family
Principal Correspondents: Vienna, Austria: Creditanstalt; Montreal,
    Canada: Bank of Montreal; Frankfurt, Germany: Deutsche
    Bank; Paris, France: Banque Nationale de Paris; Milan, Italy:
    Banca Comerciale Italiana; Amsterdam, Netherlands: ABN

AMRO Bank; New York City, US: Citibank
Management Chairman: Andre Alois Wicki
President: Hyder M. Habib

KREDIETBANK (SUISSE), SA
7 Boulevard Georges-Favon
P.O. Box 334
CH-1211/11 Geneva, Switzerland
Telephone: (41-22) 311-63-22
Fax: (41-22) 311-54-43
Telex: 427303 KBS CH
Cable: KREDIETGEN
S.W.I.F.T. address: KSUI CHGG
Web site: www.kbl.lu
Type: Commercial bank established 1970
Member: Swiss Bankers' Association–Basel; Association of Foreign
Banks in Switzerland–Zurich
Ownership: Kredietbank, SA, Luxembourgeoise, Luxembourg
Principal Correspondents: Hong Kong: HSBC Bank PLC; SGD:
HSBC Bank PLC; XEU: Kredietbank Luxembourgeoise
Manager: Pierre Joye

ZURCHER KANTONAL BANK
Bahnhofstrasse 9
P.O. Box 715 CH-8010
Zurich (CHH-8001), Switzerland
Telephone: (41-1) 220-1111
Fax: (41-1) 221-6539
Telex: 812140 ZBK CH
S.W.I.F.T. address: ZKBK CH 22
Web site: www.zkb.ch
E-mail: serviceline@zkb.ch or info@zkb.ch
ZKB Service Line: Sibylle Egli
Telephone: (41-1) 802-9686
Fax: (41-1) 802-5715
Type: State-owned universal bank established 1869
Ownership: Canton of Zurich (100%)
Member: Swiss Bankers' Association, Association of Assis
Cantonal Banks
Chairman: Hermann Weigold

VANUATU

EUROPEAN BANK, LTD.
International Building, Kumul Highway
P.O. Box 65

Port Vila, Vanuatu
Telephone: (678) 27700
Fax: (678) 22884
Telex: (771) 1023 EURTRUST NH
S.W.I.F.T. address: EUBL VU VI
Type: Private bank established 1972
Member: Finance Centre Association, Swiss Bankers' Association, Association of Assis Cantonal Banks
Ownership: European Capital Holding Corporation (100%)
Principal Correspondents: Standard Chartered Bank in Sydney, London, Hong Kong, Tokyo, and New York City
Managing Director: Michael J. Harkin
General Manager: Kelly Irich
Senior Vice President and Operating Manager: Brenton W. Terry
President and CEO: Robert M. Bohn

Application for Opening of Account

I/We request you to open an account with the following specifications (mark if applicable):

☐ Individual Account   ☐ Current Account   ☐ In Swiss Francs (Sfr)
☐ Joint Account   ☐ Deposit Account   ☐ In U.S. Dollars (U.S.$)
☐ Corporate Account   ☐ Managed Portfolio,   ☐ In German Marks (DM)
        Type _____   ☐ Other _____

Personal Information (Please Print or Type):

Family Name(s)
   or Company Name _____

First Name(s) _____

Street and No. _____

City, State, Zip Code _____

Country _____

Nationality _____

Occupation or Type of Business _____

Date of Birth or
   Company Formation _____

Telephone No.: _____   Telex No.: _____

Correspondence Is to Be:
☐ Retained at the bank and forwarded only on special request
☐ Forwarded regularly to the following address (if different from above): _____

_____

Initial Deposit in the Amount of _____
☐ Is Enclosed   ☐ Will Be Mailed Separately
☐ Will Be Wire Transferred Through (Bank Name): _____

Place: _____   _____
                                (Signature)

Date: _____   _____
                                (Signature)

POWER OF ATTORNEY

I/We the undersigned (please print) _____

residing at _____

_____

hereby grant _____ (hereinafter called "the Bank")
full powers with a view to represent me/us validly within the limitations
of the following provisions:

1. The Bank is authorized to dispose, on behalf of the principal(s), of the securities and assets whatsoever of the undersigned principal(s), lodged with the bank, insofar as these deposits and assets may be increased or reduced as a result of purchases, sales or conversions of securities, and for this purpose any possible subscription rights may be exercised or sold at best.

2. The Bank is furthermore authorized, in a general manner, to do everything it will deem necessary or appropriate for the management of the assets lodged with the Bank.

3. However, the Bank is not authorized to carry out, in any way whatsoever, any withdrawals of all or part of the funds and securities deposited or to pledge the assets and securities in question; nor is it empowered to order bonuses, except when these are destined for taking over securities of an equivalent amount.

4. The principal(s) expressly approve(s), and they/he do(es) so in advance, all acts of management or abstentions of the Bank and recognize(s) that the bank does not assume any responsibility whatsoever for the consequences of the transactions which the Bank, acting in good faith, will have made or will have abstained from making. In addition, the principal(s) undertake(s) to compensate the Bank for any expenses or damages it might have incurred on account of this power of attorney.

5. The power of attorney will remain valid until and unless revoked in writing.

6. It is expressly agreed that this power of attorney will not become void upon the death or loss of exercise of the civil rights of the principal(s), but will continue in full effect.

7. The parties agree that the constitution and validity of this power of attorney are governed by the laws of the jurisdiction in which the Bank is domiciled and that transactions carried out by virtue of said power of attorney will be judged in accordance with such laws. Any litigations between the parties will be brought before the competent courts of said jurisdiction. The Bank, however, is authorized to assert its claims at the legal domicile of the principal(s).

Signed at this place: _____

And on this date: _____

By the principal(s): _____

_____(signature)_____

_____
(signature)

Account No.: _____

INDEX

Product Order Form

QTY	PRODUCT	DESCRIPTION	PRODUCT #	S&H* (U.S. ONLY)	PRICE/ EACH	NET PRICE
___	*How to Own Your Own Private International Bank*	The complete source for starting your own bank.	WPC-020	$6.95	$40.00	$ ___
___	*How to Start Your Own Offshore Investment Fund*	How to raise capital and start your own fund.	WPC-011	$6.95	$29.95	$ ___
___	*The Complete Guide to Offshore Money Havens, 4th Edition*	Jerome Schneider's bestseller revised and updated.	WPC-006	$6.95	$30.00	$ ___
___	*Global Investing for Maximum Profit and Safety*	Jerome Schneider's strategies for global investing.	WPC-005	$6.95	$30.00	$ ___
___	*Hiding Your Money*	Everything you need to know about keeping your money safe from predators and greedy creditors.	WPC-008	$6.95	$30.00	$ ___
___	*Finding Your Own Offshore Wealth Haven Set*	Audio and video program.	WPC-014	$12.50	$99.95	$ ___
				Subtotal Before Shipping		$ ___
				Add Shipping & Handling**/Rush/Courier***		$ ___
					TOTAL ORDER	$ ___

NOTES:
*International standard shipping $12.50
**Shipping prices quoted are for 1 item (Please add $2.00 for each additional item)
***UPS/FedEx extra (Call 800-877-3777 for rates)

Method of Payment
I have enclosed a check for $ _____ made payable to Wilshire Publishing Company Ltd.

Mail Payment To: Wilshire Publishing Company, 902-1185 West Georgia Street, Vancouver, BC V6E 4E6

OR

Please charge my (cirle one) Visa   MasterCard   Amex   Discover

Credit Card # _____   Expiration Date: ___ / ___

Name of Cardholder: _____

Signature of Cardholder: _____

Please Ship to:
Name: _____
Company: _____
Address: _____
City/State/ZIP: _____
Phone: _____
Fax: _____

FOR RUSH ORDERS CALL (604) 444-1234 or (800) 877-3777 FAX (604) 608-4000 Webpage: www.offshorewealth.com